The Early Modern Englishwoman:
A Facsimile Library of Essential Works

Series II

Printed Writings, 1641–1700: Part 1

Volume 1

Life Writings, I

The Early Modern Englishwoman:
A Facsimile Library of Essential Works

Series II

Printed Writings, 1641–1700: Part 1

Volume 1

Life Writings, I

Selected and Introduced by
Elizabeth Skerpan-Wheeler

General Editors
Betty S. Travitsky and Patrick Cullen

Ashgate

Aldershot • Burlington USA • Singapore • Sydney

Published by
Ashgate Publishing Ltd
Gower House
Croft Road
Aldershot
Hants GU11 3HR
England

Ashgate Publishing Company
131 Main Street
Burlington, VT 05401–5600 USA

Ashgate website: http://www.ashgate.com

British Library Cataloguing-in-Publication Data
The early modern Englishwoman : a facsimile library of
    essential works
    Series 2: Printed writings, 1641–1700, part 1: Vol. 1: Life
    writings, I
    1. English literature – Early modern, 1500–1700   2. English
    literature – Woman authors   3. Women – Biography – Early
    works to 1800   4. Women – England – History – 17th century –
    Sources
    I. Skerpan-Wheeler, Elizabeth   II. Travitsky, Betty
    III. Cullen, Patrick
    820.8'09287

Library of Congress Cataloging-in-Publication Data
The early modern Englishwoman: a facsimile library of essential works. Part 1. Printed writings, 1641–1700/general editors, Betty S. Travitsky and Patrick Cullen.

See page vi for complete CIP Block 00–64294

The image reproduced on the title page and on the case is from the frontispiece portrait in *Poems. By the Most Deservedly Admired Mrs. Katherine Philips* (1667). Reproduced by permission of the Folger Shakespeare Library, Washington, DC.

ISBN 0 7546 0208 7

Printed in Great Britain by Antony Rowe Ltd, Chippenham, Wiltshire.

CONTENTS

Library of Congress Cataloging-in-Publication Data

Life writings. Volume 1 / selected and introduced by Elizabeth Skerpan-Wheeler.
    p. cm. -- (The early modern Englishwoman. Printed writings, 1641-1700, Part 1 ; v. 1)
    Includes bibliographical references.
    Contents: Mris. Cooke's meditations / Frances Cook(e) -- Svsanna's apologie against the elders, or, A vindication of Svsanna Parr / Susanna Parr -- This is a short relation of some of the cruel sufferings (for the truths sake) of Katharine Evans & Sarah Chevers / Katherine Evans and Sarah Cheevers -- A Christian woman's experiences of the glorious working of God's free grace / Katherine Sutton -- Clavstrvm regale reseratvm, or, The Kinges concealment at Trent / Anne Gerard Wyndham -- Heaven realiz'd, or, The holy pleasure of daily intimate communication with God / Sarah Davy.
    ISBN 0-7546-0208-7
    1. Christian women--Religious life--England. 2. Autobiography--Women authors. 3. Women--England--History--17th century--Sources. I. Cooke, Frances, fl. 1649. Mris. Cooke's meditations. II. Parr, Susanna. Svsanna's apologie against the elders. III. Evans, Katharine, d. 1692. This is a short relation of some of the cruel sufferings (for the truths sake) of Katharine Evans & Sarah Chevers. IV. Sutton, Katherine, ca. 1630-1663. Christian woman's experiences of the glorious working of God's free grace. V. Wyndham, Anne. Clavstrvm regale reseratvm. VI. Davy, Sarah, ca. 1635-1667. Heaven realiz'd. VII. Skerpan-Wheeler, Elizabeth, 1955- VIII. Title: Mris. Cooke's meditations. IX. Title: Svsanna's apologie against the elders. X. Title: This is a short relation of some of the cruel sufferings (for the truths sake) of Katharine Evans & Sarah Chevers. XI Title: Christian woman's experiences of the glorious working of God's free grace. XII. Title: Heaven realiz'd. XIII. Title: Clavstrvm regale reseratvm. XIV. Series.

BV4527 .L54 2000 vol. 1
274.2'07'0922--dc21

                                          00-6429

PREFACE
BY THE GENERAL EDITORS

Until very recently, scholars of the early modern period have assumed that there were no Judith Shakespeares in early modern England. Much of the energy of the current generation of scholars has been devoted to constructing a history of early modern England that takes into account what women actually wrote, what women actually read, and what women actually did. In so doing the masculinist representation of early modern women, both in their own time and ours, has been deconstructed. The study of early modern women has thus become one of the most important—indeed perhaps the most important—means for the rewriting of early modern history.

The Early Modern Englishwoman: A Facsimile Library of Essential Works is one of the developments of this energetic reappraisal of the period. As the names on our advisory board and our list of editors testify, it has been the beneficiary of scholarship in the field, and we hope it will also be an essential part of that scholarship's continuing momentum.

The Early Modern Englishwoman is designed to make available a comprehensive and focused collection of writings in English from 1500 to 1750, both by women and for and about them. The three series of *Printed Writings* (1500–1640, 1641–1700, and 1701–1750), provide a comprehensive if not entirely complete collection of the separately published writings by women. In reprinting these writings we intend to remedy one of the major obstacles to the advancement of feminist criticism of the early modern period, namely the limited availability of the very texts upon which the field is based. The volumes in the facsimile library reproduce carefully chosen copies of these texts, incorporating significant variants (usually in appendices). Each text is preceded by a short introduction providing an overview of the life and work of a writer along with a survey of important scholarship. These works, we strongly believe, deserve a large readership—of historians, literary critics, feminist critics, and non-specialist readers.

The Early Modern Englishwoman also includes separate facsimile series of *Essential Works for the Study of Early Modern Women* and of *Manuscript Writings*. These facsimile series are complemented by *The Early Modern Englishwoman 1500–1750: Contemporary Editions*. Also under our general editorship, this series will include both old-spelling and modernized editions of works by and about women and gender in early modern England.

New York City
2001

vii

INTRODUCTORY NOTE

Readers coming to the volumes of *Life Writings* looking for intimate details or stories tracing their subjects from birth to adulthood will be disappointed. Early modern women and men represented their lives very differently from twentieth-century autobiographers. Writers today describe the process by which they have come to be what they believe they are: distinctive, unique individuals. In contrast, early modern writers sought connections between particular events in their lives and the larger pattern of Christian salvation. These writers frequently omit the names of their husbands and children, mentioning them in passing as they focus on the most important part of their lives–their quest for salvation. Their narratives interconnect their experiences and feelings with scriptural passages as they attempt to understand daily life in spiritual terms. The persons most frequently described are those who make the greatest impact on the writers' spiritual development. While modern writers strive to emerge from their context, these early modern writers attempt to justify and then subsume themselves in divine history.

With one exception, all the women represented in *Life Writings* would have been considered by their contemporaries religious radicals–Independents, Baptists and Quakers. All lived through an extremely turbulent time in English history. The English Revolution (1642–1660) saw the temporary disestablishment of the Church of England, the rise of open religious experimentation and regular interpretation of political events in religious terms. Restoration of the Stuart monarch in 1660 brought harsh laws against Protestant Dissenters from the reestablished Church, forbidding unlicensed preaching and worshipping, and requiring prison terms for religious lawbreakers. A few of the writers collected here spent time in prison, and the works are marked by a sense of persecution, interpreted as spiritual challenge. Response to a palpable threat is a common theme. Mary Rowlandson, the best known of these writers, describes the months she spent as a captive of North American Indians, while Katherine Evans, Sarah Cheevers and Barbara Blaugdone endure prison as a result of preaching the faith of the Society of Friends. Hannah Allen faces a different kind of captivity in a prolonged fight with depression. Anne Wentworth encounters the hostility of an entire congregation when she decides to leave a bad marriage; Susanna Parr is excommunicated for disagreeing with her pastor. Frances Cook has her faith severely tested by a terrible storm at sea. Katherine Sutton, Sarah Davy and Susannah Blandford recount their battles with doubt and their coming to refreshed understanding of their faith. Elizabeth White (d. 1669) recounts her crises of faith, her spiritual growth, and the challenges it entailed. However, *The Experiences of Gods Gracious Dealing with Mrs. Elizabeth White* (Wing W 1762), published in Glasgow by Robert Saunders in 1696, could not be included here because the condition of the two extant copies precludes reproduction. Theodosia Alleine and Mary Penington offer testimony to the hardships their clergyman husbands endured as a result of defying the Stuart government's religious laws. The lone exception, Anne Gerard Wyndham, tells a pure adventure story of the wartime rescue of Prince Charles from the hands of the parliamentary army by herself, her husband, and several other royalist men and women. While she seeks no religious explanation for events, Wyndham follows the pattern of the other writers in subordinating details about herself to the particulars of her narrative.

The works have been arranged in chronological order so that readers may get a sense of the progression of the historical events surrounding the writers as well as the gradual emergence of the Quakers as the newest of the Independent sects and the continuity over time and place of particular themes and methods of exposition. With the exception of Rowlandson's captivity narrative, these works are making their first complete, unexcerpted modern appearance.

Frances Cook(e) (fl. ?1646–60)

Little is known of the life of Frances Cook, other than that she was the wife of John Cook, barrister and chief prosecutor in the trial of Charles 1, executed in 1660 for his role in the regicide. Frances visited John in the Tower of London before his execution; his letter to her is printed in *A Complete Collection of the Lives, Speeches, Private Passages, Letters and Prayers of those Persons Lately Executed* (1661), edited by S.W. Possibly the Frances Cutler John Cook married in 1646, Frances was the mother of a daughter, Freelove. In January 1650, while John and Frances Cook were traveling to Ireland so that he could assume his newly appointed position as Chief Justice to the Court of Munster (which he held until 1654), they encountered the terrible storm that is the subject of Frances's book, and of one by John, also.

M$^{ris.}$ Cookes Meditations

M$^{ris.}$ Cookes Meditations is printed in 4°, with a title page of ornamented printer's rules and central ornament. Frances's book was published together with her husband's *A True Relation of Mr Iohn Cook's Passage by Sea from Wexford to Kinsale and of the Great Storm and Eminent Danger*, in 1650 at Corke and reprinted in London by Thomas Brewster and Gregory Moule. John's book went through a second edition in 1652, but Frances's exists only in the first printing. While both editions of John's book exist in numerous exemplars, probably because of the fame or notoriety of its author, only four exemplars of Frances's book survive. There are no modern editions. Her efforts at understanding the experience through her reading of scripture and her concluding psalm, modeled on the psalms of David, place her firmly in the Protestant tradition of spiritual autobiography. Students of literature and gender may wish to read Frances's narrative together with John's: the existence of both narratives provides a rare opportunity to compare the responses of a woman and man with similar sympathies to the same event.

The base copy reproduced in Volume 1 is the exemplar owned by The British Library. It was selected for both its clarity and its inclusion in the famous collection of bookseller George Thomason, universally recognized by seventeenth-century scholars as the most inclusive collection of books and pamphlets from the revolutionary period

Susanna Parr (fl. 1635–69)

Married and the mother of seven children, Susanna Parr was living in Exeter when in 1657 she and another woman, Mary Alleine, were–for asserting themselves, speaking in church, and hearing the minister of another congregation–excommunicated from the Baptist fellowship headed by Lewis Stucley (or Stycley) of which Parr herself had been a founder. Her actions apparently precipitated by the death of one of her children around 1654, Parr, together with Mary Alleine and Alleine's husband Toby, a prominent serge-maker, criticized Stucley's increasingly radical, separatist ministry. The incident prompted six pamphlets, including Parr's work and a tract by Toby Alleine. A full account of the episode appears in Patricia Crawford, *Women and Religion in England 1500–1720*.

Svsanna's Apologie against the Elders

Svsanna's Apologie Against the Elders was published in Oxford by Henry Hall for T. Robinson, on 12 May 1659, according to the bookseller George Thomason, who made the note on his own copy of the book. An 8° edition, without distinguishing ornaments, the book went through one printing and exists in only four exemplars. Written in response to verbal and published accusations, Parr's book coherently argues her case, dividing the text into a Narrative, which lays out the circumstances surrounding her excommunication, and a Vindication, which provides a meticulous refutation of all the charges published against her. The book opens with Parr's own preface 'To the Impartiall Reader'. While pleading the infirmity of her sex, Parr insists on speaking for herself, providing the voice missing from the pamphlets written about the case by the male participants. In presentation and argumentation, Parr's work compares favorably with those of other political and religious controversialists. An excerpt appears in Graham *et al.*, *Her Own Life: Autobiographical Writings by Seventeenth-Century English Women*.

The base copy reproduced in Volume 1 was chosen for its availability, clarity, and inclusion in the noted Thomason Collection, owned by The British Library.

Katherine Evans (d. 1692) and Sarah Cheevers (d. 1664)

Both members of the Society of Friends, Katherine Evans and Sarah Cheevers were married and the mothers of several children when in 1658, while traveling to Alexandria to preach, they were detained in Malta, where they subsequently spent three years in the captivity of the Inquisition. Redeemed after three years through the actions of Daniel Baker and other Friends, they returned to England by 1663 and continued to publish accounts of their experiences. A determined spiritual seeker from a well-to-do family, Evans had by her own account been a Lutheran, Baptist, Independent and Puritan before joining the Friends. Evans's husband, John, died in prison in 1664; she herself lived until 1692. About Cheevers, whose family home was in Slattenford, or Slaughterford, Wiltshire, and whose husband's name was Henry, little else is known. Several letters by both Evans and Cheevers appear in Besse.

This is a Short Relation of Some of the Cruel Sufferings (For the Truths Sake) of Katharine Evans & Sarah Chevers is a cheaply printed 4° with a densely printed, descriptive title page ornamented by printer's rules, printed in London for Robert Wilson in 1662, while the women were still in prison. The title page and Daniel Baker's introductory 'Epistle to the Readers' clearly indicate that the publication is both an attempt to enlist support in the campaign to free Evans and Cheevers and an argument against the charge that Friends were Roman Catholics and agents of the Pope. As the title suggests, it is not a single account; rather, it is a complex and dazzling intermingling–in changing voices–of personal narratives, copies of letters by Evans and Cheevers and others, hymns, and connecting commentary by Baker. After their return to England in 1663, Wilson published a revised and expanded edition under the title of *A True Account of the Great Tryals and Cruel Sufferings* (8°), which included a description of the process by which the women regained their freedom and appended a narrative of the experiences of fellow Friend George Robinson, captured while traveling to Jerusalem. In the same year, Wilson also published Evans's revised version of her experiences, titled *A Briefe Discovery of God's Eternal Truth and a Way Opened to the Simple Hearted Whereby They May Come to Know Christ and His Ministers, from Antichrist and His Ministers* (4°). Five exemplars exist of *Short Relation*, two of *A True Account* and four of *A Briefe Discovery*. Versions of the narratives were reprinted twice in the eighteenth century, but there are no modern editions. The writings of Evans and Cheevers illustrate the spiritual gender equality within the Society of Friends, as readers may see by comparing the women's accounts of captivity to those of Barbara Blaugdone, in Volume 2, and of George Robinson, as well as to numerous letters to Friends collected by the Society and preserved at the Friends House Library in London and in the libraries of Swarthmore and Haverford Colleges in the United States. An excerpt from *A True Account* appears in Graham et al., *Her Own Life: Autobiographical Writings by Seventeenth-Century English Women*.

The base copy reproduced in Volume 1 is the Huntington Library copy of *This is a Short Relation*, the earliest version of the narrative, and the clearest copy available.

Katherine Sutton (fl. 1630–63)

Katherine Sutton, a married woman and the mother of several children, was praised by the Baptist minister Hanserd Knollys for the depth and sincerity of her faith. Her experiences with family life, including the death of one child and disagreements with her husband, contributed to the intensity of her spiritual quest. Inspired by dreams and visions and blessed most especially, she felt, by her 'gift of singing', which she dated to February 1655, she composed both narratives and hymns. The manuscripts of some of these were lost in a shipwreck in a crossing to Holland around 1662 and rewritten for *A Christian Womans Experiences*.

The text, a 4° edition, was printed by Henry Goddæus in Rotterdam. The title page bears a beautifully detailed printer's ornament. The book opens with a preface by Knollys, who was passing through Rotterdam around 1663, continues with the narrative proper, and concludes with Sutton's address to the 'Courteous Reader' and several of her hymns which, Sutton asserts, were composed spontaneously and presented without revision. This text went through one edition; three exemplars exist. There are no modern editions, although there is some discussion of the hymns in Ian M. Mallard (1963), 'Hymns of Katherine Sutton', *Baptist Journal*, January (pp. 23–33). Sutton's text is a spiritual autobiography comparable to John Bunyan's *Grace Abounding to the Chief of Sinners*, stressing the author's conviction of sin and her quest for grace, punctuated by a series of hardships. Knollys, who may have been impressed by Sutton because of her gift of singing (his last published work defends the right of women to sing in church) and who would prove to be the nemesis of Anne Wentworth (see Volume 2), cautions readers about 'some suddain and unexpected Transition' in Sutton's writing, but offers its lack of polish as evidence of 'Heavenly communications'. Sutton echoes Knollys's concern about style in her concluding address to the readers, but urges them to judge the quality of her work for themselves, guided by the spirit.

Owned by Cambridge University Library, the base copy of this very rare book, reproduced in Volume 1, is distinguished for its clear, legible printing.

Anne Gerard Wyndham (1632–98)

Alone of all the women in these two volumes, Anne Gerard Wyndham was a committed royalist. The daughter of Thomas Gerard of Trent, Somersetshire, she married Col Francis Wyndham, also of Trent, whose mother had cared for the young Prince of Wales before the civil wars. Both Anne and her husband actively participated in hiding the future Charles II after the royalist defeat at the Battle of Worcester (1650). In May 1667 Anne petitioned the king for a pension in recognition of the help she and her husband gave him. The book may have been an attempt to support the petition. Wyndham counted several aristocrats among her friends and acquaintances, including Lord Henry Wilmot, later Earl of Rochester.

Clavstrvm Regale Reseratvm

Wyndham's narrative, *Clavstrvm Regale Reseratvm*, or *The Kinges Concealment at Trent* is a brief, 4° volume, with a title page in script and without other ornament, published in London for William Nott in 1667. It opens with a dedicatory epistle to the Queen, Catherine of Braganza, and explains why the book is appearing in 1667, rather than at a date closer to the actual events. The remainder of the text is a third-person narrative describing how Wyndham, her husband and others designed and carried out their plot to rescue Prince Charles. Wyndham explains that her story provides the missing piece of a larger narrative of Charles's escape, already published, and that this narrative, originally written by her husband, remained in the king's custody until he himself gave permission to publish it. While the book went through only one printing, it survives in eleven known exemplars. It was also reprinted in its entirety in the third edition of Thomas Blount's *Boscobel* (1681). There is no modern edition. Her dedication to the queen places Wyndham among a significant group of royalists who, although not part of the court, played a crucial role in sustaining and unifying opposition to the governments of the 1650s. Her book appeared at the time of the Second Dutch War (1666–67), when supporters of the king, who at no time in the 1660s trusted in a universal royalism, were publishing works designed to make the king the center of popular patriotism. Wyndham's narrative–depicting a young and vulnerable prince dependent upon the goodwill of his people, and subjects willing to undergo risk and hardship for their prince–thus indirectly serves the interests of contemporary politics.

Of the surviving eleven exemplars, the copy owned by The Huntington Library was chosen for reproduction in Volume 1 because of its legibility and availability.

Sarah Davy (?1635–67)

Characterized as a young gentlewoman by her publisher, Sarah Davy was born Sarah Roane around 1635. When she was eleven years old, her mother died, precipitating the spiritual journey that is the subject of Davy's book. She married around December 1660 and died after a long illness in 1667. Her book was published posthumously.

Heaven Realiz'd

The text, printed in 8°, with a simple, unadorned title page, was published in 1670, probably in London, by A.P., who also contributed an extensive introduction. The text includes personal narratives, reflections on Davy's experiences and meditations on religious subjects; it concludes with several hymns and a table of contents. Printed only once, the text exists in five exemplars. As presented by A.P. (tentatively identified by Elaine Hobby as Baptist clergyman Anthony Palmer), the book is at once a book of devotions, a memorial and a didactic example for other young persons, who are living 'in an Age of the *great corruption of youth*, when Religion is made a by-word and a scorn'. While the text of Davy's book is highly personal, carefully describing the stages in the author's spiritual growth, A.P. emphasizes the exemplary nature of the writing of 'a blessed Soul (now in Heaven)' and addresses 'all sort of Readers' in the preface, decrying the morals of the age. For A.P., the value of Davy's writings is their testimony that her spiritual life gave her the rewards otherwise denied her in her short life. A.P.'s framing of Davy's text may be contrasted to Daniel Baker's handling of the letters and narratives of Katherine Evans and Sarah Cheevers. Evans and Cheevers clearly shared the same goals as Baker. While Davy intends to serve as an example, it is A.P. who gives her life and text their polemical cast. Excerpts from *Heaven Realiz'd* appear in Graham *et al.*, *Her Own Life: Autobiographical Writings by Seventeenth-Century English Women*.

Although the British Library copy reproduced in Volume 1 has been cropped too closely and is bound too tightly for perfect reproduction, the other exemplars are too fragile to reproduce.

Theodosia Alleine (fl. 1653–77)

Her birth and her marriage placed Theodosia Alleine at the center of the Dissenting community in mid-seventeenth-century England. Born at Ditcheat, Somerset, the daughter of clergyman Richard Alleine (1611–1681), Theodosia married relative and clergyman Joseph Alleine (1634–1668) in 1659. Educated at Oxford, Joseph began his ministry in 1654 as assistant to the Reverend George Newton at Taunton. Theodosia ran a school for local children while her husband conducted church activities. Ejected from his position in 1662, Joseph began evangelizing and in the next several years was repeatedly jailed. His health failed and, after repeated illnesses during which he was nursed by Theodosia, Joseph died in 1668 at the age of 34. Theodosia survived him by at least sixteen years, during which she remarried. She died before 1685.

'A Full Narrative of His Life'

The book *The Life and Death of Mr Joseph Alleine* was first published in London in 1671 in 8°. Although many bibliographies list Theodosia as the author, the text is in fact a series of testimonials to Joseph written by many prominent puritan clergymen, including Richard Baxter, father-in-law Richard Alleine, George Newton, and Richard Fairclough. It concludes with several of Joseph's letters and his funeral sermon. Theodosia contributed the sixth chapter: 'A full Narrative of his Life from his silencing to his Death; by his Widow Mrs. Theodosia Alleine, in her own words; wherein is notably set forth with what patience he ran the race that was set before him, and fulfilled the Ministry that he had received in the Lord'. Theodosia's chapter, included in this volume, incorporates one of her husband's speeches, an 'Exhortation to his Fellow Sufferers', delivered in prison before they, but not he, were released.

   The book proved to be extremely popular. It was reprinted once in 1671 (five exemplars surviving from the two printings), three times in 1672 (a total of twenty-four exemplars), once in 1673 (seven exemplars), once in 1677 (nine exemplars) and once in 1693 (two exemplars). The 1672 printings corresponded to the publication of Joseph's book *An Alarum to the Unconverted* which, according to the *Dictionary of National Biography*, sold 20,000 copies in its first edition, and another 50,000 in 1675 when it was reprinted as *Sure Guide to Heaven*. *The Life and Death of Mr. Joseph Alleine* thus presented an exemplary life of a puritan clergyman at a time when Dissenters were subject to harsh laws and governmental repression.

   In contrast to the works of many of the other writers in these volumes, Theodosia's account reached an exceptionally wide audience. Her narrative is the sixth of nine chapters, all testifying to the high moral character of Joseph. The unidentified editor stresses the difficult circumstances of all the writers, commenting that two anonymous chapters were 'written by two Conformable Ministers' who clearly ran a risk of losing their livings if their friendship with Joseph were known. The same editor advises readers that Theodosia had prepared her contribution as notes to be used by 'a worthy Divine' in his own work, but he and others 'upon perusal, saw no reason to alter it, but caused it to be printed as it is'. Theodosia's chapter is noteworthy for the honesty with which she describes the hardships of life married to a man who appeared at times to be more devoted to the church than to his family. Moreover, it presents a rare example of a woman writer 'framing' the words of a man, as Theodosia inserts Joseph's 'Exhortation' in the middle of her chapter. The inclusion of her chapter in the commemorative volume dignifies both the private life of a public figure and the insights of an articulate woman.

'A full Narrative of his Life', excerpted from *The Life and Death of Mr Joseph Alleine*, and reproduced in Volume 2, is taken from the fine copy owned by Cambridge University Library, one of the few surviving exemplars of the first printing of 1671.

Anne Wentworth (fl. 1650s–77)

Married around 1653 and often in failing health, Anne Wentworth led a difficult life with her husband until her healing and conversion in 1671 (Old Style 1670). From that time onwards, her marriage worsened until, after considerable provocation, she left it in 1674 (Old Style 1673). Her actions precipitated great public arguments with her Baptist church in London, headed by Hanserd Knollys. These experiences prompted her to write the two works discussed here as well as *England's Spiritual Pill* (?1678) and *The Revelation of Jesus Christ* (1679). Several of her letters appear in *CSPD* 1677.

True Account

Wentworth's first publication was *A True Account of Anne Wentworths Being Cruelly, Unjustly, and Unchristianly Dealt with by Some of those People Called Anabaptists*, a 4° edition, printed in 1676, probably in London, with a simply-designed title page. It bears the author's name not only on the title page but at the end of the narrative. Only two exemplars exist, and the work went through only one printing. The text itself is a narrative describing Wentworth's view of her miserable marriage and the harsh judgment she received from members of her church. It also is noteworthy for its insistence that God's word was never meant to justify the mistreatment of a wife and that she had a right to redress of grievances.

The base copy of this extremely rare book reproduced in Volume 2 is owned by the Folger Shakespeare Library.

A Vindication

The following year saw the publication of *A Vindication of Anne Wentworth, Tending to the Better Preparing of All People for Her Larger Testimony, which is Making Ready for Publick View*. This text, a 4° edition, includes a supporting but unsigned letter 'by an eminent Christian' and a hymn by Wentworth, called by her a 'Song of Tryumph'. Like her previous work, this text was printed once. Two exemplars survive. In this work, Wentworth elaborates on her previous narrative, this time presenting more scriptural references to underscore the rightness of her leaving her husband. The supporting letter calls attention to *A True Account*, asking Baptist preachers 'Can you prove that God hath not spoken to her and by her? No, you dare not produce that Book of hers ... you too well know it would demonstrate her to be in the Truth, and your selves shameless Lyars'. Readers may compare Wentworth's two books to Susanna Parr's *Svsanna's Apologie Against the Elders* (in Volume 1). Both assert their right to independent action and challenge criticism of them based on gender, but for Wentworth gender is at the heart of her dispute with her church as she makes the case for her right to leave her marriage. Excerpts appear in Graham *et al.*, *Her Own Life: Autobiographical Writings by Seventeenth- Century English Women*.

The base copy of this very rare book reproduced in Volume 2 is the exemplar owned by The British Library. The sole other existing copy, owned by the William Andrews Clark Memorial Library, is cropped at the top, affecting page numbers.

Mary Penington (c. 1625–82)

The daughter of Anne (Fagge) and Sir John Proude, Mary Penington was born around 1625 in Kent and was orphaned by 1628. The heiress of both her parents, trained as an oculist and druggist, she married Sir William Springett in 1642. He became a colonel in the parliamentary army, dying in 1644. Mary and William had two children, including daughter Gulielma Maria, who later became the wife of prominent Quaker William Penn. In 1654 Mary married the clergyman Isaac Penington, son of Isaac Penington, Alderman and Lord Mayor of London in 1642, who was subsequently imprisoned for his antiroyalist activity and died in the Tower of London in 1661. At some time subsequent to their marriage, Mary and Isaac joined the Society of Friends. By 1656 her house at Chalfont St Peter (Buckinghamshire) had become a meeting house. Isaac wrote extensively for the Society, and, after he died in 1679, his works were collected and published. After his death Mary wrote several manuscript accounts of her life which she prepared for her family and which were published by Quaker printers in the late eighteenth and early nineteenth centuries: *A Brief Account of My Exercises from Childhood* (1668–80), published in a work by Christopher Taylor (1797); and *Some Account of the Circumstances in the Life of Mary Penington, from Her Manuscript, Left for Her Family* (1821, 1848). Mary died in 1682 and was buried next to her husband at Jordans, Buckinghamshire. The Chalfont Meeting was established with assistance from Mary's estate.

'Mary Penington her Testimony'

'Mary Penington her Testimony concerning her Dear Husband' was her only work published in her lifetime. It is a two-page account that forms part of the preface to *The Works of the Long-Mournful and Sorely-Distressed Isaac Penington, Whom the Lord in his Tender Mercy, at length Visited and Relieved by the Ministry of that Despised People, called Quakers*, a handsomely-produced folio volume published in London by Benjamin Clark in 1681. Mary's text accompanies the testimonies of many prominent Quakers, including George Fox and the Peningtons' son-in-law William Penn. Mary is the only woman represented. *The Works* was frequently reprinted throughout the eighteenth and nineteenth centuries. Sixteen exemplars of the first edition survive. In a concluding note, Mary comments that she wrote her account 'between 12 and 1 at night, while I was watching with my sick child'. Her text focuses on Isaac's character, especially his '*hidden life*', known only to herself and God. Like Theodosia Alleine, Mary Penington offers her unique perspective as a further way of understanding and appreciating her husband. Unlike Alleine, Mary describes her great sense of loss and the companionate nature of her marriage.

Because of its high degree of legibility, the exemplar owned by The Huntington Library was chosen as base copy for Volume 2.

Mary Rowlandson (?1635–1711)

Although she was probably born in England, Mary Rowlandson is best known as one of the earliest American writers. Born around 1635, she was the daughter of John White, one of the founders of Lancaster, Massachusetts, where her family moved in 1653. Around 1656 she married Joseph Rowlandson, minister of Lancaster, with whom she had four children. Little is known of their lives until 10 February 1676 (Old Style 1675) when Mary and her children were captured by Indians in an attack on Lancaster that was part of King Philip's War. Mary was moved several times by her captors, living with them until she was ransomed in May. Her three surviving children were released shortly thereafter. In the following year she and her husband moved to Wethersfield, Connecticut, where he was called to the ministry. According to the *Dictionary of American Biography*, Wethersfield voted Mary an allowance when her husband died in 1678. Remarried in 1679 to Captain Samuel Talcott, she died in 1711.

A True History of the Captivity & Restoration

The first edition of Rowlandson's narrative was published in Boston in 1682, under the title *The Soveraignty & Goodness of God ... Being a Narrative of the Captivity and Restauration of Mrs. Mary Rowlandson*. Only fragments survive. A second edition, 'Corrected', was printed in Cambridge, Massachusetts by Samuel Green in 1682 and reprinted in London in the same year under the title *A True History of the Captivity & Restoration of Mrs. Mary Rowlandson, A Minister's Wife in New-England*. In the English version, but not the American, Mary's narrative is framed by an opening preface, signed "Per Amicum", and concludes with what is identified as Joseph Rowlandson's last sermon. Six exemplars survive of the American edition, twelve of the English. The existing copies of the American edition, an 8°, are in poor condition: the type is still clearly legible, but many pages are torn or have portions missing. The extant copies of the English edition, a 4°, are in much better condition, although the typeface is smaller and more difficult to read than in the American edition. One of the earliest books by an American woman, Rowlandson's work is also one of the first examples of the New World captivity narrative. Its form and sensibility established many of the features repeated in subsequent narratives through the nineteenth century. The book went through some thirty printings before the advent of modern editions, and remains one of the most frequently anthologized works of early American literature. The American edition most recently has been edited by Neal Salisbury for the Bedford Series in History and Culture (Boston: Bedford, 1997). Because of its pivotal position in both American and European history, the book continues to attract extensive critical attention. Of all the works in these two volumes, Rowlandson's is the only one with a substantial secondary bibliography. Earlier twentieth-century scholars studied the text as a step in the formation of a national identity. Recent studies have considered Rowlandson's narrative as a microcosm of colonialism, seeing in her text the psychological damage feared by Europeans in their encounters with alien 'others'; and as a vehicle for self-assertion amid conflicts of gender roles and expectations. Both feminist and historical scholars have incontrovertibly established Rowlandson's work as a key text in the development of modern identity.

Because of the poor condition of existing American editions and many of the London editions, the London edition owned by The Huntington Library has been chosen as base copy for Volume 2.

Hannah Allen (fl. before 1670–83)

Born around 1638, Hannah Allen was the daughter of John Archer of Snelton, Derbyshire, and his wife, the daughter of William Hart of Uttoexeter Woodland, Staffordshire. Her father died when she was a child, and she was raised partly by her mother in Snelton and partly by her paternal aunt in London. Around 1654 she married the merchant Hannibal Allen, who died at sea around 1662. This event precipitated a serious depression, from which Allen suffered for several years, aided by her relatives, several members of the clergy and her Baptist faith. Some time after 1667 she married Charles Hatt of Warwickshire; she died before 1683.

A Narrative of God's Gracious Dealings

The account of Allen's depression, *A Narrative of God's Gracious Dealings with that Choice Christian Mrs. Hannah Allen*, published with the running title *Satan's Methods and Malice Baffled*, was printed in 8° in London by John Wallis in 1683. The text begins with an extensive, anonymous preface describing the exemplary nature of the mental struggles of this 'Now-glorified Soul' who presumably died before publication. The narrative follows, giving a detailed description of the onset and progress of Allen's depression and its treatment, and concludes with several scriptural passages that Allen found especially comforting. Seven exemplars exist of this work, and apparently all are missing pages 75 through 78. There are no modern editions. The preface to the work explicitly urges the reader to regard this narrative as an aid in combatting what the writer perceives to be a common problem confronting the faithful: the depression that sometimes arises from an overwhelming conviction of one's own sinfulness. The writer compares Allen's experiences to those of '*an eminent and holy Minister of Christ, that once counted himself a Reprobate*' and finds in their experiences strong reasons to avoid sin and assert one's commitment to one's faith in light of the irreligion of the times. Like the work of her sister Baptist Katherine Sutton, Allen's text may be compared to Bunyan's *Grace Abounding to the Chief of Sinners* and other Baptist spiritual autobiographies, many of which describe encounters with despair. Allen's experiences are noteworthy because they form the principal subject of her book and because she describes at length the efforts of others to respond to her with compassion. As presented, her depression was the central, formative experience in her religious life, challenging her as others were challenged by prison and government persecution. Excerpts appear in Graham *et al., Her Own Life: Autobiographical Writings by Seventeenth-Century English Women.*

Although it is severely cropped, we have chosen as base copy for Volume 2 the exemplar owned by The British Library because of its superior legibility. Unfortunately it, like all other known exemplars, is missing pages 75–78.

Barbara Blaugdone (1609–1704)

A determined Quaker traveler and preacher, Barbara Blaugdone was probably born in Bristol around 1609. She died in London in 1704 at the age of 95. Introduced in 1654 to the Society of Friends by John Audland, husband of Anne Audland, who herself was a distinguished pamphleteer for the Friends, Blaugdone journeyed throughout England and Ireland 'on my own Purse', facing such hardships as robbery, whipping, death threats and an accusation of witchcraft. Imprisoned for her religious activities in 1655, 1664, 1681 and 1683, Blaugdone occasionally supported herself as a schoolmistress.

An Account of the Travels

Blaugdone's sole publication, *An Account of the Travels, Sufferings & Persecutions of Barbara Blaugdone*, was published in small 8° by Quaker printer Tace Sowle in London in 1691. The book has a plain, unadorned title page and begins with Blaugdone's narrative, with no intervening prefatory matter. Four exemplars survive. There are no modern editions. Blaugdone gives very few details of her own life before her conversion. In effect, her life begins at that point, and her narrative is filled with specific references to people and places, and to the events that frequently sent her to prison. The text is a chronicle of the author's determination to preach in the face of opposition and hardship, once even being accused of witchcraft. Her method of presenting her experiences compares to Katherine Evans and Sarah Cheevers's narrative of their own experiences in captivity. All confront others who do not share their religious convictions but, in contrast to Rowlandson's account of her captivity, reproduced in Volume 2, all three Quaker women emphasize not their loss of freedom but their efforts to assert and witness publicly for their faith.

The base copy reproduced in Volume 2, chosen for its legibility, availability, and association with the Society of Friends, is owned by the Friends House Library.

Susannah Blandford (fl. 1658–1700)

The S.B. of the title page of *A Small Account* is believed to be Susanna Blandford, a follower of the Quaker preacher William Rogers from Northamptonshire. S.B. was born around 1658, brought up in the Church of England, began to suffer from spiritual troubles in her teens and experienced conversion at the age of 24. She was married, had several children and also wrote *A Small Treatise Writ by One of the True Christian Faith; who Believes in God and in his Son Jesus Christ*, published in London in 1700.

A Small Account

Blandford's personal narrative, *A Small Account Given Forth*, was printed in 8°, in 1698, probably in London. The book opens with a brief preface by Blandford declaring her desire to share her experiences with others. The narrative follows, and the text concludes with a poem and several postscripts defending the beliefs and actions of the Quakers. The book was published once; three exemplars survive. There are no modern editions. In contrast to the works of other Quaker women included in these volumes, Blandford includes no account of prison or physical hardship. She emphasizes instead her spiritual journey, the teachings that most influenced her and her opposition to extensive preaching, especially by women. The concluding postscripts exemplify her confidence in discussing the politics of religion in a climate unfavorable to Dissenters.

Chosen for its availability and legibility, the exemplar owned by Cambridge University Library is reproduced in Volume 2.

References

Wing C 6008 [Cook(e)], Wing P 551 [Parr], Wing T 935 [Evans and Cheevers], Wing S 6212 [Sutton], Wing W 3772 [Wyndham], Wing D 444 [Davy], Wing A 1011B [Alleine], Wing W 1355A [Wentworth, *True Account*], Wing W 1356 [Wentworth, *Vindication*], Wing P 1149 [Penington], Wing R 2094 [Rowlandson], Wing A 1025 [Allen], Wing A 410 [Blaugdone], Wing B 3163A [Blandford]

Bell, Maureen, George Parfitt, and Simon Shepherd (eds) (1990), *A Biographical Dictionary of English Women Writers 1580–1720*, Boston: GK Hall

Besse, Joseph (1753), *A Collection of the Sufferings of the People Called Quakers, for the Testimony of a Good Conscience*, 2 vols, London

Bevan, Joseph Gurney (1831), *Memoirs of the Life of Isaac Penington; to which is Added A Review of His Writings*, Philadelphia: Thomas Kite

Blain, Virginia, Patricia Clements, and Isobel Grundy (eds) (1990) *The Feminist Companion to Literature in English: Women Writers from the Middle Ages to the Present*, New Haven and London: Yale University Press

Blount, Thomas (1681), *Boscobel, or, The Compleat History of His Sacred Majesties Most Miraculous Preservation after the Battle of Worcester, 3 Sept. 1651*, 3rd ed., 2 vols, London

Crawford, Patricia (1993), *Women and Religion in England 1500–1720*, London: Routledge

Derounian-Stodola, Kathryn Zabelle and James Arthur Levernier (1993), *The Indian Captivity Narrative, 1550–1900*, Twayne's United States Authors Series, 622, New York: Twayne Publishers; Toronto: Maxwell Macmillan Canada

Ebersole, Gary L. (1995), *Captured by Texts: Puritan to Postmodern Images of Indian Captivity*, Charlottesville and London: University Press of Virginia

Edwards, Karen (1997), '*Susanna's Apologie* and the Politics of Privity', *Literature and History*, 6

Graham, Elspeth (1990), 'Authority, Resistance and Loss: Gendered Difference in the Writings of John Bunyan and Hannah Allen' in Anne Laurence, W. R. Owens and Stuart Sim (eds), *John Bunyan and his England, 1628–88*, London and Ronceverte: Hambledon Press

Graham, Elspeth (1996), 'Women's Writing and the Self' in Helen Wilcox (ed.), *Women and Literature in Britain, 1500–1700*, Cambridge and New York: Cambridge University Press

Graham, Elspeth, Hilary Hinds, Elaine Hobby, and Helen Wilcox (eds) (1989), *Her Own Life: Autobiographical Writings by Seventeenth-Century English Women*, London: Routledge

Greene, David L. (1985), 'New Light on Mary Rowlandson', *American Literature*, 20

Hobby, Elaine (1992), '"Discourse So Unsavory": Women's Published Writings of the 1650s' in Isobel Grundy and Susan Wiseman (eds), *Women, Writing, History 1640–1740*, Athens: University of Georgia Press

Hobby, Elaine (1988), *Virtue of Necessity: English Women's Writing 1646–1688*, London: Virago

Jansen, Sharon (1996), *Dangerous Talk and Strange Behavior: Women and Popular Resistance to the Reforms of Henry VIII*, New York: St. Martin's

Knollys, Hanserd (1691), *An Answer to a Brief Discourse Concerning Singing in the Publick Worship of God in the Gospel-Church* [London]

Mack, Phyllis (1992), *Visionary Women: Ecstatic Prophecy in Seventeenth-Century England*, Berkeley: University of California Press

Mallard, Ian M. (1963), 'Hymns of Katherine Sutton', *Baptist Journal*, January

Mendelson, Sara Heller (1985), 'Stuart Women's Diaries and Occasional Memoirs' in Prior, Mary (ed.), *Women in English Society 1500–1800*, London and New York: Methuen

Pratt, Mary Louise (1992), *Imperial Eyes: Travel Writing and Transculturation*, London and New York: Routledge

S., W. (1661), *A Complete Collection of the Lives, Speeches, Private Passages, Letters and Prayers of those Persons Lately Executed*, London

Smith, Joseph (1867), *A Descriptive Catalogue of Friends' Books, Or Books Written by Members of the Society of Friends, Commonly Called Quakers, From their First Rise to the Present Time*, 2 vols, London: Joseph Smith, rpt (1970) New York: Kraus Reprint Co.

Warburton, Rachel M. (1999), 'Not a Description of Sodom's Glory: Quaker Women Travelers and Biblical Geography', Women and Knowledge in the Seventeenth Century, Renaissance Society of America Annual Meeting, The J. Paul Getty Museum and Research Institute, 27 March

ELIZABETH SKERPAN-WHEELER

M^{ris.} Cookes Meditations (Wing C6008), shelfmark E. 600. (9), is reproduced by permission of The British Library. The text block of the original measures 154 × 94 mm.

Reading where the British Library copy is obscure:

5.31   some
5.32   that
5.33   as

M^{ris.} COOKES

MEDITATIONS,

Being an humble thankſgiving to her

HEAVENLY FATHER,

For granting her a new life, having conclnded
her ſelfe dead, and her grave made in the bottome of the Sea, in that great ſtorme.
Ϳan. the 5th. 1649.

Compoſed by her ſelfe at her unexpected ſafe
Arrivall at C O R C K E.

C O R K E, Printed,
And reprinted at *London* by *C. S.* and are to be ſold
by *Thomas Brewſter* and *Gregory Mould*, at the three Bibles
May. 9 at the Weſt-end of *Pauls*,

M^{ris}. COOKES

MEDITATIONS,

BEING

An humble thanksgiving to her Heavenly Father, for
granting her a new life, having concluded her selfe dead,
and her grave made in the bottome of the Sea.

Aving solemnly promised to the most high God in the grea
storme, that if his Majesty would be pleased to prolong my
dayes, and deliver me from so great a danger, I would studie
to prayse and glorifie his Name all the dayes of my life, and
call upon others that were in the storme so to doe, if I shall
neglect so to do these broken Meditations may be an evidence
against me; written suddenly after my comming to *Corke*, *Psal.* 118. 17.
verse. I shall not dye but live and declare the works of the Lord : 66. *Psal.* 16.
Come and heare all yee that feare God, and I will declare what he hath done
for my soule, 19. *verse*, I cryed unto him with my mouth, and he was extolled
with my tongue. *Psal.* 56. 12. thy vowes are upon me oh God! I will render
prayse unto thee, for thou hast made a path in the great waters for thy redeemed to passe through, and hast brought thy ransomed ones safe to land, therefore blesse the Lord oh my soule, and forget not such mercies, who hast forgiven all mine iniquities and saved my life from so great a danger! oh that I could
spend this new life wholly in thy service, and that I might live to the prayse and
glory of his grace, wherein he hath made me accepted in his beloved, *Eph.* 2. 6. *v.*

Landing in *Kinsale*, I said, am I alive or dead ? Doth not the ground move
under mee ? I have been dying all this storme, and I cannot tell whether I am
yet alive ; I finding my body much out of frame, and my heart fainting, having been ten dayes at sea without eating, but the next day the Lord made mee
more sensible of my new life : and when I came to dive into the mighty depth of
the love of God, in granting mee deliverance from so great a danger, my heart
was so brim-full with the apprehension of his tender mercies, that. I could not
containe my selfe, but must needs burst forth in teares, for feare I should not
live sutable to so great a mercy, and I said to my friends, that I would gladly be
with my Saviour, if it pleased him to take mee : for the mercy I received was so

great

great, that I should never be able to walk answerably in holinesse to the Lord and my care is, that I might not be found a fruitlesse figtree in the garden of my God, when Christ said, I am come into my garden my sister, my spouse, it was but to gather fruit; but when he expected fruit and found none, he was displeased.

I know it is a great mercy to blesse God for mercies, and they which have a heart to blesse God for mercies, ought to have a tongue to prayse him for the same; and a pen to record them, we being too prone to let them slip out of our memories, which if I shall do, I desire my hand may be brought to testifie against me, my heart and tongue shall not only prayse him, but with my pen also will I stirre up my self, and intreat all others that were in the same storme partakers with me of the same deliverance, to magnifie the Lord for ever. Oh ye couragious Sea-men that said, you were at your wits end, and knew not what would become of you, prayse ye the Lord; O ye that came into the great Cabbin to dye with us, blesse his name for ever. O ye that said you would give all you had to be landed even in your enemies Quarters, that you might fight for your lives, prayse him that is Lord of the Sea, that now we see the faces of our friends in peace, and can joyfully meet together to keep dayes of thanksgiving to the Lord.

Jesus Christ took speciall notice of the Lepers, *Luke* 17. 15, 16. *verses*: but one of them when he saw that he was healed, turned back, and with a loud voyce glorified God, and fell downe on his face at his feet, giving him thanks, but Jesus said, were there not ten clensed, but where are the nine? It is all Christ requires of a Saint to be praised for deliverances; as he saith, *Psal.* 50. 15. Call upon me in the day of trouble, I will deliver thee, but thou shalt glorifie mee.

But no soule can glorifie and praise God, but those whose hearts He hath wound up, and tuned to such a spirituall note, because they are birds which fly high upon the wing of faith, and may have place to sit and sing neer the altar of God: and those that are thus admitted into the holy of holyes to sing *Hallelujah's* to the Name of the most high God, and to the Lambe, are the spirits of just men made perfect already in heaven and those who are kept through the power of God by faith, **1** *Pet.* 1. 5. while they are in the world untill they come to be made one with the Father, and the Son, when this mortality shall be swallowed up of life, and we crowned with an incorruptible crowne of glory, and come to be made perfectly glorious through Christ, and perfectly holy, then shall we be fit to come into the presence of our God and, behold his glory, and admire him who is the King of Saints, and then shall we worship and sing everlasting prayse to the Lord God Almighty, who is great and marvellous in all his

workes

workes, and juft and true in all his wayes. Thus to prayfe God is the worke of Angells, which they doe, and fhall doe to all eternity, who are glorious creatures without finne, which are fet apart onely for the worke of prayfing God. Oh the difproportion betwixt Men and Angells! And yet God requires and looks for prayfe from men as well as from Angells. But Lord, who is fufficient for thefe things? who is worthy to undertake the worke of Angells? whofe fpirits are thus afcended up on high to make an Evangelicall harmony in the eares of fo holy a God? whofe hearts are fitted and tuned to fing everlafting prayfes and *Hallelujah's* to the mighty Lord God of mercies to our foules, redeeming mercies juftifying mercies, temporall deliverances? God requires prayfe of every one that he workes deliverance for, whether fpirituall or temporall.

He that eateth after ten dayes fafting let him give thanks, yee that have efcaped the rocks remember the Lord. Ye whom God hath kept from finking and perifhing in the deepe waters praife him: Ye which are living monuments of his late mercy, and have been preferved by the immediate wonderfull hand of God, praife him. Ye for whofe fakes he rebuked the Sea, and made the proud waves calme, and hath fet your feet upon dry ground, declare that God is a prefent help in time of trouble, *Pfal. 46. 1. verfe.* and tell his goodneffe to the fons of men. The Lord would not have his people to forget his mercies, but he puts them in mind of deliverances. How often doth he tell us in Scripture, that he is our God, and that he brought us out of the Land of *Egypt*, and that with his holy Arme he hath wrought falvation for his chofen. *Ingratitude* is a very great fin, becaufe it is a breach of the Commandements of God; you fhall glorify me, faith he, when *I* deliver you, and *I* will be praifed by them that dwell upon the earth. The Lord Commands, and requires his people to be thankfull for mercies, and he takes it very unkindly when they will not fo much as returne thanks. 50. *Pf.* 8. The Lord cares not for burnt-offering and facrifices nor cattell upon a thoufand hills, nor for all the fowles of the mountaines nor the beafts of the fields, but, faith he gather my Saints together unto me, 5. *v.* thofe that have made a Covenant with me.

⹂ And what doth God require of his Saints, when they fo affemble together to remember fuch mercies, but prayfe and thankfgiving, and fpecially to pay their vowes unto the moft high *verfe* 14? Yet many of Gods people are very backward in duty of thankfgiving, and that we fee by the Lords oft putting them in mind to pay their vowes, and to performe their Covenant which they make with him in the day of their afiliction. The Lord knowes very well when his people moft frequent him, as he faith, *Hofea 5. 15. verfe*, In their afliiction they will feeke me early, but in the day of their profperity they forget their maker, *Hofea*
8. 14.

8. 14. So that the Lord complaines, that he knowes not what to do with thefe people. He findes fuch ebbings and flowings in their unconftant affections, that he compares them to the clouds *Hofea* 6. 4. Oh *Efraim* what fhall I do unto thee? oh *Judah*, what fhall I do unto thee? for your righteoufnefs is as the morning cloud, and as the early dew it goeth away.

I am confident that there is not one that was in this ftorme of tryall, as I may fo call it, or a ftorm wherein we might found our hearts & have the bottom of the inward vitalls difcovered to our felves, efpecially fuch as feared the Lord, and have had former acquaintance with him, by way of communion through his Son, but did folemnly enter into a Covenant with God, and made vowes unto the moft high, in the great ftorme, that if he fhould come and ranfome them now when they were almoft finking from the power of the grave, which to all apprehenfions was prepared in the feas, and redeeme them from the jawes of death, which then prefented it felfe moft dreadfull, and fave their lives when they faw no way to efcape death.

That they would give up themfelves wholly unto the Lord all the dayes of their lives, and ftudy how to live anfwerable to fo great a mercy, and that they woul live as refined ones whom God hath pluckt out of the fire, and out of the water, and if they knew any way more pure or holy then other wherein they might glorify God & advance his praife, they would do it, and that they would not value the world, nor men of the world, but that they would live like thofe whofe hearts God hath melted downe and overcome with loving kindnefs and mercyes, prefervations and deliverances: a heart that God hath melted downe with a fenfiblenefs of his fpirituall and temporall deliverances will be faying, Lord, what wilt thou have me to do? Loe I come to do thy will oh God; I am ready not only to be bound, but alfo to dye for the name of Jefus.

Therefore let me fpeake a word to them to whom God hath given new lives, and it may be hath added fome yeares to thefe renewed lives, give me leave to put you in minde to remember your vowes all the dayes of your lives, and live by faith and not by fenfe: *Job* would not reject the counfell of his fervant and therefore I fhall prefent fome Scriptures to your confiderations. *Jonah* 1. 16. we may obferve there, that when men are in ftormes and diftreffes; then they make vowes unto God, as you may fee in the 16. *verfe*: then the men feared the Lord exceedingly, and offered facrifice unto the Lord, and made vowes. *David* faid in *Pfal.* 61. 8. *verfe*. I will praife the Name of the Lord forever, that I may daily performe my vowes. *Pfal.* 116. 17. *verfe*: I will offer unto the Lord the facrifice of thankfgiving, I will pay my vowes unto the Lord in the prefence of all his people. When thou voweft unto the Lord, deferre not to pay it, *Ecclef.* 5. 4. *v. Job* 22. 27. *verfe*. Thou fhalt make thy prayer un-

A 3

to the Lord, and he shall heare thee and thou shalt pay thy vowes. *Numb.* 30. 2. *verse.* If a man vow a vow unto the Lord, or sweare an oath to bind his soule with a bond, he shall not breake his word, but he shall do according to all that proceedeth out of his mouth, *Deut.* 23. 21. When thou shalt vow a vow unto the Lord thy God, thou shalt not slack to pay it, for the Lord thy God will surely require it of thee, and it would be sin in thee.

God hath granted me the thing I prayed for, although he did not evidence to my heart then, that it should be granted, but he calmed and contented my heart, by giving me a quiet rest of spirit to submit to my Fathers good wil & pleasure; that living or dying it should goe well with me, and that I was not my owne but bought with a price 1 *Cor.* 6. 20. and therefore must glorifie God, both in my body and soule which are his.

The Lord comes to the quick, and puts me to the tryall, that I might know what temper I was made of, and what was in my owne heart, whether I had improved my talent, and what stock of grace I had gained to support at such a time of need, and if I had a spirit that durst encounter with death, let him appeare never so terrible, and in this trying condition the Lord kept me under water, as I may say, and expostulated the case with me, and put questions to my soule, and pleaded with me about life and death.

I mean onely this temporall death, for I blesse God I know that my Redeemer lives, all the time of the storme the Lord did sweetly smile upon my soule, and I found a strong sensiblenesse of his love and favourable presence in supporting my faith to believe, and in giving me assurance of my eternall salvation, thorough Jesus Christ my Lord and Saviour.

But concerning the being delivered from the power of the waves, the rage of the sea, and the danger of the rocks, the Lord hid it from me, and I could not believe that I should be preserved, neither could I tell whether God would put a period to my life, the Lord revealed it not to me concerning living and dying: but he fitted me for both, in believing that I was his, and I blesse his Name, the Lord kept me all the time of the storme in a submissive, humble, believing and quiet frame of spirit. and he spake to my heart by way of questioning with me, that suppose the Lord should spare my life now, and at another time should call for it : would I be contented to suffer for him by way of being a witnesse to his truth, and the faith of Jesus Christ, if he should call me to it? unto which I found my spirit willingly to submit, and I resolved with all my heart and soule to repay this dying life to my ever living God, whensoever he calls for it, and howsoever he will have me to come to him at sea or land, And I will not feare the King of terrors, as *Job* calls death, let him bring me to my Fathers house which way he will, whether through the fire or through the water, I

hop:

hope I shall be willing to suffer any death that might bring glory to him that hath suffered death to bring me to life, believing that Christ would not bring me into any condition but that he would be with me therein, and then I know that I can do any thing through him which strengtheneth me. 4. *Phil.* 13. *v.* For I blesse the Lord, I never once repined all the time, but I patiently lay expecting every houre when I should be dissolved and be with Christ in his glorious and triumphant Kingdome, and after the Lord had searched my heart, and had wrought in me a willingnesse to submit to him, and had shewed me what a solemne action it was to dye, and had made me sensible that there was a cloud of griefe, but faith would pierce thorough that, and see life in the midst of death, and that in finishing my course, and in resigning my spirit to God that gave it, I should find my fraile nature sinking, but the Divine Nature supporting, and that there is a little agony to be gon through about the time dissolution when the soule will be heavie unto death, notwithstanding a submission to its Fathers will. *Matth.* 26. 38, 39. *v.*

After the Lord had given me a taste of death, he gave me life, conditionaly that I should be willing to dye and suffer death for him at another time, if he called me to it, whereupon I solemnly promised & covenanted with God, and mad my vowes unto the most high, in the hearing of my dearest friend on earth & others: That if the Lord would deliver me out of this terrible storme and bring me safe to land againe and renew my dayes, I would give up my selfe and my new life wholly to the Lord & that I would walke more closely with him in holy Communion then ever I had done formerly & that I would no more live to my selfe, nor to the world but wholy to the Lord & that I would study to live more Gospel-like, declaring and holding forth to the world: that the Lord had overporwrd my soul by his free grace & overcome my heart with loving kindnes & many & extraordinary deliverances which cal for extraordinary praises; & if it pleased God to mak me partaker of such a singular mercy, I would not only record it in my heart all the dayes of my life, but in all places render thanks unto the Lord while I have any being; and tell all the world, that I have my life from Christ, and therefore must spend it for him. And the Lord did suddenly accomplish the thing which I had so earnestly prayed for, when the sea had done threatning it was mercifull ere I was aware of it, as if God would surprise me with deliverance, and I could scarce believe that I was come to a harbour when I was told so, the newes was so unexpected and sudden to me, that I was like those men that had prayed long for the returne of the captivity of *Babylon*, and it was the conclusion of many prayers, and when they saw that the Lord did accomplish it on a sudden, and the thing was done in a trice, they were as men in a dream. *Psal.* 126. 1. *verse.* they could scarce believe it was so, so the Lord wrought

deliverance

deliverance for *Peter* suddenly, when he was fast asleepe, and did not so much as think of it; and so the Lord delivered *Joseph* out of prison on a sudden, which shewed he had heard his prayer; therefore blessed be his Name for ever. And this the Lord doth to overcome the heart and to draw out the affections unto himselfe, and that he might be admired of his Saints, that they finding him giving in sweet and unexpected deliverances may returne everlasting praises unto him, and glory in the God of their salvation. *Psal.*40. 10, 11, *verses.* that they may learne alwayes to trust him for we had the sentence of death in our selves, that we should not trust in our selvs but in God which raiseth the dead, who delivered us from so great a death; and doth deliver, in whom we trust that hee will yet deliver 2: *Cor.*1.9.10. The Lord hath his path in the whirlewinde and in the storme *Nahum* 2.3. *verses,*

And the Lord answered *Job* out of the whirlewind *Job* 38. 2. *verse* and said *verse* 4 Where wast thou when I laid the foundations of the earth? hast thou entred into the springs of the Sea? or, hast thou walked in the search of the deeps? hath the gates of death been opened unto thee? or, hast thou seen the doores of the shadow of death? *verse* 7. 2 *King* 3. 11: And *Eliah* went up in a whirle winde into heaven, so that wee may see when the Lord descends to the creature, *Exod.* 19 18. or calls for it to ascend up to him, it is in some mirvelous and extraordinary manner, as by stormes and whirle-windes, fiery Chariots, and thick clouds, and hee gives us the reason why he doth so in *Exod* 19:9. that the people may believe for ever when he speakes to them. God hath severall wayes to speak, and after severall manner he doth reveale himselfe to the sons of men under the *Gospell* as well as under the Law, although some will not believe although one should come from the dead to speak to them: when the morning starres sing together, and all the the sons of God shout for joy, or who shut up the Sea, with doores when it brake forth as if it had issued out of the wombe and said, hitherto shall thy proud waves come and no further, and here shall they be stayed. Where the Lord Jesus is broken forth in spirit, where he is risen forth from the dead there is a glorious appearance of the presence of God which fills the soule with joy, when *Mary* came to *Elizabeth*, she said, what am I that the mother of my Lord should come unto mee? as soone as the voice of thy salvation sounded in my eares the Babe leaped in my wombe for joy, and shee said, *My soule doth magnifie the Lord, and my spirit doth rejoyce in God my Saviour,* if there be such rejoycing betwixt the Babe and his Mother for hearing the voice of the Mother of her Lord, what infinite transcendent happinesse, admirable delight and over-comming and ravishments of joy & abundance of rejoycing wil there be when the *Lord* himself shal apeir in

his

his glorious presence to the soule arayed with all his excellent
and glorious apparrell, travelling in the greatnesse of his strength
and power, having all his artillery of graces following him who
is the bright and glittering Morning Star that shineth in such
luster and brightnesse, and is the perfection of Beauty that it da-
zells the beholders ; and when the salutations of the Lord Himself
are heard thus to a Soule, saying, my lips Oh my Spouse drop as
the Hony-combe, speaking peace to the Soule, as when Christ
appeared unto His Disciples and said, Peace be unto you, His
Voyce is sweete, and His Countenance is comely, and a Soule
that Christ hath taken into Union with Himself, and saith, thou
art comely through the comelinesse that I have put upon thee,
I have crowned thee in the day of thy Espousall : so that in
the presence of Christ there is infinite cause of rejoycing, and the
Salutations of Christ are but invitations to come above and live
aloft in the highest Regions of light. *Revel.* 4. 1,2. And I heard
a voyce saying unto me, come up hither ; and immediatly I was
in the Spirit. Christ takes a soule into Communion with Himself, and sheweth it a glimpse of His glory that must be hereafter, whereupon the Soule concludes with the Disciples, when
they saw Christ transfigured on the Mount, that it is good for
them to be there, and *Stephen* being full of the Holy Ghost, said,
I see the Heavens opened, and Jesus standing at the right Hand
of God, and *Iohn* saw wonders in Heaven above : a Soul which
Christ hath taken up into his Presence Chamber, and pleads with
it there, shewing it the Thrones of God and the glory of His
Fathers Kingdom, will be transformed to the Image of God ;
when *Moses* had been talking with God upon the Mount the
People could not behold his Face, this glory and spirituall joy is
for the Children of the Bride-chamber, unto whom when Christ
appears he makes them so amiable and lovely a Spouse that he
admires the beauty and glory of his own Worke saying, thou art
all faire my love, thou hast no spot in thee, thou hast ravished my
Heart, my Sister, my Spouse ; thou hast ravished my Heart with
one of thy Eyes, *Cant.*6.5. Turne away thine Eyes from me for
thou hast overcome me. Hence Christ is overcome with the
beauty of a flourishing Soul and admires it, and the Spouse, hearing the voyce of her beloved, eechoes back again, admiration of

B   her

her love than he was the chiefest of ten thousand, *Cant.* 5. 10. He
is white and ruddy, His Countenance is excellent, His Mouth
is most sweet, he is altogether lovely, here the Spouse would, if
it were possible outvye Christ by way of admiration : here is the
displaying the colours of each other, as if they would see which
could advance highest in exaltations, and needs must there be
joy in such a Soul that is betrothed unto Christ; and made one
with Him, very well may it break forth into a singing note; my
Beloved spake and sayd unto me; Rise up my love and faire one
and come away. *Cant.* 2. 10. For loe the Winter is past, the
Raine is over and gone, the Flowers appeare on the Earth, and
the time of singing of Birds is come; now will I sing unto my well
beloved a song of prayses and thanksgiving. *Psal.* 47. 6. Sing
prayse unto God, sing prayse, sing prayse unto our King, sing
yee prayses with understanding. *Psal.* 59. 17. unto thee O my
strength will I sing, for God is my defence and the God of my
mercies, *Hebr.* 2. 12. I will declare thy Name unto my Brethren
in the middst of the Church, I will sing prayse unto thee, 1 *Chro.*
16. 8. Give thanks unto the Lord, call upon His Name, make
known his deeds amongst the people, sing unto him, sing Psalmes
unto him, talke yee of all his wondrous Workes, glory yee in
his holy Name, let the heart of them rejoyce that seeke the Lord,
Job. 29. 13. Let the Widdowes heart sing for joy when the blessings of him that was ready to perish came upon me saying, I will
give her the valley of Achor for a door of hope, and thee shall
sing there as in the dayes of her youth, and as in the day when she
came up out of the Land of *Egypt*. That temporall deliverance,
God records as remarkable for praise to be sung unto him, and
puts it in the forefront of his ten holy Commandements; When
Davids soule lay under sin he heard nothing of joy and gladnesse,
as we may see in his complant. *Psal.* 51. 6. *Verse* 3. He cryed,
make me to hear of joy and gladnesse, *Verse* 8. Restore unto me
the joy of thy Salvation, so that we may see the times of restoration, either out of a relapse from sin, or by deliverance from danger of death are rejoycing times.

The thoughts of God from everlasting, were thoughts of
mercy, love and peace, and when he doth show mercies by
wonderfull deliverances, he doth act but in his own element, for
he

he delights to show mercy unto the sons of Men; I will have
mercy on whom I will have mercy; Gods Will and Mercy
is the fountaine and spring of our eternall Salvation and of our
temporall deliverances, I remember very well in the middst of
the storme, that I fled for refuge to the anchor of Faith, and the
VVill of God, saying to my friend, that the Lord saith, I will
never leave thee, nor forsake thee, and I will not cast thee off,
assuring my self, that it was the VVill of God that I should receive the welcome of my Father pronounced by the Son. Come
yee blessed of my Father, inherit the Kingdome prepared for you
before the foundation of the world.

Notwithstanding all the comfort and encouragement that my
deere Husband gave me, saying, that I had no cause to be
troubled at all, in respect of any danger, and bad me sleepe
and be still, for all was as well as Heart could wish, and I should
land safely, saying he was as sure of safety as if he was on shore,
and said; he would not give a farthing to have his life secured
him, nay, if the Ship brake in pieces yet we and he should be
safe he knew, thereupon I asked him if he knew what he said,
surely he was in a Dreame, why would he be so confident of
safety when the Captaine and all the rest said, they knew not
what would become of them, expecting every minute nothing
but Death, and he replyed, that he had Dreamed, that Jesus
Christ told him so, and therefore he would believe it. I find
that God had formerly revealed Himself to His servants by Vi-
sitions and Dreames: as in the 1 Kings 3. 5. Verse: when
the Lord so lovingly appeared to Solomon, and asked him what
he should doe for him, as if he would lay aside all his VVill and
desires, and condescend to Solomons request. Aske what I
should give thee, saith God, as if he would refer Himself to Solomons demands, and say not as I will, but as thou wilt, which
is the highest expression of love from the Lord to the Creature,
as I have found in all the Booke of God, and yet we see that
it was in a Dreame that the Lord thus revealed his infinite Love,
so that we may here learne there is no time excluded from
GODS manifesting Himself to His People, but that it is all
one to Him to speak in a Dreame by Night, as in a Cloud by
Day, Verse 5. Yet I marvelled at His confidence, and could not

believe

believe it, as to assure my self of my life, but my fears were much above my hopes, I confess I had a submissive hope to have life, but no assurance at all of life, *It was enough*, as *Jacob* said, *that my son Joseph is yet alive*; it was enough for me that my Soul should ever live with the Lord, and upon this rock he brought me, and set my feet upon that rock that was higher then I, which only is my rock and my salvation, *Psal.62.2.* Upon which rock the foundation of my eternal comfort was built, when the rain descended, and the flouds came, and the wind blew and beat upon my soul, my heart fell not from my God, & when we were like to have been split in pieces upon the rocks in the Sea called the 3 *Stags*, I said I would cast my soul and body into the arms of my sweet Saviour, and if I perished I would perish there. And now seeing it hath pleased God to give us new lives, let us desire one thing more of our good God, which he would not deny, *Psal. 27.4.* and say with *Elijah*, 2 *King.2.9.* I pray thee let a double portion of thy Spirit be upon me, as my life is doubled: So let it be our souls desire to have a double portion of the Spirit of God upon this new life, and withall an understanding heart, 1 *King.3.9. Then opened he their understandings, that they might understand the Scriptures, Luk.24.45.* And although *Elijah* said to *Elisha*, That he had asked a hard thing, yet God delights that we should ask of him hard things, for it is for a great God to give great things, as you shall see in 1 *King.3.10.* And the speech pleased the Lord, that *Solomon* had asked understanding, and he gave it him; and said, That he had given him also that which he had not asked for, which was a long life; but it was but conditionally that God said, *Solomon* should have it, 1 *King.3.14. And if thou wilt walk in my Ways, and keep my Commandments, as thy father David did, then will I lengthen thy days:* and upon this condition the Lord gives *Solomon* a new life; Verf.15. *And Solomon awaked, and behold, it was a dream*; yet notwithstanding the thing was accomplished, for in the 28. verf. the people admired him, and why ? because *they saw that the Wisdom of God was in him to do Judgment*; and they came from all parts of the earth which had heard of *Solomon* to hear him.

And here do I conclude humbly, spreading before the Lord my earnest desires, that all we Sea-partners may obtain with *Elisha* a
double

double portion of the Spirit of God, and with *Solomon* understanding hearts, that we may understand the Scriptures, for which I shall humbly wait at the feet of my sweet Saviour for a more glorious manifestation of his presence, and for a more enlightning revelation by his blessed Spirit, discovering the hidden Mysteries of the glorious Gospel of Jesus Christ unto my soul, which is life eternal to know God and Jesus Christ his Son whom he hath sent.

Come my fellow-sufferers, we that have had a tryal of ten days tribulation in our Sea Voyage, seeing it hath pleased God to redouble our obligations in miraculous preservations, let us multiply our fervent prayers and praises, and redouble our thanksgiving unto the Lord of Glory, that seeing these dangerous storms, and tempests, and sickness, which we have had, were not unto death, but for the glory of God, and that the Son of God might be glorified thereby, *John* 11.4. Let us joyn with one consent to give him praise which is due unto his Name all the days of our pilgrimage, which are few and evil. Let us exceedingly rejoyce in our God while we are hereupon earth, and cry *Hosanna* to the highest; Let us so run, as we may obtain a never fading Diadem of Glory amongst the Saints of that new *Jerusalem* which is above: Let us be faithful to the death, and we shall have a crown of life, *Rev.* 2. 10. For our God will surely come, and his reward is with him, and he will give to every one according to his works: Therefore God that is rich in mercy to all that call upon him, and a present help in time of trouble, fill your Souls with graces of his most holy Spirit, and accept all our Praises, and help us to perform all our Vows, and grant all our Petitions, so prays,

Your Weak Remembrancer in

all Christian Love and Duty,

FRANCES COOK.

A Pſalm gathered out of the Pſalms of David at my landing
after the great ſtorm at ſea, in Ianuary 3. 1648.

COme forth and hanken deareſt friends,
    all ſuch as loue the Lord,
What he for my poor life hath done,
    to you I will record.

For ſafety from the raging Seas,
    vnto him I did cry;
And thou my tongue make ſpeed apace,
    to praiſe him by and by.

To render thanks vnto the Lord,
    how great a cauſe haue I.
My voyce and prayer, and my complaint,
    that heard ſo willingly.

Of his good will he hath call'd back
    my Soul from Hell to ſaue;
He did revive when help did lack,
    and kept me from the grave.

I to the Lord will pay my vowe,
    that I to him did make,
That if he would deliver me,
    and not my Soul forſake:

Then finally while breath did laſt,
    on his grace I would depend,
And in the houſe of God always
    my life for ever ſpend.

Therefore open to me the gates
    of truth and righteouſneſſe,
That I may enter into them,
    the Lords praiſe to expreſſe.

God

God is my glory, & I will sing
   with praise unto his Name,
That all my vows I may fulfil,
   and dayly pay the same.

Thy Servant Lord, thy Servant lo,
   I do my self confesse:
One of thy handmaids, thou didst hear
   my prayer in my distresse.

Who with the Lord is equal then,
   in these his works of wonder?
That kept me from so many deaths,
   and brake the waves in sunder.

I will before the living Lord
   confesse his kindnesse then:
That shewed his wonders in the storms,
   unto the sons of men.

For with his Word the Lord did make
   the sturdy storms to cease:
So that the great waves from their rage,
   he brought to rest and peace.

Then was I glad when rest did come,
   which I so much did crave:
And was by him to Haven brought,
   which I so fain would have.

This was the mighty mark of God,
   this was the Lords own fact,
And it is marvellous to behold
   with eyes that noble act.

I will perform with heart so free,
   to God my vows alwayes:
And I O Lord all times to thee
   will offer thanks and praise.

My Soul from death thou didst defend,
   and kepst my heart unmight:

That

That I before thee may ascend,
with such as live in Light.

I will not hide within my brest,
thy goodnesse as by stealth:
But Ile declare, and will expresse,
thy truth and saving health.

Ile keep not close thy loving minde,
that no one should it know;
Thy love, which in the deeps I finde,
to all the Church Ile show.

Yea, good to me that was at Sea,
his Mercies did exceed;
Lo all thy works do praise the Lord,
and to thy honor spread.

Thy Saints do blesse thee, and they do
thy Kingdoms glory show;
And blaze thy praise, to cause the sons
of men their power to know.

God is the Lord, by whom alone
Salvation cometh plain;
He is my God, by whom I scapt
all danger, death and pain.

As God hath given power to me,
so Lord make firm and sure
The work that thou hast wrought on me,
for ever to endure.

Until the day of Iudgment comes,
and I am call'd to rest,
With all thy holy company
of Saints and Angels blest,

To praise the Lord Omnipotent,
triumphantly each houre;
To him be all dominion,
and praise for evermore.

FINIS.

SVSANNA'S
Apologie againſt the
ELDERS.

OR
A Vindication of
SVSANNA PARR; one of
thoſe two Women lately *Excommunica-*
ted by Mr LEWIS STVCLEY, and his
Church in *Exeter.*

Compoſed and Publiſhed by her ſelſe, for the clearing of her own Innocency, and the Satisfaction
of all others, who deſire to know the true
Reaſon of their ſo rigorous Proceedings againſt her.

*Whoſe hatred is covered by deceit, his wickedneſſe ſhall be ſhewed
before the whole Congregation.* Prov. 16. 26.

*They ſhall put you out of the Synagogues, yea the time cometh, that
whoſoever killeth you, will think that he doth God ſervice.* Joh. 16. 2.

*Let us go forth therefore unto him without the Campe, bearing his
reproach,* Heb. 13. 13.

may: Printed in the Year, 1659. *May 12*

IT is a thorny path, and a myrie way that I am compelled to walke in; a way wherein there is a danger of loosing more in all likelyhood, rather then of regaining what is already lost. A way, the walking wherein, all the comfort I have, is the hope of getting out of it at last, and so it concerns me to hasten as fast as I can. In it I meet with the Enemies Sword, covered over with zeale for God and his glory, when as nothing of this hath appeared in the least, either in the worke, or in the managing thereof: Satan is now transformed into an Angel of light, But my hope is, that he will in the end appear to be no other than he is, a prince of darknesse, a black grisely Divel, Jealousy, and censorious Slander; the discovery of which, is the worke I am at present engaged in, the designe of this following Vindication: a worke it is no lesse difficult and dangerous, then troublesome, and unpleasing, in respect of my selfe who write, the things whereof I write, and the persons against whom I write.

Weaknesse is entailed upon my Sex in generall, and for my selfe in particular, I am a despised worme, a woman full of naturall and sin-

full

full infirmities; the chiefest of Sinners, and least
of Saints: should the Lord contend with me, I
must lay my hand upon my mouth, I must acknowledge him to be just and righteous in suffering
them to deale thus with me; neither should I put
my selfe to the trouble of a Vindication, but leave
the clearing of my Innocency to that day which
he hath appointed to judge the world in righteousnesse; I have cause to remember, and be ashamed
before the Lord, there being iniquity even in my
holy things; yet as to them, my heart doth not reproach mee, but on the contrary, I have great cause
of rijoycing, in the uprightnesse of my heart, as to
the things of God, and in my abundant love and
affections unto them, my heart was enlarged in
love towards them, and therefore my mouth was
opened upon all occasions for their good: though I
was of a stamering Tongue, slow of speech, and
wanted eloquence, yet the desire I had of their perfection, made me forward to speake to them in generall, and in particular: the Lord knowes I lie
not, my conscience also beaking me witnesse: I
mourned with them that mourned, rejoyced with
them that rejoyced; when any were under temptations, or afflictions, I did labour to sympathize
with them, as if they were mine owne, and did engage for them at the Throne of Grace as for my
selfe. And as for that which I did oppose among
them, it was matter of mourning unto mee, when
I apprehended the glory of Christ and their partis-
culart

cular interest, could not stand together, I then
withstood them, resolving not to spare any that
stood in the way of Christ, and the Gospels enlarge-
ment. It is my comfort that the Lord seeth not
as man seeth, man looketh on the outward appearance, but the Lord looketh on the heart: not he
that commendeth himselfe, but he whom the Lord
commendeth is approved. Though they have
proceeded to Censure me, and have been full of
Cursing and bitternesse, returning evill for good;
yet I shall pray, Lord lay not this sin to their
charge: they know not what Spirit they are of.

Besides my personall weaknesses, the many
Family-cares that lie upon me, must needs unfit
me for such a worke, and very much disinable me
to write even of those things which were newly
done, and fresh in my memory, much more to
write of these, which they charged me with, being
some of them transacted Seaven or Eight yeares
since: In the laying down of which, if my memory
should fail me, I need not tell thee (if thou knowest
Mr. Stucley and his Congregation) what an
improvement they will make thereof, for the ju-
stifying of their late unchristian Censure, of
whom I have cause to complaine, as the Church
in the words of Jeremiah, Lam. 3. 53. they
have cut off my life in the dungeon, and cast a
stone upon me, which they threaten to eternity. Surely they who have been so wicked as to
censure me without any ground, will not stick to
take hold of the least occasion for the maintaining

A 3   of

of it, and though I have in part been cleared by the
Ministers of Exeter from their forged accusations, who received me jointly into communion
with them, yet my Adversaries being so crafty,
cruell, and powerfull, it will be no hard matter
for them to beare downe all their gain-sayers;
whosoever shall dare to contradict them, unlesse the
Lord himselfe take them in hand, and then though
they are mightier then I, yet they will find to their
cost, that he is higher then they, to him I have committed my way, in him is my trust, therefore my
confidence is, that he will bring it to passe; seeing
my undertaking is not so much for my selfe, as for
the Lord, for his servants and for his people.

It cannot be (whatever Mr Stucley sayes to
the contrary, p. 46. of his answer to Mr Toby
Allen.) but that a slur is cast (by their censuring
mee) on the Ministers and people of God, in this
City, it must needs reflect very much on them,
who have received such a daughter of Belial, such
a lyer, &c. (as he tels the world confidently enough
I am) into communion and fellowship with them.
I looke on it as my duty, to keep the house of God
pure, to the uttermost of my power; which in this
case I cannot doe, without clearing my selfe from
those crimes layd to my charge. Had Mr Stucley
dealt ingeniously with his Readers, in discovering
the right and true grounds of his Excommunication (viz:) my hearing another Minister,
whiles I was with them, and after my leaving
them, my refusing to returne, unlesse I might have

the liberty of communion with other of Gods people
in this City, then it would have beene apparent,
that their censuring mee was no other then the
smiting of tha watchmen; for seeking after my
beloved, and so have freed mee from a great deale
of trouble. But seeing he hath dealt so craftily as
to omit them, and lay other things to my charge in
their place, it will be worth the while a little to
uncase him in his cōparisons; for the undeceiving
of those, who (by his two Books) may be perswaded to thinke that Mr. Allen and my selfe are indeed children of hell, and fitter for fellowship with
damned spirits, then to be associates of the Lords
people, p. 11. True Acc: And that they on the o-
ther side are a selfe-denying people, trampling the
world under their feet; keeping judgement and
doing righteousnesse at all times; having their
hands filled with both the Tables; and an equall
respect to all Gods Commandements, pag. 13.

To this end I shall declare,

First, the ground of my joyning with them, and
here I cannot but take shame to my selfe, for being
so rash; as because of their specious pretences, to
forsake the societie of Gods people, and joine with
them, before I saw what worke they woul make.

Secondly, the manner of our joining together,
and my coming in unto them.

Thirdly, some remarkable passages I observed
whiles I was with them, together with my behaviour in reproofe, admonition, and admission of
members,

           A 4   Fourthly,

Fourthly, declare the grounds of the difference
between us, and of my leaving them; and also
how I left them.

Lastly, wipe off the reproaches they have cast
upon mee, since my leaving them.

All which I shall set upon, in the strength of
Christ, who is able to make the foolish things of
the world to confound the wise, and the weake
things of the world to confound the mighty: And
never had a poore creature greater cause to flie
for refuge to the hope set before mee in the Gospel,
to get within the vaile, and shroud my selfe under
the wings of the Almighty, till these calamities
be overpast, then I have: my enemies are many,
and I am single; they wise, or rather crafty, I
simple; they mighty, I weake; they have witnesses
(as Mr. Stucley affirmes) I none, and which is
worst of all, by accusing mee of lying, by making
me a notorious lyar, they have endeavoured to
stop the eares of the people, and take them off
from believing, and giving credit to what I
write: so that if the Lord doth not bring forth
my righteousnesse as the light, and my judgement
as the noone day, I can looke for none other then
to become a Pray (by my writing) unto those who
wait for my halting, who have (as farre as I
can perceive) taken up a resolution, (according
to the Elders threatning) to make my going away
cost mee dearer, then my coming among them,
tis true, I have not yet resisted unto blood,
yet

*yet I know not how soon, I may, they have endea-
voured to deprive mee of my good name, which
is of more worth then riches, and the next in
esteeme to life it selfe. And what they will do
next, had they power in their hands, the Lord
knowes! it is to be feared that they who have
beene so forward to Smite with the Tongue, will
not be backward to strike with the hand, when
occasion shall serve: The Papists, when they
had put a Cap upon the head of* John Husse,
*on which were painted severall ugly devils, pre-
sently after cast him into the fire: if that which
was his lot, and the lot of other servants of
God, be mine, the will of the Lord be done:
It is my resolution to part with all, rather then
returne to such a backsliding, and selfe-seeking
people: And therefore my request is unto you,
the* Ministers *of Christ in this Nation, that
you would take my case into your serious consideration, and call* Mr Stucley *to an account,
for his disorderly smiting his fellow-servants:
That you, who have so openly declared against
Separation, and charged it as a duty on stray-
ers to returne into the fold of Christ, would en-
courage others to follow our example, by defending us against the assaults and endeavours of
those who have dealt so outragiously with us,
upon no other account then our leaving them,
and returning unto you, as it will appeare in
the following Narrative and Vindication, from*
which

which I shall no longer detaine you, but conclude and shut up all with this request; that you would in the examination of what I have said, not looke to words or expressions which may not be so fitly placed, but to the things themselves, and the truth of them, which was the chiefe ayme (in writing) of her, who still professeth herselfe to be an engaged servant to Jesus Christ in Gospel bonds.

SUSANNA PARR.

NAR.

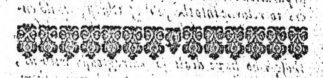

NARRATIVE.

Ee were told in the time of the Warres, that when the Lord did turne our Captivity, there must be a thorough Reformation, every thing must be brought to the patterne in the Mount; and by some, that rather no Reformation, then a partiall Reformation; and in speciall, the last warre by many was stiled a Sacramentall warre.

Considerations of this nature made me willing to engage where was most purity as to the Ordinances; and the great affection and good opinion I had of the *New-England* Churches, made mee in liking with the Congregationall way: Besides it is well knowne, how much was spoken of a Church State, and the priviledges thereof: A greater effusion of the Spirit, more purity and holinesse, more union and communion, more liberty of Conscience, and freedome from that yoke of being servants unto men, in this Church State, then could be found elsewhere: Many such considerations made me engage in this way, which we did after this manner.

Explicit Cov.

M

Mr *Stucley* being at *Torrington*, and coming
often to this City, speaking very much in
commendation of Mr *Bartlets* Church at *Brideford*, and the order therein, and also exhorting
mee, and others to meet together, telling us
that we did not live like Christians, because we
had not communion one with another, and that
we must come together, so that we might be
in a capacity of having the ordinances, we thereupon met very often, the time was spent in
praying, and speaking one to another, what
God had done for our soules : And to this we
were enjoyned secrecie, the reason was given,
because we might be put upon such tēptations
(if it were knowne) as wee could not resist.
This practise wee continued once or twice a
weeke for a long time, M. *Stucley* promising to
be at our meetings, which he accordingly performed sometimes. At length some of us desired to have the Sacrament of the Lords Supper, and because of that confusion which was
among us, in that we wanted abilities for the
right managing of our weekly Exercises, wee
desired likewise to have a Minister, M. *Hanmer*
was pitcht upon by some, but opposed by o-
thers, in the end wee agreed to leave it to M.
Bartlet of *Brideford*, whether M. *Hanmer*, or
M. *Stucley* was the fittest for us, hereupon wee
sent messengers to M. *Bartlet*, who when they
came to his house found M. *Stucley* himselfe
there, M. *Bartlet* told the messengers, he conceived

ceived M. *Stucley* was fittest for the present; but however hee would acquaint M. *Lothly* with the businesse, which he did, but M. *Hanmer* refused it. After this M. *Stucley* came to continue in this City, yet not quitting *Torrington* till the meanes was setled on him here. And now againe some of us (the greater number were very indifferent) renewed our former desires of having the Sacrament, and sent about it to M. *Bartlet*, who said, we were not as yet in a capacity to have that Ordinance; that it was necessary we should be first in a Gospel order embodied: and said moreover, that then wee should see much of God, that the day of our embodying would be such a day as we had never seene. A while after M. *Bartlet* came to the City with his Church officers, he himselfe prayed and preached on *Zach* 6.13. in the morning, afterwards seven or eight persons spake out the experiences they had of the change of their condition, with which I was much affected, and through M. *Stucleys* perswasion did the like. Afterwards there was a confession of faith read, being a Copy of that which was composed by M. *Hughes*, which Copy we had not from the Author, but from another, this confession of faith was subscribed by every one of us: And then M. *Bartlet* made some proposals unto us by way of *quare*; to this effect as I remember.

                      1. Whether

1. Whether we would take Christ for our Judge, King, and Law-giver?

2. Whether wee would renounce all wayes of false worship?

3. Whether wee would worship God in all his Ordinances?

4. Whether we would give up our selves to the Lord, and one to another, and would engage our selves in all duties of Christianity each unto other?

5. Whether wee would hold communion with other Churches?

6. Whether wee would relieve the Saints that were in Communion, according to our abilitie?

7. Whether we would not rest in the light that we had received, but would study to know the mind of God, and live up unto it?

This is the substance of our engagement, as I remember. At this time and somewhile after, there was never a woman of the Church but my selfe; and yet at every meeting about Church affaires Master *Stucley* would send for mee, and when I pleaded for my absence (at such times) from the meetings, that of the Apostle, *Let your women keep silence in the Church, for it is not permitted unto them to speake,* he replyed, he would do nothing without the consent of the whole. And when I was present, he himselfe would constraine me to speak my opinion of things proposed.   Wee

We were as I said formerly very desirous of the Sacrament, in order to which, our first work was to get a Minister that might administer it. Although Master *Stucley* was with us, yet the people of *Torrington* claimed an engagement from him, that Towne having been visited with the plague, and deprived of their Ministers maintenance. Master *Stucley* (who was their Minister) for those reasons left them, but with a promise of returning so soon as the Lord should remove his hand, and sufficient maintenance for a Minister should be procured, both which being at this time effected, we could not chuse him) to be an Officer, untill he were by them freed from his engagement: in order hereunto much meanes was used, Master *Bartlet* was imployed to perswade them unto it; but they with one consent refused it, saying, that seeing he had promised to returne, they expected that he should keep promise with them. Hereupon we wrote for counsell to some of the Congregationall Churches in London, Master *Feake*, and Master *Harrison* (in their answers to our Letters) affirmed that Master *Stucley* was bound in conscience to goe unto *Torrington*, that it would be dishonourable to the Gospel to leave them, unlesse he could get their consent for his dismission. At length Master *Stucley* himselfe accompanied with two or three of the Church rode thither, where having

made

made an agreement with the people, those that
rode with him were called in to consent thereunto, which they accordingly did.

At their returne Master *Stucley* required each
one of us to consent likewise unto the agreement they made at *Torrington*, without declar-
ring what it was; which being done by all the
men, he desired the sisters (there being other
women now added to the Church) to do the
like, which my selfe and some others refused,
resolving that we would not act by an implicite
faith. Master *Stucley* thereupon said, that what
was done was a Church act, because they who
went with him consented thereunto (viz.) that
we were engaged to get a Minister for the people of *Torkington*. Accordingly there was one
procured, who continued with them for a time.
This Serpentine subtilty of his I tooke speciall notice of, and did for it reprove him to his
face: we were in the meane time (and so continued for so many yeares) in a wildred condition, without either of the Sacraments; some not
having their children baptized in a long time, o-
thers did procure some Congregationall Minister to do it. And as for the Lords Supper, they who would partake of it, rode to o-
ther places in the Country: most of the people
were very indifferent whether we had the Ordinances or no, seeking themselves, getting places and offices, designing how they might build
their

their owne houses: and as for Mafter *Siucley* himfelfe, he was fo diftracted with Law-fuits, Intangled with the world and mony engagements, as that he was feldome with us at our fafts and times of prayer.

Hence I began to fufpect, that they intended nothing but feparation, and fetting up of themfelves and their owne interefts and defignes, which did exceedingly trouble mee.

Upon our private faft dayes, when wee had done praying, it was our cuftome (for the help of thofe that were to pray) to fpend a little time in Conference, and at fuch times did I take occafion to fpeak of the diforders among us, & told the plainly, that I feard we did feparate frō others more godly then our felves, as *Cain*, who went out from the prefence of the Lord to build citties; that there was little regard had to what we at firft pretended, the fetting up of pure ordinances; I often told them that I never heard or read in Scripture, or other hiftory, that the Lord did make ufe of a people of fuch an earthly, luke-warme, and indifferent fpirit, in any publique worke of reformation; that it was not a party, or confederacy that I looked after, but to have the Gofpel more difcovered in greater light and beauty; and the ordinances to be enjoyed in greater purity: the beauty of Gods ornament to be fet in Majeftie, and more purity and felfe-deniall to appeare in us, who

B had

had separated from all mixtures.

Because I conceive that purity lay onely in this way, therefore was I very forward and zealous in it, hoping to leave posterity the ordinances pure, and the name of God glorious in the brightnesse of the Gospel: for this cause did I deale so plainly with them; with which plaine and faithfull dealing, they pretended many times to be much affected, and thereupon would do something more in order to Religion, then they had formerly.

Master *Stucley* (as I said before) being troubled about the things of this world, left us to our selves very often in our meetings: so that it is not to be wondred at, if in them there were much strange fire, both in prayer and exposition of the Scriptures, they being meere Novices, and in the entrance of Christianity, and many of them scarce well principled, I feared that the name of God was often taken in vain in prayer, sure I am that much ignorance, pride, and selfe confidence, and a *Diotrephes* spirit strongly working, appeared in many of them.

N.E.　One of them affirmed, that there was no iniquity of the holy things &c. this being delivered without any caution when the meeting was publique, I told him of it in private the same day.

Owen.　Another who had formerly beene an Anabaptist, then a Seeker, next (as I was informed)

a

a Papift, or little better, very much addicted to
the ftudy of their bookes, the moft conviction
that he had (as was reported) was by *Jonas
Ware*, fince a Roman Catholique, who went to
Rome, and then turning to prelacy, and the
booke of Common-prayer, and afterward an
Independent, the fame perfon was very forward at our meetings, and did often put forth
himfelfe in the duty of prayer, which was a great
trouble to mee to heare how the name of God
was taken in vaine by him, infomuch as that I
earneftly defired Mafter *Stucley* to hinder him
from engaging in that duty, till he underftood
the nature of it better.

I acquainted him likewife of other diforders
and mifcarriages very frequent at our meetings,
declaring how much I was troubled at them;
for redreffe of which, I intreated him to be
conftantly with us. But he endeavoured to
quiet me with this, that they, were honeft,
though weak, and further perfwaded me to be
conftant at the meetings, to be faithfull unto
them, in minding them of what was amiffe.
I told him it was more fit for me to be in private meditation, to be gathering rather then
fcattering: but he replyed, that the time was
now not to be Clofet-Profeffors, but to fay,
*come, let us go up to the houfe of the Lord, to feek
the Lord together, with our faces Zion-ward.*
And though I pleaded my Sex, my naturall

B 2   and

and finfull infirmities, which made me unfit to
fpeak unto others, yet he preffed it on me as
my duty. And when there was any Jarring
between them and my felfe, he defired me not
to be troubled, though I met with oppofition,
that one was of a Souldierly fpirit, another of
a dull Spirit, that it was meere Envy, promifing to fpeak with them about it himfelfe.
Yea when I refolved to be filent at fome meetings, Mr. *Stucley* himfelfe would fingle me
out, and even conftraine me to fpeak.

As concerning my Carriage at the Admiffion of members, I fhall give a briefe account
of it as followeth.

They who defired admiffion into the Society, were fometimes defired in a private meeting to fpeak what experience they had of the
worke of grace upon their Soules: after which
we were every one of us both men and women
to declare our thoughts of what was fpoken,
it being laid down as a ground, that we muft
have an account of a change from a naturall and
legall eftate, into an eftate of grace and believing, of thofe whom we admitted into communion with us. I among the reft did according to my weak meafure declare my felfe a-
gainft that which I thought would not ftand
for grace. I was fo far from delighting in this
work, as that it was a trouble to me, an Imployment from which I would willingly have
been

been freed : I conceived it more needfull for
my felfe to ftudy the worrd, and compare my
own heart with the rule, then to be fo taken
up about the condition of others. But this
was our principle, we were to keep the houfe
of God pure, we were fet as Porters at the
door, it was our duty, we were not to be wanting at fuch times, yea it was our liberty, that
we, who were to have communion with thofe
vvho came to be admitted, fhould give in our
affent, or diffent in reference to their admiffion. I did therefore at fuch times declare my
thoughts afvvell as the reft, but left the determination to themfelves, as it appeares in *Ganicle*, vvho vvas admitted, though I vvas at the
firft againft his admiffion. I mention him, becaufe he vvas brought by Mr. *Eveleigh*, as an
Inftance of my cenforioufneffe. I vvas blamed
for difliking him, vvhom they faid vvas one
of the moft eminent among them, and yet it
vvas not long after, before he difcovered himfelfe, by Renouncing the principles of Chriftianity, and turning *Quaker*. He in fpeaking
out his Experiences pretended unto much
Joy and ravifhment of Spirit, but (the Lord
knovves) vvhen he fpake of fuch enjoyments,
he fpake as a ftranger that never intermedled
vvith this Joy, never declaring any povverfull
effect thereof, but only that vvhich vvas, only
but a *Balaams* vvifh. I the rather inftance in

him,

him, becaufe he was the firft that kindled the fire of Contention, which then brake out in that manner, as it is not quenched to this days, here began the Quarrell on their part. When I was called by the Elder to give in my thoughts concerning a Perfon propofed, he moft diforderly intercepted me , for which there vvas not the leaft admonition given him: but not long after his folly was made manifeft, by his Cafting off the very forme of godlineffe. This is one and the Cheife one of thofe perfons whom I difliked, though approved of by the Church. If I be contentious for oppofing fuch a one, let me be contentious ftill; though none among them will witneffe for me, yet he doth, he ftands to this day as a fad witneffe between me and them, whether I were contentious in my oppofitions, or they infallible in their determinations. Befides, as for fome who continue among them, if you look for diftinguifhing Characters , they are fcarcely vifible, much leffe eafy to be difcerned.

Thus I did from time to time, whilft we were without Officers and Ordinances, partly through the great defire I had to promote the worke of Reformation among us, partly through Mr *Stucley's* inftigation reprove them for their indifferency of Spirit, ftir them up to that which I conceived vvas their duty, for vvhich I alvvaies gave them my grounds and

reafons

reafons. But after the officers vvere chofen, I never medled (to my remembrance) vvith Church affaires, nor fpake in the meetings, after I heard by Mr. Stucley my fpeaking vvas difrelifht; unleffe a Queftion vvas propofed, and I vvas defired to give my Anfvver unto it.

Not long after, the Officers vvere chofen, I being at Mr. Stucley's houfe, defired him to refolve me concerning a true Church, he then confeffed that the Churches of New England did acknovvledge the Churches of old England, from vvhence we had feparated, to be true Churches: I told him thereupon that vve could not juftifie our Separation. At length vve falling into difcourfe of other things, he faid my fpeaking vvas difrelifht by fome, I anfvvered, that I did not like it my felfe, and therefore vvould be from thenceforth filent, though I looked on it as my duty formerly, he told me no, he vvould have me fpeak, but it muft be by a Brother; for a ftander by may fee more then he that plaies the game, promifing likewife if I did fpeak by him, to deliver my words in the fame manner as I fpake them.

After this it pleafed the Lord to exercife me with a fmarting affliction, the death of a dear child, the fuddenneffe of the ftroke, and fome other circumftances made it a very melting affliction. When my Bovvels vvere yerning

ning towards my child, I called to remembrance the Lords tender bowels towards his children, for whom he had given his only Son; when I confidered the breach that the Lord had made in my family, I beheld how terrible it was to make a breach in his family. Then the worke I was ingaged in, this Sin of Separation, appeared nakedly unto me to be no other then a vvounding of Chrifts body; vvhich is his Church, the Church vvhich he hath purchafed vvith his ovvn blood: I then looked on Separation to be a dividing of Chrift. Truly I beheld it vvith terror, this fin of vvounding of Chrift it made a vvound in my foule, vvhich vvas kept open in a terrible manner; the Lord bringing to my remembrance his Juftice and feverity, and vvrath revealed from heaven on families and nations, yea on his ovvn people, ever fince the beginning of the vvorld: as alfo his Judgments vvhich are in the earth to this day , from *Genefis* to the *Revelation* vvas brought to my remembrance, and kept hard upon me. Having thefe Impreffions on my Spirit, I vvas almoft overwhelmed, and in mine ovvn apprehenfion upon the Borders of Hell, vvhere the Lord made me to behold the Execution of his vvrath upon finners: I could then have told vvhat hel vvas, I felt the flafhings of helfire in my foule, the vvrath of God that lay hard upon me, the effects vvhereof vvere very terrible,

terrible, infomuch as I was even fwallowed up,
only the Lord was pleafed to keep me following after him, refolving to lie at his feet,
though he fhould fpurne me to hell. Having
thus been under a fentence of death with the
very terrors of hell in my foule, providence fo
ordering it, I came (by following the people)
where Mr. FORD preached. I no fooner
came into the Congregation, but I was fo exceedingly troubled, as that I vented my felfe
in Paffionate teares ; fearing left I might be
unfit to hear, but in prayer recovered my
felfe. His text was in *John* 16: laft. *Be of
good cheere, I have overcome the world.* He
inftanced, in all the enemies of the new creature, the World, the God of this world, Sin,
Death, and Hell: the Lord fetting it home
every fentence was to me as the rivetting of
the nailes, fet on by the great mafter of Affemblies, and in prayer afterward (the Lord
fo providing) thofe very particulars which
were the burden of my foule, were put up
unto God. I went out of the congregation
with another frame of fpirit then when I came
in, bleffing the Lord for giving his Son Jefus
Chrift, who hath loved us, and wafhed us from
our fins in his own blood, and hath made us
Kings and Priefts unto God. But afterwards
I began to queftion whether I had not taken
that, which did not belong unto me, Chrift
                                        then

then speaking comfort to his disciples in reference to that hardship they were to meet with
in the world; among the rest of their sufferings this was one, that they should be put out
of the Synagogues, yea the time would come
that whosoever killed them, would think he
did God good service, which things Christ
told them that they might not be offended:
But yet the Sermon being in generall of all
the Enemies of the new Creature, I could not
put it off. Furthermore the appearance of God
was so remarkable in the change of my spirit,
as that I could not but take it home, that Sins
of the right hand and left hand, and separation
also, and death and hell should be cast into the
lake that burneth with fire and brimstone, that
in the meane time Christ hath overcome the
world, the Prince of this world is judged, condemned already, only the execution is defer-
red till the time appointed by the father. And
as for sufferings, that we must look for them,
having such provision so remarkably laid in
before, I cannot but take notice of it at present.
But then I could not conceive how it was
likely for me to suffer in that kind, there being
then so much love pretended. But now the
time is come, and therefore I mention it: Christ
saieth, these things have I spoken unto you,
that when the time shall come, you may remember that I told you of them. Now I can
make

make application of all the Sermon which is food for my faith to live upon, although I suffer as an evill doer. I mention it with admiration, that the Lord even then when he spake peace unto me after my being convinced of Separation, should lay also provision against Excommunication.

But now after my conviction of Separation, it troubled me very much, because I knew not how to avoid it: my fear was lest I should be constrained to live in it, had I presently come off, I should have made a breach there. They pretended so much love unto me, as I knew not which way to break this bond, which the Apostle calls the bond of perfectnesse; wherefore I resolved to wait upon the Lord, for the opening a way unto me, which he did afterwards in manner following.

The Lord was making such abundant Provision for me in Mr. *Ford's* ministry, I did constantly attend thereon, hearing him once a Lords day for the most part, unlesse it were when we had the Sacrament of the Lords Supper administred among us. This was my practice ever since he came to this City, of which Mr. *Stucley* took no great notice before he was in office; but afterward both he and the people were displeased with me for it, on which began the quarrell on my part between us. Mr. *Stoneham* being a stranger was employed

to

to take me off from this practice, who at firſt pretended that it did very much trouble him, but ſince he hath told me that he wiſhed that he had never been put upon it.

He ſent a Meſſenger unto me to perſwade me to leave Mr. *Ford's* miniſtry: I then ſhewed my grounds for that practice, what proviſion I found there, and how the Lord had made that miniſtry effectuall unto me, and withall that when I came among them, I took up a reſolution to attend upon that miniſtry.

The ſame day in a publique meeting they accuſed me firſt of Contention, and ſecondly for my hearing Mr. *Ford*, which (as the Elder ſaid) the Church neither could nor would bear, however they would not medle with it for that time.

As to the Article of Contention *I* appealed to the Church, and charged them to be faithfull as they would anſwer it another day, in making it known whether they had found me Contentious.

Upon which, *I* having withdrawn my ſelfe, they entred into a debate about it, every one declaring their thoughts of me: the reſult of which debate was this.

That they neither could nor would charge me with contention for a world, but did fear that through a mixture of Corruption it might tend to contention. This buſineſſe was ended
three

three daies after, they declaring that they were
satisfied.

But as to the other Article the Elder told
me the very next day, when I preſſed him to
declare whether he knew of any thing againſt
mee, he told mee that there was nothing elſe in
the world but my hearing Maſter *Forde*, and
then deſired me to leave off that practiſe, which
I did ſometimes to content them, but the little
peace that I found in it, made me quickly to take
it up againe.

After this meſſengers were ſent unto me ſeverall times from the Church, to informe me
how my practice was diſliked by ſome, to
whom I gave my reaſons for it as formerly, and
told them farther, that I was engaged to ſtudy
the mind of Chriſt, and becauſe of their diſ-ſa-
tisfaction, to ſeeke the Lord in this thing, I promiſed likewiſe to ſubmit my ſelfe to the Officers, ſo as to be accountable to them of my hearing Mr *Forde*. I informed them alſo, how the
Lord had made uſe of that Miniſtry for my good
in theſe times of diſtraction, I gave them thanks
for the great love, & good will they ſeemed to
bear towards me, but withall deſired them not to
be offended if I made uſe of my Chriſtian liberty,
till I was better informed, and told them *where
the Carkaſſe is, there will the Eagles reſort.*

Maſter *Stneley* alſo ſent me two long letters,
wherein he endeavored to perſwade me to have
dependance

dependance only on their miniſtry without hearing any other.

But when they ſaw that I could not be taken off from this practice, they began to quarrell with me, telling me that I was contentious, that it was heighth of ſpirit, and ſo by little and little eſtranged themſelves. But the Word was a light unto me, and ſo evident, as if it had been appointed on purpoſe for direction, they themſelves being judges; inſomuch as ſome of them asked me whether I did not uſe to viſit Mr. *Ford.*

As for Mr. *Stoneham* he declared in his publique miniſtry oftentimes, That it was out of the way of order to hear any other miniſter, when our own officers preached, that no bleſſing was to be expected in ſuch a way, and if ſo be there were any profit received, it was a deluſion, a temptation, yea a judgment of God upon ſuch a ſoule; it was a going out of the boſome of Chriſt into the boſome of ſtrangers; Rebellion againſt Chriſt; and that ſuch muſt be dealt with as Traytors and Rebells.

At length a faſt, a day of humiliation was appointed for the diſorderly walking of ſome, and that with obſtinacy in the generall.

Hereupon I went unto Mr. *Stoneham* to know for what end this faſt was intended, whether it was in reference to my ſelfe; if ſo, I ſhould remove the occaſion, reſolving with

my

my felfe, if the liberty of hearing other minifters were denied me, to leave them. But he
and Mr. Stucley whom I found with him, in
ftead of informing me fell into a difpute about
true Churches, a fubject that I was unskilfull
in, and he by reafon of his deafneffe unfit to
treat of, and withall let fall fome ftrange Expreffions concerning the people of God. I told
him that I did delight in the image of God
where ever I found it, in thofe that were the
Excellent of the Earth, that did excell in virtue: he then endeavoured to perfwade me that
I was to have my affections tyed up to thofe
of their Society, alleadging that I might afwell
delight in another man that was not my hufband, becaufe the Image of God fhined more in
him then in my husbad. I being troubled at this
groffe difcourfe told him that thofe relations
were of a different nature, and that I thought
I did owe more duty where God in his Providence had caft me, and where I had the opportunity and ability to performe it, then I was
engaged unto or could difcharge unto others,
where I had no fuch opportunities: yet I did
not look upon it as that which could cut off
my affections from the people of God, from
thofe who had the Image of God renewed in
them. Something alfo was fpoken of Church
ordinances, Mr. Stucley faid the preaching of
the vvord vvas not a Church ordinance, be-
                                        caufe.

caufe that it might be preached by one that was not a Church officer, and it might be ufed out of a Church, even in a family. For my own part I knew not how to underftand thefe diftinctions, but accounted them ftrange doctrines.

Mr. *Stucley* fome dayes after in a letter taxed me for acknowledging an affembly of people to be a Church meeting, and the wednefday meeting to be a Church meeting which formerly I lookt upon as *Babylon*. To which I returned Anfwer by letter, that I accounted thofe from whom we did feparate a true Church, as he had told me the New England minifters did; that I lookt upon the wednefdaies meeting to be a Church meeting, the Minifters as ambaffadors of Chrift, the preaching of the word a Church ordinance, that which Chrift hath appointed for the gathering in, building up, and edifying of his body, which is the Church, that I did put no difference between hearing there and among our felves in point of efficacy, and that my feparation from them was not in doctrine and worfhip, but in difcipline. Much I wrote likewife for the removing of fome prejudices, complaining how I was preached againft, and prayed againft; informing him likewife that I was neither able to live in the fire of contention, nor fit down under a miniftry that I could not profit by, and
therefore

therfore fhould willingly withdrawe from them,
I alfo defired him that whileft wee contended
for pure ordinances we fhould not fuffer the
Gofpell to be corrupted, and that I feared we
did not walke up to our owne principles, and I
likewife defired direction from him.

When the day appointed for the faft was
come, I went to the meeting not knowing for
what it was intended, The practice of the hearing of other minifters was then made to be as
the Sin of *Korah* and *Dathan* And betweene the
feverall prayers Mr *Stonehā* propounded fomewhat by way of queftion, how to know an heri-
ticke: one difcovery was when perfons went a-
gainft their owne principles as thofe did, who although they have given up themfelves on unto
another fhall notwithftanding fay they delight
in the Image of God where ever they finde it, in
the Excellent ones of the earth, which was contrary to their principles and deftructive to the
very fundementalls of the Church.

This being contrary in my apprehenfion to
that of the Apoftle. 2 *Col*, where he tels us,
That he had greate conflict not for them only
which he knew, But alfo for as many (of the
Saints) as had not feene his face in the flefh, And
in *Chap*: 1. 4. where he commends them for
their love to all the Saints, *I* did in the conclufion tell fome of the privately, There was that deliver'd which could not be prov'd by the word.

C   The

The Sacrament of the Lords Supper had
beene about this time omitted for neer halfe a
yeare, sure I am it was very long, I enquired of
some the reason thereof, who told me because
I could not sit downe with Master *Stoneham's*
ministry, whereupon I went to Master *Stoneham*
to know the reason why the Sacrament was
kept from us, at the first he gave me no answer,
but when I was earnest with him to give me satisfaction, he said, that he did not know what use
I would make of it: I then told him, hee looked
upon me as under a temptation, when I was in
an ordinance of Jesus Christ; but I had cause to
feare that he was under a temptation, in neglecting such an ordinance of Jesus Christ, which he
had a command often to make use of; and then
intreated him that if he thought me unworthy
to partake of it, that I onely might be kept off,
that the ordinance might not (upon that account) be laid aside: to this he replied, that the
prayers they had put up, would be answered,
which was all the satisfaction I could get from
him at that time : A weeke after I pressed him
againe for the Sacrament, he then told me, that
if I would not sit downe under his ministry he
would be no officer unto mee, and for a
close told mee, there was one who had somewhat against mee : whereupon the same day I
went to Master *Stucley* to know what it was
that some body had against mee, what the evill
was

was they could charge me with; I told him that it was my desire and endeavour *to keep a good conscience void of offence both towards God and towards men*: that if there were any evill, with which they could charge mee, upon information what it was, I would not continue in the practice thereof, and therefore desired him to tell mee what it was, that one had against mee: to which Master *Stoneham*, then being at Master *Stucleys* house, answered, that I must first resolve to sit down under their ministry, and then they would conferre about that: *I* replyed that *I* did not separate, but in distinguishing ordinances, unto which this answer was returned, that there was as much reason for a woman to goe after another man, because of fruitfulnesse, as to make use of another Ministry because of more benefit. At which grosse discovery of themselves *I* resolved with my selfe to take my leave of them: Master *Stucley* at my going forth came with mee to the doore, and then desired me to deny my selfe-holinesse for God, and look for a reward in heaven: This was the last time that ever *I* was in his house.

After this two or three times *I* went to Mr. *Eveleigh* the Elder, to know what it was they had against me, but *I* could never speak with him, untill *I* met him at the meeting, where *I* desired to speak with him, and went to his house, and desired him to informe me, what

they

they had to Charge mee with, who instead of answering directly to my question, sayd, there would bee a Sacrament the next Lords day, which (as I remember) was putt of, and that some body did desire mee to forbeare; my Answer was, that I should not giue offence to any; he then told mee what a doe they had to please mee, instancing in his wife, dead and buried long before.

This being all I could learne of him, I went about to seuerall persons (att their houses) to know what it was that they had against mee, but they told mee there was nothinge but my goeing to heare others; then I asked whether the Church had any thinge against mee, they did assure mee the Church had nothing against mee, Having done this, I beheld the doore standing so wide open, as that I might fairely take my leave, which yet I did not, before I had for a while seriously and sadly considered of these following particulars.

1. The strangenesse of their opinions and practises in reference to the ordinances of Jesus Christ. Preaching was affirmed to be no Church Ordinance, as also Catechizing.

The ordinance of Fasting exceedingly perverted, in which they walked in the wayes of *Ahab*, and statutes of *Omry*; Making it like *Ismaels* weeping to fall on poore soules, when they go to worship the Lord, like the tumultu-

ous

ous concourse of people, *Act.* 19. 32. by con-
cealing the perticular occasions and ends of their
fastings, *fasting rather for strife and debate*, then
to keepe the *unity of the spirit in the bond of peace*
with Gods people.

The Sacrament of the Lords Supper was for
a long time detained, not only from my selfe in
particular without giving any reason, but from
the whole Congregation in generall, new, and
unheard of, and unscripturall qualifications were
required of those who would pertake thereof:
They must subscribe and engage not to heare
any, but their owne Officers at such times as
the Officers did preach, and must believe that
a greater blessing was to be expected on their
Ministry, then on the Ministry of others; when
(as the Apostle saith) *He that planteth, and he*
that watereth are all one, 1 *Cor.* 3. 7, 8. To come
out from among them upon this account I was
very much encouraged by Master *Burroughs*,
who in his *heart divisions*, p. 174. sayeth, *If*
Gouernors enjoyne any thing vppon the Church,
on any member thereof that is Sin, or if they shall
mingle Euill in the Publique worship, so that there
can be noe Ioyning with their worship, but there
must be Ioyning likewise with their Sin: In this
case they are the Schismaticks, not those who with-
drawe from them.

Yea farther. If they impose that, which is not
necessary though in it selfe not sinful, and will not

beare with the weaknes of such as thinke it Euill:
If upon that, they are forced to withdrawe, in this
the governors are the Schismaticks; the cause of
the Rent is in them, they ought in such things to
beare with the weaknesses of their brethren, and
not imperiously require of them those things of
which there is no necessity, if such things be Sinne
to their Brethrens consciences; if they will stand
upon it to enjoyne them, they lay a necessity on
them to withdraw. God will not lay the Indictment of Schisme thus, such a one departed from
the Communion of such a church; because he
would not doe what was lawfull to be done. But.
thus,——you imposed that upon your brother,
which there was no necessity of, and would not
forbeare him in what I would have you to forbeare
him, but caused him by your imperiousnesses and
stifnesse to depart from communion with you. It's
true, God faith, the things might have been done,
but it was not necessary, it was own of conscience
to ma that they forbore, the weaknesse is theirs,
but the Schisme is yours.

2. From the ordinances I turned my thoughts
unto the Churches, both that from which I had
separated, as also that whereof I was then a
member, as to the Churches of England, I
considered that they were right in respect of
Doctrine and worship; and not onely so, but
that they were united likewise by an *implicit
covenant*, which upon enquiry that they of

New-

New-England make to be the same for substance with that which is *explicit*, contrarie to
what I believed at the first (viz.) That an *Explicit Covenant* was necessary to the *Constituting* of a *visible Church*, and therefore upon
this account, there was no reason to separate
from them: I considered that the work of
this generation was not the *Constituting*, but
the *reforming* of Churches, which I conceived
separation did hinder. It made my heart bleed
within me to think that I should have a hand in
the hindering of *Reformation*, for which so
much precious blood had been spilt in the late
Warre.

As to the Church whereof I was then a member, I feared what it would come to in the end,
there being in so short a time, such a visible
difference between our first Ingagements, and
the present state thereof. At the first, *liberty
of conscience and freedome* from the Intolerable
yoke of being Servants unto men was pretended; But now we were in greater bondage then
ever, all liberty of dissenting from them being
denyed. Our officers were swayed by such a
Prelaticall Spirit, as that every one must rest
satisfied with their determinations, otherwise
it would be lookt upon as a *non-conformity*,
contention, and the Lords Supper forthwith
denyed them.

At

At the firſt we were not to reſt in the light we had allready received, but engaged to ſtudy the minde and will of God, and live up unto it, to have Chriſt for our *Judge*, our *Lawgiver* and *King*; but now the voice of the Church (two or three of them) carries all before it, he that did not hearken unto this, he that was not obedient unto this, muſt be preſently accounted contentious, cenſorious, a Rebell againſt Jeſus Chriſt, and dealt withall as ſuch. When I demanded, whether that which they ſaid to be the *voice* of the *Church*, were the *voice* of *Chriſt* ?

Anſwer was returned, that the *voice* of the *Church*, was the *voice* of *Chriſt*.

If this be true, then we muſt believe as the Church believes, we muſt believe that the Church cannot erre, contrary to that in *Rev.3.* where we read that the Church of *Laodicea* ſaid one thing, and *Chriſt* another, where every one is commanded to *heare what the ſpirit ſaith unto the Churches.*

And as for the people, the generalitie of them I plainly perceived that they made it their buſineſſe to ſtudy conformity, without the leaſt heeding what they had formerly engaged, or enquiring what, for the time to come this might grow unto; *Iſachcr-like they bowed their ſhoulders to beare, and became Servants unto whatſoever tribute was impoſed.*

In

In the laſt place I took a briefe view of their behaviour abroad in the world-where they were ſtriving who ſhould be foremoſt in get_ ting of offices and places of profit; ſo imployed they were in enriching themſelves, and building their *own houſes*; as that they little minded the *houſe of God*. And as for Mr. *Stucley*, he was ſo entangled with the world as that it took up a great part of his time every week, which ſhould have been ſpent in the worke of the miniſtry, contrary to that of the Apoſtle, 2 *Tim.* 2. 4. So troubled he was about many things, as that he very much neglected that one thing needfull, the feeding of the flock,—— He ſeemed to me to be led captive by *ambition* and *covetouſneſſe*, which made him more crafty and politick then could (in my Judgment) ſtand with the *Sim-plicity of the Goſpell*: So that I queſtioned whether or no, he had not applied himſelfe to the ſtudie of wiſedome, onely for her left hand bleſſings of riches and honor.

I cald to mind his ſubtilty in the manageing of many buſieneſſes, his ſetting Mr *Stonham* a worke about that which he durſt not appeare in himſelfe; but eſpecially his *trecherouſneſſe* and deceitfull dealing in uſeing means for the opening reading and Coppying of poſtletters; the letters of the chiefe mageſtrate of this Cit-ty, this I was enformed of by one of their mem-bers, and ſince hath been confirmed by others;

And

And his appointing a day of *thankſgiving* for the Succesfulneſſe of his deſignes furthered by ſuch unlawfull meānes; whether this were not a bringing of *Thankſgiving* with leaven, I leave it to others to Judge. I could not but withdraw from that *thankſgiving*: I conſidered with my ſelfe, how unlike it was that he ſhould be a faithfull miniſter of Chriſt, who dealt ſo unfaithfully with men, and therefore that it could not be ſafe for me to continue any longer under his paſtorall charge; eſpecially ſeeing I could not be faithfull to them, becauſe of their crafty ſeeking advantages to enſnare: All the remedy I had left was to withdrawe from them.

Thus being convinced of *Separation* and the evill thereof, and having pondred a while of their *Unchriſtian* or rather *Antichriſtian* practiſes, I went on the 24 of *March* 1654. to Mr *Eveleigh* the Elder, whom *I* deſired to acquaint the Church, that I ſhould continue no longer with them, for ſeverall reaſons which I then gave him; And that *I* would willingly (if they deſired it) give them farther Satisfaction; he replyed that there was nothing but would be made up: *I* know that very well, ſaid *I*, but for ſeverall reaſons *I* am reſolved to withdraw from your ſociety.

About foureteen daies after, (being ſent for) *I* went to their meeting according to my promiſe,

mife, fuppofing they would require an account
of my leaving of them ; but Mr *Stucley* altogether waved that, and infteed thereof having
queftioned me a little concerning Mr *Stoneham*,
demanded how long I had ufed to heare M*r* *Ford*,
I anfwered a year at the leaft, the truth of which
affertion when he feemed to queftion, I added
farther that my writing books would make it
appeare that I had heard him much longer.

Then he afked me concerning Mris *Eveleigh*,
whether I did not fpeak againft her?

To this I returned Anfwer, (1) by asking
him whether he did not fay to Mr *Eveleigh* in
his own houfe within a few daies after that fhe
was admitted, that I was fo farre from fpeaking
againft her, as that I had fpoken for her, and
therefore would cleare me.

To this he anfwered never a word, but was
filent. (1ly) by acknowledging that I had Spoken againft her ; but not to have her kept off,
as Mr *Eveleigh* had charged me.

Why did you then Speake againft her, said
Mr *Stucley* ?

I anfwered becaufe fhe had gone contrary to
the *law of Charity*, in that fhe did partake of the
ordinance of the *lords Supper* with the *Presbyterians*, which we did not : If fhe looked on this
as her duty, fhe could not but looke on the neglect thereof, as our Sin, and fo fhe walked *un-
charitably*: fhe being in *Societie* with vs, and not
admonifhing

admonishing vs. of our neglect, in suffering Sin
uppon us.

To this Mr *Stutley* replyed, what that lawe of
Charitie was (for his part) He knew not, he
knew noe such law, Mr *Roles* said It was a word
hastily spoken, and so it might be taken.

After this Mr. *Stutley* asked me, how I
could go amon the *Presbyterians.*

To this I answered, that I looked on it as
my dutie to wait upon God amongst a profes-
sing, reforming people.

And then he told me, how that in my letter
unto him, I had acknowledged that for a *true
Church*, which I had formerly called *Babylon.*

To this I answered, that I had called to mind
so much as I could against my selfe, as to that
particular of *Babylon*, and so far as *I* could remember any such expressions, I did acknowledge my evill therein, for which *I* had cause
to be humbled: and withall that *I* did not *separate* as from *Babylon*, that *I* looked upon them
from whom vve *separated* as true Churches in
doctrine and *worship*, that *I* did not *separate*
from either of these, but only from their *di-
scipline*: that the chiefe ground of my *separation* vvas a *Mistake*, I supposing that a Church
rightly constituted must be joined together by
an *Explicite Covenant*, vvhich *I* found to be
othervvise novv.

I vvas likevvise questioned for opposing in

a

a publique meeting Mr. *Stucley*, as to his being *Paftor* at that time, vvhen they chofe him
to be the *Paftor*, and that in fuch a *Contentious*
manner, as to caufe an hovver and halfe debate
in the meeting. Mr. *Whitehorne* fent them a
paper, vvherein he profered to affirme vvith
oath this charge.

Which being denied by me, becaufe I knevv
I vvas not prefent at the meeting at that time,
Mr. *Role* and Mr. *Slade* faid they did believe
that Mr. *Whithorne* vvas miftaken (or to that
effect) and Mr. *Sprague* expreffely affirmed,
that it vvas othervvife then Mr. *Whithorne*
had vvritten, for (faid he) vve did agree to
conceale that meeting from her, leſt ſhe ſhould
oppofe him.

I asked Mr. *Roles* and Mr. *Slade* where ever
they knew me oppofe Mr. *Stucley* in a publique
meeting? They faid no, they never knew it.
Thus after they had fpent fome time in fuch
Cavills, Mr. *Stucley* faid to me, you are accufed of a flip of your Tongue, of an Untruth.

To which I replied, that this was a new
thing, and defired to know what ground he
had for it?

He anfwered here is Teftimony, here are
they who will witneffe.

I told him my witneffe might be taken as
foon as theirs, and had been formerly before
theirs.

Mr.

Mr. *Rols* then turning himselfe towards Mr.
Stucley, said, that he believed there was never
an untruth spoken, and it being things long
before, and that every one spake as they remembred: and farther said, that he wondred
he made so much adoe about nothing.

To which Mr. *Stucley* replied, here is a *negative* and an *affirmative*, and therefore a lye;
although he never examined where the lye
was.

At the conclusion I told them that I should
come no more among them.

This is the Substance of what I can remember concerning this daies discourse, it being
more then three yeares since. Whereby it appeares that I have just cause to charge the lye
on themselves.

A few daies after they sent for me againe,
but I told the messenger, seeing they had so
grossely abused me, as to charge a lye upon me,
I would come no more among them: that they
were a people not to be trusted, and that I
would be drawn in sunder by wild horses rather then go unto them.

However the same day I sent unto Mr. *Slade*,
one of the Officers, to know what they would
have of me, who told me that they were very
much troubled at my leaving them, and that
they would look on my *Returne* as a *Resurrection mercy*.

I

I defired him to returne this as my anfwer unto them, viz. Let them ftudy the Word, and convince me from the Word what is my dutie in fuch a Cafe, and I would gladly re, ceive it, and willingly fubmit to it, fo unwilling was I to offend them, yet to come any more among them I durft not, becaufe of their former Carriage, neither was it (as I conceived) fafe for me to adventure fingly and without witneffe among them, who were my *accufers*, *witneffes*, and *judges*, Since that day of the meeting abovefaid I never fpake with Mr. *Stucley*, though I defired it feverall times.

Some daies after Mr. *Eveleigh* and Mr. *Slade* Officers, and a member with them came unto me, and (as they faid) expected Mr. *Stucley's* comeing likewife, but he came not.

I then complained of their *Carriage* towards me, telling them how much I was troubled at it, and defired them alfo to fhew me from the word what they could expect, and then I fhould fubmit.

One of them replied you muft returne, and do otherwife, I anfwered, that I had too much to do with *Separation* already, and therefore fhould not returne; then faid one of them, then they will never be fatisfied.

As for Mr. *Eveleigh* he told me, that my going away fhould coft me dearer then my coming in, and that they would proceed according

ding to the order of the Churches: this was heard by another.

I anfvvered, vvhatever I fuffered by them, could not be fo much as had fuffered for them.

After this others came to me; I told them I did expect to fpeak vvith Mr. *Stucley*, that I might knovv vvhat he had againft me, and that I vvas ready to fubmit to the vvord, that they fhould convince me thereby hovv I ought to be affected.

Mris *Roles* alfo came unto me in vvay of a vifit, vvho defired me to confider vvhat a dif-honour it vvould be unto the Church, if I left them: and as for vvhat you have at any time fpoke unto them (faid fhe) I believe it vvas in the uprightneffe of your heart, and fo doth my hufband.

I told her that I did not juftify my felfe in every parricular as to the manner of it, faid fhe, you fpoile all in faying you vvill leave them, and if you do fo, vvhat vvill they fay of my *Cozen Stucley?* and what will they fay of us? confider, we are rifing, and more will come into us continually.

And after this Mris. *Stoneham* came unto me, asking with teares in her eies, whether I would not returne, and whether fhe was the caufe of my going away.

I demanded of her whether Mr. *Stoneham* knew of her coming? She anfvvered, that fhe

did

did not see him at her coming away. I then told her that it was reported by some of them, that they could not partake with me in ordinances now.

: For my part (said she) I was never of that mind, neither do I know any who are, but on the contrary we are all much troubled that you will leave us.

About two months after, *Ezekiel Pace* was sent from Mr. *Eveleigh*, to tell me that I was *suspended* by the *Church*.

I told him that I had left their *Society*, and that I had no communion with them.

He answered, they conceived that they could not otherwise discharge their dutie unto me, and as for what they had done, it was in order to my return.

I replyed that my purpose was never to returne unto them.

After I had made my Addresse to the Ministers of the City, desiring to be admitted into fellowship and communion with them in ordinances. Mr. *Stucley* understanding thereof sent Mr. *Eveleigh* unto Mr. *John Bartlet* Minister, to give him notice that they had severall things against me: upon which it was by Mr. *Bartlet* desired that they would produce their charge, which they promised to do, although it was long first, yet at length (after often desiring of it) a meeting was appointed at Mr. *Fords*

D   house

houfe the Minifter: Between Mr. *Ford* and
Mr. *Bartlet* on the one fide, and Mr. *Stucley*
and Mr. *Eveleigh* on the other. At which meeting I was prefent, there they did declare what
they had againft me, concerning Mris *Eveleigh*
and *Babylon*, where they charged me with an
untruth. And the refult of this *conference* was
this, the *Articles* wherewith they charged
me, being after ferious *Examination* by all the
minifters of the City found partly doubtfull
and proofeleffe, and partly frivolous, I was
fhortly after (according as I defired) received
into Communion with them; and fo continued neer three yeares, till Mr. *Stucley's* Curfing
began to make a noife in the world, which was
neer three yeares after I deferted them.

Neer three years after my leaving of them,
Mr. *Eveleigh* acquainted me with a *faft* in order to their *Excommunication*. I then defired
that the bufineffe might be brought to a new
triall before the minifters, whom they had acquainted with it formerly, and with whom I
was in *Communion*, without whofe advice I
would do nothing.

But this was not hearkned unto, they being
(it feemes) refolved on their worke of *Excommunication*, how caufeleffe and unjuft foever.

Let that letter that Mris. *Allen* and my
felfe jointly fubfcribed and fent to Mr. *Stucley*
to be communicated to the Church, ftand as a
vvitneffe

witnesse between us and them, to testifie to all
the world how unjustly they charge us with
Contumacy and refusing of *Admonition*, whereby it evidently appeares that we honoured
them so far as to receive their Summons, and
to return them our *Answer*, wherein we did

1 Desire a fair triall botvveen them and us
before understanding and impartiall men.

2 We did professe our desire to submit to
the lavv and vvill of *Christ*, vvhen vve should
see reason from *Scripture* to Convince.

3 We did in the generall professe our *Repentance* for those Evills that vve knevv our selves
guilty of.

Thus far vve condescended to them. And
let the impartiall Reader judge vvhat they
could expect more from us, vvho had upon
Conscientious principles withdrawne from *communion* with them, as Master *Allen* hath already
declared of his wife, and my selfe having deserted them neere three yeares before (being convinced of the groundlesnesse of *separation* for
severall particulars I declared to the *Elder*, & the
cause of my withdrawing being not removed,
but more offence being still given by them,
how could *I* acknowledge them so as to put my
selfe upon their tryall . Besides how could wee
with safety put our selves on their triall ; who
were enraged with us since we left them, which
they discovered by their *Calumniating* and *de-
faming* of us.　　　D 2　　　Be-

Besides we having been in fellowship with the Lords people in other congregations; my selfe severall yeares, and Mris. *Allen* for some time, we being so aspersed by them as we were, how could we cleer our selves, so as to satisfie them that we were in Communion with (without a tryall) so as that they might not suffer by us; for what we were aspersed with, did in some manner reflect upon them, who had received us into fellowship with them.

And whereas Mr. *Stucley* in his book Intituled (*Manifest Truth*) pag. 22. pretends that it robbes particular Churches of that power and authority which Christ hath intrusted them with, of Trying and censuring their own *delinquent members* &c.

Resol. This is nothing to the purpose, we were not their members, but reall members of some other congregations. If they have power to censure their own *delinquent members*, we doe not hinder them from exercising their power. But have they therefore power to Censure the *members* of other Churches? we had withdrawen from *Communion* with them, and they having not satisfied us so as to remove the occasion of our leaving them.

May he not therefore reflect upon himselfe, who hath contrary to his own professed principles robbed the Church of their power, and of their *members* in *Censuring* of us, without the

Ap-

Approbation of thofe *minifters* and *congregati-ons* to which we ftood related? May we not therefore aske him, who gave you this *Autho-rity* of lording it over *Churches* and their *mem-bers* without their Counfell or confent? Is not this practice of his too much like thofe that the Apoftle foretells of *Acts* 20. 24. *For I know this that after my departure fhall grievous wolves en-ter in among you, not fparing the flock,* and our Saviour tells us *there are wolves in fheeps-cloa-thing, ye fhall know them by their fruits, Matth. 7.* 15, 16. Befides, let it be confidered, in denying of us this liberty to have a fair Triall, hath he not hereby denyed *Communion of Churches,* he being fince defired feverall times by feve-rall minifters of the City, that the bufineffe might be brought to a Triall; they judging it unreafonable that we fhould be excommunica-ted by them, untill the caufe be clearly proved, and we be permitted to Anfwer for our felves. But this he hath evaded for feverall months; and in ftead thereof takes liberty to preach and print what he pleafeth of us, that fo he may render our names and perfons odious to them that know us not.

And for farther Anfwer to him in that he pretends that it robs the *Church* of the power that Chrift hath given &c. It being a point of *controverfie* I fhall leave it to the learned. Let him confult the Judgments of thofe that are

D 3 for

for the *Congregationall way.*

The *Apologeticall Narration* presented to the house of *Parliament,* and subscribed by T. G. P. N. S. S. I. B. W. B. in answer to this objection, viz. That in such a *congregationall go-vernmēt,* thus entire within it selfe, there is not allowed sufficient Remedy for miscarriages or wrongfull sentences, or persons injured there-by, no Room for complaints, no powerfull or effectuall means to reduce a *Church* or *Churches* that fall into heresie, or schisme, but every one is left, and may take liberty, without controle *to do what is good in their owne eyes.*

Pag. 14. We could not but judge it a safe, & an allowed way to retaine the Government of our severall *Congregations* for matter of *disci-pline* within themselves, &c. yet not claiming to our selves an *independent power* in every *Con-gregation,* to give account, or be subject to none others, but onely a full and entire power com-pleat within our selves, untill we should be chal-lenged to erre grosly: such as *Corporations* en-joy, who have the power and priviledge to passe sentence for life and death within them-selves, and yet are accountable to the State they live in.

Pag. 16. An instance they give of their owne practice in a businesse of this nature of *Excom-munication,* wherewith some *Churches* were offended.

In

In this Cafe our *Churches* did mutually and univerfally acknowledge and fubmit to this as a Sacred and undoubted Principle and fupreme Law to be obferved among all Churches. That as by vertue of that *Apoftolicall Command*, Churches as well as particular men are bound to give no offence, neither to *Jew* or *Gentile*, nor the Churches of God they live amongft: fo that in all cafes of fuch offences or difference, by the obligation of the *common law of Communion of Churches*, and for the vindication of the glory of *Chrift*, which in common they hold forth, the Church or Churches challenged to offend or differ are to fubmit themfelves, upon the challenge of the offence or complaint of the perfon wronged, to the moft full and open triall and examination by other neighbour churches offended thereat, of what ever hath given the offence. And farther that by vertue of the fame and like law of not partaking of other mens fins, the Churches offended may & ought(upon the Impenitency of thofe Churches perfifting in their error and mifcarriage) to pronounce that heavy fentence againft them of withdrawing and renouncing all Chriftian Communion with them, untill they do repent. And farther, to declare and proteft this, with the caufes thereof to all other Churches of Chrift that they might do the like.

D 4   Pag.

Pag. 21. It was openly and publiquely professed in a speech, that was the Preface to that
discussion, to this effect. That it was the most
abhorred *Maxime*. that any *Religion* hath ever
made Profession of, and therefore of all other
the most contradictory and dishonourable unto that of *Christianity*, *That a single and parti-*
cular Society within themselves should farther ar-
rogate unto themselves an Exemption from give-
ing account, or being Censureable by any other,
either Christian magistrate above them, or neigh-
bour Churches about them. So farr (say they)
were our Iudgements, from that Independent
liberty, that is imputed to us.

So Mr *Borroughs*, heart division *p.* 43. where
he sayes, Those in the *Congregationall way* acknowledge that they are bound in *conscience*, to
give account of their wayes to the Churches a-
bout them, or to any other who shall require it,
this, not in an *Arbitrary way*, but as a duty they
owe to God and man.

Reader, here you see how wide and dissonant,
the judgements of those (more) learned of the
Congregationall way are from the practice and
proceedings of Mr *Stucley* & his Church: Those
of that way acknowledging, but hee denying,
submission to any *examination*, or *triall* by
neighbour Churches, and hee and his Church
claiming an *Independent* power, or liberty to
give

give no account, or be subject to no others,
though accused and challenged for erring grosly
in point of their Arbitrary unjust proceedings
against us, which is plainly manifested in Master *Allen's* booke called (*Truths manifest revived*) and will farther appeare in my ensuing
Vindication, to which I hasten ; This being
(to my best remembrance) a true Relation of
what passed between us, untill the *Excommunication*.

THE

VINDICATION.

BY that which hath been said in my *Narrative*, it is manifest that I was never
questioned, much lesse admonished for
lying, untill my coming off from them, that
they

they never accounted me (whiles I was with them) such a vile person as now by their *slanderous pamphlets* they endeavour to make the world believe me to be : and here I cannot but wonder at Mr *Mall*, that he, being a stranger to me, and altogether ignorant of my manner of life and conversation, should yet be so rash and inconsiderate, as meerly upon *reports* to defame me in *Print*, for which he is bound in conscience as he is a *Minister* (if he be one) a Christian, yea, as he is a man, to give the Church of God, mee, and the world, satisfaction.

The Notes, (saith he in his *Epistle to the Reader*) of Mr *Stucleys Sermon*, I am glad I took in short hand from his mouth, or otherwise thou mightest never have seen a true Copy of them.

Surely, if the *Copy* do agree with the *Original*, (which some question) I shall be so bold to affirme of both that they exceedingly disagree with the *Truth*, in laying those *Crimes* to my charge which they are never able to prove, as will sufficiently (I beleive) appeare in these my following *Answers* to their Severall *Articles*.

I shall begin with that of *lying*, it being that which my accuser begins and almost ends with, which he in many places of his book mentions with a great deale of pretended *zeale* and *indignation*, which he indeavours to equall with the sin of *Incest*, which he saith is a fault detestable to the very *heathens*. Some of them, this is
the

the *Gryme* which he and his party especially
charge me with both in *Citie* and *Country*,
crying out every where, I am a lyar, yea an
egregious one, and therefore justly *Excommunicated*, This is in fine, the Article on which the
whole *charge* depends.

Before I come to the *Charge* it selfe in particular, I shall crave leave to speake something in
the generall concerning the apprehension I have
of this *Sin*, as also somewhat concerning Master
Stucleys practice in reference unto it, whereby it
will be evident, both how improbable it is that
I should be such an *Egregious lyer*, as hee hath
made mee in his booke, and also how unlikely
it is, that hee should be so *zealously* affected against *lying* as he therein pretends.

For the first of these, *Lying* is that *Sin*,
which my *Parents* from time to time, so represented unto me in the severall aggravations and
deformities thereof, as that I alwaies (since I
came to yeares of discretion) abhorred, and detested it, both in my selfe and others.

I account a *lyar* unfit not onely for *Christian
Communion*, but also *civill Commerce*.

From the word, and my own sadd experience, I finde it to be an *hereditary evill* in all the
sons and daughters of *Adam: That the heart
is deceitfull and desperately wicked above all
things, who can know it ?* That there is a way
of

of *lying* in the best of men by nature, in this sense, *let God be true, and every man a lyer*. The guile, deceipt, falshood, and hypocrisy which is in the heart, is that which is a chiefe part and member of the *bodie of death*, and that which makes it out of measure sinfull, and an intollerable burthen to be borne.

As to the practice of this *sin*, I do believe that it is not confistent with the worke of grace; That he which lives in the practice thereof, is not a *member* of *Chrift* but a *limbe* of the *divell*; it is fo contrary to the God of truth, fo contrarie unto Chrift, who is *the Truth*, and fo contrarie unto *the Spirit of Truth*, and fo contrary unto the work of *Regeneration*, as I cannot believe that fuch a foule as lives in the practice thereof, or hath flight thoughts of it, was ever begotten againe by *the word of Truth*, neither is it (I conceive) poffible for fuch a one to enjoy comfortable comimunion with God.

I looke on it as a *diftinguifhing Character*, whereby the Children of God are known from the children of the divel, *The Remnant of Ifrael fhall not doe iniquity, nor fpeak lies, neither fhall a deceitfull tongue be found in their mouthes.* *Lyers* are excluded from the *New Jerufalem*, that cometh down from God out of heaven, whofoever loveth and maketh a lie is in the number of thofe who are without: The hundred fortie and four thousand that ftand with
.the

the *Lambe* on *Mount Sion*, having his fathers
name written on their foreheads, which follow
the *lambe* wherefoever he goeth, which were
redeemed frō among men, being the *firſt-fruits*
unto God and to the *lambe*, in their mouth
was found no *Guile.*

I hope through *grace* in fome meafure I can
fay, That I have feen fuch a defireable beauty
in *Truth*, as with *David* to hate and abhorre
lying, & whatfoever is contrary unto *truth*, guile,
deceit, hypocrifie, falfhood, a falfe heart, falfe
wayes, falfe doctrines, though under never fo
faire pretences, when once they are throughly
difcovered.

And as to my *practice*, as I defire to lay
afide every weight that preffeth down, and the
Sin that doth fo eafily befet me, So is it my endeavour in all my approaches unto the *Throne of
Grace*, the word & ordinances, to obtain ftrength
for the purging out more & more of the Guile,
hypocrifie, falfhood, and deceit that is in my
heart, and is ftill difcovering it felfe before the
Lord, and ready to break out on all occafions,
which doth continually adminifter matter of
lamentation unto me.

And becaufe I find by fad *experience* that this
body of death doth not lie idle, but is ftill
bringing forth fruit unto death, and being
not willing to reft in my own *Teftimony*,
confidering often that of *Solomon*, he that
         trufteth

trusteth his own heart is a fool: and fearing also left through *corruption* I might forget the miscarriages laid to my charge *f.* some yeares being expired ere ever I was questioned for them). or put them off, I did earnestly desire againe and again to speak with Mr. *Stucley* himselfe, that I might know his *grounds* in charging me with *lying,* but all to no purpose; he could not be spoken with.

And so also since the *Excommunication* did I write unto him to know the particulars whereof I am accused in reference to *lying,* that so I might accordingly either *justifie* or *condemne* my selfe. But he in stead of satisfying my just and reasonable demand, most imperiously and prelatically sends me a letter full of bitter *Calumniations,* accusing me to be a *Contentious, dividing,* and *lying Spirit;* without so much as naming any particulars.

As to the Second, I might referre the *Reader* for proof hereof to his *practice.* It will be found upon triall that he is not of *Davids* minde in *Pfal.* 101.7. to *Banish* from his house and fight, every one that worketh deceit and telleth lies; and though he pretend to banish mee (upon that account) from his *society* and *fellowship,* yet he never questioned me for lying, untill I departed from him, untill I sent him word that I would come no more among them.

When

When he and Master *Eveleigh* accused me to Master *Forde*, and Master *Bartlet* of *lying*, Master *Forde* asked him whether he had ever admonished me for those things whereof he accused me, To which he answered that he had not been faithfull unto me, and that I had told him of it my selfe, And Master *Eveleigh* added, That they had much a doe to please me.

Had I continued with them I should, without doubt, notwithstanding all those *lyes* I am now accused of, have been as favorably dealt with, as two other of their *members*, who were notoriously guilty of *lying*.

As to the first of them, it was briefly thus; we having beene enjoyned *Secresie* by Mr *Stucley*, there was notwithstanding somewhat of our *private Conferences* divulged and made knowne.

Hereupon the next meeting every one was examined, and charged in a solemne manner to declare whether they knew who it was that had revealed it: To which a negative answer was returned by every one, and when I desired Master *Stucley* to search after it more narrowly, and presse it more closely upon them, that the *Lyar* might be found out, he put mee off with this, that it had beene so in another Church, and though he knew who it was afterward (as I am informed) yet the party was never admonished at any of our meetings.

Here was (to be sure) a *negative* and an *affirma-*

*firmative,*a breach of promise, and then a denying of that which was fresh in memory, and
(which is more)the words spoken in prviae betweene our selves were mif-reported, and yet
Mr *Stucley* could quietly passe it over.

The other is *John Whitehorne,* who offered
to affirme with oath, that which was by two or
three of the members presently contradicted;
and yet Mr *Stucley* hath beene so farre from admonishing him for it, as that I heare he is now
become an Elder.

By all which it is more then probable, that
there is little of truth to be expected in his *lying
charge,*which he expresseth in these words.

Charge. As for Mris *Parr* she is accused amóg
other things for *lying* more than three times
sufficiently proved, in *pag.* 18. of his booke
published by Mr *Mall.* But when she was under Church admonition concerning severall
things, she was found tripping very much in reference to her Tongue, and *lying egregiously;* so
that the *whole Church* could beat witnefs against
her.

Resol: If this *Charge* be throughly sifted, it
will be found faulty more wayes then one, and
so *egregiously tripping,* and *halting,* as that every
unbyassed Reader may witnesse against it. For,

1. It runs altogether in the generall, in affirming mee to be under *Church admonition,* for
severall things, without naming any one: And
when

then in accuseing mee only of *lying* in generall, without inftancing in fo much as one particular, whereby others are poffeffed with a *prejudice* a-gainft mee ; and my felfe difenabled to alleadge any thing in mine owne *defence*, not knowing how the particulars will be framed.

2. Secondly, it confidently afferts me guilty of *lying* more then three times fufficiently proved, and that fo *egregiously*, as all *the Church could witneffe againft mee* ; when as one of their prin-cipall *members* declared (at that time when I was accufed of Tripping) in their meeting that hee thought there was never an untruth fpo-ken, but that every one fpake as they remem-bred.

3. Thirdly and laftly, it fayes, I was under Church admonition for feverall things.

What hee meaneth by *Church admonition* I fcarce underftand ; if by *Church admonition* hee meanes that difcourfe which wee had together at the very time (being ten dayes after I left them ; when as he faith , I was found tripping) I fay it was no *admonition* (as I conceived) but onely an *examination*, as appeares in my *Narra-tive*. If he would infinuate thereby that I was under *Church admonition* before that time : Then I fay it could be but for one thing onely which is omitted ; neither is there any mention made of it throughout the whole booke ; And that was my hearing Mr *Forde*.

E   Its

Its true Mr *Stucley* told me, my speaking
was difrelished, whereupon I left that practice
neere two yeares before I left them; Its true
likewife that the Elder accufed mee of contention, upon which I made my appeale unto the
Church, who with one confent acquitted me
of that charge,

The Elder alfo accufed me of *cenforiousnes*
for oppofing (*Ganicle*)who not longe after turned *Queker*, and therby cleered me of that im-
putation; fo that I could not be at this time,
when as they fay I lyed fo egregioufly, under
church admonition for either of thefe,

And as for any other things I cannot remeber
any that they did ever manifeft the leaft diflike
of, unleffe my practice of hearing Mr *Forde*,
(which is the thing (not things) for which I was
under *Church admonition*) the thing which hath
occafioned all this trouble; and for which, (as
Mr *Stucley* in a letter formerly threatned) they
have proceeded to *cenfure* mee, though it be
daubed over with lying & other forged crimes.

This practice of hearing Mr *Forde* was permitted mee, or at the leaft winked at by them,
fo long as I had a friend that might pleafure
them in the City, and in the Parliament—. Mr
Stucley prefently upon his being an *officer*, told
mee that he did expect I fhould heare him, and
no other, to which I prefently replyed, that it
would be hard for mee to leave that Miniftry
                                                    which

which the Lord had made so profitable unto
mee, and withall gave him my grounds for that
practice. At length at the close of our discourse,
he said, we should not disagree about it, and yet
afterwards Master *Stoneham* was put upon it to
preach and pray against mee for this practice.

   To take mee off from this practice also was
Mr *Sprague* sent unto me, by Mr *Stoneham*: the
very same day at the meeting the Elder told
me, they had two things against me, one was
Contention, the other my hearing Mr *Forde*,
which the *Church* neither could nor would bear:
the Elder the next day after the businesse of
contention was ended, told mee that he had nothing against mee but my hearing Mr *Forde*.

   Mr *Slade* also, and Mr *Rolls* came to mee as
messengers from the *Church* (as they said) to
admonish me in particular of hearing Mr *Forde*:
Mr *Stucley* himselfe wrote me two long letters,
about this very thing, & in one of them threatned to *censure* mee for it: they kept a fast for
this very particular the 24. of *February* 1654.
They omitted the administration of the Lords
Supper for this reason (as Mr *Raddon* told me)
yea Mr *Stoneham* said, that if I would not sit
downe under his Ministry, he would be no Officer unto mee.

   When I was desired afterwards to forbeare
coming to the *Sacrament*, without giving any
other reason then this, That some body did

desire

desire me to forbeare (who this somebody was
I could never learne) I went forthwith to severall members, to know what they had against
mee, who answered, they had nothing, but my
going to heare others, which practice (they said)
was destructive to the Church. By all which it
is manifest that this was the onely thing they
had against mee, untill I had left them, and yet
this is omitted, and other things are pretended.
Let all the world judge whether this be not *Serpentine subtilty* : As to this charge of (lying) I
shall desire the Reader to consider farther these
three or fower particulars.
  1. The time when they found me Tripping,
(as he saith) it was after I had left them. Before
I had sent them word that I was resolved to
withdraw from their *Society* I was never questioned for a lye : what doth this imply, but that
they resolved my going off should cost mee
dearer then my coming in among them, according to the Elder Mr *Eveleighs* threatning.
  Again, it was at that time when I went to the
in *love*, in *the simplicity of my heart*, to give
them *satisfaction* why I left them, as I did at
the first why I associated my selfe with them;
thinking as little to be charged with lying, as
with theft, murder, or other sins not to be named among *Christians*. And here I cannot but
commend Mris *Allen* her discretion, in refusing
to adventure her self singly among them, which
                                            had

had she done, they would have made her as great a lyer, as my selfe, thereby Mr *Stucley* would have been freed from the trouble of framing two indifferent bills of indictment against us.

2. Secondly, the matters about which they examined me at that time were such as had been done and past long before, some yeares: so that if through weaknesse of memory, my tongue had tripped, how will it follow hence that *I* lyed so *egregiously* as to deserve *Excommunication*? How could they be sure that *I* made a lye, though *I* had spoken an untruth, unlesse they knew certainly, that *I* spake against my knowledge?

3. Thirdly, *I* did in my answers to their frivolous and cavilling questions insert by way of *caution* (*viz.*) *as I remember: according to my best remembrance,* &c. which might have satisfied them, as it did M*r Rolls* at that time, had they not beene fully bent to slander mee for leaving them.

4. Fowerthly, *I* was onely accused, not convicted, of lying: M*r Stucley* said, here are they who will witnesse, but yet they did not witnesse any particular, that I absolutely denied, except *John Whitehorne,* whose testimony (though he offered to confirme it with oath) was presently contradicted by another of their members. Why did not M*r Stucley* according to the man-

ner

ner even of heathenish Romans, *Act. 25. 16.* (who in this shew the worke of *the Law written in their hearts*) require as an Officer, every one to speake out what they had to say against me ? was it for feare lest they should be found *Tripping* as *John Whitehorne* was ? I appeale to all impartiall Readers, whether it be not a most *unrighteous judgement* thus to condemne mee without being convicted, yea when I was cleared by Mr *Rolls.*

And farther let it be considered that I was so farre acquitted by the *Ministers* of this *City,* as that they gave mee the right hand of fellowship, notwithstanding their *impeachments,* which I believe they are ready to witnesse unto the Church, of God when it shall be required of them. This may suffice to be spoken in reference to the charge of *lying* in the generall.

I shall in the next place proceed to Answer the Particulars of this *lying Charge,* as I find them laid down by Mr. *Stucley* in another Pamphlet of his, Intituled *Manifest Truth.* Being an *Angry Answer* to Mr. *Toby Allein,* in in which he hath unbosomed and discovered himselfe more fully then in Mr. *Mall's* Book. In pag. 41. and so onwards, he reduceth the grounds of my *Suspension* to three heads, *Contentiousnesse, Censoriousnesse,* and *Lying,* each of which he instanceth in severall particulars. The last of these I shall begin with, and answer in

the

the first place, which I shall do, having briefly
considered what he saith concerning the grounds
of my *Suspension*.

As to that *suspension* that *Ezekiel Pace* gave
me notice of, I say that it was neer two months,
after I had left them, after I was withdrawen
from their *communion*; which *suspension* (as the
messenger said) was in order to my *returne*. By
which I gather that the chiefe ground thereof
was my going away: and that it is so, as also
their *Excommunication*, almost three yeares
after, will be manifested fully by my following
answer; wherein I shall shew that they had no
ground at all to *suspend* or *excommunicate* me
for any of those three particulars mentioned by
Mr. *Stucley*.

And first of *lying*, which in pag. 44,45. he
endeavours to prove in six particulars.

Instance 1. She affirmed, that she alwaies
acknowledged *Presbyterian Churches* to be
true Churches in respect of *Doctrine* and *worship*, and that it was hard for her to *separate*
from the *Presbyterians* in distinguishing ordinances; whereas she excepted against Mr. *Toby
Allein*, for having his child Baptized by Mr.
Ford, and opposed his admission on that
ground: there were 4 witnesses to this.

Resolut. This instance hath more of *Craft*
(if I understand it) then either truth or reason,
and may very well (I think) answer it selfe.

E 4   I

I am here brought in opposing Mr. *Allens* *suspension*, and in other pages of his book he saith Mr. *Allen* consented to my *suspension*.

As Mr. *Allen* denies the one, so do I the other. But suppose I should have done it, they all know it was my judgment and my practice at that time: where is the lye?

I told them it was very hard for mee to *separate* in distinguishing Ordinances. And they may remember the same time I told them also what was my ground why I did *separate*: what can be gathered hence, but that I did that which was very hard for me to do, *separate* in distinguishing Ordinances, and dislike Mr. *Allen*, because he was not of the same mind?

But I am very much dissatisfied and offended with this *charge*, because it doth differ from the *charge* which I was charged with by them, which was this, namely for speaking against Mr *Allen*, because he did partake of the ordinance of the *Lords supper* with the *Presbyterians*.

And this I denied, my reason was, because I had never heard at that time, that Mr. *Allen* did partake with the *Presbyterians* in that ordinance; its now Seaven yeares since.

Instance 2. She affirmed that she never opposed Mris *Dorothy Eveleighs* admission, but was for it, whereas the generality of the then members of the Church witnessed, that a

long

long time she openly contended against it to
the griefe of the Church.

Resolut. 1. I have marveild many times
why they should question me about opposing
of her, who was long before in her grave, and
with whom *I* had loving and *Christian converse*
to her dying day.

2ly, That *I* affirmed that *I* never spake
against her is false, neither could *I* get any advantage by it, seeing others of the Church did
the like, in whom it was not lookt upon as an
evill. *I* might say more, but that *I* am unwilling to rake in the ashes of the dead.

3ly, *I* gave Mr. *Stucley* a Reason why *I* spake
against her at the first, (which he himselfe mentions pag. 43. in the 4th. particular of *Contention*) not to have her kept off, but that she
might acknowledge her sin in breaking the law
of Charity &c.

4ly, That *I* did speak for her *admißion*, Mr.
Stucley himsele witnessed it to Mr. *Eveleigh*
in his own house, and also another of their
members E.B. hath (as she told me) declared
unto them that it was *I* who prevailed with her
to consent unto the admission of Mris *Dorothie
Eveleigh.*

Instance 3. She denied that she ever called
the *Presbyterian Churches* by the name of *Babylon,* whereas most of the Church witnessed
that she had often so called them.

Resol:

Resol. What I answered Mr. *Stucley* when he did in a manner reprove me for acknowledging that to be a *true Church*, which formerly I had called *Babylon*, appeares in the Narrative. To which I shall farther adde

1 Suppose it were true, that I had in the heat of *Contention* at our first *separation* vented some rash and inconsiderate expressions in reference to the *Presbyterian Churches*, or the *Presbyterians* themselves, yet it ill becomes Mr. *Stucley* and the rest to be my accusers, who continue in the same practice, in judging me for this, they do but condemne themselves, according to that of the Apostle *Rom. 2. 1.* Why do they censure me now for this, seeing I am not guilty of it at present? why did not they admonish me for it formerly, when I was with them?

2 Would they even now be so faithfull unto me, as to name any particular time, place, or other circumstance that might bring such expressions to my remembrance, they should find me as ready to condemne my selfe, as they are to accuse me, if done in an orderly manner.

(3^ly) It may be that which occasioned this report, was my mentioning of *Babylons brats*, at the time when I spake my *Experiences*.

I did then declare how hard it was for me to *Separate* from those who were godly, and whose ministry had bin so profitable unto me: But

when

when I considered the command of god, *Touch
noe uncleane thing, and I will receive you. &c.*
I conceived it did sufficiently warrant our *Se-
perating* from them: And farther I declared that
there were many litle ones, *Babylonish Brats,*
which must be dasht against the stones, which
(I then told them) I did understand of things,
not persons. But they, many of them, being
newly crept into a *forme of godlines,* were so ignorant of that *distinction,* as what I spake of
things, they interpreted of persons, which was
so farr from my thoughts, as that when I began
to read the Booke Intituled, *(one blowe more to
Babylon.)* I lay'd it aside, as not being able to
Close with the Author thereof, because of his
many *Reflections* therein, though (as they all
know) *I* had a high esteme of him, and did not
use to slight him.

(4ly) When *I* did at any time afterward name
Babylon, I never meant it but of *Babylon* in the
Mystery, consisting either in the joyning of
mens *Inventions* with Chrifts institutions; or
in pressing of things indifferent upó the conscience, as necessary; or in the setting up of mixtures in the Ordinances of Chrift, So far as *I* apprehended any of these, *I* did declare against
them: And for these very things doe *I* now declare against that *Congregation* from which *I*
have departed, which *I* little thought at first
would have bin found amongst them.

Instance

Inftance. 4. She denied that ever ſhe endeavoured to have Mr *Stoneham* paſtor, and under her owne hand were theſe words, *J never laboured to bring him to that office,* whereas the contrary was witneſſed by three perſons.

Reſolut. What I affirmed in my letter I believed to be truth, neither have I reaſon to think the contrary : if it were as Mr *Stucley* ſayth, More then three would have been able to witneſſe it : 'tis true, he being an ancient *non conformiſt*, and very ſenſible of the evils under which the Church of God did formerly groane, I had a good eſteeme of him ; but that I laboured to have him Paſtor, will never (I believe) be clearly proved, yea two or three of the chiefeſt of them, did witneſſe in the meeting, that they never heard mee ſpeake for him.

Inftance 5. She affirmed that ſhe never profitted by Mr *Stonehams* preachings, and never approved his Miniſtry, the contrary hereunto was witneſſed by three perſons.

Reſol. What I affirmed concerning Mr *Stoneham* was in a letter in theſe words, (*viz.*) *As for M.* Stonehams *preachings, J have had little benefit by it, but J have imputed it to my owne dulneſſe in hearing, and did hope that when J was better acquainted with his method in teaching J ſhould profit more by it:* they that vvitneſſe other then this vvitneſſe a lie.

Inftance 6. Shee denyeth in a letter, That ſhee

shee suspected those that had Kindred and Relations among the *Presbyterians,* whereas many vvitnessed the contrary.

Resol. 1. If the contrary vvere true, then I must have suspected my selfe having Kindred and acquaintance that vvere *Presbyterians,* vvith whō I had daily *societie,*& intimate *communion,* and vvhom I did highly honour, for the image of God shining in them, though our judgments differed.

2ly. Let them shew me the persons vvhom I suspected, and I vvill shew other grounds of my suspicion:

3ly. They themselves questioned me for my affections to those of different judgements, even *Presbyterians,* and therefore I cannot but vvonder, that they should dare to charge mee vvith this.

This may (I hope) suffice vvith all judicious and impartiall *Readers,* for the vviping off that filth, vvhich they flung after mee at my leaving them, in reference to *lying,* one of those three generalls to vvhich he reduced the ground of my *Suspension;* the other two are *contentiousnesse,* and *censoriousnesse,* so he is pleased to miscall, Love and Faithfulnesse.

Contention. The first of these (*Contention*) he saith, *pag.* 41 in his Answer to Mr *Toby Allen,* vvas proved by many vvitnesses in six particulars.

Ansf.

Anf. As to this *I* anſvver, that *I* vvas cleared by the vvhole Church of this *Impeach-ment*, (as in my narrative) vvhich all of them can vvitneſſe if they vvill; ſince that time none of them ever undertook to prove it to my face.

I vvas ſo far from delighting in *Contention*, as that I complained of it to Mr. *Stucley* ſeverall times, and alſo in a letter I told him plainly, that I was not able to live in the fire of *Conten-tion*, nor ſit down under a *miniſtry* that I could not profit by, and therefore I ſhould willingly withdraw from them; which I did accordingly for this and other reaſons, & therefore he hath little reaſon to accuſe me of *Contention*. But he ſaith it was proved in theſe particulars.

Inſtance I. In very many, if not in moſt of thoſe debates which have been in the Church ſince our firſt coming together, ſhe hath been uſually ſilent, untill the *Church* have been rea-dy to come to ſome determination, or had de-termined, and then ſhe would object againſt what ſhe perceived was the Judgment of the *Church*, and purſued it with much *violence*. This the generality of the then *Church* witneſ-ſed.

Sol. I. Was I ſilent till the laſt? why may not *Elihu's* Apologie be mine? *Job.* 32. 4, 5, 10, 11, 12.

2 My *Aſſent* was required to their *deter-minations*,

minations, and therefore it was very fit I should know what ground there was for them; especially confidering that the *then Church-members*, the generality of them were *novices* in *Chriftianity*, and very weak in the firft principles, fo unacquainted with the Rule, as that they knew not how to behave themfelves in the *Church of God*, knew not how to direct either themfelves or others, in matters of faith or order, without inftructions from abroad; yea we vvere then in a bevvildred condition, without officers and fome of the ordinances; and profeffed our felves to be a people that had loft our way, and that vvere feekers of the way to *Syon*.

3. As for my purfuing it vvith *much violence*, I knovv not vvhat he meanes, unleffe it be that I refufed to be fatisfied vvith their *determinations*, vvhen they gave me no fufficient ground for them.

Inftance 2. Secondly, vvhen it vvas moved in the *Church* to this effect, That it vvas very neceffary to have refpect in our admiffion of *Church-members* to union in Judgment, (at leaft in all the ordinances of Chrift) that peace and love in the *Church* might be preferved, fhe did eagerly contend againft this motion, and occafioned long and fad difputes betvveen the *Church and her felfe*, efpecially concerning *finging of Pfalmes*, the practice of vvhich fhe
abfolutely

absolutely denied, and declared *That praises and thankſgivings unto God in prayer were only that ſinging which the Scripture requireth.* This alſo the generality of the then Church members did vvitneſſe.

Sol. 1. Mr. *Stucley* vvas not preſent at this meeting.

2. Thoſe vvho made this motion vvere ſome of them very vveak and erronious in their Judgment.

3. When this motion vvas made, vve were without ſome of the *ordinances,* and ſo continued for ſome yeares after this, And they who made this motion were of a very *indifferent Spirit,* as to the procureing them, untill they had ſetled themſelves in publique offices. This was ſuch a burden unto mee, as that I was very much diſſatiſſied, when as they (who needed ſome to enforme their Iudgments) who made ſo litle Reckoning of the *ordinances,* ſhould yet be ſo forward after union in Iudgment: I conceived the worke we had to doe, was to free our ſelves from that *Confuſion* in which we were, by getting officers and ordinances.

4. As to Singing of *Pſalmes,* It's true, I did at that time queſtion it, which doth adminiſter matter of daily humiliation unto me, to conſider and remember the darknes of my minde, that hath and continually doth, cauſe mee to wander from the way of the lord to the right hand and

to

to the left; But yet Mr *Stucley* hath litle Reason to Charge me with it, for,

1. He was the firſt that *unſetled* mee as to this *practiſe*, by Speaking againſt it himſelfe, &c

2. Some of his members have ſpoken more ſlightingly of this ordinance then ever I did, in affirming that one who was poſſeſſed of the divell would ſinge *Pſalmes*, that they who ſunge *Pſalmes*, ſunge lyes, &c.

3. The generality of the People that were for *ſeperation* every where Scrupled *Singing*, as to the matter, manner, place or time: So that it was a vaine thing at ſuch a time to Expect vnion as to this ordinance, much more to preſſe it ſo eagerly, as to make it a neceſſary qualification of Church member ſhip, when as the Apoſtle ſayth, *Him that is weake in the faith receiue you, but not to doubtfull diſputations*: whereupon I did oppoſe, not union, ſo much as the pride and irregularity of three members, Mr *Owen*, and *John Whitehorne* (then ſervant to Mr *Mayne*) who tooke upon them to deny *Admiſſion* unto two perſons who propoſed themſelves, becauſe they differed in judgment about the *Circumſtance* of this *ordinance*, and that before it was debated by the Church (conſiſting at that time onely of eight or nine perſons) when as admitting or refuſing of perſons was then accounted a *Church act*, that which was to be debated by the whole. Theſe perſons did

F   affe-

affectionately declare, that they were in the darke about the manner of *singing*, not knowing whether it were a praising of God in a musicall tune, or praising of him in prayer: one of them being asked,whether shee looked on *singing of Psalmes* as an ordinance of God, shee answered, that she lookt on praising of God, as an ordinance of God, and as for *singing*, as now used, she could not say but it might be an ordinance of God, however it was doubtfull to her: This person was afterwards received into the *Church*, and hath attested this under her owne hand, so that its evident, these words were spoken by others, and if I did afterwards speake them, it was on the behalfe of those persons whose judgement I spake,more then mine own. And farther, the desire I had to be informed concerning it, put mee upon objecting many things against it, especially vvhen Mr *Stucley* vvas prelent: for this caule alfo vvas I very earneft vvith them to procure an able Minifter, as all the then *Church* can vvitneffe.

Inftance 3. Thirdly, she hath oppoled feverall perfons in their *Admiffion*, vvho have beene knovvne to be of approved *godlineffe* and *integrity*; and thofe vvho have beene moft lyable to *Exception*,she hath moft contended for,infomuch that the *Church*, having refpited the admiffion of a perfon concerning vvhofe *converfation* they vvere not fufficiently fatisfied; she did

did openly declare againſt it, in theſe vvords,
That it was an *unrighteous ſentence:* this particular vvas vvitneſſed by foure perſons.

Reſol. As to the former part of the *Accu-*
ſation, my oppoſing perſons (reputed godly)in
their admiſſions, I anſwer,

1. They themſelves have done the ſame, as
appeares in my anſvver to the *Accuſation* immediately preceding this: They denyed admiſſion to tvvo perſons, eſteemed godly, becauſe
they ſcrupled *Singing,* and for their unwilling-
neſſe to ſpeake their Experiences in a publique
meeting.

2. I never oppoſed any for their godlineſſe,
and as for any who were eſteemed godly, I never oppoſed them alone, without other members, why am I therefore more *Contentious*
then they?

3. They vvere not all godly vvhom I oppoſed, as is evident in *Ganicle,* vvho after his *Ad-*
miſſion (vvhich I vvithſtood) turned *Quaker.*

As to the ſecond part of the *Accuſation,* my
contending for thoſe vvho vvere moſt lyable
to *exception,* I anſvver. The perſons I contended for are novv many of thē *Church-members,*
and ſuch(I conceive) as Mr *Stucley,* and the reſt,
do not novv looke upon as lyable to *exception.*

As for the *perſon* concerning vvhom *I* uſed
thoſe vvords, that it vvas an *unrighteous ſen-*
tence, it vvas *A. P.* one generally accounted
F 2   godly,

godly, yea Mr *Stucley* himfelfe hath given this *Teftimony* of her often, that fhe vvould oppofe *Sin* vvhere ever fhe found it, that fhee vvould not feare to *Reprove* it, vvhere ever fhe came, fhee being in *fellowfhip* vvith us from the firft beginning, did at length propofe her felfe to be admitted a *Church-member*, but this vvas denied her, becaufe of her unwillingneffe to declare her *Experiences* in a publique meeting, this vvas the onely reafon (that ever *I* heard) vvhy fhe vvas then kept off.

Aftervvards, vvhen the *Admiffion* of *members* began to be in private, fhe propofed her felfe againe, but vvas refufed the fecond time, becaufe that fome had a *prejudice* againft her, for vvhich (as *I* conceived) they had little reafon, the things vvhereof fhe was accufed were triviall, neither were they fufficiently proved, yea Mr *Stucley* himfelfe cleared her, as to fome one of the particulars : and although fhe vvas in *focietie* with us for fome yeares, yet fhe was not permitted to fpeake for her felfe: Her *companion* alfo, a *Church-member*, who lived continually with her by reafon of her many weakneffes, was ready to anfvver for her, but it vvould not be permitted.

After this meeting vvas difmift, *I* defired M. *Stucley* that *I* might not be prefent at fuch debates, for *I* lookt on this as an *unrighteous judgement*, of vvhich he feemed then to take no

great

great notice: if he vvere offended at that *expref-fion*, vvhy did he not prefently examine vvhat ground I had for it? vvhy did hee not convince me of the *Equity* of their proceedings ? vvhich untill it be done, I cannot but looke on it to this day as an *unrighteous fentence*, fuch a *fentence* as they have caufe to be humbled for. It is not un-knowne to thofe, vvho vvere acquainted vvith her, how that fhe vvas a perfon that had beene under great *Terrours of minde*, and *affliction of fpirit*, even from her youth, that fhe vvalked very fadly continually; partly by reafon of the vveakneffe of her body, and partly by reafon of thofe *temptations*, vvith vvhich her vvhole life was accompanied. fo that it is not to be won-dred at, if fhe vvere troubled at her being twice refufed *admiſſion*, by thofe vvhom fhe did fo highly honour; and that fhe vvas fo exceedingly troubled at it, appeares by what fhe faid to mee tvvo daies before her death, vvhich vvas vvith-in fevv dayes after they had denyed to admit her, fhe then told mee that their *cruell dealing* vvas the caufe of her *fickneffe*, and would be the caufe of her *death*. And vvhen fhee vvas told that *death* could not come till his *commiſſion* vvas fealed by him vvho had the keyes of *hell* and *death*; fhe anfvvered, fhee knevv that very vvell, but yet they vvere the inftruments, vvhich had effected it: fhee defired mee likewife to tell them of their *pride* and *cruelty*, and to beware of

them

them, she likewise grieved very much that Mr.
Stucley came not unto her when she sent for him
in her *sicknesse* : however she testified her love
unto the *Church* and him, by leaving them both
Legacies : the morning after she dyed Mr *R.* (as
I heard) came to the house, and did with teares
in his eyes, tell her companion to this effect,
that he and his wife had blessed God solemnly
for that they had no hand in this *censure*. Mr.
Stucley himselfe honoured her so farre after shee
was dead, as to preach her *funerall Sermon*: by
all which it appeares how little reason hee hath
to charge mee with being dissatisfied with their
censuring her, and calling it an *unrighteous sen-*
tence, when as others besides my selfe did not
looke on it as *righteous*.

Instance 4. Shee opposed the *Admission* of D.
E. for her Ioyning with the *Presbyterians* in the
ordinance of the *lords Supper*, & insisted upon
it with much Earnestnes, shee then declareing
that shee could not be satisfied otherwise, then
by her acknowledging it to be her *Sin* in breaking the *law of Charity*: This was witnessed by
Seaven persons.

Solution. This cannot prove me *Contenti-*
ous, any more then the generality of them, who
have acknowledged that they did speak against
her; and some of them told me, that whereas
I had one thing against her, they had twenty:
yea Mr. *Stucley* himselfe was so dissatisfied with
her

her, as that he took advice with another minister about her; but I remember the *law of Charity* to the dead, and therefore forbear to adde
any more, but refer the Reader to my *Narrative,* where she is brought in as a witnesse
against me for *lying,* as she is here to prove me
contentious. Surely if Mr. *Eveleigh* did ever
love her whiles she lived, the best *testimony* he
can give of it will be by letting her alone, to
rest quietly in her grave, and not urge me any
more to publish that, which the *law of Charity*
requires to be concealed.

Instance 5. She caused a great deale of *disturbance* amongst us after the Officers were
chosen, in pressing with much earnestnesse that
Mr. *Stoneham* might be chosen Pastor: this
was witnessed by three persons.

Resol. I know not what he meanes by *disturbance,* nor who was *disturbed,* neither have
I any ground to believe that I caused the least
disturbance to any, as to this *particular.* If I had
caused such a great deale of disturbance amongst
them, it might have been witnessed by more
than three witnesses. And as for Mr. *Stoneham*
I wonder they should alleadge him as an Instance of my Contentiousnesse now he is absent, who when he was present in the name of
the Church pronounced me innocent, as to
this very *impeachment,* after he was Officer.

Inst. 6. She did a long time contend for *womens*

mens speaking in the Church, and being *admo-shed* for practifing accordingly, she did openly professe that she would not be present at *Church meetings* when matters were debated, unlesse she might have that *liberty,* and being denied, she ever since contemptuoufly negle-cted *Church meetings,* and slighted the *officers* of the Church.

In pag. 20 of Mr. *Mall's* book, he laies down the charge in these words. *She took liberty of speaking in the Church for some time, and being reproved by me for it, from time to time there was a visible decay of affection to me &c.*

Solut. That it is false, as to the whole charge taken together, appeares, in that there are none (as in the former particulars) menti-oned who did witnesse it, neither will he ever find any (unlesse they be *desperately hardned*) that dare affirme it, which I shall make *evident* in my Anfwers to the severall particulars there-of.

As to the first particular (viz.) she took the the liberty of speaking, and she did a long time contend for *womens speaking &c.*

To this I anfwer,

1. As for *womens speaking* it was ufually practifed amongst us by the rest of my *Sex.* And it is well known that the power was pre-tended at first to be in the body of the people, in the *multitude,* so that every one had the liberty

berty of *assenting* or *dissenting*, of *arguing* and *debating* any matter proposed, whether *men* or *women*. If *women* were denied the liberty of *speaking*, how could they declare their *Experiences*: yea *A. P.* was kept off for refusing this.

2. It is false that I took the *liberty of speaking*, it was not only given me, but the *liberty* of being *silent* was denied me, and that by Mr. *Stucley* himselfe, who would send for me at the meetings, even then, when there was never a woman of the *Church* but my selfe: and afterwards many times he would single me out in the meetings, and urge me very earnestly to declare my *Judgment* in reference to what had been proposed.

3. As to my contending for *womens speaking*, by my former Answers it appeares, that Mr *Stucley* hath little reason to charge me with it, unlesse he expected that I should be as fickle as himselfe, in taking up, and laying down *opinions* and *practises*, as they suited with, or thwarted his *humour* and *interest*.

As to the second particular, whereas he saith he *admonished* and *reproved* me for it from time to time, I answer,

That all the *Admonition* and *Reproofe* I had from him, was that mentioned in my *Narrative*, viz: that my speaking was disrelishd by some, whereupon I resolved *Silence* for the

future,

future, although I had looked on the Contrary
as my duty formerly; which resolution I ac-
cordinglie kept alwaies after the Officers were
chosen, unlesse it were when I was required to
give in my thoughts concerning a person, proposed or asked a question; yea Mr. *Stucley*
witnesseth for me in the charge it selfe, where
he saith, it was a long time that I contended
for *womens speaking*, and in Mr *Mall's* book for
some time &c. By which it is evident that I
did not continue in the practise thereof to the
last: how can then my speaking be brought as
an Instance to prove me *contentious* (one ground
of their *Suspension*) neer three yeares after *I* had
left of this practise.

As for what he saith followed on his *Reproving* and *admonishing* me, viz. 1 A decay of
Affection to him.

I answer, if there were such a visible decay
of *affection*, he mistook the cause of it. *It* was
not his *reproving* of me, no, the *reproof* was so
mild and gentle, and at such a distance, as that
I had litle reason to be *angry* with him for it.
But it was his *selfe-seeking*, and minding his
own things more then the *things of Christ* &c.
against which *I* did declare my dislike both
before and after this *reproof* and *admonition*.

As to what he saies, *that after their denying
me the libertie of speaking, I contemptuously neglected Church meetings, and slighted the officers.*   I

I answer that it is a *groffe lye*, a lye fo *egregious*, as that the whole *church* can vvitneffe (if they pleafe) againft it.

For I was after this conftantly at *church meetings*, the liberty of *fpeaking* by a Brother being allowed me; yea I declared that I was very much diffatisfied, becaufe the meetings (after the Officers were chofen) for conferring one with another, were not continued as formerly, I never abfented my felfe, but upon fome neceffary hindrance, which was not often.

As for *flighting of the Officers* —

I anfwer, that I gave them fo much honour as was due unto them according to my power; if they had not fo much as they defired, let them confider whether they did not defire more then they deferved. *They that rule well, are worthy of double honour.*

3d *Charge.* The *Cenforioufneß* of her *Spirit* was evidēced in her *uncharitable language* cōcerning the *Prefbyterians*, and us alfo: reporting one to be *fallen from the faith*, another to have *nothing of God in her*; charging Mr. *Stoneham* to have walked contrary to the *Apoftles Counfell*, 2 *Cor.* 4. 2. And to have fuch expreffions in *preaching* and *prayer*, as were but as *chaffe* to the *wheat*. And imputing the afflictions of fome of the *church* to their unworthy receiving of the Lords body. Thefe were proved by many witneffes, and her own letters.

Anf.

Anſ. As to the firſt *Article*, vvhich con-
cernes the *Presbyterians,* I anſvver, I muſt acknovvledge & confeſſe, that difference in *judge-*
ment did likewiſe cauſe ſome breach in *affection,*
that I vvas too much ſvvayed vvith a *ſpirit of*
ſeparation, vvhich made mee prone to *cenſure*
thoſe vvho differed from mee in *judgment,* more
then vvas fit ; vvhich I have cauſe to bevvaile
and lament. But yet I cannot but vvonder that
Mr *Stucley* ſhould be ſo farre blinded vvith *paſ-*
ſion, as to cenſure mee for this, vvhen it is vvell
knovvne that neither himſelfe , nor any of his
Congregation , are in a *capacity* to fling ſo much
as one ſtone at mee upon this account. It
is now the fifth time hee hath mentioned the
Presbyterians in his threefold *Accuſation;* for
what reaſon, though he himſelfe knowes beſt;
yet others cannot be ignorant of, and as for
the hope he puts in this, I believe it will prove
but a *Spiders web.* I ſhall onely adde this, That
if my *Tongue* were againſt the *Presbyterians ,* ſo
would my hand likewiſe, had I harkened to Mr
Stucley.

As to my *uncharitable language* concerning
themſelves, he doth inſtance in ſeverall particulars, which I ſhall anſwer in that order he layes
them downe, having deſired him in the generall
to conſider thoſe reproachfull, bitter, unchriſtian *Raylings* againſt Mris *Allen* and my ſelfe,
wherewith both his *Pamphlets* are full, and ſee
whether

whether they doe not farre exceed all the hard
fpeeches I have given of them.

As for the particulars they are (*viz.*) 1. My
reporting one to *be fallen from the faith.*

Refol. I do not remember that ever I ufed
fuch an *expreſſion* in *reference* to any of them,
as *(fallen from the faith.)* There was (its true)
one, concerning whom, when they were about
to choofe him to be an *officer*, I faid, that I did
feare he was not *found in the faith* , for which I
had good ground, neither did I hereby intend to
reproach that perfon , but to prevent the evill
that might follow, in cafe one not found in the
faith were chofen an Officer.

2^{ly}. That another had nothing of God in her.

Refol. I never heard the leaft hint from them
of any fuch expreſſion, neither do I remember
that I ever ufed it concerning any among them.
If it be that perfon which I admonifhed, that is
meant by Mr *Stucley*, as I have fome ground to
conjeĉture , for I cannot conceive who it fhould
be elfe. Then I fay that it is a groſſe miſtake, if
no worfe, to affirme that I reported, that fhee
had nothing of God in her.

Shee was a perfon that pretended to a great
deale of *Aſſurance*, whereupon I was willing to
have fome conference with her, to know if fhee
had any ground for fuch an *aſſurance.* To this I
was the more willing, becaufe a *member* of the
Church did fomewhat queſtion it , who defired
me

me to try whether it were so or no, which *I* did: in my discourse *I* told her, that they who had this *assurance* knew how they came by it, that where there is *assurance*, there is likewise *adherence*, a closing with the *promises*, the workings whereof will be evident to that soul which hath attained it, that therefore she should do well to look to the *ground* of her *confidence*, and be sure that she had *Scripture* for it. What her answers were *I* shall not here mention; but it seemes she did not like this my plaine and faithfull dealing with her, as appeares by her complaining of it to some, who hereupon have now accused mee for being so *censorious* as to affirme that she had nothing of God in her, which is false; yea, *I* was so unwilling to dishearten her, as that I told her, that *grace* was in the *hidden man of the heart*, and not *discernable* many times where it is, though *assurance* hath alvvayes its *evidence*. Had *I* knovvne that they had been offended vvith me for this, *I* should have given them a full *Account* of vvhat passed betvveen us, whereby they vvould have knovvne the truth of vvhat was reported concerning her: this had beene farre better then to accuse mee for it so many yeares after.

3. As to that of Mr. *Stoneham* &c.

Resol. I must confesse that when Mr *Stoneham* refused to declare the End of that *fast* mentioned in my *Narrative*, I did look upon
it

it as walking in *Craftinesse,* contrary to that of
the *Apostle,* 2 *Cor.* 4. 2.

And as to his *Expreßions* in preaching &c.
I conceived Mr. *Stucley* the fittest to admonish
him of his weaknesse; and therefore in a letter,
I wrot unto him these following words. " I
shall intreat you to speak to Mr. *Stoneham* of
those Expressions he doth often use to expresse
spirituall things by; the *word* (I conceive) is
fittest to expresse *spirituall mysteries and du-*
ties: I am sure that is the *sword of the Spirit,*
and *that is able to make the man of God perfect,*
throughly furnished to all good works. The more
wise the preacher was, the more he sought to teach
the people wisdome, and to find out acceptable
words, words of wisdome, that are as nailes and
goads fastned by the master of the *Assembly:* I
must confesse I cannot close with his Expressions which are usuall and ordinary both in
prayer and preaching, which is as the Chaffe to
the wheate; and what is the chaffe to the wheat?
I should speak to him my selfe, but I fear he
will not hear it from me.

The ground on which *I* went, was that of
the Apostle: *say to Archippus, take heed to thy*
ministry that thou fulfill it. Would it have been
an *ingenuous* returne of *Archippus* to censure,
suspend, or *excommunicate* a person for giving
him such an *admonition?* let Mr· *Stucley* judge.

Lastly, concerning my imputing the *afflicti-*
on

on of some of the *church* to their unworthy receiving &c.

Resol. For answer hereunto, *I* shall here set down what I wrote in the same letter concerning it, viz.

" *It* is and hath been a great trouble to me, that there is no meanes of instructing by *Catechising*, which is like, in my apprehension, to put a stop in the way of the *Gospell*. And *I* conceive the ordinance of the *Lords supper* cannot be kept pure, without *instructing* those that are of the Church, younger ones especially, in the mystery of discerning the *Lords body:* for this many are weake and sick, the Apostle laies it down as a Cause of that *sicknesse* and *death* that was amongst them. For my part it is my *feare* that the Lord hath a *controversie* with us for not discerning the Lords body, and not judging our selves. Surely the Lords hand that is upon us, and those afflictions that have been upon me, hath put me upon serious enquiry after the Lord in his word; and *I* am afraid we do not walk up to our own *principles,* and keep the *ordinances* pure.

, Behold Mr. *Stucley's* discretion and ingenuity in censuring me for censuring my selfe, which *I* did in that letter as well as others. *I* did impute the *afflictions* on my selfe and them, either to the omitting of the *administration* of the *Lords supper* for a long time, without giving
any

any reason, or to our not discerning the *Lords
body*, which *I* was perswaded that many
amongst us by reason of their ignorance could
not do, *I* did verily think that the Lord was
angry with us for this. *I* was so sensible of
Gods *afflicting hand*, as that *I* could not but
discover my fear unto Mr. *Stucley*, that he
might set upon reforming whatwas amisse, for
I thought *I* had herein to do with *Christians*,
and not with *Scorners:* it was the least of my
thoughts, that ever *I* should be censured for it.

Having finished his threefold charge, he
proceeds to adde somewhat concerning my
contumacious refusall of admonition in pag. 45.
of his Answer to Mr. *Toby Allen*, in these
words: *I might tell thee I have severall times
endeavoured to convince her of her sin, yet I doe
not remember that ever she acknowledged her
selfe guilty, and that severall persons that were
sent to her (or that went voluntarily) about
the worke of admonition, came away from her
with a burdned spirit. But I shall referre thee to
20 & 21 pag: of my Sermon in the true Account
&c.*

Here he tells the world that I refused *admonition*, first from *himselfe*, secondly from *others*,
and then refers the Reader for farther Satisfaction to the *true Account*, &c.

1 As to his *admonition* he saith, *I might tell
thee I have severall times &c.*

G

Resol.

Refol, You cannot tell this without *telling a lye*, for I was never admonifhed by you for any fin that I continued in after admonition, either before my leaveing you or fince.

Not before. This you acknowledged to me when I asked, whether you had ever admonifhed me, you told me you had not: this you confeffed to Mr. *Ford* and Mr. *Bartlett*.

Not fince. For I could never fpeak with you, after you had accufed me of *lying*.

Its true you *admonifhed* me for hearing another minifter; but that this is a fin, you dare not (it feems) affirme or maintaine: for it is not fo much as named among thofe *Crimes* laid to my charge either in the *true account*, or in your Anfwer to Mr. *Toby Allen*. And therefore what reafon is there that I fhould acknowledge my felfe guilty?

2 As to the Second (viz.) that feverall perfons that were fent unto her &c. came away with *burdened Spirits*.

Refol. The errand they came about was not to *admonifh* me for lying &c. But partly to take me off from hearing other *minifters*, and fince I left them to perfwade me back again: it was my not confenting unto them in this, that made them go away with a *burthen'd fpirit*, and not becaufe of my *proud and loftie Carriage* (as he faith pag. 20 *True Acc:*) for I alwaies treated with them *Civilly*, returning
                                           them

them thanks feverall times for their (pretended love) to me; I never baulkt difcourfe with them. And alwaies at their departing, faid, let me be convinced from the word what my duty is, and I fhall fubmit.

I defired the *Elder* before the faft in order to their *Excommunication*, and fince that *faft* others alfo, that they would bring the bufineffe to a new Triall before the minifters, whom they themfelves had acquainted with it formerly, and with whom I was then in *Communion*: had the Inceftuous perfon done fo, I am perfwaded he would never have been delivered to Satan.

The letter likewife fent Mr. *Stucley* by Mris. *Allen* and my felfe makes it evident, that neither of us *contemptuoufly* refufed *admonition* according to the rule of Chrift.

3 As for his referring the reader to pag. 20. 21. of the *true Account*, as if there were other *Crimes* mentioned there, for brevities fake he omitted here, I fay.

That in pag. 20 of the *True* (which yet fome think to be a very *defective*) *Account*, there is only one *Crime* mentioned, which he hath not accufed me of here in this other Book, and that is my *unfaithfulneffe* in not reproving privately.

Charge. I am confident (faith he) that there is fcarce one *Brother* or *Sifter* that can bear witneffe of her faithfulneffe in *Reproving*

private-

privately, though fhe fo much Blazon'd abroad
fuppofed or reall infirmities, &c.

Refol. 1, I am Confident that fome can (if
they will not *hold the truth in unrighteoufneffe*)
bear witneffe of my *faithfulneffe* in reproving
them privately, I reproved Mr. *Raddon* and
his wife, Mr *Eveleighs maide*, yea Mr. *Eveleigh*
himfelfe, both privately, and publickly when
his offence was publick, according to that of
the Apoft. 1 Tim. 5.20. And if none of thefe
will witneffe, yet Mr *Stucley* himfelfe can, if he
call himfelfe to mind, he can bear me witneffe,
that I reproved him for his *indifferency of Spirit* in the worke of God, for his preaching *funerall Sermons*, for his *Serpentine fubtilty* in his
Entrance on his Office, and in reference to his
Carriage in Mr. *Madder*'s bufineffe, yea he
hath witneffed that I reproved him for the *unrighteous fentence* in reference to. A. P.

2 As for Blazoning abroad their fuppofed
or reall infirmities, I know not what he meanes,
or of what thing he fpeaks it, whether whiles
I was with them, or fince I left them.

If he mean thereby that when I was among
them, *I* did difcover the nakedneffe of a *Brother*
or *Sifter* to others who were not in *Communion*
with us, *I* fay it is falfe, and dare him to inftance
fo much as in one particular.

If by *abroad*, he meane others of the *Society*,
I acknowledge it. But then it was to fuch as
by

by reafon of their intimacy and familiarity with the *offendors* might in all probability prevaile, more vvith them then I could.
And for this very reafon did I feveral times ad-
dreffe my felfe to Mr. *Stucley*, which he acknowledgeth a litle before this charge, though,
through *Envy*, he call it an *Impeachment* and
accufe me for it, though I had the houfe of *Cloe*
for my Example.

Laftly, If (*By abroad*) he meane that I have
divulged their mifcarriages to others fince I left
them, To this I anfwer.

That even fince my leaveing them, It was
my defire to continue a good opinion of many
among them : So unwilling was I to make
knowen that which might blemifh any of them,
As that I fuffered in mine owne name, by con-
cealing their mifcarriages, untill fuch time as it
was noifed abroad, that I had not left them, but
that they had caft me out as a *lyer*, a *contentious*
and a *troublefome perfon*, whom they could no
longer Suffer, nor have *communion* with: Then
indeed I did begin to pull off their *masking robes*
and *vizards*, as Mr *Stucley* expreffeth it in the
true Account, that fo it might appeare to the
world, how unlikely it was, that fuch (as many
of them were) fhould caft off any upon the *Account* of *lying*. Againe,

Charge. In *pag.* 21. He brings in a *paffionate
expreffion* of mine in thefe words, And being.
farther

farther preſſed to heare the Church, ſhe refuſed, and (if my memory faile not) ſhe ſaid, *She would be drawn aſunder by wild horſes rather then come among us.*

Reſol. I confeſſe the *expreſſion*, whether there were not cauſe for it, let others *judge*, they having dealt ſo baſely with mee as to accuſe me of *lying*, when I went unto them a little before to give them a reaſon why I left them. *A burnd child* (we ſay) *dreads the fire:* I had been burnd once by adventuring ſingly among them, therefore I durſt not do it againe the *ſecond* time. So that Mr *Stucley* needed not here to inſert this *parentheſis* (if my memory faile me not) it would have done better in all the other *Articles* of his *accuſation*, in which, if his memory did not faile him, he will never be able to free himſelfe from that, for which he pretends he hath *Excommunicated* mee.

But that I did not refuſe to heare the *Church*, the ſeverall anſwers I gave to the meſſengers ſent me can witneſſe. Beſides, when M. *Eveleigh* came to acquaint mee with the Faſt, in order to *Excōmunication. I* deſired that the buſineſſe my might be referred to Mr *Forde,* and Mr *Bartlet,* who had formerly heard it : and after the Faſt *I* told two other of their members, that they ſhould bring it to a new tryall before the Miniſters of *Exeter* with whom I was in *Communion,* promiſing to ſtand to their *determination.*

The

The letter likewise Mris *Allen* and my felfe sent the *Church*, doth witnesse sufficiently, that neither of us refused to heare the *Church*.

Unto this Charge he addes that of *separation*.

Charge. And though shee had lifted up her right hand to heaven to walk in fellowshiß with us, yet hath shee *separated* from us, and to this day sought not *reconciliation*, neither hath shee expressed *Repentance* for her *Sinne*, &c.

Resol. This is likewise confest and acknowledged that *I Seperated* from them, The grounds of my *Separation* are layed downe in my *narrative*. To which I shall farther adde.

1. That there was a clause in our first *Engagement* binding every one of us not to rest in the light then received, but to Studie to knowe the minde of God, and live up to it, and so accordingly haveing Studied the minde of God, concerning our *separation* from other Churches of Christ, I founde it to be *Sinfull*, and therefore durst no longer to continue therein.

2. If I engaged so to walke in *fellowship* with you as to deny it to others of *God's people*, of which there are many (I hope) in this *Citty*, I am Sorry for it, and to shew my *Repentance* I have reformed, by leaveing your *Society*. in which I could not continue without the guilt of *Sin*, If a man should promise, yea Sweare to that, which is *Sin* he had better to breake then to keepe his oath.

Yea

yea we were likewife engaged to hold *communion* with other *Churches of Chrift*, But this is now denyed, unleffe it be with thofe that are *Congregationall*.

As for what he addes concerning my not ex-preffing *repentance* for my fin:&c.

Refol. I fhall anfwer with *Job:c.27.God forbid that I fhould juftify you*(by confeffing that which I am not guilty of) *till I die,I will not remove my integrity from me. My righteoufneffe* (as to your impeachment) *I hold faft, and will not let it goe: my heart fhall not reproach me* (for bafely fub-mitting to any thing againft my confcience) *fo long as I live.*

In pag. 23. He fpeaks of my undervaluing, *Excommunication* & flighting it, in thefe words (*viz.*)

The other (meaning me) as little valued this *Inftitution of Chrift* for (as I am informed) fhe faid, *Excommunication was but as the breaking of a horfe over the hedge,&c.*

Refol. I have been heretofore, and am at prefent fo far from flighting *excommunication* rightly adminiftred, as that it makes me trem-ble to behold my felfe accufed thereof, as if I flighted the *ordinance* it felfe: *I* look on it as an ordinance of *Jefus Chrift*, as that *Sword* which he hath given his *Church* for the cutting off *contagious members*, as that, which he hath appointed and ordained to as high an end (for
ought

ought *I* know) as any other ordinance, (*viz*) *the destruction of the flesh, that the spirit may be saved in the day of the Lord* Jesus.

And as for the *slighting expression* concerning this ordinance, with which he chargeth me. *I* say it is a *notorious slander*, as he hath laid it down, the truth is, that to some, who spake about *excommunication I* told them how it had been formerly abused in this nation by many who (as it was reported) would *excommunicate* for such a *Trespasse*, as a horse to break over a hedge, and farther added, that I valued an unjust *excommunication* no more then *I* did that: and because *I* look on Mr *Stucleys* late *excommunication* as such, therefore do *I* set light by it: as *Luther* did by the *Popes bull*, for which he was never charged by any *Protestant*: in doing of which I am no more to be condemned for slighting this ordinance in generall then he. It will be found upon triall that Mr *Stucley* hath a farre lower esteeme of this *ordinance*, then my selfe, otherwise he would never have so abused it as he hath, for the promoting his own *interest* and *carnall designes*, which is the ready way to make it contemptible, in the Judgment and opinion of those who are not well acquainted with it.

Thus I have done with the *true account*, and now returne to what he saith farther concerning me in his answer to Mr *Toby Allen*: pag. 45.

Her

Her Crimes and contumacy being very great; the Church thought themselves obliged to suspend her from Communion before ever she joyned in the Sacrament with any other.

Resol. That this *Suspension* was for no other *crimes or contumacy*, then my leaving them, and my refuseing to returne unto them: And therefore it was not thought sufficient to debarre me from *communion* with others of Gods people in this City, by those who heard the whole businesse, and throughly examined the Circumstances thereof.

Char. In the next place he chargeth Mr *Allen* with a lye, for affirming, That the *Quarrell* between the *Church* and me began, becaule I had a mind to heare some other *ministers* which (he faith) is abominably false, and farther, that this was no particular for which I was ever admonished by the *Church* in pag. 45. 46. And again, he faith, That the *Quarrell* began in my *contentious Spirit* and sowing Divisions, and was increased by *lying*.

Ref. 1 That *I* was admonished, for hearing other ministers, by the *Church* it is manifest by what is allready set down.

2 That the *quarrell* did not begin in my *contentious Spirit*, and sowing divisions, nor was encreased by *lying*: it is also apparent, as for *lying*, I was never charged with it till I left them: and as for *contention*, &c. I never medled with

Church

Church affaires after the officers were chosen,
unlesse it were once in reference to a person
proposed, when *Ganicle* interrupted me.

The *Qurarell* Brake out at a *Tuesdayes meeting*,
Mr. *Stucley* was absent from that meeting and
so knowes nothing of it but by the report of o-
thers, it so much concerning mee, I have reason
to know it better then others: The account
whereof according to my best Remembrance
is this.

On the day before, being munday after dyn-
ner Mr. *Stonham* and his wife came to visit me,
Before *I* could come to them, my husband, in
discoursing with them sayed, that *I* had heard
Mr. *Ford* the day before, when *I* came into the
Roome, Mr *Stonham* looked on me with an *Angry countenance* and would scarce Speak, whereupon I asked his wife what did aile him, who answered that he was not well pleased with me
for my goeing away to heare, she told me likewise that he did not like Mr *Eveleighs* maide,
and farther added, that she heard that I had
somewhat against her, she is (said I) a stranger
unto me, and therefore it is my desire that she
may be kept off one week longer untill I have
informed my selfe concerning her, Then (said
she) do you be present at the meeting to speak
to have her kept off, this she desired with much
earnestnesse.

On the *Tuesdaie* following after dinner. Mr
Sprague

Spraigue the younger came to me frō Mr *Stone-ham* (as he faid) who had been with him the day before, and defired him to take me off from hearing Mr *Ford.* To this end (among other things) he told me, *that thofe fheep, which had been ufed to meane feeding, were not fit for fat pafture, it was the way to bring them to the fcab:* he likewife fpake fomething about Mr *Eveleighs* maid, and earneftly defired me to be at the meeting. I told him that I then lay under fome *trouble of fpirit,* and fo could not be fit for fuch an *Imployment,* however upon his earneft intrea-ty, I fitted my felfe to goe.

When I was come, they began (contrarie to their ufuall practice) to talke of the maid, before ever the Lord had been fought unto in *prayer:* Mr *Owen,* fitting at the table neer me, I willed him to acquaint them, that it was my defire fhe might be kept off a week longer (as I remem-ber) untill I had informed my felfe concerning her.

Mr *Eveleigh,* prefently replyed, that he would give *Teftimony* for her: I told him that a mafter or fuperior was not fo fit to give *Tefti-mony* for a fervant or inferior, and withall in-ftanced in *Gehazi,* who carried himfelfe fairly in his mafters prefence.

After this one *Ambrofe* a fhoomaker was pro-pofed, who (it feemes) wrought with *Ganicle,* concerning whom Mr *Eveleigh* asked me whe-ther

ther I had any thing againſt him ? I anſwered
that I had nothing, and alſo that though he
were a ſtranger unto me, yet I had heard a good
report of him : upon which *Ganicle* ſaid that I
would take his *Teſtimony* for his man, and not
Mr *Eveleighs* for his maid, yea (ſaid Mr *Eveleigh*) that is the very thing, becauſe it is my
Teſtimony, therefore ſhe will not take it, adding
farther that it was *ſcandalous*, and that I was offenſive or *contentious*, and had hindred their
proceedings for many yeares, inſomuch as he
could not partake with me in the *Ordinances*,
untill he was *ſatisfied*.

I replyed, that this would not be borne, and
that if my *carriage* had bin ſo offenſive, I ſhould
have heard of it, in ſome other place and in ſome
other manner: and then I preſently appealed to
all the *Congregation* deſiring them to be faithfull unto me, as they would *Anſwer* it another.
day, by declaring wherein my *carriage* had been
offenſive, and what evils they had ſeen in me :
And when I perceived they were unwilling to
meddle in it, *I* told them plainly, that *I* would
come no more among them, unleſs they would
ſatisfie me herein.

At length Mr *Stoneham* began his *prayer* after this manner: *Lord, we have waited for a prayer, and now thou haſt given us in a prayer, it may
be, the returne of many prayers*, and then bewai-
led *that the ſerpent was gotten into the garden:*
.After

After the prayer, *Mr. Eveleigh* and my selfe were to withdraw, but Mr *Eveleigh* (before he went out) told them, he left it to the *Church* to determine, whether I were not *contentious.* Two things (said he) I have against her, *Contention*, and her going away to hear Mr *Ford*, which the *Church* neither can, nor will bear. And he farther charged *John Whitehorne* (the chiefest then in this businesse) that he should insist upon *Contention*, and if he wanted an *Instance*, that he should name *Agnes Pullen*.

When we were withdrawne, the generality of them said, they did believe I was a good woman &c. But then they were asked againe, whether through a mixture of *Corruption* it might not tend to *Contention?* to which this reply was made, That they did not know but it might. Mr. *Stoncham* told me, that they would not for a world charge me with *contention*, but did fear left through a mixture of *Corruption*, it might tend thereunto.

Many of them were offended with the *Elders* dealing so disorderly with me, but knew not how to help it, and desired me to take no notice of it.

By all which it appeares

1 That they were very much displeased with me for hearing others besides our own Officers, though they were unwilling to quarrell with me openly about it. Mr. *Eveleigh*

(tis

(tis true) accuſed me thereof at this meeting,
but (as I am informed) ſome of them did very
much diſlike his mentioning of that particular;
and refuſed to medle with it, becauſe they
thought it fitter to be concealed, then that it
ſhould be publickly taken notice of.

2 That it is very probable they had a reſolution (ſome of them) to *quarrell* with me
about Mr. *Eveleigh's* maid, in caſe I could
not be prevailed with to leave off hearing of
other miniſters, why elſe ſhould they be ſo
earneſt with me (after I had given a *ſufficient
Excuſe* for my abſence) to be preſent at the
meeting? why elſe ſhould Mr. *Stoneham* uſe
ſuch *expreſſions* in his prayer.

3 That although Mr *Eveleigh* at this time
(when the *Quarrell* brake out) accuſed me of
Contention; yet that the *Quarrell* did not begin in my *contentious ſpirit*, and ſowing diviſi-
ons, is apparent. 1 Becauſe I did no more
then Mr. *Stoneham* approved of, and Mris.
Stoneham deſired me to do; ſo that I could be
no more *contentious* in oppoſing Mr. *Eveleighs*
mayd, then they. 2. This buſineſſe was ended in three daies; they had nothing after this
againſt me, but my hearing other miniſters,
as Mr. *Eveleigh* himſelfe told me.

4 And therefore notwithſtanding the quarrell brake out at the time, when I oppoſed Mr.
Eveleigh's maid, yet it is very apparent that it
began,

began, was continued, carried on, and increafed even to a breach, only for my hearing of another minifter: for as to the charge of *lying* I never heard of it till my coming off, as I have already declared.

In the next place he *takes fhame to himfelfe,* that he did not fooner excite the *church* to their duty, as to the laft *Remedy* for the healing of this woman, &c.

Refol. I believe in the end he will fee more caufe to *take fhame to unto himfelfe,* in that he hath fo rafhly excited them to this *cenfure,* before he ever difcharged the duty of *admonition.*

Let him confider whether he hath not run before the Lord fent him, let him produce his warrant to *Excommunicate,* before ever he proved the *Crime,* or admonifhed me of the Evills, for which he faies *I* am *Excommunicated.*

He addes, that there are fome full of evill furmifes about this matter, as if the Church would never have proceeded againft her, but upon a defigne to hinder others from deferting us.

Refol. It is no furmife, for
1 One of their own Officers (Mr. *Slade* by name) talking with an *Alderman* of this City about this *Excommunication,* told him that if they had proceeded againft me fooner, Mris. *Allen* would not have left them.

2 Mr.

2. Mr. *Stucley* doth not in plain termes deny it. And though that which follows concerning the *unquietnesse of his spirit* about my not *Repenting* may imply a deniall, yet

3 It is that which he hath in a manner acknowledged in pag. 10. of the *True Account*, in these words, *If we had discharged our duty sooner on the lyar, we might have prevented the others fall, her disobedience and perversenesse of spirit.*

As for that he professeth, he had no quiet in his Spirit, that a Person should lie so long suspended, and give no *Evidence* of *Repentance,* but the Contrarie &c.

Resol: The *Suspension* vvas tvvo moneths after I had left them; the messenger that vvas sent to give me notice thereof sayd it vvas in order to my *Returne*, a *Returne* to them, this is the *Repentance* they expected, and I resolved against, unlesse (as *I* told the *Elder*) I might have *communion* vvith them, and not to *separate* from others that vvere godly.

But vvhat quiet can Mr *Stucley* have novv, that he hath passed a *Sentence of Excommunication* vvithout *admonition,* seeing I so earneftly desired it? vvhat comfort can he have in passing this *Censure* three yeares wanting a few daies after *I* had left them? when as in all probability by reason of *forgetfulnesse,* there could not be a *charging of sin,* so as to convince and work a kindly *Repentance.*

If his *conscience* had troubled him, becaufe

H   of

of my lying in *Sin*, without evidencing Repentance, then his *conscience* is either *blind* or *baffled*; else why had not his *conscience* checkt him, when he discovered no *zeale* against *lying*, when he was so often prest unto it by me? why had not his *conscience* troubled him, when there was a *lye* affirmed with so much *Confidence* by *John Whitehorne*, when he offered to depose it upon Oath, and yet there was clear *Testimony* brought by some of their members to prove it to be a *lye*? this person is under his *charge*, yet here his *conscience* hath not disquieted him.

And for what he addes, *That to quiet his conscience he tooke advice with severall Ministers, and so concluded the matter by them and his own Conscience.*

Resol. 1. Why did he go so farre away? had he desired to have the truth brought to light, then why should he refuse to advise with those *Ministers* that he himselfe acquainted with the businesse; and when *I* so often desired them to bring it to a new tryall before them, with a promise to *submit* unto their *determinations*, without expecting any favour from them.

2. How could those *Ministers* (whoever they be) perswade him to such a *censure*, without advising him to bring the businesse to a *Triall*, without hearing both parties speake? will not *Festus* rise up in judgement against them? Did these *Ministers* in their *advice* duly weigh the
weight

weight of this *Ordinance*, and the pretiousnesse of
soules for which *Christ* did *Sweat, Bleed* and *died*, for
which hee ever lives to make *intercission?* Durst they
upon the Report of one partie without Examination,
give such advice in a corner? the Lord lay not this sin
to their charge: 'Tis not the first time that *Satan*
hath made use of such *instruments*, Christ saw him
in a *Peter* &c. I confesse it would have been more ea-
sily borne, if they had been such as have not knowne
the Father, nor the Lord *Jesus*, that had given this
wicked advice; but that it should come from them,
who have (or at least pretend to)more *acquaintance*
with Christ then others, this is as the *Vineger* and the
Goll.

  Charg.p. 47. In the last place hee gives the world a
Catalogue of *lying defamations,* spoken by mee since
my *Suspension.*

  I *Resol.* As for those *lying defamations,* I answer
briefly: That many of those Reports are no *lying*
Defamations, but manifest truths, as I have made it
already to appeare in my *Narrative* and *Vindication,*
and make no question but shall be able to do the like
of the rest, if called unto it, even as many of them as
he shall prove to proceed from mee, farre better then
Mr *Stucley* will be able to make good (in a regular
and orderly proceeding) those *slanderous reports* concerning mee, with which he hath filled the world, notvvithstanding he *boasts* so much of *witnesses*; at the
end almost of every *Charge.*

  And novv *I* suppose the *Reader* is sufficiently tired
vvith perusing an unpleasing and broken *History*, I

        shall

shall therefore now hasten to an End.

If the *Gospell* be the great *Salvation* that is delivered by *Christ* himselfe, and the *Revelation* of it compleated, and it be once delivered to the *Saints*, and no other *Revelation* to be expected till *Christ* come, and this *Salvation* being so glorious, as that the *Angels* desire to look into it, and there being such a *Curse* by Christ pronounced on such as shall adde to it, or take from it, then let it serve as an *Apology* for me in my learning of them. This was that which I did desire and aime at, that I might be instructed in the *mystery* of this *great Salvation, God manifest in the flesh* &c. 'Tis that was in my eyes, and that I still follow after (although I have not yet attained) *to comprehend with all Saints what is the bredth, and length, and depth, and heighth, and to know the love of Christ, which passeth knowledge;* yet through grace this was, and is that one thing, that I may *know Christ and him crucified;* and that I may with the Apostle *Phil. 3. 12, 13, 14. know him, and the power of his Resurrection, and the fellowship of his Sufferings, so as to be made conformable to his death,* that I may know this great mystery which hath been hid *from other ages, but is now revealed unto us by the holy Apostles and Prophets by the Spirit, Eph. 3. 1.* Know him so, as *to bear about in my body the dying of the Lord Jesus;* that the life of Jesus may be made manifest in this mortall flesh, that *the old man may be Crucified with him, that the body of Sin might be destroyed, that I might not serve sin;* This was that which to the glory of *free grace* I can say in some measure
(if

(if thy heart do not deceive me) was my desire in
Joyning with them; and in my withdrawing from
them, I finding not a *Sufficiency* in their *Ministry* for
edification and *building up*, and being difapointed of
my *expectation* in the *ministry*, and continuing my
practice of hearing Mr *Ford*, fometimes once a Lords
day meerly out of neceffity, and obferving what they
did after they were in office and fetled themfelves,
in ftead of difcovering their love and faithfulneffe to
the peoples foules in their diligent *circumfpection* and
watchfulneffe over them , and difcovering to them
the *hidden myfteries of the Gofpell*, they were very
remiffe, the worke they were imployed in was to
exalt themfelves, and bring the people into *Subjection* unto them, *filenceing* fome, and *cenfuring* others
without allowing them any liberty to clear themfelves, fuch as they fuppofed ftood in their way, and
when this was effected, then they proceeded farther
to take them off from hearing any other *miniftery*
making that practice of hearing another *miniftery*,
when themfelves preached, to be a going out of the
Bofome of Chrift into the *Bofome of Strangers*, and
fuch perfons were *Traytors* and *Rebells* to Jefus
Chrift, and fhould be fo dealt withall; and what benefit was received by another *minifter* to be a delufion and a *Temptation*, and a *Judgment of God* upon
the *foule*. And ingaging the people at their admiffion,
to believe it as an *Article of their faith*, that a greater bleffing was to be expected on their *miniftry*, then
on any others; as if they preached another Jefus, or
another Spirit, or another Gofpell when the Apo-

ftle

ſtle ſayeth, *he that planteth and he that watereth are
one,* 1 *Cor.* 3. Was there not a cauſe to *ſuſpect* what
they intended, but the liberty of diſſenting was denyed, and they proceeded to lay aſide their meetings
for to conferre together, and to conſider one another,
and the *ordinance of the Supper,* that was layd aſide a
long time, faſting was perverted to carry on their own
deſignes, and to keep the people ignorant of the occaſion and ground of their faſt.

I being troubled at this, and reſolved not to be Silent to ſee what was done by them, but rather to ſuffer, did diſcover my diſlike of theſe practiſes, and blamed them to their faces for walking in *craſtineſſe,*
contrary to the *Apoſtle,* 2 *Cor.* 4. 2; and perverting and
laying aſide of the *ordinances,* then inſteed of giving
me any *ſatisfaction* (as I expected) did they craſtily
conſpire to *entangle me,* to fall to diſpute about *true
Churches.* And to ſeek occaſion againſt me, to defame
me, and as if there had not been ſufficient *above
ground,* rakt up the *dead* out of her *grave,* and made
matter to frame an accuſation againſt me, for doing
that which themſelves the generality of them did the
ſame, as ſome of them have ſince acknowledged, and
in what they accuſed me Mr *Stuckley* himſelfe cleared me, and here is the ground of all their charge of
ſcandall, which how *cruell,* and *unjuſt,* and *unreaſonable* it is, I leave to the *impartiall reader* to Judge.

Thus ſeeing *Goſpell priviledges,* purity of ordinances, and liberty of *conſcience* lay a bleeding, and
they walking contrary to their principles, and often
engagements, and having no way to free my ſelfe
from

from partaking with them in their *evils*, not only the liberty of *speaking* but of *dissenting* being denied, vnles it were purchased upon such termes as their *ensnaring* of me, and of looseing *peace* and a *good name*, I not daring to make it known to other *members*, lest I should be accounted *contentious*, having had experience of the people formerly, and seeing the *officers* to be masters of the ordinance, insteed of *dispensors*, and to *lord it over Gods heritage*, as if they had dominion over our faith: after often seeking of the Lord and enquiry in his word according to that light *I* had received, after *I* had declared my *resolution* and my grounds to the *elder*, *I* withdrew, according to the Apostles rule, 1 *Thes*. Hoping that by my *withdrawing* they might be more *convinc't*, and that in time the Lord would make them sensible of their *Usurpations*, when they saw what effects were produced, and so might put a stop for time to come to such proceedings: and though I could expect little *favour* from them, unlesse the Lord did convince them, and so humble their *Spirits*, yet having the *Testimony* of mine own *conscience*, that I could say in in some measure with the *Apostle*, herein did *I exercise my selfe to have alwaies a conscience void of offence towards God and towards man*: and I considered that I should hereby keep and preserve mine *own peace*, in having no hand in *exalting* of men and so opening a way to bring in mens *inventions*, and to worship God according to the *precepts of men*.

And Mr. *Stacley* himselfe in his *Sermon* on that *black* and *dark day* hath acknowledged (as the *Copie*

taken

taken from his own mouth will *testifie*) that I *separa-*
ted from them on pretence of *conscience*, he might
have left out the words (on pretence) unlesse he take
upon him to Judge the *heart* and *conscience*, although
Mr *Mall* in his printed *True account* (as he cals it)
hath not afforded me so much *charity* as to put in
that perticular.

And Mr *Stucley* himselfe afterwards *pag.* 23. saith
that I went away to avoid the *censure*, here he con-
tradicts himselfe more waies then one, for 1. If I
went away to avoid the *censure*, then I could not *se-*
parate on pretence of *conscience*, but if this be denyed
(as the leaving it out of his printed *Sermon* may in-
ferre so much) 2. If I went away to avoid the *censure*,
then he must be forc't to deny that I am *excommuni-*
cated justly for *lying*, for how could I goe away to
avoid the *censure* for *lying*, afore ever I knew I should
be charged with *lying*, for I was never charged by
him with *lying* untill such time as I had really withdrawen and *separated* from them.

The like Mr *Allen* hath allready declared of his
wife, *pag.* 24. of his *Truths manifest*, that the pretended *crime* or *cause* of *excommunicating* her, was in
time long after she left them.

Therefore (Reader) take notice of his grosse *con-*
tradiction of himselfe in what he affirmes.

And whereas he pretends that he had no quiet in
his spirit that a person should lie so long *suspended*
and give no evidence of *Repentance*, and in his *prayer*,
that they have not past their *censure* in a *revengefull*
way, and that they could not answer the neglect of
their *censure* one day longer.   If

If it be so, why must he take liberty so himselfe to defame me in my name, if it were the *sinne* only he aymd at? &why did he use such *Epithites*, as, *discredited lyer, notorious lyer, egregious lyer, Bryer in our sides, companion for damned spirits,* when as his *conscience* must needs tell him, that he never accused me of one *lie* all those years that I was in *fellowship* with them: And if he found me guilty of a *lye,* let him produce what *lye* it was, I never heard of any yet, whiles I was with them, and when since I left them, he carged me at first, it was then with an *untruth.*

And although I defired in our letter fent them to have the caufe heard by underftanding and impartiall men and promift to *Submit,* yet he flighted that, and hath taken libertie in *pulpit* and in print to render our names and our perfons odious to all the world, as if the *fword of excommunication* had not been *fharp* enough, unleffe it were fharpned by him at the *Philiftins forge,* and in the meane time takes liberty to himfelfe to practice thatfor which he pretends he hath *cenfured* me as for *lying,* I could inftance in feverall of their *charges* that they are no other but lies.

Not to mention the feverall *reports* that have been fpread concerning me, as not worth the *taking notice* of, which have one *contradicted* the other, and not two of the *Reporters* found in one *tale,* as hath been taken notice of (as I am informed) by a perfon of credit, this is not worth the *taking notice of.*

But that *falfe report* that hath been raifed by them and fpread in citty and countrie on Mr *Ford* the minifter,

nifter, that he should flight *lying*, and that say lying
was the *property* of a woman.

Whereas the truth is, that when Mr *Ford* and Mr
Bartlet Ministers, and Mr *Stucley* and Mr *Eveleigh*
were met at Mr *Fords* house, Mr *Stucley* and Mr,
Eveleigh accused me of *Scandall*, and brought in a
charge of *lying* against me, instancing in Mris *Eveleigh* and my speaking against the *Presbyterians*
(which I have allready answered) Mr *Ford* still call'd
for more, more charge: then to make up their *accusation*, they said that I was fickle, Mr *Ford* answered
them, that is as much as to say, she is a woman, this
I know to be the truth; and yet the report is spread
by them in *City* and *Country*, that he said that *lying*
was the property of a *woman*: and herein have they
discovered their falsehood and rage against such an *E-
gimont labourer* in *Christs Vineyard*, who hath given
abundant *Testimony* that he seeks not himselfe but
the things of Christ.

And as for *Contention*, how hath Mr *Stucley* discovered himselfe guilty to all the world, *Doeg* like,
falling on *Magistrates* and *Ministers* whom he sup-
poseth stands in his way, as his *Sermon* and printed
books do witnesse.

Give me leave to take notice of it, as *David*, when
he heard how *Saul* had cut off the *Lords Priests* (saith
he) I have occasioned the death of all these.

And for *Censoriousnesse*, how doth it appeare? not
by secret search, but upon their severall *Accusations*,
wherein the greatest ground of their proceedings
against me, hath been a *censuring* of the *ends* of my
words

words and actions, which is Gods *prerogative* alone, who *searcheth the heart, and tryeth the reines.*

Let the *Impartiall Reader* judge whether they sought the glory of Christ, &to convince me of this *sin,* whē it is that which was & yet is usually practised by themselves. Witnesse their usuall calling Mr *Fords* preaching *Rayling* and *nonsense,* and some of them would have the Pulpit shut against Mr *Ford,* and would have had the notes of his *Sermons* to pick occasion against him, and perswaded me not to hear him, and I was questioned many times for hearing of him, not only the Lords daies, but on Lecture daies also.

I cannot but take notice of Mr *Mall* in his reasons pressing them to *renew their Covenant.* He saith, such poor wretches are given up to *Judiciall hardnesse,* so that they are sorry for nothing so much, as that they with such a *Church* entred into *Covenant* with God; and again, such wretches they have renewed their *Covenant* with *hell* and *Satan.*

For answer, what *Covenant* I have ented into with God, whether with them or any other, I desire still to own and acknowledge, that I am engaged unto to performe, and am resolved in the *strength of Christ* never to retract. And if in any particular I have denyed my *Covenant* with God, it lies upon them to *convince* me of it. It is not enough for them to charge *Covenant breaking,* and *perjury,* and *Schismes,* it lies upon them to prove their charge, otherwise I am not engaged to an *Implicite faith* to believe them.

I

I think our letter (we sent to them) will testifie, that we did not retract our *Covenant* with God, when we did professe our *submission* to the law and will of *Christ*, wherein I think we did own our *Covenant* with God more than they did, who by their *Explicite Covenant* engaged themselves to an *Implicite faith*, in subjection to Mr. *Stucley's* ministeriall guidance and teaching, without any *restriction* or *limitation*. And yet how doth he boast pag. 13. as if they were a company of believers that will part from life rather then from a little command, and their hands are fill'd with both *Tables*: is not this practice of theirs a *contradiction* to this profession, & yet pag. 29. exhorting them to keep to the Church of Christ, he tells them he cannot but approve of their purpose to *subscribe a covenant*, that will be a fence against a *lawlesse Spirit*.

Moses who was a *servant in the house of God*, and God testifies of him that he was *faithfull in all the house of God*; see *Deut.* 33. 4. *Moses* commanded us a law, even the *Inheritance* of the *congregation of Jacob*.

Is not this fence against *lawlesse Spirits*, that God hath prescribed his Church sufficient? but that Mr *Stucley* must engage the people to himselfe, as if his designe were to seek himselfe, and to espouse a people to himselfe, and not to Christ.

It was the *commendation* that the *Apostle* gives of his hearers, that *they received the word with all readinesse of mind, and searched the Scriptures dayly, whether those things be so or no* : but here they *Ingage* to absolute *subjection* to Mr *Stucleys* Ministry without

any

any *Caution*, I the rather take notice of it, because they may confider, that whiles they are *Cenfuring* us, they forget themfelves, and their *Engagements* to Chrift, and to his Lawes; that whereas they have profeft the taking Chrift for their *King* and *Law-giver*; now they fet up men in the roome of Chrift, without any mention of the Law and Septer of Chrift., And yet he pretends that his booke ('called *Manifeft truth*)' is fet forth by him to prevent the *Gofpells fuffering*; although he hah had a *Bratherly admonition* given him by the unknowne author, *Dio-trephes detected and Archippus admonifhed*, yet he never takes notice of this particular, to give any *Satis-faction* unto it, or to remove the *offence* taken by it.

And now for a clofe of all I fhall defire Mr *Stucley* to retyre himfelfe a little from the world and thofe multitudes of *defignes* hee is at prefent fo much en-tangled with; having done this, ferioufly and fadly confider a while of that great day of accounts, wherein the *hidden workes of darkneffe* fhall be fully difcove-red by him whofe eyes are as a flame of fire: if he doth thinke in good earneft that there is fuch a day coming wherein he muft by *accountable* for all his *actions*: let him I fay, confider what *account* he can give to *Chrift* of his late proceedings againft Mris *Allen* and my felfe; will it (thinks he) be enough to fay, that his *cre-dit* and *efteem* in the world could not be upheld with-out it? that the *Intereft* of that party with whom he fided confifted therein? that he had *Majors, Collo-nels, Knights, Ladies*, to ftand by him; if he account thefe these vaine and foolish pleas , now, why should hee ? how dared he act upon such grounds now ? His only way therefore will be to repent of this his *wickednesse,* and pray God, *if perhaps the thoughts of his heart may be forgiven him* ; which will be more to his *honour,* then by *Printing* any more *angry bookes* against two weake *women* (who are not able to speake for themselves in *Print* (neither is it required) so well as *men,* especially *Schollers*) to *withold the truth in unrighteousnesse,* to *oppresse the Innocent,* and to cover his own *Sin,* which whosoever doth, shall not *prosper, the mouth of the Lord hath spoken it.*

FINIS.

Readings where the Huntington copy is blotted:

title page. 9	Pope's
title page. 10	Relati
title page. 24	partakers with
title page. 25	with them in
title page. 26	with them, and what
title page. 27	Christians
A3v. 1	ning spirit
28.37	of the Lord
31.18	that were
31.19	benefit of
32.18	have fashioned
32.19	pain of death
45. 36 right	To an Image
46. 1 left	Arise oh Lord,
47. 1 right	Cross of Christ
104.1	that
104.52	blessed

This is a short

RELATION

Of some of the

Cruel Sufferings

(For the Truths fake) of

KATHARINE EVANS & SARAH CHEVᵉ⁰,

In the Inquisition in the

ISLE of MALTA,

Who have suffered there above three years, by the Po
Authority, there to be deteined till they dye; Which Re
on of their sufferings is come from their own hands and
mouths, as doth appear by the following Treatise.
These two Daughters of *Abraham* were passing to *Alexandria*, and to *Cilicia*; And thus may that part of Christendom
see their fruits, together with the Pope's, and of what birth
they are; and that those that are called Christians are worse
than Heathens: For they falling into their hands, should have
been refreshed by them with necessary things; but the provision which the Inhabitants and Knights of *Malta*, (called
Christians) provided for them, is the Inquisition. Now it was
not so when *Paul* suffered shipwrack there among the barbarous
people; which is a manifest token they are not in the love of
God, whose fruits shew they are not in the true Spirit.

*And this is to all fellow-brethren that are parte....rx with them in the Power of God
that have a feeling and fellowship wit.... ..in their sufferings, that they might see
and know how it is with th ....was unkindness they find abroad among them
that profess themselves Chr.....us.*

LONDON, Printed for *Robert Wilson* 1662.

An Epistle to the Readers.

MAny there be among the Nations in the world, that in their haste have unjustly condemned the innocent, guiltless and harmless people of the Lord of Hosts (scornfully called Quakers) viz. That they are Papists, Jesuits, and what else, adhering to the Whorish false Church of Rome; I say to such on this wise, which is my advice as a man to his friend, to whom this may come, Be not hasty to judge before the time, as many do to their own hurt, guilt and condemnation, before they have a clear and right understanding of the things that differ from equity and truth, and so the nobility of the mind which should weigh and pass true sentence of sound and perfect judgment, the same being vailed with a hasty dark spirit of prejudice, or evil surmising, which gets up into the seat of enmity, and therein passeth sentence of the pure way and things of God as evil, heresie, and what else; and thus it comes to pass, and indeed it cannot be otherwise with such that have not their minds staied and fixed in that which is perfect and true, and clear, and single, as is the clear manifestation of the grace of life, which is the Light of the Lord Jesus shining in the heart and conscience of the Sons and Daughters of men; and the same Light of the Lord which lightneth the poor and deceitful man's eyes, is the true measure and equal ballance, which all is to trie, and prove, and weigh words, thoughts, intents, ways, and actions, whether they be justifiable or condemnable; and hereby with the same measure of the true Spirit of God who is Light, a true sentence to be passed accordingly: For if that which is perfectly true be measured with a false measure, or with an unequal Ballance, it doth appear so to all that behold the same with an evil eye, or measur'd that with the same measure; save onely to them that discern the measure, weight, or ballance; as for instance, as to the thing natural, if a deceitful man with a false measure,

A 2   being

being guided by a deceivable Spirit (al-be-it his eyes are inlight-
ned with the Light of the Lord , which is true) if he

Prov. 29. measure a piece of cloth to his Customer, with his deceitful measure, though the cloth be good, yet he not
giving it its true measure, the simple hearted is thereby deceived,
and knoweth it not till it be brought to a true measure, which doth
answer the true principle, or Light of God in the conscience to justification, as doth not the false, but contrariwise; wherefore its
needful, and of absolute concernment, for the mind of every man
male and female, to be guided and exercised in the true manifestation of the Light of Jesus in the conscience; and so blessed is the
man, the people, the family that brings their deeds to the Light,
that they may be manifest that they are wrought in God who is
Light, who is Truth; and so what is here following written and
published is to be tried, and proved by the Witness of God in every
Conscience which is true, and will answer to the same things or
words that springs forth from its own clear nature.

Therefore, when thou hast honestly read this throughout with a
meek spirit of sobriety and moderation that's single and pure, then
with the same spirit of singleness, and of true discerning judge honestly, and cease from hastiness in such matters of Eternity, least a
place of Repentance become finally hid from thine eies, not to salvation, but contrariwise, which I desire not, neither doth the
Lord, whose servant a living and true Witness I am, for Him, his
Truth and People, of these things and much more.

Wherefore let the Reader see hereby, how that the Lord hath
chosen the foolish things of this life to confound the wise; and that
the living God Eternal hath chosen the weak things, to confound
and bring to nought the things that are mighty, subtil, and potent;
yea, base things which are so deemed despisable, and contemptible;
yet behold God hath chosen them, and things that are not approvable
in the sight of the prudent of this world, even to bring to nought
things that are: But may some say, Wherefore, or why doth
the most High, Wise, Invisible, Immortal God do thus?
my answer is one and the same as the Apostle saith, viz. That no
flesh should glory in his presence, who of God is made in us
Wisdom, Righteousness, Sanctification, and Redemption: And
why should it be accounted such a foolish thing in the eyes of the wise
men

men of this world, to see the wisdom of God dispensed through a weak Vessel? as is a free-born woman from above, a weaker Vessel than that of the man.

Now tell me, oh man of understanding, What must not the Spirit of Christ, or the same that is begotten of God in the female, as well as in the male, what must not (I say) the same Spirit of life from God speak, but be limited in the weaker Vessel, in the foolish Vessel, in the Vessel which is not esteemed, but base, contemptible and despised in the eyes of lofty man that must be laid low, who excels in that wisdom and knowledge which is not from above, but otherwise, bruitish, and puffeth up the fleshly mind that's enmity to God, and is therefore to be confounded and moved backward, and slain upon the Cross, which is the Power of God that crucifieth the lusts and inordinate affections of the flesh, which thereby come to be silent before the Lord, who is that one and self-same spirit that is quick and powerful; so that not any other spirit governs or rules over the members of the body, but that which created the body, and every Member, which is to have the supream authority and preheminence, as well in the female as in the male; and so he the Spirit of Truth that's to guide into all truth; he, the man, is not he to speak, viz. Christ in the male, the same in the female, where he is risen and manifest as King, Priest and Prophet, a Guide, Leader and Commander in all equitable and just things which are truly honorable.

But the woman was in the transgression against the Spirit; Flesh lusteth against the Spirit, saith the Apostle; and the Woman (that's in the transgression) is to be under obedience, and to be in silence, to learn in silence, and to ask her Husband at home; but what if she have a disorderly, drunken Husband (and not Christ the man, the true Husband, the true Lord) how can he teach her, seeing the woman is to learn of her Husband in silence, and to be under obedience (and not to usurp Authority over the man) as also saith the Law, which hath dominion over all that are under it in the transgression; but the Spirit of Grace and Truth that's poured upon sons and daughters, teacheth us to deny the sin, and guideth from the same, and so maketh free from its condemnation, and from under the Law, to be under the Grace and Truth that is in the one Seed Christ, in the Male Christ, in the Female, the quickning

ning Spirit, the Lord from Heaven; and so who are lead and guided by this, are not under the Law, which saith, the woman is not to usurp Authority over the man, as also saith the able Minister of the Mysterie of the glory and riches of Eternity, which is Christ the fulness in his Saints, their hope of life and glory; but the woman is to be under obedience, as also saith the Law; yea, but they that are led by the Spirit, are not under the Law, so are the sons of God manifest; yet under the Grace covered; the same Grace with which the Man-Child, the holy Child Jesus was covered and filled with; the same, and no other but that which did and doth save the Saints from sin, and so from under the Law, and its condemnation; and not onely so, but also the same Grace which bringeth salvation, and appeareth to all men, it teacheth them not onely to deny ungodliness and worldly lusts, but also to live soberly and righteously in this present world; and verily this Grace, is in them which saves and justifieth them; and it's not of themselves, it is the gift of God.

And such are the servants of the living and true God, that have their fruits, (and possess the same) unto holiness; and not onely so, but the end of the same, which is the pure manifestation of the Eternal substance, to wit, everlasting life, pure, clean power, which is the excellent Treasure in the Earthen Vessels, as saith the holy Scripture, 2 Cor. 4.

But Oh ye Congregations of the dead! ye gathered Churches of so many Names and Heads, to you sounds my voice, saying, What have ye done? Oh! how guilty do ye appear before mine eye that's single (in the Lord's Light) of despising prophesying, and quenching the tender Spirit of glory, which resteth at this day in, and upon many sons and daughters; and behold if ye can see how they do, and have prophesied in the Name of the Lord, and have fore-warned you of that which is justly come to pass upon you, while many of you despised and wondered, in the days of haughtiness, and its prosperity among you. But oh my soul, how hast thou been wounded in me, whilst I have travelled and mourned over you! And so you have been found despising that, and quenching that Spirit of Grace which teacheth the Saints in Light, and reproves for sin, and testifieth against the World, and its deeds, because they are evil.

And

And this same Spirit strived long with you, and in you, and would have arisen up in its Authority, Power and great glory from on high, had ye not preferred and exalted the Spirit of this World in it's proper place in you, above the just and long-suffering, which is but one and the same in male, and in female.

Oh! what have you done? Can any of you yet smite upon your thigh, and say so yet? if ye can, enquire, enquire ye, the Watch-man's voice is the same it was, and not otherwise, viz. Return, come; yea, return and come to the tender Spirit of holiness, and of the gentleness of Christ, and his yoke of self-denial, and the daily Cross, they are the two great Ordinances which ye have left behind, and so the vail and the Darkness has covered you, but the true Is-raelites have Light in their dwellings, and their habitations is in the best of the Land of the living.

Wherefore my spirit saith, Return, come and hearken to the Lamb's voice, and now see whether ye can follow him (or a stran-ger) wheresoever he goeth; that's the true Prophet raised up like un-to Moses, and obey his voice which savoureth not of this world; for so his Kingdom and servants are not. Therefore beware, lest your souls be cut off from the Land of the living, and ye perish in the outward observations, (by which the Kingdom cometh not) among the Congregations of the dead, where ye are yet seeking the living, but I as a Brother (even Joseph) tell you yet again, He is not there, but is arisen from the dead, from death to life, who is the quickening Spirit, the Lord from Heaven, over the Earth, over all the Land of Ægypt, over the Land of darkness, the same Lord, the same Spirit which hath done excellent things, is exalted in the new Heaven, and in the new Earth, wherein dwelleth righ-teousness; and let the Virgin-Daughter of Sion publish the same, even from henceforth to all generations, yea and my spirit it's ready to say, Amen.

There was one that saw a little Stone cut out of the Moun-tain without hands, and he well retained his sight so long until (in the Light of the living) he saw the same which was so little, wax so great, that it became an exceeding great Mountain.

Verily, the beloved City is manifest, set upon a holy Hill, it cannot be hid from them that see; the glory of God doth enlighten

it,

it, and the Lamb is the Light thereof, and his Light is like unto a stone most precious, clear as Chrystal.

The Fountain is opened free; come down from on high, and thou
shalt see if thou dost thirst for springs of Life. To the Light submit
thy mind, and cease from strife, is the same to behold the Bride, the
Lamb's Wife, from the false Church.

Dan. Baker,

A Salutation *to the whole Body of the* Elect of God, *whether gathered or scattered abroad upon the face of the Earth. And tender Greeting, with* Information *from the same suffering and long suffering Seed, whose Earthen Vessels are held in the Bonds of strait Captivity, under the Pope's dark and cruel Authority, in his* Inquisition *in the Island of* Malta, *for the Word of Life, which is the living Testimony of Jesus, and the truth of his Innocency which they hold and stand fast to, and in the same; having already suffered more then three years in the said Confinement, to the present* 12*th month of the year accounted* 1661. *of the same I bear Record also, and affirm to the Truth, of which I am a Servant, and living Witness,*

Daniel Baker.

O Yee Eternal and Blessed ones, whose dwelling is on high, in the fulness of all Beauty and Brightness, Glory and everlasting Joy, Happiness and Peace for evermore; We who are poor sufferers for the Seed of God, in the Covenant of Light, Life, and Truth, do dearly salute and imbrace you all, according to our measures, Blessing and honour and Glory be given to our Lord God for ever, of all who know him, who hath counted us worthy, and hath chosen us among his faithfull ones, to bear his name and to witness forth his truth, before the high and mighty men of the earth, and to fight the Lords battle with his spirituall weapons, to the breaking down of strong holds, high lofty looks and vain imaginations, and spirituall wickedness in high places.

The Lord did give us a prosperous journey hither, and when we came to *Legorne*, we were refreshed with friends [who were there before us] and they did get a passage for us (and lodging) but as soon as we heard of the Vessel, we did feel our service, So we went into the City in the living

B

power

power of the Lord, and there were many tender hearts did
visit us, to their comfort, and our joy: The little time we
staid there we gave some of our Books, and one Paper: so
journying towards *Alexandria*, the Captain told us that *Malta*
was in the way; and he must put in there a small time. But
before we came there, our burthen was so heavy, that I was
made to cry out (saying,) Oh we have a dreadfull cup to
drink at that place! Oh how am I straitned till it be
Accomplished!

And when we came there, the walls of the City were full
of people; some stood on the top of the walls, as if something
had troubled them: before we came there we stood upon the
deck of the ship, and I looked upon them, & said in my heart,
Shall yes destroy us? *If we give up to the Lord, then he is sufficient to*
deliver us out of their hands; but if we d'sobey our God, all those
could not deliver us out of his hand : So all fear of man was taken
from us. The English Consul came abord the ship (as the
Captain said) but we did not see him, and invited us to his
House, it was the seventh or last day of the week: The next
morning being moved of the Lord we went a-shore, and the
Consul met us, and we gave him a paper, who sent us to
his House, with his Servant; and when we came there at the
present we well were entertained (like Princes) their *Neigh-*
bours and *Kinsfolk* came in, and some *Jesuits*, and we gave them
Books, they read a little, and laid them down, they were too
hot; we declared our message to them in the Name of the
Lord, and we gave some Books in the Street, so they were all
set on work: Away went the Friers to the King (or Supreme
in the Island) and he would not meddle with us, but said, we
were honest women, we might go about our business, and that
night we went a-bord the Ship again, the Consul was troubled,
for their snare was laid, and we felt it; being moved of the
Lord we went in again the next day, and the Consul having
a sister in the Nunnery, desired us to go there, that she might
see us; and we went to them, and gave them a book, then to
the Consuls we returned again, and sitting to wait to know
the mind of the Lord, what he would have us to do, he said
we must give in the great Paper; and if we would go to save
our life, we should lose it,

Here

Here followeth a Copy of some more words which they had written before the former was given forth.

A True Declaration concerning the Lord's love to us in all our Voyage: We were at Sea, betwen *London* and *Plymouth*, many Weeks, and one day we had some trials; and betwen *Plymouth* and *Legorn* we were 31. days, and we had many trials and storms within and without; but the Lord did deliver us out of all: And when we came to *Legorn*, with the rest of our friends, we went into the Town after we had product, and staid there many dayes, where we had service every day; for all sorts of people came unto us, but no man did offer to hurt us, yet we gave them Books and having got passage in a Dutch ship we sayled towards *Cyprus*, intending to goe to *Alexandria*, but the Lord had appointed somthing for us to do by the way, as he did make it manifest to us, as I did speak, for the Master of the ship had no businefs in the place; but being in company with another ship which had some businefs at the City of *Malta*, (in the Island of *Malta* where *Paul* suffered shipwrack) and being in the Harbour, on the first day of the Week, we being moved of the Lord, went into the Town, and the *English* Conful met us on the shore, and asked us concerning our coming, and we told him truth, and gave him some Books, and a Paper, and he told us there was an Inquisition, and he kindly entreated us to go to his house, and said all that he had was at our service while we were there; And in the fear and dread of the Lord we went, and there came many to fee us, and we call'd them to repentance, and many of them were tender; but the whole City is given to Idolatry. And we went a ship-board that night; and the next day we being moved to go into the City again, dared not to flie the crofs, but in obedience went, desiring the will of God to be done. And when we came to the Governor, he told us that he had a Sifter in the Nunnary did desire to fee us if we were free; and in the fear of God we went, and talked with them, and gave them a Book, and one of their Priefts was with us (at the Nunnery) and had us into their place of Worship, and some would have us bow to the high Altar, which we did deny; and having a great burthen, we

went

went to the Consul again, and were vvaiting upon the Lord what to do, that we might know.

And the Inquifitors fent for us, and when vve came before them, they asked our Names, and the Names of our Husbands, and the Names of our Fathers and Mothers, and how many children vve had; and they asked us, *Wherefore we came into that Countrey?* And vve told them, We were the Servants of the living God, and were moved to come and call them to repentance, and many other queftions, and they went away, but commanded that vve fhould be ftaid there. And the next day they came again, and called for us, and vve came; but they vvould examine us apart, and called *Sarah*, and they asked, *Whether fhe was a true Catholick?* She faid, that fhe vvas a true Chriftian that worfhippeth God in fpirit and in truth, and they proffered her the Crucifix, and vvould have had her fvvare that fhe vvould fpeak the truth; and fhe faid, *fhe fhould fpeak the truth*, but fhe vvould not fvvear, for Chrift commanded her *not to fwear*, faying, *Swear not at all*: And the *English* Consul perfvvaded her vvith much entreating to fvvear, faying, *None fhould do her any harm*: But fhe denied, and they took fome Books from her, and vvould have had her fwear by them, but fhe vvould not: And they asked, *Wherefore fhe brought the Books?* And fhe faid, Becaufe we could not fpeak their Language, and they might know vvherefore vve came; and they asked of her, *what* George Fox *was*; and fhe faid, he vvas a Minifter. And they asked, *wherefore fhe came thither?* She faid, To do the Will of God, as fhe vvas moved of the Lord. And they asked, *how the Lord did appear unto her?* And fhe faid, by his Spirit. And they asked, *where fhe was when the Lord appeared unto her?* and fhe faid, upon the way. And they asked, *whether fhe did fee his Prefence, and hear his Voice?* And fhe faid, fhe did hear his Voice, and faw his Prefence; and they asked, *What he faid to her?* and fhe faid, the Lord told her, fhe muft go over the Seas to do his Will; and then they asked, *how fhe knew it was the Lord?* and fhe faid, he bid her go, and his living prefence fhould go vvith her, and he was faithful that had promifed, for fhe did feel his living prefence; and fo they vvent away.

Two dayes after they came again, and called for me, and offered me the Crucifix, and told me *the Magiftrate commanded me to*

fwear.

siseer that I would speak the truth. And I told them that I should speak the truth, for I was a Witness for God; but I should not swear, for a greater than the Magistrate, saith, *Swear not at all, but let your yea be yea, and your nay be nay, for whatsoever is more, cometh of evil*. But said they, *You must obey the Justice, and he commands you to swear*. I said, I should obey Justice; but if I should swear, I should do an *unjust* thing; for (the just) Christ said, *Swear not at all*. And they asked me, *Whether I did own that Christ which dyed at Jerusalem?* I answered, We owned the same Christ, and no other, he is the same yesterday, to day and for ever. And they asked me, *What I would do at Jerusalem?* I did not know that I should go there, but I should go to *Alexandria*; and they said, *What to do?* and I said, to do the Will of God; and if the Lord did open my mouth, I should call them to repentance, and declare to them the day of the Lord, and direct their minds from darkness to Light. Then they asked me, *Whether I did tremble when I did preach?* and I told them, I did tremble when the power of the Lord was upon me. And they asked, *Whether I did see the Lord with my eyes?* I said, God was a Spirit, and he was spiritually discerned.

That day that vve vvere had from the *English* Consul to the Inquisition, the Consul's Wife brought us meat to eat, and as she past by me, I was smote with an Arrovv to the heart, and I heard a voice, saying, *It is finished, she hath obtained her purpose*; I did not taste of her meat, but went aside, and wept bitterly. The Consul did affirm to us the night before, that there was no such thing (as to ensnare us) intended; but it was in us as fire; and our souls were heavy even unto death; for many dayes before we saw in a Vision of our going there, (to prison) and we said *Pilate* would do the *Jews* a pleasure, and wash his hands in innocency. He required *a sign of me if we were the Messengers of God*; and the Lord gave me a sign for him, that stuck by him while he lived. The same day it was, he called me, and told me the Inquisition had sent for us, and they had Papers from *Rome*, and he did hope we should be set free; which was a lye: For he knew there was a room prepared for us. And there came a man with a black Rod, and the Chancellor, and the Consul, and had us before their *Lord Inquisitor*, and he asked us, *Whether we had changed our minds yet?* We said,

said, Nay, we should not change from the truth. He asked, *What new Light we talked of?* We said, no new Light, but the same the *Prophets* and *Apostles* bare testimony to. Then he said, *How came this Light to be lost ever since the primitive times?* We said, it was not lost, men had it still in them, but they did not know it, by reason that the night of Apostacy had, and hath overspread the Nations. Then he said, *If we would change our minds, and do as they would have us to do, we should say so, or else they would use us as they pleased.* We said, The Will of the Lord be done. And he arose up, and went his way with the Consul, and left us there. And the man with the black Rod, and the *Keeper*, took us, and put us into an inner Room in the Inquisition, which had but two little holes in it for light or air; but the glory of the Lord did shine round about us.

After the *Consul* came with tears in his eyes, and said he was so sorry as for his own flesh, but there was some hopes in time; and so he went away; but never had peace while he lived. He would have given up the thirty pieces of silver again, but it would not be received; the Witness was risen much in him, but slavish fear possest him. This was upon the sixt day of the Week, and our stomacks were taken away from all meat.

The next second day came a *Magistrate*, two *Fryars*, and the man with the *black Rod*, and a *Scribe*, and the *Keeper*, to the *Inquisition*, to sit upon Judgement, and examined us apart concerning our faith in Christ. The Magistrate would have had us to *swear*, and we answered, No; Christ said, *Swear not at all*; and so said *James* the Apostle. He asked, *if we would speak truth?* We said, yea: He asked, *Whither we did believe the Creed?* We said, We did believe in God, and in Jesus Christ, which was born of the Virgin *Mary*, and suffered at *Jerusalem* under *Pilate*, and arose again from the dead the third day, and ascended to his Father, and shal come to judgement, to judge both quick and dead. He asked, *How we did believe the Resurrection?* We answered, We did believe that the just and the unjust should arise, according to the Scriptures. He said, *Do you believe in the Saints, and pray to them?* We said, We did believe the Communion of Saints; but we did not pray to them, but to God onely, in the Name of Jesus Christ. He asked, *Whether we did believe in the Catholick Church?* We said, We did believe

believe the true Church of Christ; but the Word *Catholick* we have not read in Scripture. He asked, *if we believed a Purgatory?* We said, No; but a Heaven and a Hell. The Fryar said, *We were commanded to pray for the dead; for those that were in Heaven had no need; and they that were in Hell there is no redemption; therefore there must be a Purgatory.* He asked, *if we believed their holy Sacrament?* We said, We never read (the Word) *Sacrament* in Scripture. The Fryar replied, *Where we did read in our Bibles* Sanctification, *it was* Sacrament *in theirs.* He said, *Their holy Sacrament was Bread and Wine, which they converted into the Flesh and Blood of Christ by the virtue of Christ.* We said, they did work Miracles then, for Christ's virtue is the same as it was when he turned Water into Wine at the Marriage in *Canaan.* He said, *If we did not eat the flesh, and drink the blood of the Son of God, we had no life in us.* We said, the Flesh and Blood of Christ is spiritual, and we do feed upon it daily; for that which is begotten of God in us, can no more live without spiritual food, than our temporal bodies can without temporal food. He said, that *we did never hear Mass.* We said, We did hear the voice of Christ, he onely had the words of eternal life, and that was sufficient for us. He said, *We were Hereticks and Heathens.* We said, they were Hereticks that lived in sin and wickedness, and such were Heathens that knew not God. He asked about our *Meetings in England?* And we told them the truth to their amazement. And they asked, *Who was the Head of our Church?* We said, Christ. And they asked, *What* George Fox *is.* And we said, He is a Minister of Christ. They asked, *Whether he sent us?* We said, No, the Lord did move us to come. The Fryar said, *We were deceived, and had not the faith; but we had all virtues.* We said, that faith was the ground from whence virtues do proceed. They said, *If we would take their holy Sacrament, we might have our liberty; or else the Pope would not leave us for millions of Gold, but we should lose our souls and our bodies too.* We said, the Lord had provided for our souls, and our bodies were freely given up to serve the Lord. They askt us, *if we did not believe Marriage was a Sacrament?* We said, it was an Ordinance of God. They ask't us, *if we did believe men could forgive sins?* We said, None could forgive sin, but God onely. They brought us that Scripture, *Whose sins ye remit in earth, shall be remitted in heaven.* We said, All Power was God's, and he
could

could givr it to whom he would (that were born of the Eternal Spirit, and guided by the same, such have power to do the Fathers Will, as I answered a Fryar also in the City of *Naples*,) and they were silent, the Power greatly working, We asked them wherein we had wronged them, that we should be kept Prisoners all dayes of our lives, and said, Our innocent blood would be required at their hands.

The Fryar said, *He would take our blood upon him, and our Journey into Turky too.* We told him, the time would come he would find he had enough upon him without it. They said, *The Popes was Christ's Vicar, and we were of his Church, and what he did, was for the good of our souls.* We answered, The Lord had not committed the charge of our souls to the Pope, nor to them; for he had taken them into his own possession, glory was to his Name for ever. They said, *We must be obedient.* We said, We were (obedient) to the Government of Christ's Spirit. The Fryar said, *None had the true Light but the Catholicks; the Light that we had, was the Spirit of the Devil.* We said, Wo to him that calleth Jesus accursed: Can the Devil give power over sin and iniquity? then he would destroy his own Kingdom. He said, *We were laught at, and mockt at of every one.* We said, What did become of the mockers? It was no matter. He said, *We did run about to preach, and had not the true Faith.* We said, the true Faith is held in a pure Conscience void of offence towards God and man; and we had the true Faith. And he said, *There was but one Faith, either theirs or ours;* and askt us which it was? We said, Every one had the true Faith, that did believe in God, and in Jesus whom he had sent, but they that say they do believe, and do not keep his commandments, are lyars, and the truth is not in them. He said *it was true;* but he did thirst daily for our blood, because we would not turn? and urged us much about our Faith and Sacrament, to bring us under their Law; but the Lord preserved us.

They said, *It was Impossible we could live long in that hot room.* So the next Week-day they sate in Councils but oh how the swelling Sea did rage, and the proud waves did foam even unto the clouds of Heaven, and Proclamation was made at the Prison-Gate, we did not know the words, but the fire of the Lord flamed against it, [K.] my life was smitten, and I was in a very great agony, so

that

sweat was as drops of blood, and the righteous one was laid into a Sepulcher, and a great stone was roll'd to the door, but the Prophesie was, that he should arise again the third day } Which was fulfilled. But the next day they came to sit upon Judgement again, [but I say, in the true Judgement they sate not, but upon it they got up unjustly above the righteous, and upon the same they sate, a child of Wisdom may understand] and they brought many Propositions written in a paper, but the Fryar would suffer the Magistrate to propound but few to us, for fear the Light would break forth; but they aske *how many friends of ours were gone forth in the Ministry, and into what parts*: We told them what we did know. They said, *all that came where the Pope had any thing to do, should never go back again.* We said, the Lord was as sufficient for us, as he was for the children in the fiery Furnace, and our trust was in God. They said, *we were but few, and had been but a little while, and they were many Countreys, and had stood many hundred years, and wrought many Miracles, and we had none.* We said, we had thousands at our Meetings, but none (of us) dare speak a word, but as they are eternally moved of the Lord; and we had Miracles, the Blind receive their sight, the Deaf do hear, and the Dumb do speak, the Poor do receive the Gospel, the Lame do walk, and the Dead are raised. He asked, *Why I lookt so, whether my Spirit was weak?* I said, Nay, my body was weak, because I eat no meat, [it was in their *Lent*] He offered me a *License to eat flesh*. I said, I could not eat any thing at all. The terrors of death were strongly upon me; but three nights after, the Lord said unto me, about the 11th. hour, *Arise, and put on your Clothes;* I said, *When wilt thou come Lord?* He said, *Whether at midnight, or at Cock-crow, do thou watch.* My Friend and I arose, and the Lord said, *Go stand at the Door.* And we stood at the door in the power of the Lord, I did scarce know whether I was in the body, or out of the body; and about the 12th. hour there came many to the Prison-Gate; We heard the Keys, and looked when they would come in: They ran to and fro till the 4th. hour; the Lord said, he had smote them with blindness, they could not find the way. And we went to bed, there I lay night and day for 12. days together, fasting and sweating, that my bed was wet, and great was our affliction.

C   The

The tenth day of my fast there came *two Fryars*, the *Chancellor*, the man with the *black Rod*, and a *Physician*, and the *Keeper*; and the *Fryar* commanded my dear Friend to go out of the room, and he came and pull'd my hand out of the bed, and said, *Is the Devil so great in you, that you cannot speak?* I said, Depart from me thou worker of iniquity, I know thee not; the Power of the Lord is upon me, and thou call'st him Devil. He took his Crucifix to strike me in the mouth; and I said, Look here! and I asked him, Whether it were that Cross which crucified *Paul* to the World, and the World unto him? And he said, *it was*. I denied him, and said, the Lord had made me a Witness for himself against all workers of iniquity. *He bid me be obedient*, and went to strike me: I said, Wilt thou strike me? He said, *he would*. I said, Thou art out of the Apostles Doctrine, they were no strikers; I deny thee to be any of them who went in the Name of the Lord. He said, *he had brought me a Physician in charity*. I said, the Lord was my Physician, and my saving-health. He said *I should be whipt, and quartered, and burnt that night in Malta, and my Mate too: wherefore did we come to teach them?* I told him I did not fear, the Lord was on our side, and he had no power but what he had received; and if he did not use it to the same end the Lord gave it him, the Lord would judge him. And they were all smitten as dead men, and went away.

And as soon as they were gone, the Lord said unto me, **The last Enemy that shall be destroyed, is Death**; and the Life arose over Death, and I glorified God. The Fryar went to my friend, and told her, *I called him worker of iniquity.* Did she, said *Sarah*, *Art thou without sin?* He said *he was*; Then she hath wronged thee. [But I say, the wise Reader may judge.] For between the eighth and ninth hour in the evening, he sent a Drum to proclaim at the Prison-Gate; We know not what it was, but the fire of the Lord consumed it. And about the fourth hour in the morning they were coming with a Drum and Guns; and the Lord said unto me, arise out of thy Grave-Clothes. And we arose; and they came up to the Gate to devour us in a moment. But the Lord lifted up his Standard with his own Spirit (of Might) and made them to retreat, and they fled as dust before the Wind: praises and honour be given to our God for ever. I went to bed again, and

and the Lord said unto me, Herod will seek the young childes life to destroy it yet again; and great was my affliction.; so that my dear fellow and labourer in the Work of God, did look every hour when I should depart the body for many dayes together, and we did look every hour when we should be brought to the stake day and night, for several weeks, and *Isaac was freely offered up.* But the Lord said, he had provided a Ram in the Bush. Afterwards the Fryer came again with his Physician; I told him, that I could not take any thing, unless I was moved of the Lord. He said, *we must never come forth of that Room while we lived, and we might thank God and him it was no worse, for it was like to be worse.* We said, if we had died, we had died as innocent as ever did servants of the Lord. He said, it was well we were innocent. They did (also) look still when I would dye.

The Fryer bid my friend *take notice what torment I would be in at the houre of Death, thousands of Devils (he said) would fetch my soule to Hell.* She said, she did not fear any such thing.

And he asked *if I did not think it expedient for the Elders of the Church to pray over the sick?* I said, yea, such as were eternally moved of the Spirit of the Lord. He fell down off his knees and did howle; and wish bitter wishes upon himself if he had not the true faith; but we denied him. The Physician was in a great rage at *Sarah*, because she could not bow to him, but to God onely.

The last day of my fast I began to be a hungry, but was afraid to eat, the enemy was so strong; but the Lord said unto me, If thine enemy hunger, feed him; if he thirst, give him drink. In so doing thou shalt heap coales of fire upon his head; be not overcome of evil, but overcome evil with good. I did eat, and was refreshed, and glorified God; and in the midst of our extremity the Lord sent his holy Angels to comfort us; so that we rejoiced and magnified God; and in the time of our great trial, the Sun and Earth did mourn visibly three dayes, and the horror of death and pains of Hell was upon me; the Sun was darkned, the Moon was turned into Blood, and the Stars did fall from Heaven, and there was great tribulation ten dayes, such as never was from the beginning of the world;

and

and then did I see the Son of man coming in the Clouds, with power and great glory, triumphing over his enemies; the Heavens were on fire, and the Elements did melt with fervent heat, and the Trumpet sounded out of *Sion*, and an Allarum was struck up in *Jerusalem*, and all the Enemies of God were called to the great day of Battle of the Lord. And I saw a great wonder in Heaven, the Woman cloathed with the Sun, and had the Moon under her feet, and a Crown of 12. Stars upon her head, and she travelled in pain ready to be delivered of a Man-child, and there was a great Dragon stood ready to devour the Man-child as soon as it was born; and there was given to the Woman two Wings of a great Eagle to carry her into the desert, where she should be nourished for a time, times, and half a time; and the Dragon cast a Flood out of his mouth, &c. And I saw War in Heaven, *Michael* and his Angels against the Dragon and his Angels, and the Lamb and his army did overcome them; and there was a Trumpet sounded in Heaven, and I heard a voice saying to me, The City is divided into three parts; and I heard another Trumpet sounding, and I looked and saw an Angel go down into a great pool of water, and I heard a voice saying unto me, Whosoever goeth down next after the troubling of the Waters, shall be healed of whatsoever Disease he hath. And I heard another Trumpet sounding, and I heard a voice, saying, Babylon is fallen, is fallen, Babylon the great is fallen. And I looked, and saw the smoke of her torment, how it did ascend; and I heard another Trumpet sounding, and I heard a voice saying, Rejoice and be exceeding glad; for great is your reward in heaven: for he that is mighty hath magnified you, and holy is his Name; and from henceforth all generations shall call you blessed: And I heard another trumpet sounding in Heaven, and I heard a voice saying unto me, Behold: and I looked, and I saw *Pharoah*, and his Host pursuing the Children of *Israel*, and he and his Host were drowned in the Sea.

Dear Friends and People, whatsoever I have written, it is not because it is recorded in the Scripture, or that I have heard of such things; but in obedience to the Lord I have written the things which I did hear, see, tasted and handled of the good

Word

Word of God, to the praise of his Name for ever.

And all this time my dear Sister in Christ Jesus was in as great affliction as I (in a manner) to see my strong travel night and day; yet she was kept in the patience, and would willingly have given me up to death, that I might have been at rest; yet she would have been left in as great danger, woe and misery, as ever was any poor captive for the Lord's truth; for they did work night and day with their divinations, inchantments and temptations, thinking thereby to bring us under their power; but the Lord prevented them every way, so that great was their rage, and they came often with their Physician, and said it was in charity; I askt them whether they did keep us in that hot room to kill us, and bring us a Physician to make us alive.

The Fryar said, *the Inquisitor would lose his head if he should take us thence; and it was better to keep us there, than to kill us.*

The Room was so hot and so close, that we were fain to rise often out of our bed, and lie down at a chink of their door for air to fetch breath; and with the fire within, and the heat without, our skin was like sheeps Leather, and the hair did fall off our heads, and we did fail often; our afflictions and burthens were so great, that when it was day we wished for night; and when it was night we wished for day; we sought death, but could not find it; We desired to die, but death fled from us; We did eat our bread weeping, and mingled our drink with our tears. We did write to the Inquisitor, and laid before him our innocency, and our faithfulness, in giving our testimony for the Lord amongst them; and I told him, if it were our blood they did thirst after, they might take it any other way, as well as to smother us up in that hot room. So he sent the Fryar, and he took away our *Ink-horns*, (they had our *Bibles* before.) We asked why they took away our goods? They said, *it was all theirs, and our lives too, if they would.* We asked, how we had forfeited our lives unto them; they said, *For bringing Books and Papers.* We said, if there were any thing in them that was not true, they might write against it. They said, *they did scorn to write to fools and asses that did not know true La-time;* And they told us, *the Inquisitor would have us separated, because I was weak, and I should go into a cooler room; but Sarah should abide there.* I took her by the arm, and said, *The Lord hath joined us to-*
gether

gether, and wo be to them that should part us. I said, I rather chuse to dye there with my friend, than to part from her. He was smitten, and went away, and came no more in five weeks, and the door was not opened in that time. Then they came again to part *us*; but I was sick, and broken out from head to foot. They sent for a Doctor, and he said, *We must have air, or else we must dye.* So the Lord compelled them to go to the Inquisitor, & he gave order for the door to be set open *six hours in a day*; they did not part us till ten Weeks after: But oh the dark clouds and the sharp showers, the Lord did carry us through! Death it self had been better than to have parted in that place. They said, *we corrupted each other, and that they thought when we were parted, we would have bowed to them.* But they found we were more stronger afterwards than we were before; the Lord our God did fit us for every condition. They came and brought a Scourge of small Hemp, and asked us, if we would have any of it. They said, *they did whip themselves till the blood did come.* We said, that could not reach the Devil, he sate upon the heart. They said, *All the men and women of Malta were for us, if we would be Catholicks, for there would be none like unto us.* We said, the Lord had changed us into that which changed not. They said *all their holy women did pray for us, and we should be honored of all the world if we would turn.* We said, we were of God, and the whole world did lye in wickedness; and we denied the honor of the World, and the glory too. They said, *We should be honored of God too, but now we were hated of all.* We said, it is an evident token whose servants we are; the servant is not greater than the Lord, and that Scripture was fulfilled which saith, *All this will I give thee, if thou wilt fall down and worship me.*

Upon a first day of the Week, we were fasting and waiting upon the Lord till the second hour (after mid-day) and the Fryars came and commanded us *in the Name of the Lord to kneel down with them to prayer.* We said, we could not pray but as we were moved of the Lord. They commanded us the second time. Then they kneeled down by our bed side, and prayed, and when they had done, they said, *they had tryed our spirits, now they knew what spirit we were of.* We told told them, they could not know our spirit, unless their minds were turned to the Light of the Lord Jesus in their Consciences. The English Fryar was wrath, and shewed ed us his *Crucifix*, and bid us *loook there*. We faid, The Lord faith, *Thou shalt not make to thy self the likeness of any thing that is in heaven above, or in the earth beneath, nor in the water under the earth; thou shalt not bow to them nor worship them, but I the Lord thy God only*. He was fo mad, he called for the irons to chain *Sarah*, becaufe fhe fpake fo boldly to him : She bowed her head, and faid to him, *Not onely my feet, but my hands and my neck alfo for the Testimony of Jefus*. His wrath was foon appeafed, and he faid, *He would do us any good he cou'd*; he did fee what we did was not in malice, the power had broken him down for that prefent; they came to us often, faying, *If you would do but a little, you should be fet at liberty*; *but you will do nothing at all, but are against every thing*. We faid, We are against nothing that is of God, but would do any thing that might make for God's glory.

Many did think we fhould not have been heard nor feen after we were in the Inquifition, but the Lord did work wonderfully for us and his Truth: For they new built the *Inquifition*, and there were many *Labourers* for a year and a half, and the great men came to fee the building ; and we were carried forth with great power to declare in the Name of the Lord Jefus, not fearing the face of man; the Lord was our ftrength. But behold they threatned us with *Irons* and *Halters*, for preaching the Light fo boldly, and they faid, *None ought to preach but Prelates to a Bishop*, (as they ufe to fay in *England*.) Now their *Lord Inquifitor* (fo called)and the *Magiftrates* were kept moderate towards us, and gave order, we fhould have *Ink and Paper to write to England*. But we were hindered ftill; and vve do believe they would have fet us at liberty, had it not been for the Fryars ; it was they that wrought againft us ftill to the *Pope* and to the *Inquifitor*; and we told them fo. They fought three quarters of a year to part us, before they could bring it to pafs; and when they did part us, they prepared a bed for *Sarah*, and their own *Catholicks* lay upon the boards, that had not beds of their own. When we were parted, the Lord would not fuffer me to keep any money, I knew not the mind of God in it. Their Fryars came and faid, *We should never fee one anothers faces again, but the Inquifitor should fend me my food*. But the Lord would not fuffer him to fend it, *Sarah* did fend me fuch as fhe could get neare three Weeks : then the Fryar came and askt me, *what I did want* ? I faid, one to wafh my

Linnen

Linnen, and something hot to eat; I was weak. He sent to *Sarah*
to know *if she would do it for me.* She said she would. And by that
means we did hear of each other every day. The Fryar said, *You*
may free your self of misery when you will; you may make your self a
Catholick, and have your freedom to go where you will. I told him,
I might make my self a Catholick, and have a name that I did
live, when I was dead; and said, he had Catholicks enough already; he should bring some of them to the Light in their Consciences, that they might stand in awe, and sin not. He said, *He would*
lose one of his fingers if we would be Catholicks. I said, it was *Baby-*
lon that was built with *blood,* Sion was redeemed through Judgement. They would have had me to a Picture set at my beds head,
for a representation, I askt them if they did think I did lack a
Calf to worship? And whether they did not walk by the Rule
of Scripture? The Fryar said, *They did, but they had traditions too.*
I said, if their traditions did derogate or discent from the funda-
mentals of Christ's Doctrine, the Prophets and Apostles, I denied them in the Name of the Lord. He said, *they did not.* I askt
him where they had their Rule to burn them that could not join
with them for Conscience? He said, *St. Paul did worse; he gave*
them to the Devil; and that they did judge all damned that were not of
their Faith. And he askt whether we did judge them so? *I said,*
No, We had otherwise learned Christ. I askt him why they did
bind that which the Lord did not bind? and set tyes, chains and
limits, where the Lord did not, as in *meats* and *drinks,* or in respect
of *dayes* or *times,* which the Apostle called *beggarly Elements,* and
rudiments of the world, and *forbidding to marry,* (*a Doctrine of De-*
vils said I:) He could not tell what to say, but told me, *That Saint*
Peter *was the Pope of* Rome, *and did build an Altar there; and the*
Pope *was his Successor, and he could do what he would.* (I denied that)
and said, We never read any such thing in Scripture; for Peter
Christ's Apostle had no money to build Altars; he himself did
offer Sacrifice upon the Altars made without hands. And he
said, *We were but a few, and risen up but late, and they were many, and*
had stood fourteen hundred years, and God was a lyar if they had not the
true faith, for he had confirmed it to them by a thousand miracles. I
said, the few number, and the little Flock is Christ's Flock. He
askt if we were? then all the world, said he. I said, our faith
was

was from the begidning. *Abel* was of our Church; and *the world by wisdom did not know God*. He went to *Sarah* with the same temptation, and she told him also, that *Abel was of our Church*: He said *Abel was a Catholick*, and *Cain and* Judas *were so*. She said, Then the Devil was a *Catholick*, and she would not be one. He threatned her, and told her *how many they were*.

She said, *Daniel* was but one; and if there were no more but she her self, she would not turn; but took her fingers and shewed them, if they would tear her joint-meal, she did believe the Lord would enable her to endure it for the Truth.

So they went from one to another thinking to entangle us in our talk; but we were guided by one Spirit, and spake one and the same thing in effect, so that they had not a jot nor tittle against us, but for righteousness sake: Our God did keep us by his own Power and Holiness out of their hands; honor and praises be given to his powerful Name for ever

He (the said Fryar) came to me another time like a Bear robbed of her Whelps, and told me, if *I would be a Catholick, I should say so, otherwise they would use me badly, and I should never see the face of* Sarah *again, but should dye by my self, and a thousand Devils should carry my soul to Hell.* I asked him if he were the Messenger of God to me. He said he was. I said, What is my sin, or wherein have I provoked the Lord, that he doth send me such a strait Message? He said, *Because I would not be a Catholick*, I said, I deny thee and thy Message too, and the Spirit which spake in thee; the Lord never spake it. He said, that *he would lay me in a whole Pile of Chains, where I should see neither Sun nor Moon*. I said, he could not separate me from the love of God in Christ Jesus, lay me where he would. He said, *He would give me to the Devil.* I said, I did not fear all the Devils in Hell, the Lord was my Keeper; Though he had the Inquisition, with all the Countreys round about, on his side, and was alone by my self, I did not fear them; if there were thousands more, the Lord was on my right hand, and the worst they could do, was but to kill the body, they could not touch my life no more than the Devil could *Job's*. He said, that *I should never go out of that Room alive.* I said, the Lord was sufficient to deliver me: But whether he would, or would not, I would not forsake a living Fountain to drink at a broken Ci-

D   stern

stern: And they had no Law to keep us there, but such a Law as Ahab had for *Naboth's* Vineyard. He curst himself, and call'd upon his gods and went forth, and as he was making fast the door, he put in his hand at the hole of the door and said, *Abide there Member of the Devil*. I said, The Devil's Members did the Devil's Work; the Woes and Plagues of the Lord would be upon them for it. He went and told the Inquisitor of it, and he laught at him: I saw it, and felt it in that which is Eternal. I was moved out of that Room before he came again, and when he came, he brought one of the Inquisitors men with him, and two very good Hens, and said, the Lord Inquisitor had sent them in love to me. I said, his love I did receive, but I could not take his Hens, for it was not the practice of the servants of the Lord to be chargeable to any while they have of their own. He said, *We must not count any thing our own; for in the primitive times they did sell their possessions, and laid them down at the Apostles feet.* He said, *We should not want any thing if they did spend a thousand Crowns.* I believe he would have had us lay down our money at his feet. He said *I was proud, because I would not take the Inquisitors Hens when he sent them me in Charity.* I asked whether he kept me in Prison, and sent me his Charity. He said, *it was for the good of our souls he kept us in prison.* I told him, Our souls were out of the Inquisitors reach or his either, he told me before, *if we had not been going to preach, we might have gone where we would.* I askt him, What should our souls have done then, and why their love should extend more to us, than to their own family? They could not charge us with sin and they did commit all manner of sins; they might put them into the Inquisition and bid turn. *He said again We had not the true Faith,* and shew'd me his Crucifix, and askt me if I thought he did worship that? I askt him what he did do with it? He said *it was a Representation.* I said, it did not represent Christ; for he was the express image of his Father's glory; which is Light and Life. I said if he could put any life in any of his images, he might bring them to me. And I askt him what *Representation Daniel* had in the *Lyons Den*, or *Jonah* in the *Whales belly*; they cryed unto the Lord, and he delivered them. He said, *I talks like a mad woman, I talks so much against their idols.* He was in a rage, and said, *He would give me to the Devil.* I bid him give his own, I am the Lords. He stood up, and said,

said. He would do by me as the Apostles did by Ananias and Saphira. He stood up and opened his mouth; and I stood up to him and denied him in the Name of the Lord, the living God; and said he had no power over me. And away he went to *Sarah* with the Hens, and told her *that I was sick, and the Lord Inquisitor had sent two Hens, and I would be glad to eat a piece of one if she should dress one of them presently, and the other to morrow.* [Mark, this Deceiver! this Lyar!] But she standing in the Counsel of the Lord, answered him accordingly as did; and he carried them away again. We did not dare to take them, the Lord did forbid us. He said, *You would fain be burned, because you would make the World believe you did love God so well as to suffer in that kind.* I said, I did not desire to be burnt but if the Lord did call me to it I did believe he would give me power to undergo it for his truth; and if every hair of my head was a body, I could offer them up all for the Testimony of Jesus. He came twice to know *whether I had not been inspired of the Holy Ghost to be a Catholick since I came into the Inquisition.* I said, No; he said, *we were*; he said, *We called the Spirit of the Holy Ghost the Spirit of the Devil.* We said, the Spirit of the Holy Ghost in us will resist the Devil. We told him the inspiration of the Holy Ghost was never wrought in the Will of man, nor in man's time, but in the Will of God, and in God's time. He asked, *How we did know a clean from an unclean Spirit?* We said, an unclean spirit did burden the Seed of God, and dam up the Springs of Life; and a clean spirit would open the Springs of Life, and refresh the Seed; it was a Riddle to him, but he said it was true: He would assent to pure truth sometimes

We asked him. Whether every man and woman did not stand guilty before God of all the sins they ever committed before Regeneration? He said, *Yea.* And he did confess all their Learning and Languages (in their places) was but to serve the Lord. We told him, all their Praying, Preaching and Crouding, was no more accepted than *Cain's* Sacrifice, unless they were moved of the Eternal Spirit of the Lord. We askt him, if he that was in them, was greater than he that was in us; and why they had not overcome us all that time? We were very sensible of their workings day and night. He said, *Because we resisted still.* We askt him for our Bibles? He said, *We should never see them again, they were false.*

D 2   We

We said, if they were conjuring Books, they had no warrant from the Lord to take them from us.

They always came two Fryars at a time, and they would fall down and howl, and wish bitter wishes upon themselves if they were not in the truth. We would deny them, and preach truth to them, the Light of the Lord Jesus in the Consciences of every one, to lead them to a pure life, and did ask them where the pure and holy life was, and what all of them did do, that the people did live in sin and all manner of wickedness? And whether words and forms would serve without life and power? He was as bloody a fiery Serpent, as ever was born of a Woman, and did strike as hard at our lives & would hold up his hand often to strike us, but had never the power, he would quickly be cut down, that he would say, we were good women, and he would do us any good. He was compell'd to work for us sometimes, and would say it was for God's sake, and would have us thank him for it. We would tell him, those that did any thing for God, did not look for a reward from man. He said, *We were the worst of all creatures, and we should be used worse than any; the Turks, Arminians, Protestants and Lutherans should be used better than we.* We said, the pure Life was ever counted the worst, and we must suffer; we were the Lords, and could trust him; let him do what he would with us, we did not fear any evil tydings; we were setled and grounded in the truth, and the more they did persecute us, the more stronger we did grow; We were bold and valiant for God's Truth, that whatsoever we did suffer, we could not fear. We were separated two years; I had neither fire nor candle in that time above two hours, none did bring me any, nor I had not freedom to call for any.

The Fryars went to *Sarah*, and told her, if she would, she should go forth of the Prison, and say nothing, nor do nothing. She said, she would upon that account. He said, they would come in the morning, and so they did; but the Lord saw their deceit, and fore-warned *Sarah*, and bid her mind *Esau, who sold his Birth-right for a morsel of meat; and* Judas, *that betrayed his Master for thirty pieces of Silver:* That when they came, she (was strengthned against them, and) said, she stood in the Counsel of God, and could take up nothing in her own will; they had not power to have her forth. They said the Inquisitor said, if we did want Linnen, Woollen, ten, Stockins, Shooes or Money, vve ſhould have it.

But there was a poor *Engliſh* man heard that *Sarah* was in a room
vvith a Windovv next the Street, it vvas high, he got up, and ſpake
a tevv vvords to her; and they came violently, & hall'd him down,
and caſt him into priſon upon life and death : And the Fryars
came to knovv of us vvhether he had brought any Letters. We
ſaid no; I did not ſee him. They ſaid, they did think he would be
hang'd for it. He was one that they had taken from the *Turks*,
and made a Catholick of him. *Sarah* wrote a few lines to me of
it, and ſaid ſhe did think the Engliſh Fryars were the chief actors
of it, (we had a private way to ſend to each other.) I vvrote to
her again, and after my Salutation, I ſaid, Whereas ſhe ſaid the
Fryars vvere the chief actors, ſhe might be ſure of that, for they
did haſten to fill up their meaſures, but I believe the Lord wil pre-
ſerve the poor man for his love ; I am made to ſeek the Lord for
him with tears: And I deſired ſhe would ſend him ſomething once a day, if the Keeper vvould carry it, and I told her of
the glorious manifeſtations of God to my ſoul, for her comfort,
ſo that I was raviſhed vvith love, and my Beloved was the chiefeſt
of ten thouſands ; and how I did not fear the face of any man,
though I did feel their arrows, for my Phyſician is nigh me; and
how I was vvaiting upon the Lord, and ſaw our ſafe return into
England, and I was talking with *G.F.* to my great refreſhment: The
Name of *G.F.* did prick them to the heart. I ſaid, it vvas much
they did not tempt us vvith money. I bid her take heed, the Light
vvould diſcover it, and many more things, let it come under what-
ſover it vvould.

And this Paper came to the Fryar's hands, by vvhat means vve
could never tell, but as the Light did ſhew us ; the Lord vvould
have it ſo; it ſmote the Fryar, that he vvas tormented many days,
and he tranſlated it into *Italian*, and laid it before their Lord Inquiſitor, and got the Inquiſitor's Lievtenant, and came to me
with both the Papers in his hand, and askt me *if I could read it ?* I
ſaid, *Yea,* I writ it. *O ! did you indeed !* (ſaid he). And *what is it
you ſay of me here?* That which is truth ſaid I. Then he ſaid, *Where
is the Paper* Sarah *ſent ? bring it, or elſe I will ſearch the Trunk, and
every where elſe.* I bid him ſearch where he vvould. He ſaid, *I muſt
tell what man it was that brought me the Ink, or elſe I ſhould be tyed
                                                        with*

with Chains presently. J told him J had done nothing but what was just and right in the sight of God, and what J did suffer would be for Truth's sake; and J did not care. J would not meddle nor make with the poor Workmen. He said, *For God's sake tell me what* Sarah *did write?* J told him a few words, and said it was truth. Said he, *You say it is much we do not tempt you with money.* And in few hours they came and tempted us with money often. So the Lieutenant took my ink and threw it away; and they were smitten as if they would have fallen to the ground, and went their way. J saw them no more in three Weeks; but the poor man was set free the next morning.

They went to Sarah, and told her *that J had honestly confest all, and that she was best to confess too; and threatned her with a Halter, and to take away a Bed and Trunk, and her Money, to have half of it for me.* She answered, she might not send to me any more. She askt him, Whether he was a Minister of Christ, or a Magistrate? if he were a Magistrate, he might take her money, but she would not give it him: And they that were with him, said, *No, he should not meddle with any thing.* He was a bitter wicked man. He told her, *She was possest:* She answered and said, she was with the power of an endless life.

The Lord was not wanting to us at any time, for Power nor Words to stop the mouths of gain-sayers of his Truth, neither in Revelations nor Visions; Praises be to his Name for ever. He kept us in our weakest condition, bold for his Truth, declaring against all sin and wickedness, so that many were convinced, but did not dare to own it, for fear of *Faggot* and *Fire.* There were none that had any thing to say against what we spake, but the Fryers, but would have us to join with them. There were none did come into the inquisition but the judgements of the Lord would be upon them, so that they would cry and foam, and send for a Physitian to any of them. The unclean spirits would cry out as much as ever they did against Jesus, and would gnash with their teeth when we were at prayer; there was a Fryer and other great men, the Fryer would run as if he had been at his Wits end, and call to the Keeper, and he would run for the *English* Fryer, and he would go the Jnquisitor for counsel, and sometime they would send them word they should have a remedy, J should be sent to

Rome;

Rome, and sometimes the Fryers would come, but had not power to say any thing to me of it) The Lord did say to us, Lift up your Voice like the noise of a Trumpet, and found forth my Truth like the shout of a King. There was one that life was arisen in him but they were upon him as Eagles til they have destroy'd him; he did undergo terrible Judgements all the time he was in the *Inquisition*.

Our money served us a year and seven Weeks; and when it was almost gone, the Fryars brought the *Inquisitor's Chamberlain* to buy our Hats. We said, we came not there to sel our clothes, nor any thing we had. Then the Fryar did commend us for that, and told us *we might have kept our money to serv us otherwise*. We said, No we could not keep any money, and be chargeable to any; We could trust God. He said, *He did see we could, but they should have maint ined us while they kept us Prisoners*.

And then the Lord did take away our stomacks; we did eat but little for three or four Weeks; and then the Lord called us to fasting for eleven dayes together, but it was so little, that the Fryars came and said, that *it was impossible that Creatures could live with so little meat*, as they did see we did for so long time together; and asked *what we would do*. And said their Lord Inquisitor said, We might have any thing we would. We said, We must wait to know the mind of God, what he would have us to do. We did not fast in our own Wills but in obedience to the Lord. They were much troubled, and sent us meat, and said the *English Consul sent it*. We could not take any thing till the Lord's time was come. We were weak, so that *Sarah* did dress her head as she would lye in her Grave, (poor Lamb) I lay looking for the Lord to put an end to the sad trial which way it seemed good in his sight. Then I heard a voice, saying, Ye shall not dye. I believed the Lord, and his glory did appear much in our waiting; he was very gracious to us, and did refresh us with his living presence continually, and we did behold his beauty to our great joy and comfort, and he was large to us in his promises, so that we were kept quiet and still, (the sting of Death being taken away,) our souls, hearts and minds were at peace with the Lord, so that they could not tell whether we were dead or alive but as they did call to us once a day, till the time the Lord had appointed we should eat; and they were made to

bring

bring *many good things*, and laid them down by us ; so that Scripture we witneſſed fulfilled, *Our Enemies treated us kindly in a ſtrange
Land*, ſaid I. But we were afraid to eat , and cryed to the Lord,
and ſaid, We had rather dye, than eat any thing that is polluted
and unclean. The Lord ſaid unto me, *Thou mayeſt as freely eat, as
if thou hadſt wrought for it with thy hands : I will ſanctifie it to thee
through the Croſs*. And he ſaid to *Sarah*, *Thou ſhalt eat the fruit of
thy hands, and be bleſſed*. We did eat and were refreſhed , to the
praiſe and glory of our God for ever. We did eat but little in two
Months; and they did bring us what ever we did ſpeak for, for 8.
or 10. dayes ; and afterward we were ſo ſtraitned for want of
food, it did us more hurt than our Faſt. Yet the Lord did work
as great a Miracle by our preſervation, as he did by raiſing *Lazarus* out of the Grave. The Fryars did ſay, *the Lord did keep us alive
by his mighty power , becauſe we ſhould be Catholicks*. We ſaid, the
Lord would make it manifeſt to us then ; they ſhould know the
Lord had another end in it one day.

But ſtill they ſaid, *There was no Redemption for us*. We ſaid, with
the Lord there was mercy and plenteous Redemption. We bid
them, take heed ye be not found fighters againſt God. They ſaid,
We were fooliſh women. We ſaid we were the Lord's fools , and the
Lord's Fools were right dear, and precious in his ſight, and wo to
them that do offend them. He ſaid, *they were the Lord's fools*, and
ſhewed us their deceitful Gowns, and their ſhaven Crowns , and
ſaid, *they did wear it for God's ſake, to be laught at of the world*. We
ſaid, they did not wear it for God's ſake, unleſs they were moved
of the holy Spirit of God to wear it. He ſaid , *it was no matter,
they did wear it becauſe of their Superiors*. [mark, and before it was
for God's ſake, as he ſaid] He thought to bring us under him for
our food, and did make us ſuffer a while , though the Inquiſitor
and the Magiſtrates had taken a courſe we ſhould want for nothing. But the Lord did torment him and all the reſt , till they
did bring us ſuch things as were fitting. Then he did work all that
he could to ſend me to *Rome*, and was coming two or three times
(for what I know) to fetch me forth , but the Lord vvould not
ſuffer them ; and vvhen they ſavv they could not prevaile that
vvay, they ſaid vvo ſhould go both; but the Fryar ſhould go firſt,
becauſe he vvas not vvell; he got leave to go , he vvas ſo vveary

of

of coming to us, that he did beseech the Lord Inquisitor he might come no more to us. He told *Sarah, I was a Witch, and that I knew what was done at London*, and he vvould come to me no more, he said, Because vvhen he did tell me a company of lyes, I said, *I had a witneſs for God in me, which was faithful and true, and I did believe God's witneſs.*

The Diviners did vvax mad, and did run as at their vvits end, from Mountain to Hill, and from Hill to Mountain, to cover them: They ran to the Inquisitor, and vvrit to the Pope, and vvent to him, their King did not hide them at all; some of them did gnath vvith their teeth, and even gnavv their tongues for pain: Yet the reſt vvould not repent of their blasphemy, sorcery, nor inchantments, but do post on to fill up their meaſures; Oh! the Lord revvard them according to their vvorks. A little before the Fryar vvent to *Rome*, he came to the *Inquiſition* Chamber vvith a Scribe, to vvrite concerning us, to carry it vvith him; I savv him, as God vvould have it; the Lord said, *There is thy deadly foe.* They vvere vvriting part of three dayes; and vvhen they had ended it, the Lord would not let me eat till the Scribe did come where I was, that I might pronounce vvo againſt it, and defie it, which I did do in the Name of the Lord, and it did wither vvith all the reſt: After it vvas gone, the *Engliſh Conſul* came to us with a Scribe, and he brought us a doller from a Maſter of a Ship that came from *Plymouth*; I told him, I did receive my Countrey man's Love, but could not receive his Money. He askt me, *What I wou'd do if I would take no money?* I said, the Lord was my portion, and I could not lack any good thing. I said to him, We were in thy Houſe near 15. Weeks, didſt thou see any cauſe of Death or Bonds in us? He said, *No.* I askt him, how he would diſpence with his Conſcience for telling us, *He would have us before the Inquiſitor*, and thou didſt know that Room vvas provided for us; and had not we been kept alive by the mighty Power of God, we might have been dead long ſince. He said, *How could I help it!* I said. We are the Servants of the living God, and were brought here by permiſſion, and in the Spirit of Meekneſs gave in our Teſtimony for the Lord in faithfulneſs, and told you the truth as it is in Jeſus, and called you all to repentance, and fore-warned you in love to your ſouls, of the evil the Lord is bringing upon you, if you do not

E   repent

repent. He said, *However it be, it will go well with you.* [Mark that.]
I told him, he required a sign of me when vve vvere at his house,
if we were the servants of the Lord God; I gave him a sign from
the living God, and my friend gave him another from the Lord,
to his shame and destruction for ever. I askt him, Whether it vvere
not true we spake to him, he said it was, *but how should he help it?*
I said, Thou art a condemned person, and stands guilty before
God; yet nevertheless repent, if thou canst find a place. He
smil'd upon the Scribe in deceit, but his lips did quiver, and his
belly trembled, and he could scarce stand upon his legs. He was
as proper a man as most was in the City, and full, and in his prime
age. O! he was consumed as a Snail in a shell, which was a sufficient sign for the whole City, if their hearts were not harder than
Adamants, He said, *How should he help it?* He might have helpt
it, but he was as willing to prove us, as any of them all. He was
sworn upon his Oath to protect the *English*; and their Ruler bid
him let us go about our business, and said, *We were honest women*;
and then he might have let us go before we were under the black
Rod.

Then he went to *Sarah* with the Doller; she told him she could
not take the Money; but if he had a Letter for us, she should be
free to receive that. He said, *he had not any.* He askt her *what she
did want?* She said, the Lord was her Shepherd, she could not
want any good thing; but she did long for her Freedom. He said,
That you may have in time. He told us, *we should have ink and paper
to write:* But when he was gone, they vvould not let us. The next
time we heard of him, he was dead; We could have rejoiced if he
had dyed for righteousness sake; for the Lord delighteth not in
the death of a sinner.

The Fryar was gone to *Rome*, and they said, *he must stay there
till we came.* There was great working to send us there, but the
Lord did prevent them, that they could not send us there. Then
the Lord did work to bring us together again after so long time
we had been parted. There vvere five doors between us with
Locks and Bolts, but the Keeper had not power to make them
fast, but as *Sarah* could undo them to come where I could see her,
but could not speak to her; for there were them that did watch
us night and day; yet she being moved of the Lord, did come to

my

my door by n'ght; she must come by the Fryars door, he and the Doctor of Law were together, and they did set a trap to take her in, and many did watch about the Prison, and would complain. Then she was lockt up again; but they had no peace in that, till the doors were open again; then we did sit in the sight of each other, to wait upon the Lord, so that our voices were heard far; the Magistrates vvould hear and bow to it sometime; then the complainers were weary, and did work to have us brought together; and we did wait and pray, and the Magistrates would come in and look upon us many times, but would say nothing to us: There were of divers Nations brought into the Inquisition Prisoners, and the Fryars, and the rest that were great, would go in their way to make Christians of them; and we were made to stand up against them and their vvays, and deny them in the Name of the Lord, and declare the truth to the simple-hearted continually, if vve did suffer death for it; We could not endure to hear the Name of the Lord blasphemed, nor his pure Way of Truth perverted, nor the ignorant deceived. They did vvrite all they understood of vvhat vve spake, and sent it to the Court-Chamber before the Inquisitor and Magistrates, but the Lord did blast it vvith the Mildevvs of his vvrathful indignation, and burnt it up vvith the brightness of his Son, and vve rejoiced in our God; but still our burdens continued very heavy, and our righteous souls vvere vexed vvith the filthy Conversation of the Wicked, and the pure Seed of God vvas prest from day to day, that our spirits did mourn, and our hearts vvere grieved because of the hardness of their hearts, and their Rebellion against their Maker, vvho vvas so gracious to them, to suffer them so long in all their abominations, and vvaited to be gracious to them, and knock at the Door of their hearts, calling for *Justice*, *Mercy* and *Humility*; but behold *Oppression*, *Cruelty*, and *Self-Exaltation*, notvvithstanding the Lord did strive so much vvith them, and sent so many undeniable truths, and infallible testimonies of the coming of his Son to Judgement, and so clear a manifestation of the vvay to eternal Salvation, given forth of his ovvn mouth, by his eternal Spirit, and having us for an example vvho vvere kept by his Povver and Holiness; they had not a jot nor tittle against us, but for righteousness-sake, though they had vvinnovved and fanned us so long:

E 2   Glory

Glory, honor and praises be given to our God for ever. O they would not let us know of any *English* Ship that came into the Harbour, as near as they could, but the Lord would make it manifest to us; We had a great working and striving in our bodies, but we knew not what it meant; the arrows of the Wicked did flye, so that my soul was plunged and overwhelmed from head to feet, and the terrors of the unrighteous had taken hold of us, and the flames of Hell compassed us about; then the Lord appeared unto me in a dream, and said, *There were two English Friends in the City which did plead for our liberty in our behalf, and he had taken all fear away from them, and made them bold.* And in a little while after the Magistrates sent for us forth, and askt us, *whether we were sick*, or *whether we did want any thing* and were very tender to us, and said we *should write to England*, and bid the Scribe *give us Ink and Paper*; he said he would, but he was so wicked he did not. They did not tell us of any *English* that were there; but there was one *Francis Steward* of *London*, a Captain of a Ship, and a Fryar of *Ireland*, which come to the City together (for what we know) and they did take great pains for us, and went to their Ruler, and the Inquisitor, and to several Magistrates and Fryars, and the new *English* Consul with them, and wrought much amongst them, that all were willing to let us go, save the Inquisitor; they said, and he said, *He could not free us without an Order from the Pope.* But we had many heavy Enemies besides, which would not be seen; but they obtained the favour to come and speak with us, which was a great thing in such a place.

They sent for us to the Court-Chamber, and the *English* Consul askt us, *if we were willing to go back to* England? We said, if it were the Will of God we might. The Captain spake to us with tears in his eyes, and told us what they had done for us, but could not prevail; It is this Inquisitor (said he) the rest were made free; *you have preached among these people* he said. We told him we were called upon the Testimony of our Conscience and the truth that we have witnessed forth among them; we should stand to maintain with our blood. He said, *if they could get us off, he would freely give us our passage, and provide for us,* and he Vessel was his own. We told him, his love was as well accepted of the Lord, as if he did carry us. He offered us monky, he saw the Lord would

not.

not suffer us to take any. He took our Names. We told them they took us out of our way, and put us into the Inquisition, and bid us change our minds; and we could not, the Lord had changed us into that which changed not, if they would burn us to ashes, or chop us as Herbs to the Pot. The Fryar said, *We did not work;* which was false; we had Work of our own, and did work as we were able. We told him, our Work and Maintenance was in *England.* And they said, *it was true.* He said, *We would not accept of the Inquisitors Dyet.* We did not know who did prepare for us, we did receive our meat as we had freedom in the Lord. Then he said, *We had suffered long enough, and too long, but we should have our freedom in ex days, and that they would send to the Pope for an Order.* And there were many English ships that way; but the Captain saw it was a very hard thing; so that it grieved him to the heart: He prayed God to comfort us, and he went away; and we do beseech God to bless and preserve him unto everlasting life, and never to let him nor his go without a blessing from him, for his love: he did venture himself exceedingly in that place. But after he was gone, they arose up against us with one accord; the Inquisitor came up into a Tower, and lookt down upon us as if he would have eaten us, and they did try us for our lives again, and did shut up our doors many Weeks; we could not tell for what; at length the Inquisitor came into the Tower again, and *Sarah* was moved to call to him, to have the door opened for us to go down into the Court to wash our clothes. Then he gave command for the door to be opened once a Week; and in a little while 'twas open every day. But great was our affliction indeed; and she told him, if we were the Popes Prisoners, we would appeal to the Pope, and he should send us to him. But them in the prison with us, especially the Fryar, were mortal Enemies to us, but yet they would have fed us with the choicest of their meat, and would gladly give us whole Bottles of Wine, if we would receive it, and were greatly troubled because we did refuse to eat and drink with them, and did persecute us exceedingly; but the Lord did visit them with his dreadful Judgements, the Fryar was tormented night and day, his body did perish, the Doctors and Chyrurgions did follow him a long time.

And

And there were two or three *English* Ships there, came into harbour, and *Sarah* saw the coming of them in a Vision of the night, and there was great pleading for us, that we saw; but she heard a Voice, saying, *We could not go now.* So we were made willing to wait the Lords time.

Then they sent for us forth when the Ships were gone, and askt us *if we would be Catholicks*: And we said, we were true Christians, and had received the Spirit of Christ, and he that had not the Spirit of Christ, was none of his. The *English* Consul told us of the Ships, and said, *they would not let us go unless we would be Catholicks; and that we must suffer more imprisonment yet*; and said, *he did what he could for us.* One of the Magistrates shewed us the Cross; We told them, and said, We did take up the Cross of Christ daily, which is the great Power of God to crucifie sin and iniquity. So we told them that one of their *Fathers* did promise us our liberty. We did think that Fryar was too tender-hearted to stay among them; he did take a great deal of pains for us (the Captain said) we told him, he would never have cause to repent it; the blessing of God would be upon him for any thing he should do for us; for we were the Servants of the living God, and he promised us our freedoms in a little time.

This following I received from them in other Papers to Friends. D. B.

O Dearly beloved Friends, Fathers and Elders, and Pillars of Gods Spiritual House, and Brethren and Sisters in the Lord *Jesus Christ*, in the measure of Love and Life of our God, do we salute you all, and do embrace you in that which is Eternal, and we do greatly rejoice and glorifie the Name of our Heavenly Father, that he hath counted us worthy to be partakers of the death and sufferings of his blessed Son, with you; though we be the least of Gods Flock, yet we are of the true Fold, whereof Christ *Jesus* is Shepherd; and he hath had as tender a care over us, as he hath had of any of his Lambs which he hath called forth in this the day of his Power, and hath carryed us through, and over as great afflictions as most of our Brethren and sufferers for his

Name

Name, both in mockings, scoffings, scornings, reproaches, stripes, contradictions, perils at Land, and perils at Sea, fiery tryals, cruel threatnings, grief of heart, sorrow of soul, heats and colds, fastings and watchings, fears within, and frightings without, terrible temptations and
persecutions, and dreadful imprisonments and buffetings of Satan: yet
in all these our tryals the Lord was very gracious unto us, and not absent himself from us, neither suffered his faithfulneß to fail us, but did
bear us up, and keep us from fainting in the midst of our extremity; we
had not another to make our moan to, but the Lord alone, neither could
we expect a drop of mercy, favour or refreshment, but what he did distil
from his living Presence, and work by his own strength; for we sate one
in one room, and the other in another, near a year, as Owls in Deserts,
and as people forsaken in solitary places; then did we enjoy the presence
of the Lord, and did behold the brightneß of his Glory, and we did see
you our dear Friends, in the Light of Jesus, and did behold your order,
and stedfastneß of your Faith and Love to all Saints, and were refreshed in all the faithful hearted, and felt the issues of Love and Life which
did stream from the hearts of those that were wholly joined to the Fountain, and were made sensible of the benefit of your prayers.

O the sorrows, the mournings, the tears! but those that sow in tears,
shall reap in joy. A true sorrow begets a true joy; and a true Croße, a
true Crown: For when our sorrows did abound, the Love of God did
abound much more; the deeper the sorrows, the greater the joys; the
greater the Cross, the weightier the Crown.

Dear Friends and Brethren, marvel not that Israel is not gathered,
our Judgement remains with the Lord, and so do our Labours; for it was
not for want of travel, nor pain, nor love to their souls; for we could
have been contented to have fed upon the Graß on the ground, so we
might have had our freedom amongst them : For had it not been for the
great opposition, they would have followed after us as Chickens after a
Hen, both great and small : But oh the swelling seas, the raging and
foaming Waves, Stormy Winds and Floods, and deep Waters, and high
Mountains and Hills, hard Rocks, rough wayes, and crooked paths, tall
Cedars, strong Oaks, fruitleß Trees, and corrupted ones, that cumber
the ground, and hinder the righteous Seed to be sown, and the noble
Plants from being planted : Oh! they shut up the Kingdom against the
simple-hearted, and hide the key of knowledge from the innocent ones,
and will not enter into the Kingdom themselves, nor suffer them that

                                                              would

would enter, but ſtir up the Magiſtrates to form carnal Weapons, thinking to prevent the Lord of taking to him his Inheritance, and to diſpoſ-
ſeſs his Son who is heir of all, that he might not have a dwelling-place
amongſt them, nor a habitation nigh them; becauſe that his Light will
diſcover their darkneſs, and his brightneſs will burn up all their abominations, and marr their beauty, and ſtain their glory, their pomp and
their pride, that it may periſh as the untimely Figs, and fall as the Flower of the Field, and wither as the Graſſe upon the houſe-top. Oh the
Belly of Hell, the Jaws of Satan, the whole Myſterie of iniquity is at
the height, and all manner of abominations that make deſolate, ſtands
where it ought not, and is upholden by a Law, That upon pain of
death none muſt ſpeak againſt it, nor walk contrary to it. But praiſes to
our God, he carryed us forth to declare againſt it daily. Oh the blind
Guides, the ſeducing ſpirits that do cauſe the people to err, and compel
them to worſhip the Beaſt and his Image, and to have his mark in their
fore-heads, and in their hands, and to bow to Pictures and painted Walls,
and to worſhip the things of their own hands, and to fall down to that
which their own fingers have faſhioned, and will not ſuffer them to look
towards Sion upon pain of death, nor to walk towards Jeruſalem upon
pain of Faggot and Fire, but muſt abide in Babel, and believe whatſoever they ſpeak or do, to be truth. But oh the wayes, the worſhips, the
faſhions, forms, cuſtoms, traditions obſervations and imaginations which
they have drawn in by their dark Divinations, to keep the poor people in
blindneſs and ignorance, ſo that they periſh for want of knowledge, and
are corrupted, becauſe the way of truth is not made known among them;
they are all in the many wayes, out of the one true and living way, and
their ways be ſo many and ſo monſtrous, that they are unrehearſible; but
the Lord our God hath kindled a fire in the midſt of them, that will con-
ſume all forms, faſhions, cuſtoms and traditions of men, and will burn
up the bryars, thorns and tares, ſtubble and fruitleſs Trees, and corrupted ones, and will blaſt all the fruits, works and labours of wicked and
ungodly men, with the Mill-dews of his wrathful indignation, and will
ſcatter all his Enemies with the Whirl-winds of his diſpleaſure. They
do not know the Scriptures. Their Bibles would grieve any honeſt heart
to behold them, becauſe of the corruption: They ſaid, our Bibles were
falſe: I asked wherein? The Fryar ſaid, Maccabees was not in them.
I ſaid, if any were taken from them, yet the reſt might be pure; but if
any were added to them, then they were corrupted. He askt me, Whether

ther I did not think it meet for every one to bow at the Name of *Jesus*. I said, *Yea*. He said, *Jesus*, and bid me fall down, or bow my body. I told him, My heart and whole body was bowed under the Name of *Jesus*; but should not stoop to his will, nor any man's else: He that departeth from iniquity, boweth to the Name of *Jesus*; but those that live in sin and wickedness, do not stoop to the Son of God. And he told me, they stood in the same Power the Apostles did, and were guided by the same Spirit as they were. I asked why they did abuse their Power then, and make use of Carnal Weapons; He said they did not, they were all spiritual, their Inquisition, & their Chains   * The wise and Irons, and all is spiritual *. And he asked, Whether   may judge. we judged them all damn'd that were not of our Judgement. I said, Nay, we had otherwise learned Christ; those that were in a Reprobate condition to day, the Lord may call them out of it to morrow, for what I know. He said, They did judge us damn'd, and all that were not of their Faith. I told him, Man's Judgement we did not matter.

A VISION.

IN a Vision of the night I saw in the Firmament six Suns, one at a distance from the rest, that did appear to be but half an hour high; the other five stood four-square, one in the middle, and they did cross over each other; the highest did not seem to be above an hour high. And when I did awake, I was troubled in my spirit to know the Vision; and I waited upon the Lord, and he signified to me in the Light, The six Suns were six Nations, whose Lights were near out; and the five which crossed each other, signified to me some rising amongst them.

And the Fryar came to me, and said, *It was God's will we should be kept there, or else they could not keep us.* I told him the Lord did suffer wicked men to do wickedly, but did not will them to do it. He did suffer *Herod* to take off *john Baptist's* head, but he did not will him to do it; and did suffer *Stephen* to be stoned, and *Judas* to

F   betray

betray Christ, but he did not will them to do it; for if he had, he would not have condemned them for it. He said, *Then we are wicked men*: I said, They are wicked men that work wickedness. The Fryar would say still, *We had not the true Faith.* We said, By Faith we stand, and by the Power of God we are upholden; dost thou think it is by our own power and holiness we are kept from a vain conversation, from sin and wickedness? He said, *That was our pride.* We said, No, We could glory in the Lord, we were children of wrath once as well as others; But the Lord hath quickned us that were dead, by the living Word of his Grace, and hath washed, cleansed and sanctified us through soul and spirit, in part, according to our measures, and we do press forward towards that which is perfect. He then did say, *We were good Women, but yet there was no redemption for us except we would be Catholicks.*

Now the Lord said, *Fear not Daughters of Sion, I will carry you forth as Gold tryed out of the fire.* And many precious promises did the Lord refresh us with, in our greatest extremity, and would appear in his glory, that our souls would be ravished in his presence; I had the Spirit of Prayer upon me, and I was afraid to speak to the Lord, for fear I should speak one word that would not please him. And the Lord said *Fear not Daughter of Sion, ask what thou wilt, and I will grant it thee, whatsoever thy heart can wish.* I desired nothing of the Lord but what would make for his glory, whether it were my liberty or bondage, life or death, wherein I was highly accepted of the Lord.

The Room wherein I was separated, was near the Chancery, where all the Bishops Courtiers did resort, and would come into the Inquisition Courts, and I had Work amongst them daily; they would come on purpose to their condemnation : some would be smitten, and run as if they hunted; and some would be set on fire, and cry, *Caldere, caldere*, and *fuoco, fuoco*, and many would pitty us because we were not Catholicks ; the Fryars would say, *We might be Catholicks, and keep our own Religion too : and we should not be known we were Catholicks, except we were brought before a Justice of Peace.* We askt if we should profess a Christ we should be asham'd of ?

But as for the poor Workmen, they were willing to do any thing for us, and were diligent to hear us, the Witness of God in them

'them did answer to the truth; there were many eyes over them; had it not been for the great opposition, there were hundreds would have flown to the truth.

And because I said I did talk with *G.F.* he (the Fryar) asked, *Whether* G.F. *did bring me money to maintain me in prison;* I said, no, but though I was absent in body, yet I was present in spirit, and was refreshed in him, and in hundreds more besides. They said, *I had seen Revelations, and had talkt with* G. F. *and he was God's Revelation.* Sarah said, Christ was God's Revelation; he said, *she came under the Halter for saying Christ was God's Revelation.* She answered, St. *Paul* said, *As soon as it pleased God to reveal his Son in me, I did not consult with flesh and blood, but immediately I went and preacht him;* and is not Christ God's Revelation then? He said, *who denyed that?*

What they would have done to *Sarah* if they had taken her forth, we know not; but the Lord did work so wonderfully that night for the preservation of her poor soul out of their net, that he is worthy to be glorified for ever.

The next time he came to me, he came in sheeps clothing, but he had a Woolf under his Gown; he gave me words as soft as Butter, and as smooth as Oyl, when he had a Sword in his heart, and a Spear in his hand, when they speak most fairest, then beware of them.

He desired us *we would not think so hardly of him, as if he were the Author of all our wrongs and troubles; he was not* (he said) *but would do any good he could for us, were it with his blood.* But we thought he had been the chiefest that cast the poor man in prison, but he was the man that hope him out without any punishment at all, though the Inquisitor did say he should be severely punished. I told him he did well, he would have peace in it, and would never have cause to repent it. He did entreat us, *he might not bear all the burthen.* We told him of many wicked things he did act against us, and of his lying and cruel words. He bid us, *take no notice what he did speak.* But we did feel his spirit, that what he spake, he would do, if he had not been chained. I did use to tell him, My Conscience was not seared with a hot iron, I was not past feeling. At last he was so weary of coming to us, he did entreat the Inquisitor he might not come to us any more; the Judgements of the Lord did follow him fo, it was like to kill him.

When we were parted, the Lord did vvork mightily for us, and we vvere kept by the Power of the Lord over our Enemies, and vvere bold for God's Truth, and did make war vvith them in righteoufnefs, fo that they could not gain-fay us in the truth: So that Scripture was fulfilled, *The wicked mouths muft be ftopped*; and they vvere put to filence, praifes be to our God, and were made to confefs or fay, *Of a truth God was in us*; our God was a confuming fire to them, they were not able to ftand in his prefence, but they vvould howl and make a noife like Dogs, and cry, *Jefu, Maria*, and flye as people driven by a mighty rufhing Wind; the Power of the Lord did purfue after them like a Svvord; that Scripture was fulfilled, which faith, *Chrift came not to fend peace on earth, but a fword*, to cut down his Enemies; the Lord was on our fide, and did take our part, and did fight for us, and did tread down our Enemies under our feet, that they could not hurt us. Mighty vvas the Work of God daily, our tongues cannot exprefs it; they did vvork day and night vvith their Inchantments and Divinations, Sorceries, unclean, Spirits crying and foaming, infomuch we could take little reft day or night fometimes; but the Lord vvas vvith us, and did work mightily by his power, and kept us over them in the life of the Son of God. My Prifon was nigh to the Pallace, and to their Worfhip, that I could be heard of both; and it was laid upon me of the Lord, to call them to repentance, and to turn to the Light vvherevvith they vvere enlightned, vvhich would lead them out of all their wicked Ways, Works and Worfhips, to ferve the true and living God in fpirit and in truth; the Power did raife the Witnefs in many, and troubled them; they did figh and groan; and fome did ftay to hear me, to long as they durft; for there were many did watch; and it was upon pain of death, or at leaft to be imprifoned: As was the poor *Englifh* man that did come and fpeak to me, whom they hail'd down violently, and put him in prifon; but the Lord delivered him for his love.

And we were parted near a year, but great was the Work of the Lord, and great was the Power to carry it on. He was not wanting to us, glory be to his Name; but did give us Words and Wifdom according to our Work: So that Scripture was fulfilled which faith on this wife, *Ye need not premeditate afore-hand what* to speak, or what to say ; for it shall be given you of my Heavenly Father what ye ought to speak , that the Enemies shall not gain-say; they were so tormented, that they did run to the Hills and to the Mountains to cover them from the presence of the Lord , and from the Wrath of the Lamb which sits upon the Throne to judg them righteously, and to condemn them for all their wicked deeds which they so ungodlily had committed against him.

Oh the goodness of the Lord, and his long-suffering and forbearance which would lead them to repentance, but they would not hearken to his counsel, but turned his laws behind their backs, and hated to be instructed by them; therefore the Lord did laugh at their destruction, and did mock when their fear came : Their wickedness was so great, and my burthens so heavy to bear it that I cryed to the Lord, and said , It is better for me to dye, than to live; and would gladly have given up my life in testimony against them all; I was (as twere) compell'd to declare against all their ways, works and worships, insomuch that they ran to the Inquisitor to have me chained, or punished some other way ; but the Power of the Lord chained them, that they could not diminish a hair of my head; the Lord was my safety, praises be to his Name for ever.

Now some as they passed to their Worship Houses , would sigh, and some pray, and some did throw stones at my Window; they did work night and day about the Prison , as though they would have broke through to slay me ; but the Lord was with me, and did fight for me, and did scatter his Enemies as the dust before the Wind : Glory be to his Name for evermore.

I cannot express the large love of our God, how he did preserve us from so many deaths and threatnings , as they did come to me with falling down upon their knees , saying Mass , and would have me to say after them; but in the Name of the Lord I denied them. They would howle like Dogs , because they could not beguile the innocent, and slay my righteous life; but praises be to the Lord our God, who did preserve me from the Wools and the Devourers, denying them and their Sacrifices.

And when they saw they could not prevail to betray us from the truth, then they said , they would give us to the Devil to be tormented, and deliver us over to their bad Catholicks, to do by us as they

pleased.

pleafed; for they would ufe us badly, and fo they did feek to do:
Oh the curfed noifes and cryes the *Sodomites* did make, crying,
Quake, Quake; running about the Prifon raging, and fome finging and crouding round the Prifon night and day, as if they
would have broke through to flay me; and the fons of *Belial* did
run to bear falfe witnefs, fo that I looked every hour when they
would fetch me out, and flay me. The Enemy did fo work to
perfwade, that they had preft my dear yoke-fellow with ftones,
vvhich vvas a great trouble to me, becaufe I could not fuffer death
with her ; I did yeild fhe had been flain : And afterwards this
great tribulation being ended, then they faid my (dear and faithful) yoke-fellow fhould be fent to *Rome*, and I fhould tarry at
Malta, which did fo encreafe my forrow, and wrought upon my
fpirit to try and examine wherefore the Lord fhould deal fo hardly with me, as to leave me behind; or whether he did not count
me worthy to go and give in my teftimony vvith her to *Rome*, and
offer up my life for the Teftimony of Jefus, than to have my liberty to return to *England* vvith her, and I cryed day and night
to the Lord, and vvould not give my foul reft, nor my eyes fleep,
till the Lord did anfvver me; glory and praifes be to his Name for
ever. But vve favv *Jacob* muft part vvith all, *Benjamin* muft go too.
So vve vvere vvilling to give up in obedience to the Lord; our
trials were unfpeakable. Oh the unclean fpirits ! they vvould
fpeak to us at noon-day ; but the Lord did give us power over
them, that we did not fear the wild Bores out of the Wood, nor
the vvild Beafts out of the Field.

Then there vvas one came and faid, that *Catherine and I muft*
be fent both to Rome; Which did rejoice my foul, and renevved my
ftrength, becaufe the Lord did count me Worthy to go and give
in my Teftimony for his Truth, the Word of his Prophefie, before
the great and mighty ones of the Earth. The Lord faid, *I fhould not*
be afraid; and he fhevved me in the Light how he had bowed them
down before us, and faw them in the Light of Chrift, how the Pope,
the Fryars and Sorcerers ftood in ranks, bowing dovn before us.
So we faw our Dominion in Spirit: They did work to fend us to
Rome, but the Lord did blaft it, and fought againft them, that they
could not fend us.

Now

Now our Testimony was as largely given in at *Rome*, as at *Malta*: The Fryars came to me, and shewed me *Mary* and her Babe pictured against the Wall, and would have me look upon it. I stampt with my foot and said, Cursed be all Images and Image-makers, and all that fall down to worship them, Christ Jesus is the express Image of his Fathers brightness, which is Light and Life, who doth reveal the mysterie of iniquity, the cunning working of Satan, to draw out the mind to follow him, from the pure life, and to veil over the Just One from beholding the Presence of the Lord. But glory be to the Lord, who hath made him manifest in thousands of his, in this Day of His Power, When we were separated, we spake one and the same thing, being guided by one Spirit. They would go from me to *Catharine*, they would bid her speak as *Sarah* did, and so she did to their condemnation: Praises to the Lord, *Amen*.

A Paper sent from them to the Pope's Lord Inquisitor in MALTA.

For the Lord Inquisitor and his Council, &c.

MEns persons I cannot admire; they that do admire and respect any man's person, do it because of advantage; and such are transgressors, the Apostles (*St.* James and Jude) say.

In obedience to the Lord, in love to your souls, from the Fountain of Love, and Springs of Life that stream forth to the refreshment of the whole City of God, am I constrained to visit you with these few Lines; and I beseech you to read it with the Spirit of Moderation and Meekness, and see that nothing in you arise up against it, for it is God's Truth.

Christ Jesus who is the Light of the world, which hath enlightned every one that cometh into the world, saith, This is Life eternal, To know thee the onely true God, and Jesus Christ whom thou hast sent.

sent. Now the knowledge of God is Life Eternal; and there is no other way to come to this knowledge, but to have the mind turned from darkness to the Light, out of the visible, to that which is invisible, viz. the Light in the Conscience, which convinceth of sin and iniquity, when no mortal eye can see you; and as you come to love it, and to have your minds staid upon it, you will feel the incomes of God's Power to administer condemnation upon the transgressor, that keeps the pure Seed in bondage in you; For Sion is redeemed through Judgement, and her Converts with Righteousness.

Saint Paul saith, If thou believest in thy heart the Lord Jesus, and confessest with thy mouth that God hath raised him from the dead, thou shalt be saved; for with the heart man believeth unto salvation; and we do believe, and see, and taste, and handle of the good Word of Life, and have received the Spirit of Truth, to lead us into all truth, and doth bring all things to our remembrance, without any visible thing. And Saint Paul wrote to the Galatians, saying, My little Children, of whom I travel in birth till Christ be formed in you. Where Christ is formed within, there needs no form without; the outward form is called an Earthen Vessel, or an Earthen Tabernacle, or an Earthen House; but Christ Jesus is the express Image of his Father's Glory (or Substance) which is Light and Life.

Now the Image of Christ is a pure and a holy Image, a meek and a Dove like Image, an innocent and a Lamb like Image, a righteous and a glorious Image, Christ in you the hope of glory, saith the Apostle to the Saints.

The Lord our God hath given to every man a measure of the manifestation of his own Spirit to profit withall, which is the Light in the Conscience, the true Teacher of his People; it is the Grace of God that bringeth salvation, that appeareth to all men, and it teacheth all that come, to believe in it, and to love, and to be guided by it, to deny all ungodliness and worldly lusts, and to walk soberly, righteously, holy and godly in this present world; and it will deal plainly with every one; none need to fear being deceived by that in them which doth condemn them for sin and evil: But they that live in pride, are deceived already; they that live in covetousness, are deceived already; and they that live in Lusts or Drunkenness, are deceived already; or in Lying, Swearing, Adultery or Idolatry, are deceived; or in Hypocrisie and Deceit, hard heartedness or Cruelty, they are deceived already; for their

you

you know, are fruits which do proceed from a deceived heart, being corrupted for want of knowledge: My people perish for want of knowledge (saith God) He that hath not the spirit of Christ, is none of his, and he that hath the Spirit of Christ, ought himself to walk as Christ walked: Now Christ was no persecutor, he never imprisoned any, nor ever put any to suffer, but he and the holy Prophets and Apostles were made to suffer as evil doers, this we know.

The Day of the Lord is hot and terrible against all sin and iniquity, and that nature from whence it doth proceed; and we are a WO for all them that are laying up of a Fuel for it: This is God's Truth, whether you can receive it, yea or nay, I am ready to seal it with my blood, if the Lord shall call me to it.

Whosoever shall interpret this Paper before the Lord Inquisitor, (so called) I charge thee in the Name of the living God, as thou wilt answer before his dreadful presence, to interpret it word by word, as it is written, without adding or diminishing.

Katharine Evans.

THe Fryar then came to me, and askt me, why I did not work? I said unto him, What Work dost thou do? He said he did write. I told him I would write too, if he would bring me a Pen, Ink and Paper; and I would write truth. He said, He would not that we should write; for St. Paul did work at Rome, and we might get nine or ten grains a day, if we would knit, that is three half pence. I told him, if we could have that priviledge amongst them, that St. Paul had at Rome under Cæsar, which was a Heathenish King, we would have wrought, and not have been chargeable to any. St. Paul lived in his own hired House two years, with a Souldier to look to him and had friends of the same Occupation to work with him, and could send where he would, and whosoever would come to him, might, and he taught them in the Name of the Lord Jesus, and no man forbad him. So I askt him, Whether he knew the holy War of God, yea or nay? if he did, I told him he then did know we could not be without exercise day nor night. Then his mouth

G

was

was stopped, and he spake no more to me of work : But though. our affliction of body was very great, and our travel of soul was greater, yet we did knit Stockins , and give to them that were made serviceable to u., and did make Garments for the poor prisoners, and mended their Clothes which had need, and were made helpful to them all, to their condemnation , that did persecute us. But we could not vvork at the Fryar's Will , nor any man's else, but as we had freedom in the Lord.

As I vvas vveak in my bed , the Fryar came to me, and said *We did deny the Scriptures*: I told him , they did deny them , we did own them, and hold them forth, thou dost know it : He was in a rage because I said , they denyed the Scriptures, bid me *eat my words again, and threatned death upon me*. I said , Christ Jesus was the Light of the World, and had lighted every one that cometh into the World, which Light is our salvation that do receive it, and the same Light is the World's condemnation that do not believe in it. Then he said, *He would lay me in Chains, where I should neither see Sun nor Moon*. They say, *The* Father *hath almost killed you*, said he, *but I will kill you quite, before I have done*. He had a Book in his hand, and he did study in it; I told him he did comprehend the Words in his carnal mind, and he vvas vvrath , and said *he would give me to the Devils to be tormented*. I said, I deny the Devil and all his Works and Workers.

Some would come unto the Prison upon their Saints days, and ask us *what day it was*? We did answer, We did not know, neither did we observe dayes nor times, months nor years. Then answer would be made, *It was St.* Joseph's *day*, or some other Saint ; and, *St:* Joseph *should punish us that night, because we did not observe his day*. We answered , We did know the Saints to be at peace with us, and we did not fear them. We further said, St. *Paul* did call it beggarly Elements and Rudiments of the World, to observe days, times, months and years; and their mouths vvould be stopt for a time. Then came the Fryar another time, and told me, *it was seventeen dayes to their Christmas*, and said, *the Virgin Mary conceived with child that day*, being the same day he spake to me on; as if she did go with Child but seventeen dayes. And he said , *the next day was Lady Ann's day, the Virgin Mary's Mother, a Saint.*

I was

Then as I was crying to the Lord in Prayer becaufe of our longfuffering, & our ftrong travel & labour, & no fruit (as did appear),
the Lord faid unto me, *Be not grieved, though Ifrael be not gathered;
the feed of* Malta *fhall be as the ftars of the skie for multitude: That
which ye have fown, fhall not dye, but live : Glory be to the Name of
the Lord for ever.*

A Copy of a Writing from their hands, fent in purfuit after the Fryar.

MALACHY;

THou faidft thou wouldft try whether we had the true Spirit, yea or
nay, and thou haft tryed day and night, but thou never triedft the
right way; the Seed of God is not tryed with deceit, lying, hypocrifie,
nor cruelty : But if thou hadft turned in with thy mind to the Light of
God in thy Confcience, thou wouldft foon have known us; or had the
love of Chrift been fhed abroad in thy heart, thou might'ft have
comprehended us ; or hadft thou found the Ballance of the Sanctuary of
the true Tabernacle, which God hath pitched, and not man, thou mightft
have weighed us ; or hadft thou laid Judgement to the Line, and Righteoufnefs to the Plummet, thou might'ft have fathomed us ; or could'ft
thou have opened the Book of Life, thou might'ft have read us; or hadft
thou went into the Houfe of Ifrael, thou might'ft have had fellowfhip
with us, &c. Contrary to our wills were we caft in amongft you, and
have given our teftimony for the Lord, and called you all to repentance, and have forewarned you of the evil the Lord is bringing upon
you; but you have flighted the day of your vifitation, and have done de-
fpite to the Spirit of Grace, and have caft many hard fpeeches and falfe
afperfions upon the Truth, and the Meffengers thereof, and the Lord will
vifit for thefe things; and you have blinded your eyes that you will not
fee, and ftopped your ears that you might not hear, and hardened
your hearts that you might not underftand; leaft you fhould fee
with your eyes, and hear with your ears, and underftand with your
hearts, and turn to the Lord, and be converted, and he fhould heal you.
Oh that you had known in this your day, what had belonged to your
peace; but now it is hid from your eyes. The defire of our fouls is, That

G 2   every

every one may repent that can find a place; and whatever you have done to us, we desire it may not be laid to your charge; for we count our selves happy that we were found worthy to suffer for the Name of the Lord.

Written in the Inquisition-Prison   *Katharine Evans,*
   in the Isle of *Malta.*   *Sarah Chevers.*

Behold victorions Hymns, Songs, Praifes, all in Verfe,
the fame fprung from the Seed of Life, its perfect Righteoufnefs.

OH Lord my life is given up,
thy truth for to declare;
Lord keep me in thy Arms,
and guide me in thy fear.
Thy Bow is bent, thy Sword is
thy enemies to deface, (drawn
Thy fire's kindl'd 'gainft all thofe
that Truth wil not embrace.
Thine Arrows fharp and keen,
upon their heads fhall fall,
Thy double-edged Sword alfo,
to cut them down withall.
So plague the Heathen, & correct
the people in thy wrath, (Name
That they may fear & dread thy
and come to know thy truth.
Throughout the World fo wide,
thy truth thou doft declare,
Thy faving health for to enjoy,
by thy Light doth appear.
Thou doft fend forth thy Meffen-
glad tydings to proclaim, (gers.

To call the hungry forth to feed
on thy Lamb being flain.
Feafts of fat things thou doft pre-
the hungry for to feed, (pare
And cloath the nak'd with Garments fair, (drawn
that want and ftand in need.
Heaven's glory is appearing,
its brightnefs fhineth forth,
Over all Nations it is clearing,
the Lords Eternal Truth.
Every one that's in darknefs,
and under its fhadow lye,
May come forth into the bright-
out of obfcurity. (nefs,
Oh Lord teach me thy wayes,
that I may walk therein,
And lead me in thy Path of life,
and cleanfe me from all fin,
How gracious is our God,
and kind to Ifrael,
With us he doth make his A-
his prefence doth us fill. (bode,

So

So that we are not desolate,
  nor yet distrest with woes,
Because the Lord doth take our
    part,
  and doth confound our foes,
Every one that is opprest
  and cast in danger deep,
If that in God they put their
  he will them safely keep. (trust,
Right dear and precious to the
  are all his little ones,   (Lord
That suffer for his holy Name,
  he will avenge their wrongs,
And in his wrath he will destroy
  his enemies so stout,
And suddenly will make a way,
  and lead his servants out.
And he himself will them restore
  to joy and comfort both,
And will preserve them ever-
    more,
  because they do him love.
But as for men of corrupt minds
  whose wayes defiled are,
The Lord will visit with all
    kinds
  of judgments, and not spare.
He will pursue them with his
    Sword,
  and cut them to the ground,
That do reject his holy Word,
  his Plagues shall them con-
    found,
Because that they do not obey
  his Mercies and his Grace,
Which he so free to them doth
    give
  if they would them embrace.

But as their Fathers did,
  so they requite the Lord with
    wrong,
And persecute thy Messengers,
  and make them suffer long
Because that they the Truth de-
  as Scripture telleth plain, clare
That Christ himself, th: Lord's
    own Heir,
  is come, and he will reign
Both Lord, and Prince, and King
    also,
  throughout the World, that's
    wide,
And Antichrist will overthrow,
  and Babel in her pride :
It's not their golden Candle-
    sticks,
  nor Lamps that be so many,
That can shine through the
    Clouds so thick,
  to give a Light to any.
To lead to a true resting-place,
  where they may still behold
The beauty of God's glorious
    face,
  more bright than fined Gold.
Thou seest oh Lord, what man
    hath done
  for to exalt himself
Against the Lord thy blessed
    Son,
  who is our saving health.
They have changed his glorious
    Form
  and Image that's so bright,
And fashion'd it like sinful man,
  corrupted in thy sight,
                         Arise

Arise oh Lord, arise in haste,
and punish for these things,
These men that have sought thy
disgrace,
that they might reign as Kings
Over thine own Inheritance,
contrary to thy will,
To keep them still in ignorance,
without knowledge or skill.
But now the God of Power is
come,
to raise up Sion bright,

And to build up Jerusalem
in all the Heathens sight,
The Gates of Hell shall not prevail,
though they be wide & strong,
Against the gathering in of all
that to the Lord belong.
All glory, honor, laud and praise
be to the Lord of Might,
Who hath made known in these
our dayes,
his Way, his Truth, his Light.

Concerning the Cross of Christ, which is not a visible sign, or a piece of Wood, but the invisible and immortal Power of the Lord God, and his Wisdom unto salvation, to and in all them that believe, is the same Christ, the Power of God, and the wisdom of God: But the same Crosse is to the outward Jew, (or Christian, a stumbling-block, and to the wise Greek (that's exalted and puft up in the knowledge above, and over the meek life) foolishness, as saith the Scripture, 1 Cor. 1, 18, 19.

CHrist's Cross I do embrace,
Which gives me an entrance
into Grace;
Sin and Death it doth deface,
And makes me run a glorious
race,
A Crown of Life and Grace I do
obtain,
And sin and death is daily slain,
And Christ himself alone to reign
Through the Cross I do obtain.

The Cross of Christ is more
to me
Than all the Treasures I can see:
It brings me to my resting place
For to behold God's lovely face,
The Cross of Christ is Power in-
deed
Against the Serpent and his seed.
And salvation it doth bring
To all that do believe therein.

The

The Cross of Christ is my delight,
It doth uphold me day and night;
It keeps me from the power of sin,
Through Christ who is my Heavenly King.

Without the Cross I cannot be
From sin and death at all set free,
The Cross alone doth crucifie
Transgression, sin, iniquity.
It doth break down the middle Wall,
And slays the enmity withall:
And makes of twain one perefect man,
And so renews Christ for me again.
The Cross of Christ it doth destroy
That Nature that doth disobey,
In those that do themselves deny,
And take it up most willingly,
And daily bear it after him,
Who is our Lord, and Prince, and King;
And not at all to let it down,
Till they come to enjoy the Crown.

The Cross of Christ is power and life,
It doth destroy all mortal strife;
It keepeth from the Power of sin,
All those that love to walk therein.
All that do own Christ Jesus Cross,
Through self-denial they must pass,
For to be purged from their sin,
And no longer live therein.
The Cross of Christ doth operate
Through every vein and vital part,
The heart and reins to cleanse from sin,
Of them that's exercis'd therein.
They that live in sin and wickedness,
are enemies to Christ Jesus Cross;
For all sin and uncleanness doth pierce the life of Christ Jesus.

Per

Perfect Love, and breathings of undefiled Life, to the Seed of God, greeting.

THe ſtreams of beauty, pure
   and bright,
That ſpringeth up both ¡day and
   night.
MY love to truth doth me con-
   ſtrain
In Priſon ever to remain;
If it be ſo that even I
Cannot in truth be ſet at liberty,
My deare Redeemer's face ſo
   bright,
Doth ſhine upon me day & night:
His count'nance doth exceed all
Captivity and bodage, thrall,
    Amen. K. E.

My Love,
It cometh from a harmleſs Dove,
Within vvhoſe breaſts doth ſtill
   remain
God's perfect praiſes to main-
   tain.
I have not time nor place to
   ſhovv
The love vvhich from my ſoul
   doth flovv.
The bleſſing of the Almighty be
   upon thee,
And upon the vvhole *Iſrael* of
   God, *amen.*

THeſe Writings follovving are Copies of divers Letters which they had written to their Friends and near Relations in the time of my viſitation of them: But it came ſo to paſs, that as they were handing the ſame through the Grare of the Priſon, by the hand of another man to be communicated to my hand, being then preſent in the Room alſo, that the ſaid Letters were Intercepted, and in the firſt place communicated to the Pope's Lord Inquiſitor, and he forthvvith ſent for the Conſul, and charged him to get the ſame truly copied forth. Then the Conſul vvas vvrath vvith me that he ſhonld be exerciſed vvith ſo much trouble: But in the Light and Counſel of my God I ſeeing and knovving that there vvas nothing in them but vvhat came from a good ground of innocency and truth, and pure natural affecti- on, I was moved in bovvels of tender love, leſt the ſaid Letters ſhould be finally miſcarried, or ſhut up in obſcurity, therefore I
                               pro-

propounded to the Consul, If that were such a trouble to him,
if he would let me have the Letters, I should copy them out truly. And after some time he consented, and gave them into my
hand, and laid it upon my Conscience to perform as I had said,
which I did with gladness of heart, not in submission to his Will,
but in obedience to the God of Love and Peace which guided me
in the same; and so after I had finished them, I gave the fair Copies into the Consul's hands for his Lord Inquisitor.

And so in the wisdom of the Lord, which is wiser than the Serpents, I obtained the very desire of my heart for his Truth and
Peoples sake, and retained the Original Copies, and in the endless Love and Power of the Lord Almighty, which was, and is
with me, and accompanied me (blessed and magnified be the Power of his excellent Majesty and Glory, *amen*) over the heads
of the lofty Mountains, and barren Hills, I brought the Treasures of a blessed and good ground away with this body in which
I am; so that they were not onely in my hands, but also the precious substance and virtue of the same that accompanied them,
even in my heart, within my bosom; and the Words of Wisdoms
Life did I wear as a Chain of precious Stones and Diamonds about
my neck, and as Bracelets and Ornaments of a comely and deli-
cate chaste Bride, about my hands and loins; and behold the Almighty Lord and King of Eternal Life, that had so mightily preserved me in the shadow of his hand of Almightiness, which stopt
the mouths of devouring Lyons, and chained and limited the ravening and devouring wild Beasts of the Forrest, even he the
King of blessedness and endless glory, filled my heart with his
spotless and unexpressible Love: And as I lay upon the deck of the
Vessel in which I was a passenger, and a stranger among men of
many and divers Nations, in the morning of the day I felt and
beheld the exceeding glory of the Lord under the secret shadow
of his Almightiness, in a Vision of God; and in the same I beheld
the Bride, the Lamb's Wife, prepared for the Bridegroom's coming; and why should not I declare somewhat of the felicity that
mine eye in the Eternal Life of Blessedness saw, albeit the rest is
unutterable which I felt; and know how to be silent in the Father's presence, where every Babe knoweth my voice, which is to
give a sound in their ears to whom I write; and not to spread

o I   H   Pearls

Pearls before Swine, that will defile and trample on them; That mine eye, mine eye hath seen, and perfectly beheld the Free-born from above, coming out of the Wilderness, covered with goodly and comely Raiment, white and clean, as the light of the Sun, or as a Stone most precious, clear as Chrystal, and mine eye beheld a Crown which was embraced in the Arms of the Bridegroom, and the Crown was well adorned with many Stars which did excel each other in glory, and mine eye beheld the Son as a Bride groom rejoicing over the Virgin-Bride of his Espousal, so that I was even sick with pure and undefiled love. Mine eye, mine eye did so affect my heart, so that I awaked in the same, in the morning of a clear day, and I looked, and behold the Sun was arisen above the *Horizon* of the Earth and Waters, and my Life abundantly blessed and magnified the living Lord, my King and my God, the Rock of my strength, and saving-health of his Annointed, and behold *I* had seen a Vision of God in the morning-Light, and the sweet *solution* of the same was given me to treasure up within my very heart, till an appointed time and season; the children of the Morning-light may right-well read the same as they sit together in their several places that's over and above the earth, and be comforted and refreshed at the joyful sound of the same voice that brings the glad tydings of the good things; yea and my Spirit with you the blessed of the Lord, shall bless his Name who is the mighty God in the midst of us: Even so *Amen*, *Hal-le-lu-jah.*

Praise ye the Lord, Salvation to his Name,	Among his Saints & Messengers, His fame my heart shall sound,
Ye Saints in Life,	Because their life
Free from all strife,	is free from strife,
Your voice sound forth the same	*In* love that doth abound.
My Life shall sing	My prayers in the life that's
To *Sion*'s King,	clean,
His Love in peace and glory,	shall from the same ascend,
Who hath so free	Unto the God of Love and
Begotten me,	peace,
Into his Life that's holy,	that he may you defend,

To

To perfect love and unity ,
  that it may more abound;
    for so your fame
    in his pure Name
Doth give a certain sound.

Unto the Nations round about,
  your fame aloud shall sing ,
    to call them all
    both great and small,
To bow to *Sion*'s King.

  Your Gates alwayes
  (Of perfect praise)
Full wide shall open stand,
  that all may come
  i'th free-born Son
(Th' *Light*)to dwel in your Land

  Of rest and peace
  in righteousness,
I'th living way that s holy;
  so you shall sing,
  and fruit shall spring
Within the City holy.

  The Vine that's true,
  shall compass you
That sit under his shade ,

with great delight
in his clear sight ,
None shal make you afraid.

Within the perfect love here is
  no fear,
So in the Father's sight you are
  right dear.

My bowels and my soul, my very heart
To you ye living Saints extends;
  much could *I* write
  in the true light ,
But ye can read my Friends,

Without a Book of words
Which finally may end;
  My mind that's clean,
  Come read the same,
Behold *I* am your friend.
In Jacob's Land
Where he did stand.
I'th place that's blest ,
Where he did rest,
Who like a Prince prevail'd
  with the true Lord of Might,
Who also blessed him
  even in the morning-Light,
      Selah.

And seeing that it happened so, that the Copies of the Letters of the Lords Prisoners, were left in the hands of their Enemies, in a strange Land, it is seen meet to insert them among the rest of their Writings , for the good of many of their own Nation of *England*, who may right-well favour the tender love and virtue of true and pure natural affection , not onely to their kindred and Fathers House, but also to their own Countrey; all of which they were truly called to forsake, as was good old *Abraham* our Father,

H 2   who

who in obedience to the good Word and Commandment of the Almighty God, went forth, not knowing whither he went, even as these poor, and many more, who are deemed by the wise of this world, foolish things, not well considering how that the Lord hath chosen the poor of this world, and made them rich in faith, and also chuseth base things, and weak things, and foolish things, to confound the things that are mighty, and to bring to nought things that are, to the end that no flesh should glory in his presence, who with his mighty hand and outstretched arm of Dignity and excellent Power, is defacing and staining the pride of all glory, and bringing into contempt all the honorable of the Earth that's out of order, and bringing down the haughtiness and loftiness of man, who shall know that it is the everlasting and terrible God of Eternity, when he ariseth to shake terribly the Earth, that presseth down and oppresseth the Seed of his Bowels, and trampleth on the principal Wheat that came out of the good Husband-mans right hand, for which the God of Heaven is visiting the Nations as in the ancient days: Albeit he hath long time held his peace in the habitation of his Holiness, where his Honor dwelleth; but behold, behold, he is arising in the greatness of his strength, even as a Lyon over his prey, or as a Lyonness bereaved of her young; for out of *Sion* hath he uttered his voice, and thundered forth the Majesty of his powerful Word of Salvation, through the Gate of his beloved City *Jerusalem* from on high, free-born; which hath ecchoed into the ears & hearts of the Hypocrites, & surprized the double-minded with fear on every hand; for he hath cryed, and yet will, in the spirit of his Prophesie through his Sons and Daughters, in whom he which is holy dwelleth, to make waste Mountains and Hills, and to devour at once as in the ancient dayes; and my spirit saith, Even so the Lord hasten it (*Amen*) for his Elects sake.

Katha-

Katharine Evans *to her Husband and Children.*

For the hand of *JOHN EVANS*, my right dear and precious Husband, with my tender-hearted Children, who are more dear and precious unto me, than the apple of mine eye.

*M*Ost *dear and faithful Husband, Friend and Brother, begotten of my Eternal Father, of the immortal Seed of the Covenant of Light, Life and Blessednesse, I have unity and fellowship with thee day and night, to my great refreshment and continual comfort, praises, praises be given to our God for evermore, who hath joined us together in that which neither Sea nor Land can separate or divide.*

My dear heart, my soul doth dearly salute thee, with my dear and precious Children, which are dear and precious in the Light of the Lord, to thy endless joy, and my everlasting comfort; glory be to our Lord God, eternally, who hath called you with a holy Calling, and hath caused his Beauty to shine upon you in this the day of his Power, wherein he is making up of his Jewels, and binding up of his faithful ones in the Bond of everlasting Love and Salvation, among whom he hath numbred you of his own free Grace; in which I beseech you (dear hearts) in the fear of the Lord to abide in your measures, according to the manifestation of the Revelation of the Son of God in you; keep a diligent watch over every thought, word and action, and let your minds be staid continually in the Light, where you will find out the snares and baits of Satan, and be preserved out of his Traps, Nets and Pits, that you may not be captivated by him at his will. Oh my dear Husband and Children, how often have I poured out my soul to our everlasting Father for you, with Rivers of tears, night and day, that you might be kept pure and single in the sight of our God, improving your Talents as wise Virgins, having Oyl in your Vessels, and your Lamps burning, and cloathed with the long white Robes of Righteousness, ready to enter the Bed-Chamber, and to sup with the

Lamb

Lamb, and to feed at the Feast of fat things, where your souls may be nourished, refreshed, comforted, and satisfied, never to hunger again.

My dear hearts, you do not want teaching, you are in a Land of Blessedness, which floweth with Milk and Honey, among the faithful Stewards, whose mouths are opened wide in righteousness, to declare the Eternal Mysteries of the everlasting Kingdom, of the endless joys and eternal glory, whereinto all the willing and obedient shall enter, and be blessed for ever.

My dear hearts, the promises of the Lord are large, and are all Yea and Amen to those that fear his Name; he will comfort the Mourners in Sion, and will cause the heavy-hearted in Jerusalem to rejoice, because of the glad tydings; they that do bear the Cross with patience, shall wear the Crown with joy; for it is through the long suffering and patient waitings, the Crown of Life and Immortality comes to be obtained; the Lord hath exercised my patience, and tryed me to the uttermost, to his praise and my eternal comfort, who hath not been wanting to us in any thing in his own due time; We are Witnesses he can provide a Table in the Wilderness both spiritual and temporal. Oh the endless love of our God, who is an everlasting Fountain of all living refreshment; whose Chrystal streams never cease running to every thirsty soul, that breatheth after the springs of Life and Salvation.

In our deepest affliction, when I looked for every breath to be the last, I could not wish I had not come over Seas, because I knew it was my Eternal Father's Will to prove me, with my dear and faithful Friend; in all afflictions and miseries, the Lord remembred mercy, and did not leave nor forsake us, nor suffer his faithfulness to fail us, but caused the sweet drops of his mercy to distil upon us, and the brightness of his glorious countenance to shine into our hearts, and was never wanting to us in Revelations nor Visions. Oh how may I do to set forth the fulness of God's Love to our souls! No tongue can express it, no heart can conceive it, nor mind can comprehend it. Oh the ravishments, the raptures, the glorious bright-shining countenance of our Lord God, who is our fulness in emptiness our strength in weakness, our health in sickness, our life in death, our joy in sorrow, our peace in disquietness, our praise in heaviness, our power in all needs or necessities; He alone is a full God unto us, and to all that can trust him; he hath emptied us of our selves; and hath unbottomed us of our selves, and hath wholly built us upon the sure Foundation,

tion, the Rock of Ages, Chrift Jefus the Light of the world, where the fwelling Seas, nor raging, foaming Waves, nor ftormy winds, though they beat vehemently, cannot be able to remove us; Glory, honor and praifes is to our God for ever, who out of his everlafting Treafures doth fill us with his Eternal Riches day by day; he did nourifh our fouls with the choiceft of his mercies, and doth feed our bodies with his good Creatures, and relieve all our neceffities in a full meafure, praifes, praifes be to him alone, who is our everlafting portion, our confidence, and our rejoicing, whom we ferve acceptably with reverence and God-like fear; for our God is a confuming fire.

Oh my dear Husband and precious Children, you may feel the iffues of Love and Life which ftream forth as a River to every foul of you, from a heart that is wholly joined to the Fountain; my prayers are for you day and night without ceafing, befeeching the Lord God of Power to pour down his tender mercies upon you, and to keep you in his pure fear, and to encreafe your faith, to confirm you in all righteoufnefs, and ftrengthen you in believing in the Name of the Lord God Almighty, that you may be eftablifhed as Mount Sion, that can never be moved. Keep your fouls unfpotted of the world, and love one another with a pure heart, fervently ferve one another in love; build up one another in the Eternal, and bear one anothers burdens for the Seeds fake, and fo fulfil the Law of God. This is the Word of the Lord unto you, my dearly beloved.

Dear hearts, I do commit you into the hands of the Almighty, who dwelleth on high, and to the Word of his Grace in you, who is able to build you up to everlafting life, and eternal falvation. By me who am thy dear and precious Wife, and Spoufe, in the Marriage of the Lamb, in the bed unndefiled,   K. E.

My dearly beloved Yoak-mate in the Work of our God, doth dearly falute you; Salute us dearly to our precious Friends in all places. I do believe we fhall fee your faces again with joy. Dearly falute us to T.H. R.S. and his fifter, S.B. and his daughter, N.M. and his dear Wife, with all the reft of our dear Friends in Briftol. T.C. and his deart Wife and Daughter, and all Friends in Briftol or elfe-where. J.G. and his precious Wife, Children and Servants, with all Friends. Our dear love to E.H. with her Husband and Children at Alderberry.

The original of this was written in the Inquifition in Malta, in the 11th. Month of the year 1661.

                                        Sarah

Sarah Chevers to her Husband and Children.

MY Dear Husband, my love, my life is given up to serve the living God, and to obey his pure Call in the measure of the manifestation of his Love, Light, Life and Spirit of Christ Jesus, his onely
begotten Son, whom he hath manifested in me and thousands, by
the brightness of his appearing, to put an end to sin and Satan, and bring
to light Immortality through the preaching of the everlasting Gospel by
the Spirit of Prophesie, which is poured out upon the sons and daughters
of the living God, according to his purpose, whereof he hath chosen me,
who am the least of all; but God who is rich in mercy, for his own Name
sake hath passed by mine offences, and hath counted me worthy to bear
testimony to his holy Name before the mighty men of the Earth. Oh the
love of the Lord to my soul! my tongue cannot express, neither hath it
entered into the heart of man to conceive of the things that God hath
laid up for them that fear him.

Therefore doth my soul breath to my God for thee and my Children,
night and day, that your minds may be joined to the Light of the Lord
Jesus, to lead you out of Satans Kingdom, into the Kingdom of God,
where we may enjoy one another in the Life Eternal, where neither Sea
nor Land can separate; in which Light and Life do I salute thee my
dear Husband, with my Children, wishing you to embrace Gods love in
making his Truth so clearly manifest amongst you, whereof I am a Witness even of the everlasting Fountain that hath been opened by the Messengers of Christ, who preach to you the Word of God in season, and out
of season, directing you where you may find your Saviour to purge and
cleanse you from your sins, and to reconcile you to his Father, and to have
unity with him and all the Saints, in the Light, that ye may be fellow-
Citizens in the Kingdom of Glory, Rest and Peace, which Christ hath
purchased for them that love him, and obey him: What profit is there
for to gain the whole world, and lose your own souls? Seek first the Kingdom

dom of God, and the Righteousness thereof, and all other things shall be added to you; Godliness is great gain, having the promise of this life that now is, and that which is to come; which is fulfilled to me, who have tasted of the Lords endlesse love and mercies to my soul, & from a moving of the same love and life do I breath to thee my dear Husband, with my Children; my dear love salutes you all; my Prayers to my God are for you all, that your minds may be joined to the Light wherewith you are lightened, that I may enjoy you in that which is Eternal, and have community with you in the Spirit: He that is joined to the Lord, is one spirit, one heart, one mind, one soul, to serve the Lord with one consent. I cannot by Pen or Paper set forth the large love of God in fulfilling his gracious promises to me in the Wilderness, being put into prison for God's Truth, there to remain all days of my life, being searched, tryed, examined upon pain of death among the Enemies of God and his Truth; standing in jeopardy for my life, until the Lord had subdued and brought them under by his mighty Power, and made them to feed us, and would have given us money or clothes; but the Lord did deck our Table richly in the Wilderness; the day of the Lord is appearing, wherein he will discover every deed of darkness, let it be done never so secret; the light of Christ Jesus will make it manifest in every Conscience; the Lord will rip up all coverings that is not of his own Spirit. The God of Peace be with you all. Amen.

Written in the Inquisition-Prison by the hand of *Sarah Chevers*, for the hand of *Henry Chevers* my dear Husband; give this, fail not.

I do not well remember that this was one of the surprized Letters.

I   A

A Letter to a Kinswoman of S. C.

S. P.

MY dear Kinswoman, I dearly salute thee, with thy Husband, and thy tender Babes: I am not unmindful of thee, nor of thy love that thou shewedst to me; I know thou shalt not lose thy reward; thou hast found refreshment in it; for it was of the Lord; My Burthen was weighty for the Lord; I would have fled the Cross; but praises be to the Lord that kept me to it, that I might not lose the Crown. I was straitned in it, till I gave up to it; praised be the Name of our God for ever Amen. Stand fast in the Lord; let none take thy Crown, The God of Power preserve and keep thee low and single in his fear, pressing forward to the prize of an incorruptible Crown of Glory, Peace and Rest, out of all strife. Keep to the pure life, watch the Enemy; keep thy mind staid in the measure of God's Grace, that is able to make thee wise unto salvation, and to give thee an inheritance with the rest of the Children of Light. My tender lamb, fear and dread the living God; keep in his presence, go not out to let in the Enemy, to break thy peace, and to darken thy understanding, and to vail over the pure, from beholding thy Saviour: Incline thine ear to him, give up to a daily Cross to thy own will: Stand single, empty; wait upon the Lord to be fill'd with his fulness; let him be all thy treasure, ask of him, he giveth liberally. Believe, and thou shalt receive; his promise is large, I have found it so: Having nothing, yet enjoying all things. I have tasted, handled and felt of his everlasting love, and indurable Riches; my life is wrapt up in it; I have found him whom my soul loveth; Oh what might I do to set him forth! He is the choicest of ten thousands, therefore doth my soul love him:

My life is given up for him, his truth, for to declare;
Lord guide me in thy path, and keep me in thy fear. *Amen.*

Thy dear Aunt: My dear love and life is with thee, and I do embrase thee in the Arms and Bosom of my Eternal Father's love, with thy dear Husband and little ones.

Another

Another in the same Paper to Friends.

MY dearly beloved Sisters and Friends of Truth, I dearly
salute you in the Light, Life and Love of our God, which
is shed abroad in our hearts by the Holy Ghost, wherein
I do rejoice, and have union with you. My Life is given up to
serve the Lord. O how my soul travels for the Seed of God's
Kingdom to be sown throughout all Nations, for the gathering
in of Christ's scattered Flock, and for the destruction of sin and
Satan. For our God is weighing the Mountains in Skales, and
the Dust in equal an Ballance: He is a pulling down the mighty, and
raising the meek, humble, lowly; he is a feeding the poor and hungry with good things, but the rich he sends empty away. My dear
Babes and Lambs, feed of the sincere Milk of the Word of Life,
that you may grow up in it, and wax strong in spirit to praise the
Lord and to glorifie him who is worthy. Be strong in the Lord,
and in the Power of his Might; seek him earnestly, call upon him
continually; let your whole Meditations be staid in him alway.
Seek him earnestly, deny your own thoughts and words; give heed
to the Light, bring all your deeds to it; give up all that is contrary, to be slain; stand single, empty, naked before the Lord, that
you may be fill'd with the streams of his everlasting Love. Oh my
dear hearts ! our God is full of love; stand not back, press forward, let nothing hinder you; the Lord calls for you, *My Son,*
give me thy heart : The promise of our God is as large to you as
to any, if you can believe; your straitness is in your selves ; For
God is a full Fountain ; abundance of love runs forth to them
that can trust him, I can witness it ; in the barren Wilderness he
caused streams of living water to break forth : I cannot express
it is so large ; therefore doth my soul thirst after you, my dear
ones; the love of God is to you. My dear Sisters , I have you in
my remembrance, and do pray to my God and your God that
you may be enlarged in your measures to praise the Lord, and to
be kept in a sensible feeling of his power daily; and that you may

I 2   encrease

encreafe in Wifdom, Strength and Power over Gods Enemies; The Bleffing of the Lord God Almighty be with you, and preferve you by his Mighty Power, unto the coming of our Lord Jefus Chrift, *Amen.*

Salute me to my Sifter *S. R.* there is a tender Plant in her, I do feel it to my comfort, praifes be to the Lord. I am in health I praife the Lord, and do want nothing; the Lord is my portion, I cannot want; he hath deck't my Table richly, he hath annointed my head with Balm, it runneth down the skirts of my cloathing.

Written in the Inquifiti-
on-Prifon at the Ifle
of *Malta*, a fufferer   Your dear Sifter in the Lord,
for the Seeds fake. Fare-
wel at this time, *Amen.*   *S A R A H C H E V E R S.*

Another from *K. E.* to her Husband and Children, with fomewhat from both the Lords Prifoners, to Friends, the which was taken with the reft of the Letters, in the Inquifition, and copied out for their Lord Inquifitor.

DEar Husband, with my dear Children. I befeech you together, to wait in the patience, having your minds alwayes ftaid upon the Lord: Keep out of incumbrances, for that is the Enemies opportunity to ftep in, when the mind is gone forth, and to vail the pure and darken the underftanding, and fo hinder you of the pure enjoyment of the beholding the glory of God in the face of Jefus Chrift.

Take no more upon you then you are able to perform in the Spirit of moderation and meeknefs, for that is in the fight of God of of great prize: See the Lord going before you in all your occeafions, that you may be profperous in all your undertakings; wait diligently upon the Lord, to be feafoned with his Grace, that you may come to a pure underftanding of the motions

ons of his Eternal Spirit, and to a true knowledge of the operation of his hands; So you will be able with all Saints, to comprehend what is the heigth, and the depth, and the length, and the breadth of the riches of his Grace and Love towards mankind in Christ Jesus our Lord; *Amen,* saith my spirit : This is the counsel of the Lord unto you.

I do often remember *M.H.* I do desire she may be brought up in the fear of God, and want for nothing that is convenient for her ; salute me to her dearly. I have been very sensible, dear Husband of thine, and our Children, and many dear friends more, of your sorrowful souls, mourning hearts, grieved spirits, troubled minds for us, as being Members of one body, Christ Jesu being our Head, we must needs suffer together, that we may rejoice together; a true sorrow begets a true joy, a true Cross a true Crown. We do believe it is our heavenly Fathers will and purpose to bring us back as safe to *England,* as ever he brought us thence, for his own glory, though we are some of the least of Christ's Flock, yet we do belong to the true Fold, and our Shepherd hath had as great a care of us, as he could have for any of his Lambs, and hath brought us through great affliction, praises be given to his glorious Name, of us, and you, and all that know him, for ever. Though we are absent in body in the Will of God, from you, yet we are present in spirit in the Will of God, with you, and do receive the benefit of all your prayers daily, and do feel the Springs of Life that do stream from all the faithful hearted, to our great refreshment and strengthening.

After our money was gone, the Lord Inquisitor, with the rest in Authority put a great allowance in one of their servants hands for our maintenance, because we could take no money our selves; the Lord of Heaven did forbid us to meddle with any; and he did send to know whether we did want any clothes, he would send it to the Prison to us : This was the large love of our God to us, and we were made contented with that we had, till the Lord God (who is rich in mercy, and full of all Grace, and is never unmindful of any which trust in his Name) of his everlasting love did send his faithful Messenger, whose feet are beautiful, and face is comely, cloathed with a bright shining Garment from the Crown of the head, to the sole of the foot, and came in great power and

strength

strength indeed, armed with the whole Armour of Light, and
drest in the Majesty of the Most High, and being commissioned
of the Higher Power, went to the Lord *Inquisitor* to demand our
lawful liberty, which would not be granted, except we could get
some *English* Merchants of *Legorn* or *Messana* to engage four
thousands Dollers that we should never come into those parts
again; the Lord (who alone is our Life and Redeemer) moved
our dear Brother to offer his own body to redeem ours, but it
would not be received; then he offered to lay down his own dear
and precious life for our liberty: Greater love can no man have,
than to lay down his life for his Friend; the Lord will restore it into his bosom double; his service can never be blotted out; his
Name is called *Daniel Baker*; his outward being is near London, a
right dear and precious heart he is: The blessing, strength, and
power of the Almighty be upon him and his, and overshadow
them for ever, *Amen.* Greater comfort could never be administred to us in our conditions; Glory, honor and praise to our God
for evermore, *Amen.*

This is a dear and sweet Salutation in that which never changeth, fadeth away, nor waxeth old, from us whom the Lord hath
counted worthy to bear his Name, and to suffer for, his sake, to
all our Christian Friends, Fathers and Elders, Pillars of Gods spiritual House, Brethren and Sisters in the Lord Jesus Christ;

Oh my dear Husband, with our dear and precious Children,
Lambs of God, and Babes of Christ, begotten of the Immortal
Seed of Light, Life and Truth, with us, and all the whole Family
of everlasting blessedness.

Pray for us believingly; all things are possible with our God. So
my Dearlings, in the arms of everlasting love do I take my leave
of you; the blessing and peace of the Most High be upon you
ever, *Amen, Amen.*

Oh my dear Husband praise the Lord that ever thou hadst a
Wife that was found worthy to suffer for the Name of the Lord.
Inasmuch as I can understand the moving of the Spirit of God:
My dear and faithful Yoke-fellow, Sister and Friend, is worthy

to

to be embraced of all friends for ever; the deeper the forrow, the greater the joy; the heavier the Crofs, the weightier the Crown. This was written in the Inquifition at *Malta*, of us

Malta the 11*th*. Month
 of the year 1661.   *Katharine Evans,*
                  Sarah Chevers.

From K. E. *for two Friends:*

DEarly beloved Brother in the everlafting Covenant of Light and Life, do I dearly falute and embrace thee, with thy dear Wife, my beloved Sifter, and thy dear Children, whom I dearly love in that which never changeth: My dear and faithful Friends, I am often refrefhed in you, when the Light brings you to my remembrance; then do I feel the fprings of Love and Life, which arifeth from the pure Fountain of Eternal refrefhments, to my joy and comfort; wherein I am made to praife and glorifie my God and your God, who hath redeemed us out of the Chains of darknefs, and Kingdom of blacknefs, into the everlafting brightnefs, glory, joy, and perfect bleffednefs for ever, to dwell in the enjoyment of his living prefence, as we abide faithful, to Eternity; in his prefence is fulnefs of joy, and at his right hand is pleafure for evermore.

My prayers are night and day without ceafing, to our Heavenly Father, that not one of his begetting may ever turn or flide back, but that every one may prefs forward towards the Mark of the price of the high calling in Chrift Jefus, who is our Life and glory, and fo all may come to wear the Crown of Life and Immortality, triumphing in the everlafting Bleffednefs of the Heavenly Riches and Eternal joy and happinefs that's perfect for ever, *Amen.*

Oh! my dear Brother and Sifter, we are all children of our Father, begotten in the everlafting Seed of the Promife of Eternal life and falvation. Oh my precious Friends, wait patiently with me always

always in the pure fear of the perfect and pure God, who hath an Eternal Treasure, ful of everlasting Riches and ready to distribute them to all his dutiful Children : Glory and Praises be given to his blessed Name for ever. Oh my beloved ones! your love to me is written in the Records that cannot be lost. Dear hearts, glorifie our God in my behalf, that ever he counted me worthy to suffer for his Name, I hope to see your faces again yet once more) with joy and gladness, with my dear yoke-fellow in the Lord's Work, before we go hence, and be no more seen. So in the tender bowels of pure Love, do I take my leave of you at this time. The everlasting peace and blessedness be upon you, and upon the whole *Israel* of God, *Amen*.

Dearly salute us to all Friends.

This was written in the Inquisition
at *Malta*, in the 11*th*.Month
of the year 1661.   *Katharine Evans*.

There was another Letter (and Paper) which was intercepted; but I have it not here with me, it being sent home from Legorn. Yet here followeth more of their Writings to Friends, and to my own particular, which at several times I received from them, unknown to the Oppressors.

A Copy of a Letter that I was moved to write the next day after I came to the Island and City, and communicated to their hands.

DEar Lambs, peace be unto you, *Amen*.
Now seeing that the everlasting God and Father of all truth,

truth, hath in his tender love, and Fatherly mercy, and bowels of compaſſion (through the trials of manifold ſufferings and temptations) hitherto, even to this day, upheld and preſerved you in the innocency, and its teſtimony againſt the contrary ; although ſometimes (I know that) you have taſted the ſentence of death in your ſelves, and even (as it were) ready to deſpair of life ; yet in the living teſtimony of innocency , in the anſwer of a good Conſcience, I Daniel bear you record, (in the Covenant of Life) the ſame remaineth with you, and you are in it a good ſweet ſavour to the Lord, and his Eternal Truth and People. Oh! bleſſed for ever be his Name, yea and my very heart and life bleſſeth and magnifieth the Lord on your behalf.

Wherefore my dear Friends, be faithful, full of Faith, and the living, inviſible God of Peace is with you , and will not forſake you, ſeeing it is ſo, and much more you know which might be declared.

Oh! I am moved in the Bowels of my Father's love, as one with you (in trials, and in the exerciſe of manifold temptations)to ſtir up your pure and innocent minds by way of remembrance , and alſo to beſeech you to take heed to the Teſtimony of Life that's undefiled, and manifeſt in you, and to dwell in the ſame which retains the joy and comfort of the Lord, and his peace, which you know is not of the World; and ſo to watch and beware of the Enemy that is near to tempt to make ſhipwrack of Faith and a good Conſcience, and to deſpair, and ſo to betray not only your own innocent long-ſufferings , but alſo the Teſtimony of the Lord God of our Life, for which you have ſo long ſuffered, and by the pure Divine virtue of the ſame have you been to this day preſerved ; ſo that the Lord (who is and will be your reward) hath not been wanting to you on his part. Oh faint not , but lift up your heads, and be faithful ſtill as I am not otherwiſe perſwaded concerning you; and I am well perſwaded , that in his own Covenant and Way deliverance will come to the Seed ; and ye know, if the ſame come not in his own Covenant of Truth, in the Light of his Countenance, it cannot be well ; but your nay (you know) is to be nay, and ſo to ſtand in the Truth, againſt the contrary, whatſoever our God permits unreaſonable men to inflict upon the outward or viſible body ; and the ſame alſo will

K   work

work for his glory, and also for the good and eternal peace of his innocent suffering Lambs notwithstanding.

Your tender Brother   D. B.

_____

ANd when this, with other Papers I had through not a little difficulty communicated to their hands over .the heads of our Enemies, I was moved to speak my Message as from the Lord of Life to them after I had offered up my body, and to lay down my life for these poor innocents, my dear friends; and so with my voice I saluted them in the Lord's Truth, as they stood at the prison-Grates with these words in the behalf of the general Assembly of the Saints in light; to wit, *The whole Body of God's Elect, right dearly, owneth your Testimony, and you are a sweet savour unto the Lord and his people*: And forasmuch as one of these poor afflicted Lambs replied, and said on this wise, as if it was a trouble to them that they could not be more serviceable. Then my heart being melted, and my bowels of pity, mercy and compassion, being moved, I said, That it was a wonderful mercy of the Lord, in as much as they were preserved in their own measure of Truth and pure innocency, for which my heart praised the Lord for what mine eye saw, which right dearly affected my heart, and we were well refreshed at that season, in the sweet presence of our living God, albeit our bodies were at a distance, but so as we could behold each others face through the Prison bars of Iron, in the Inquisition.

_____

Now for so much as in the Wisdom of God it is seen meet that the fore-mentioned and following Writings which came from their hands, might appear to publike view, that thereby every Member of the one Body may have a right understanding, and not onely so, but also a sensible feeling not onely of the trials and sufferings in part of these innocent Lambs, but also of the consolations of each other, as fellow-Members of the infinite Body of

which

which Chrift Jefus the Lord is both King and Head , in whom be endlefs dominion and pure glory, and eternal falvation, *Amen.*

And fo I being as it were conftrained to publifh the acceptable Words that found and favor of pure innocency and clear truth, for the Elect's fake, in the fame Love and Life I am the more free hereunto, even as a Child, that differs but little from a fervant, as I am in the Father's Love, Power and Grace of Life , fitted to ferve the undefiled Life of the leaft in the Kingdom of Bleffednefs, and to adminifter comfort or what elfe I have received from the Eternal Fountain or Fulnefs, for the ufe or fervice of either Body, Mind, Soul or Spirit, of my own Flefh or Family , feeing no man ever hated his own Flefh; and he is worfe than an Infidel that provideth not for his own Family, efpecially them of his own House.

This is a fweet Salutation to God's Elect Church in England and Ireland.

Right dear, precious and Heavenly ones , whofe Beauty fhineth bright, and at whofe Name the hearts of the Heathen do tremble : We who through the everlafting Mercies of our God, are Members of the fame Body, and are held in ftrait Captivity, and hard Bondage, for witneffing forth the fame Teftimony and Covenant of pure Light , Life and Truth of our God, with you dear and faithful ones indeed, We here in the fame Covenant of pure Love, and Bowels of tendernefs, do dearly falute and embrace you all, glorifying and praifing our Eternal Father for you all , who hath counted us worthy to partake of the fellowfhip and fufferings for the Bodies fake , with you in tribulations, fiery trials, manifold temptations, faftings, watchings, heats and colds, and cruel threatning and perfecutions, perils by Sea, and perils by Land , ftanding in jeopardy of our lives year after year , and looking every hour, day and night , for many

K 2   Weeks

Weeks together, when we should be brought out to Execution; but though Proclamation was made, and they came up to the very Gate with a Drum and Musquets, to fetch us out to destroy us, yet the Lord God of everlasting strength, who in the deepest of all dangers, and greatest extremity, when all hopes were past, did but blow upon them with the breath of his nostrils, and they did flye as dust before the Wind; for which we do entreat all Friends to glorifie our God on our behalf; for never did the Lord our God work greater deliverance for any, than he hath done for us from time to time, who are the least and weakest for what we know, that ever the Lord our God sent forth in so great & weighty a Work; but all things are possible with him, who made and created all things, it is he alone which carrieth on his own work by his own mighty Power, and the glory shal be his own for evermore, *Amen*.

Oh our dearly beloved Friends, did you know but the third part of the afflictions the Lord our God hath carried us through, you would say, The Lord hath wrought as great a Miracle in our preservation, as ever he did in raising *Lazarus* out of the Grave: And in the greatest of our afflictions we could not say in our hearts, Father, would thou hadst not brought us here; but cryed mightily to our God for power to carry us through whatsoever should be inflicted upon us, that the Truth of our God might not suffer through our weakness: And the Lord did hear us, and answered us in righteousness, and carried us on with all boldness, and made our fore-heads as Flint, and our Brows as Brass, in the faces of our Enemies; that whensoever we were brought forth upon trial, all fear was taken away, that we stood as Iron-Gates, and Castle-Walls in the faces of our Enemies, so that they said, *we would fain be burned*; but we answered, No, we would not willingly be burned; but if our Heavenly Father doth call us to suffer in that kind for his Name sake, he will give us power to go through it; and we have great cause to believe it; for our Lord God never called us to do any service for him, but he gave us power, and made way for his own Work; glory and praise be to his holy Name for ever.

Dearly beloved friends, marvel not why *Israel* is not gathered in all this time; it is not for want of labour, nor travel, nor grief, nor

nor pain, fasting, nor mourning, nor weeping, nor love to their souls; but it is because of the great oppression: For here are a willing people, but they dare not until the Lord make way for them. Truly Friends, we have not been idle since we saw your faces, nor have we had much ease to the flesh; but do travel night and day for *Sion*'s prosperity and perfect joy, and for the reparation of *Jerusalem*, and her pure praise; though our sorrows are deep, and our afflictions grievous, yet we do wait with patience to reap the peaceable fruits of righteousness, and enjoy the benefit of our uprightness; Praises be to our God for ever, he hath kept us by his power and holiness, that our Enemies have not one jot or tittle against us, but for the Truth of our God, and that we could not join with them; so they would not suffer us to have one line of refreshment, but stript us out of all, so that we could not expect one drop of mercy, favour nor affection, but what our Heavenly Father did distil upon us from his living presence, and work for us by the operation of his own Arm of strength and power. But dear Friends; though a long Winter, and many sharp and terrible storms have past over our heads, so that we cannot express our sorrows; so likewise we cannot declare our joys. Oh! in the midst of all our afflictions, our God did draw nigh unto us, and did speak comfortably unto us with many sweet and precious promises, and did never suffer his faithfulness to fail us, nor was he wanting unto us in Visions and Revelations. Oh! how doth he appear in his glory, beauty and brightness, so that our souls are ravished and wrapped up with his living presence and glory many times, so that we do not dare to look out at our long sufferings nor trials, but do press forwards towards the fulness of joy and blessedness which our Eternal Father hath prepared for all them that love him, and walk in obedience to him; and we know, the deeper our sorrow is, the greater our joy shall be; and the heavier our Cross; the weightier our Crown, as we abide faithful: And we do believe, that neither Principalities nor Powers, nor sufferings, nor imprisonment, nor persecution, nor life nor death, shall be able to separate us from the love of God in Christ Jesus our Lord and Saviour, *Amen*.

Dearly beloved Friends, though our bodies are bolted up in the Rocks and Caves of the Earth, yet our spirits (you know) none can

can limit nor confine to any place. And we do behold your order and steadfastness of your faith and labour of love, and are daily refreshed in all the faithful-hearted. Oh dear hearts! the remembrance of the least of you is precious. Oh! the Rivers of tears that have distilled from our eyes, whilst we do think upon you, for joy, because of your growth and flourishing in the Truth. Oh! you are Virgins indeed, who have Oyl in your Vessels, and your Lamps burning, and are cloathed with the long white Robes of Righteousness, and are adorned with the Ornaments of pure Beauty and glorious brightness (abundance of you) to our joy and comfort, and we do pray night and day, That every Babe of our Heavenly Father's begetting may prosper, even as we desire our own souls should prosper; and that every one may be kept out of incumbrances, and use the World as if they used it not; but every one's mind, spirit, heart and soul, may be exercised in the Eternal, by the Power of God, out of the earthly, out of the visible, out of the carnal and perishing things of this life, (so as to trust in it) into the heavenly, into the spiritual, into the invisible, into that whichnever changeth, fadeth, nor waxeth old, where every one may dwell in the enjoyment of the presence of the Lord; for in the presence of the Lord is fulness of joy, and at his right hand is pleasure for evermore. Oh! that every one may be emptied of your selves, and unbottomed of your selves, that you may build wholly upon the sure foundation, and anchored so fast upon the Rock of Ages, that neither the swelling Seas, nor the foaming Waves, nor stormy Winds, though they beat vehemently, may ever be able to remove you. Oh dear Brethren! in the life and power you may feel the issues of Love and Life, which stream as a River to every soul of you, from the hearts of us that are wholly joined to the Fountain; Glory and everlasting praises be given to his holy Name. Our whole souls, spirits, hearts and minds, are given up to serve the Lord in whatsoever he requireth of us, as he shall make it manifest unto us. And we do bless his Name for ever, that he hath found us worthy of so high a calling, as to bind Kings in chains, and Nobles in fetters of Iron. Our prayers are continually for the advancement of the Gospel of the Lord Jesus throughout the whole Earth, for the gathering of the Seed of the Elect of God, and for the raising of it up over

the

the Seed of the Serpent, in power and great glory, to bear rule, and to have dominion over the whole World, that the Kingdoms of this World may become the Kingdoms of our Lord Jesus, that he may rule in his Princely Power, and reign in his Kingly Majesty, whose Right it is; that the knowledge of the Lord may cover the Earth, as the Water covereth the Sea; that all the Children of the Lord may be taught of the Lord, and be established in Righteousness; that so the Mourners in *Sion* may rejoice; and the heavy hearted in *Jerusalem* may be right glad: The Lord God of Power hasten it for his own Name's sake, and for his Elect's sake, that lye in captivity under the hands of the dark Powers of the Earth, either spiritual or temporal; *Amen, Amen* saith our spirits.

Dear and precious Friends and Brethren, pray for us, that we may finish our Testimony to the glory of God, and to the praise of his holy Name, and to the comfort of all that love his appearing, and to our own eternal salvation, and to the shame and confusion of all that hate the Lord Jesus, and persecute his Truth. So in the pure Vnity of the Covenant of Light, Life, Peace, Love, and everlasting Righteousness, do we take our leaves of you all at this time, hoping and believing we shall see your faces once again, before we go hence, and be no more seen. Dear Friends, pray for us.

Though we were in many streights and hardships by reason of the oppression; yet whilst our minds were staid upon the Fountain, we saw no want; but our tender Father, whose heavenly eye was ever over us, saw our necessities, sent his right dear and precious Servant, and just and faithful Steward, *Daniel Baker*, to administer to our necessities both spiritual and temporal; he came not in his own time, will nor strength, but in the Will and time, Strength and Power of the Almighty God, at whose presence the Mountains were removed, the tall Cedars were made to bow, the strong Oaks to stoop. Oh wonderful! He went to the Lord Inquisitor, (the Popes Deputy) to demand our lawful Liberty, which would not be granted, unless he and we would write to *Messana*, or *Legorn*, to some *English* Merchant to be engaged for four thousand Dollers: Which Proposition being out of the Covenant of Light we durst not stoop to it; but our dear Brother in Christ Jesus offered his body for our liberty, but it
                                                        would

would not be granted; nothing would ferve but one to engage for four thoufand Dollers to be paid, if ever we come into thefe parts again. Then in obedience to the Lord he offered up his Life for our Freedom, but all would not ferve, the Will of our God be done.

Oh dear Friends! greater Love was never heard of, than for a man to lay down his Life for his Friend: Oh! it is worthy to be recorded in remembrance of him for ever; here he came up and down to adminifter to us with his Life in his hand, time after time. So the Lord God of Power reward him double into his bofome for ever. Oh how did he refresh our fouls, fpirits, minds and bodies through great tryals, which is never to be forgotten.

Written in the Inquifition at
  Malta, in the 11th. *Month*
  of the year 1661. By us

Katharine Evans,
Sarah Chevers.

Who have fuffered for the living teftimony of Jefus, and his
  pure Innocency, in Bonds, tryals and tribulations, more
  than three years, to this day.

A *fhort Relation of fome more of their exceeding great Tryals and Temptations.*

NOw in fhort time after we were taken Prifoners, we were ftung with Flyes called *Muskatoes*, in our faces and our heads, as we lay in our Beds, that were fwollen as if we had the fmall-Pox, fo that all people were afraid of us, fave the *Englifh* Conful; they thought we had been unclean perfons, fo that a Fryar told *Sarah* he faw in an evil spirit in her face, which was a great trial; they could not sleep in their beds in the house, they were so tormented, & we were told, that they had seen them that did pray and preach every day were burnt for Witches in a short time; and they would keep us to see our lives and conversations; and so they have: And glory be to our God, they cannot lay guilt to our charge, but are made to confess the truth.

In a few days after we were there, in a Vision, in the night, the Lord appeared unto me, and shewed me, that round about us, and above and beneath us, there were many Magicians of *Ægypt*; and the Lord smote me, and said unto me, *The Devil hath desired to winnow you as Wheat; but pray that your faith fail not*. And the sight was very dreadful and terrible; and the voice of the Lord did awaked me with much trembling and amazement, and a great War for the space of twelve hours, before I could get the victory; and we did witness but little ease to the flesh night nor day. We went in obedience to the Lord to one of their Tower-Houses in time of their Worship, and stood trembling in the midst of them; and I was made to turn my back to the high Altar, and kneel down, and lift up my voice in prayer unto the Lord, and he that was saying Service, drew off his Surplice, and kneeled a little beside us till I had done: and he reacht forth his hand to us, to come to him, and offered me a token; and the Lord shewed me it was the Mark of the Beast: And I refused it; and he put it into *Sarah's* hand, and she gave it him again, and shewed him her Purse, that she had to give, if any had need. And he asked if we were *Calvinists* or *Lutherans*? And we said, Nay And he asked if we would go to *Rome* to the Pope? But we denied. And he asked if we were *Catholicks*? And we told him, We were true Christians, the servants of the living God. And many of them were amazed, and came round about us; We having but little of their Tongue, gave our Testimony (for the Lord) in words and signs, as well as we could; and they were made subject to the Power at that present, praises be given to our God, and we departed in peace.

And since that, the Lord laid such a heavy burthen upon us, that we did question what he would do with us, before we knew the mind of God in it. And upon a set-day they had a great

L   Meet-

Meeting to take their holy Sacrament, (as they call it) in a high place; but we knew nothing of it, nor where it was, but where the Lord revealed to us. And we were made to go in, and stand in the midst; and there were many lights in divers places, and many Christs, as they call them, and much costliness and abominations of the Earth, they had so many sorts of holy Garments (as they call them) of so many colours, that it would make one wonder how the Devil did invent it. And there we were made to stand in the midst for the space of three parts of an hour, as near as I can judge, in great power, trembling and quaking, and bitter mourning, so that they were all amazed, and some removed further for fear, but knew not what to do; for I never did witnesse such an Earthquake. In the end one came soberly, and spake to us to go forth; and we went in the Lord's time, and sate at the door trembling and mourning, to the astonishment of them, and being so overcome with their abominations, we went along the street reeling to and fro, and staggering like drunken men, so that we were a wound to all that saw us: It was the wonderful Power of God that made way for us to go forth to them, and kept us. They have used all the Craft they have day and night to Inchant us as the Lord hath made it known unto us, Glory and prayses bee to his everlasting. Name for-ever-more. We know that there is no Inchantment against *Jacob*, nor divination against *Israel*.

Dearly beloved friends, Wee dearly salute you all in the invisible life of our God, who is our life, our peace, our stay and strength; under whose shaddow wee are Refreshed, praises, glory and honour be given unto his powerfull name of all his for ever.

Truly friends, we are not able to declare the large mercies of our God vouchsafed unto us from time to time, his born is our strength, and his Name our strong Tower in all our troubles, temptations, trials and sufferings; he is a God at hand, and not afar off, and doth make us sensible before-hand, by Visions and Revelations, what is coming upon us; and doth arm us with his own Armour, and makes us as bold as Lyons; for we fear not the face of man, because we know we shall not suffer any thing but what shall make for the glory of our God; but truly we had fainted long ago, had not the Lord upheld us by his free Spirit; but we know the Lord taketh care of the least of them that trust him:

88

him: Praifes be unto him for ever. Dear Friends, though we
be ablent in body, yet we are prefent in fpirit, and do feel you in
that which cannot be feparated, as we abide faithful, and are
much refrefhed in you; and the remembrance of you is precious
unto us: Oh! that all our Friends could prife the company and
the fight of each others faces. We do not want the company of
Fryars, Jefuits and Magiftrates, nor great women. Here are fome
that have breathings after life, but they dare not fhew it, for the
fame thing that was, is; they will not enter in themfelves, nor
fuffer them that would.

The Lord Inquifitor fent to us, that if we would (being we
are good Women, we fhould go into the Nunnery among the holy Women, and be maintained as long as we live, in regard we
have denied the World, and all we have. And the Fryar told us,
if we would come to their Maffe-houfe and receive their holy Sacrament, we fhould be the moft eminent Catholicks in all *Malta*;
but we denied them in the Name of the Lord, and all their dead
foppery which they have invented. Here we are kept under the
Inquifition, as they fay, till they have Orders from the Pope of
Rome what they fhould do with us.

We befeech you all, faithful Friends, pray for us, for great are
our trials: Did you but know the abominations that the Devil
hath invented here, you would think it were tryal enough: But
here we have cruel mockings, and the fame contradictions, trials
and temptations that ever the fervants of the Lord had, & Chrift
himfelf: It is the wonderful Power of God that we are preferved
till this time; for all the whole Ifland are Papifts, and given up to
Idolatry. We are defpifed of all people, and abhorred of all Nations; and becaufe they cannot have any juft thing againft us, they
do invent lyes againft us; but the Lord is on our fide, for elfe the
Enemy would foon deftroy us; for great is their rage; and we
have continual War with them night and day we feel; behold
their threatnings and cruelty is more than our tongues can exprefs. Great is the love of our God, for he doth refrefh us with
the fweet drops of his mercy, and doth water us every moment
with the everlafting fprings of his Love, or elfe we had fainted
long ago.

L 2   Oh!

Oh ! let all who know the Lord, praise and glorifie his holy Name for ever and ever, *Amen*. Dear Friends Friends, farewel in the Lord.

From us who are in outward Bonds in the City of *Malta*, for the Testimony of Jesus, glory be to his Name for ever, who hath counted us worthy. We are in health at present, blessed be God.

Katharine Evan.
Sarah Chevers.

Several other Writings to D.B. *whilest he was in* MALTA.

OH thou tender-hearted one, whom our God and our Eternal Father hath sent to relieve us his poor innocent Lambs, in hard bondage, and deep captivity, which thou art an eye-witness of; none can receive or discern it, but those that do see it: But our Heavenly Father, who hath respect to the rest of them that believe in his Name, hath sent thee to be an eye-witness in some measure, of what we have undergone. Oh my dear, precious and endeared one! thou meek Lamb, thou innocent Dove, who dost bear the likeness, beauty and brightness of that unspotted one that is come in the Volume of the Book to do the Will of God: We can give in our Testimony for thee, that thou camest here in the Power and Authority of the Most High, to which the tall Cedars were made to bow, and the strong Oaks to bend, praises, praises be given to our everlasting God for evermore. Oh my dearly beloved Brother, thy beauty shineth indeed, thou art all glorious within and without, thy Garments are perfumed with all delightsome scents; We smell the sweet odours thereof, and do feel the fulness of Love and Life which runs from thy tender heart day and night to us, and in the same unity of Love do our hearts stream forth to thee, and thou knowest full well: Oh how
hath

have our hearts and bowels been melted for thee ; our heads and eyes have run with tears, and our souls have been poured forth to our Heavenly Father for thy prefervation, and we do truly labor to fee thy face before thou comeft: Glory and praifes be given to our Eternal Lord God, *Amen* faith our fpirits ; that he doth vouchfafe us fo great a mercy as to behold the face of fo precious a Friend : We do befeech God to moderate us with his Eternal Spirit, that we may always be mindful of his mercies , and never to let his benefits flip out of our minds. We have been near death many times, when we had none to come near us , but thofe that preacht death and deftruction to us ; I have lain twelve dayes, or more, in a faft , in ftrong travel night and day, that my dearly beloved Yoke-Mate would have been glad if the Lord would have taken me out of the body, becaufe of my weak affliction.

Then the English Fryar which was here, came up and down to us, and down to us, and would fay to my Friend, *She is ready to depart ; fend for me, and take notice what torment fhe will be in ; a thoufand Devils will be about her, to fetch her foul to Hell, becaufe fhe will not be a Catholick,* And after we vvere parted, vve vvere called to faft, fo that my Friend vvas fo vveak, that fhe put on fuch linnen upon her head, as fhe thought to lie in her Grave : We did eat but little in a Month together , vvhen our money vvas almoft done, till vve did knovv the mind of the Lord vvhat to do. Then they did run to and fro like mad men , and the Fryars did come and fay, The Inquifitor fent them to tell us , vve might have any thing vve vvould eat; and they did fay , it vvas not poffible that ever creatures could live vvith fo little meat for fo long a time together. They bring us meat, and fay, the English Conful did fend it. It vvas a glorious Faft indeed, the Lord did appear vvonderfully in it, praifes be given to him for ever, *Amen,*

We vvere very vveak, becaufe the povver did vvork fo ftrongly ; I had no manner of food in my body five or fix days together ; We did lie in clothes , becaufe vve had no ftrength to put them off, nor one to make our bed : Then vve did fpeak to the Fryar, that vve might come together ; but he faid they had no fuch order ; if vve vvould have a Phyfician, vve might. And there vve lay, none knovving from morning to morning vvhether vve vvere dead or alive. We vvere kept quiet and ftill till the Lord's

time

time was come; they brought many things for us to eat: Then the Lord said, *Thou mayest take as freely as if thou hadst laboured for it with thy hands; I will sanctifie it to thee through the Cross.* And he said unto *Sarah, she should eat of the fruit of her hands, and be blessed.* And we did eat, and were refreshed, and glorified the Lord; We did cry mightily unto the Lord night and day, that we might not eat nor drink to offend him, vve vvould rather dye. The Lord vvas vvell pleased vvith our Sacrifice, and did encrease our strength, and administred comfort to us; honor and glory be to his blessed Name for ever. In the lowest of all our conditions, we were kept a top of all the Mountains, so that they could not make us shrink or bow one jot or tittle to any of their Precepts or Commands. Yet the Fryars have commanded us in the Name of their God to kneel vvith them in prayer.

The time is too little for me to disclose the twentieth part of the terrible trials; but whensoever we were brought upon any tryal, the Lord did take away all fear from us, and multiplied our strength, and gave us power and boldness to plead for the truth of the Lord Jesus, and Wisdom of Words to stop the mouths of the gain-sayers, that they vvould be made to say we spake truth; they could never say otherwise: But they vvould say, We had not the true faith, but we had all virtues. Oh dear heart! if it be our Eternal Father's good pleasure to carry thee away vvithout us, vve do beseech our Heavenly Father to bless, and to give thee a prosperous return, and to feed thee with the fulness of the blessing of the povverful Gospel of the Lord Jesus Christ. *Amen.* And vve do believe vve shall not vvant thy prayers, nor the prayers of all the faithful, that we may keep faithful to the end, so that our God may be glorified, his Church and People may be refreshed and rejoiced, and we may receive our Reward with the rest of the Lord's Lambs.

Our Life is with thee; for oh! thou art full of Love, thou tender-hearted one, vvho hath offered up thy sanctified body, and purified life, in obedience to the Lord, for us poor afflicted lambs vvith thee, and companions in tribulations, trials and persecutions, and in perils at Sea, and perils by Land. Oh thou precious Lamb of God, great is thy Reward in Heaven, great will be the Well-spring of joy that vvill arise in thee, in thy Journey: Oh,

thou

thou happy one indeed ! whom the Lord our God hath made choice of amongst his faithful Flock, and endued with so much povver to come into such a place as this, not the like in all *Europe* by their own report, and all others, and to stop the mouths of Lyons, and to trample upon the heads of Serpents, Scorpions and Vipers of the Earth, and they could not hurt thee; their stings are taken out of their heads, and out of their tails, glory, honor and everlasting praises be given to our God for evermore, of all that know h m; for he is worthy.

And the Lord bless thee and thine for ever *Amen*; and encrease thy strength, and multiply thee abundantly in every good gift and Grace, and prosper all thy undertakings, that thou mayest be approved for ever before the King of Saints, in the General Assembly of the Most High, and stand before the Throne of his Majesty vvith joy unspeakable; and full of glory, *Amen*; *Amen* saith our spirits.

Dearly beloved pray for us, that we fall not, nor fail, whereby our Enemies may have any advantage to rejoice, and say, We served a God that could not serve us, and called upon a God that could not deliver us; as if we were like them, to call upon stocks, stones, pictures, and painted Walls, and dead things, that cannot see, hear nor speak through their throats. We do beseech thee to tel all our dear Friends, Fathers and Elders, the Pillars of the spiritual Building, with all the rest of our Christian Brethren, that we do desire their Prayers, for we have need of them.

OH! How *strong and powerful's our KING*
To all that do believe in him?
He doth preserve them from the Snare
And Teeth of those that would them tear,
We that are sufferers for the Seed,
Our Hearts are wounded, and do bleed,
To see th' Oppression and Cru'lty
Of men, that do thy Truth deny.
In Dungeons strong, and Dungeons deep,
To God alone we cry and weep:
Our sorrows none can read nor learn,
But those that have past through the same.

But he whose Beauty shineth bright,
Turneth darknesse into Light ;
Maketh Cedars to bow, and Oaks to bend
To him that's sent to the same end.
He is a Fountain pure and clear ,
His Chrystal Streams runs far and near,
To cleanse all those which come to him,
For to be healed of their sin.
All them that do patiently abide ,
And never swerve nor go aside ;
The Lord will them deliver out of all
Captivity , Bondage and Thrall.

LEt *E.C.* know, That his Exhortations I do dearly embrace, and do witness it to be an Eternal Truth, I have had large experience of it , the Lord hath carried me on in much difficult Service, so that many times the vvay hath been stopt up , that to the eye of Reason I could not have a way made both by Sea and Land : Oh' if thou didst but know what experience I had of the mighty hand of the Lord in making a way , thou wouldst wonder. Once my vvay was stopt , and my persecution vvas so hot, that I sate in a Field all night to wait upon the Lord to make way for me to do the Work he laid upon me : I could not get lodging for money in Town nor City; it was at *Salisbury* : where I was whipt in the Market. And the next morning I went through the City by the Watchmen, and they took no notice of me. Wheresoever the Lord did send me, into what Land or City, or place soever, if they did put me out never so oft, he would make me go till I got victory ; save in the *Isle of Man*, there was a Souldier came to my bed side with a naked Sword, and took me by the Arm, and hal'd me out of the Bed at the tenth hour of the night, and carried me on Ship board : When I put on my clothes I did not dare to rise. That place lies upon me yet ; and I have motions to *Edenburgh* in *Scotland*, I was never there; the Lord did make me to do him service to almost all the mighty men in *England* and *Ireland*; insomuch that I cryed oft to my God, saying, *Lord. What wilt thou do with me that am so foolish , to go to such wise men!* If I were wise, I did not care if thou d dst carry me to the end of
the

the Earth. The Lord said, the foolish things must confound the wise; and he would carry me before the mightiest men in all the Earth, to bear his Name before them, and i should have victory wheresoever I went: And I do believe the Lord, and we both are made willing to wait the Lord's time, which is a time of peace and joy, safety and happiness. And we do bless, laud, praise and magnifie his holy Name, that he sent so heavenly a Messenger to relieve, strengthen, comfort and refresh us in our great necessity, which is a mercy beyond expression; all Friends that do understand it, will say so; Glory and everlasting praises, honor, power and dominion be given to our Eternal Lord God for evermore, of us, and all that know him, *Amen, Amen* saith our spirit.

Oh true and faithful Brother, into the Arms of everlasting power and holiness, strength and mightiness, purity and righteousness, do we commit thee, to be kept and preserved, and prosperously carried on in thy Journey: The powerful blessing, peace, joy and happiness of the Majesty of the Most High God go along with thee, to preserve, and protect thee for ever, *Amen, Amen.*

Pray for us dear heart, that we may receive strength to overcome, that we may sing the song of *Moses* and the Lamb, and the redeemed of the Lord, *Amen.*

Dear heart, it is hard for us to part with thee; thou wilt feel it.

The Will of our Eternal Father be done; in the pure unity of the blessed Spirit of Light, Life, Joy, Peace and everlasting Glory, do we here take our leave of thee at this time, hoping to see thy face again with joy in our Lord's time.

O dear heart! our hearts, souls, spirits, and our whole lives goeth along with thee.

The pure peace of our God rest upon thee, *Amen.*

Dearly salute us to all Friends, for they are dear and precious to us indeed,

Farewell, farewell dear heart, farewell.

M

Dear

Dear heart ,

THou haft cleared thy Confcience towards us in the fight of
God and man; if here had been many friends, what could
have been done more concerning us than thou haft done ? Thou
haft ftood in great jeopardy ever fince , and thy life hath been
fought for much; We have felt it, and cryed night and day to our
Heavenly Father to preferve thee, and fafely deliver thee: Whatfoever we do fuffer, we defire the Will of our Heavenly Father to
be done in all things, if the Lord doth ftir up the Earth to help
the Woman, it is his own free love ; and upon that account we
fhall receive it, and not upon any other.

This they fpake concerning the money I left with them, and for
their neceffities: And the Lord did appear unto me in a Vifion of
the Night, and fmote me on the Arm, and faid, *Look* , *there is the
Pope, he will not hurt thee* ; Where he ftood in the Room, as one
forfaken of God and man; this was at the *Englifh* Confuls, when
there was fome fear upon me concerning him. Now here is a *Romian* in the Prifon which came hither upon fome account , he is a
a Doctor of Law, and differs from them in many things; but they
are all of one fpirit : He doth conftantly affirm , that the Pope
hath fent an Order to fet us free ; and he faith, they are lyars and
falfe blafphemers if they do fay the Pope fent any fuch Order as
they fpeak of. They do meet every day concerning us; we do feel
them; fome would have it one way , and fome another , and fo
they cannot agree , becaufe they do act contrary to the Will of
God ; the Lord fets it all on fire, and hath burned all they have
done thefe three years concerning us. Now where they will look
a Reward of their charges, we do not know ; the wife are taken
in their own craftinefs, and the fubtile in their own fnare. There
have twelve of them fate in Judgement upon us three years, and
fome have ftruck hard at our lives, fo that we have been even at
death's door. I have lain very weak three Weeks at a time, There
are many for us, as far as they do dare. The Lord fays, there were
two with the Inquifitor for us, and did plead much with him: I did
fee

: feeit in a Night-Vifion, The *Englifh* Conful which is dead, was with us two feveral times after we were in the Inquifition ; he faid he would lend us five pounds when we did want : but when our money was near done, we were made to rejoice greatly, and could not take any of any one. We did not know the mind of the Lord in it; but had we had money, we had not known the mighty Power of God. Now we are able to truft the Lord wherever he fhall carry us without money. We do queftion the money in the Conful's hand. It will be hard for him to part with it. Our Life is with thee.

A few Lines to D. B.

OH our dear and faithful *Friend* and *Brother*, begotten of our heavenly Father, right dear and precious in his fight, and beautiful before his prefence. Dear heart, we do glorifie our God in our hearts, fouls and fpirits, who hath called, chofen, and elected thee to come up to the help of him againft the *Mighty*, and hath carryed thee along in fo weighty a work, and hath profpered thee therein, praifes be given to his bleffed Name for ever, who hath enclofed thee in his Bofom, and Chamber of his everlafting *Love*, and hath hid thee in his private *Pavillion*, where them that would hurt thee, cannot find thee, becaufe of the fhadowing of his Almightinefs, under whofe defence thou art kept fafe; and he doth carry thee upon the Wings of his *Power*, fo that the Mountains do become plain before thee, which we do fee clearly in the Light ; Eternal honor and glory be to his Name for ever, who is called, *Wonderful Counfellor*, the *Mighty God*, the *everlafting Father*, the *Prince of Peace*, in whom we have fellowfhip, and unity one with another, and none can hinder.

Dear heart, we do dearly embrace thy fweet *Exhortations*, thou being fenfible of the inftigations of *Satan*, who hath winnowed us with every bait, winding and twining flights that he hath, Praifes be to our God for ever, who hath preferved us, and prevented him,

The

The Enemies being busie with their Temptations, to have us enter in-
to their Covenant, thereupon I was moved to write these following
wards, which I communicated to their hands with the former
Paper, Viz.

BEhold the Word of Life arose in me, saying, (this morning)
Keep to *Yea* and *Nay*, and I will confirm my Covenant unto
thee. These Words were spoken to the true Seed that shall inherit the Kingdom; the same (you know) is but one in Male and
Female. And so the blessing of my Life rest upon you, and be
with you in the same, even in that which hath no end, neither fadeth away; yea, and my Spirit saith, *Amen.*

Dear Lambs, read within, and be refreshed, and the God of
Life and Peace encrease the same, and multiply your strength a-
bundantly, *Amen.*

Malta, the 10 *h* day of the
11*th*. Month, 1661.   D. B.

Another Paper from them to my hand.

DEar and precious heart, in the Eternal Covenant of Light and
Life of our God do we salute thee, and dearly embrace thee. Oh!
what hath the Lord made thee unto us! far more precious than we are able
to express; and great will be thy reward for thy faithfulness to the Lord,
and thy dear and tender love to us, and thy diligent care of us:

Oh! thou art the Messenger we have cried long for, to our Heavenly Father, saying, How long, Oh Lord! How long will it be before thou
wilt send thy Messenger, whose feet are beautiful, coming upon the
Mountains, bringing glad tydings of great joy to us thy poor Captives.
Now hath the Lord our God answered us at large; Praises, praises be to
his Name for evermore.

                                                             Oh!

Oh! how are our souls refreshed, and our spirits supported, and our hearts comforted, our minds rejoiced, and our bodies strengthened! Thou canst never do greater service to the Lord our God, than to come into such a place as this is, to offer up thy dear life in ransoming us: Great was the Power that brought thee, and great is the Power that doth uphold thee, and Mighty is the Strength which doth preserve thee, and great will be thy Reward. Thy labour of Love we do bear Testimony cannot be forgotten, nor thy faith unfeigned put out of remembrance; it is written in the Book of Life for ever, and it will be registred and read in the House of Israel Eternally; The mouth of the Lord hath spoken it, and he will perform it. Farewell in the Lord. By us.

Katharine Evans,
Sarah Chevers.

OH our dearly beloved and precious Friend and Brother, right honorable indeed for ever: We dare not look out at thy departure, because we stand in the will of our Maker. The blessing of the Almighty be upon thee for ever, and make thee flourish in all thy endeavours; Thou art called by the Name of Daniel Baker, in the midst of thine Enemies thou art in the hand of thy Maker: And this the Lord hath spoken, Where-ever thou dost come, thy Glass shall not be broken, until thy Sand be run. Oh! this day is this Prophesie fulfilled in our sight: When they have done dealing treacherously, they shall be dealt treacherously withall; the Lord doth steal in upon them, Praises be to his Name.

Dear heart, salute me dearly to thy dear and precious Wife, with all dear Friends, in the Covenant of Grace and Peace. Dear heart, farewell, farewell.

K. E. S. C.

Anoth

Another Letter from Sarah Chevers, to friends in Ireland, to be read among the assemblies of Saints in Light.

OH! all ye righteous ones, whose dwellings are on high, in the fulness of beauty, holiness and glory, whose Name and Fame reacheth to the ends of the Earth, to the astonishment of the Heathen, and the amazement of the ungodly, to the preparation of all Nations to appear before the dreadful presence of our Lord God Almighty to be stript of all false coverings, and to be left without excuse; Glory and praises be to our God for ever *Amen*, who hath made us eye-witnesses of his mighty Work, and helpers together with you, according to our measures, to the chaining down of the Powers of darkness, and to the defacing of that painted Harlot, *Mysterie Babylon*, with all her Lovers, to the utter overthrow of Antichrist, with all his wicked Kingdom, *Amen*.

The day is dawning, the Sun of Righteousness is arising over all Nations for to make a clear separation, to gather in his own Flock, and to scatter the proud in the imaginations of their own hearts, to feed the hungry, to heal the sick, and to bind up the broken hearted, to cloath the naked, to visit the spirits in prison, and comfort the Mourners in *Sion*, to cause the heavy-hearted in *Jerusalem* to rejoice.

Oh my dear Friends! who are precious in the sight of our Heavenly Father, partakers of his Divine Nature, living Stones, and holy Assemblies, wherein dwelleth the fulness of God Almighty's Power and Strength, Riches, Glory, Wisdom, Counsel, Knowledge and Understanding: he is the Rock of Ages, the sure Foundation, the Ark of the Covenant of the Promise of everlasting blessedness, *Amen*.

My dear and precious ones, whom my soul loveth, my heart delighteth in you, and my spirit rejoiceth greatly because of the excellency of God's Almightiness amongst you, so that you are a dread to the Nations; Kings, Princes, and mighty men of the Earth shall bow before the Power of Almighty God, by whom

we

we stand, and all shall be brought under the Foot-stool of Christ, and his Government, and he alone shall reign in righteousness, and rule the Nations in Judgement; then shall the cry of the poor be heard, and the sighing of the needy be eased, and the yoke of Wickedness be broken, and the oppressed shall be set free, the Image of Christ restored, and the Image of that subtile Serpent defaced, destroyed, and utterly cast down for ever, *Amen*, so saith my spirit: Glory, honor, laud and praise, be given to our Lord God Almighty, for ever, *Amen*.

A sweet Salutation is this, from the breathing forth of my pure Life, to the same Life, in my Spirit, joining in my measure, a sufferer for the Seeds sake, glory to the Lord, who hath counted me worthy; Farewel, farewel my dear hearts. My dear Yoke-mate *K. E.* dearly salutes all Friends.

O ye holy Assemblies! whose hearts are wholly joined to the Lord, I with you, in the Life & Power of the Almighty God do travel for the raising of the Seed, & the gathering in of the lost sheep of the House of *Israel*. Oh! blessed be the day wherein the Lord called me, and counted me worthy to suffer for the Seed's sake: Praise, praise the Lord for me ye blessed of the Lord, in whom the living praises are found in the living Fountain of God Almighty, the fulness that filleth every empty soul, in the Streams of Love, Life, Light, Strength, Riches, Immortality, and Eternal Glory; So Truth, Joy, Peace and everlasting Blessedness remain with you all for ever, *Amen*.

My Life is given up for the service of the Lord, Bonds, Chains, Bolts, Irons, double doors, Death it self is too little for the Testimony of Jesus, and for the Word of God; so the Seed be gathered, it is but a reasonable Sacrifice: Bonds and Afflictions betide the Gospel of Christ; *He that will live godly in Christ Jesus, must suffer Persecution*, it is an evident token.

My dear Friends, my Light, my Life, my Love hath perfect Union in the Eternal Spirit of the living God, and remains with you all for ever Fathers, Elders, Pillars, Nursing-Mothers in *Israel*, true *Israelites* indeed, in whom is no guile. My dear Salutation, and breathing forth of my Eternal Father's Love is to all the breathing Seed, begotten of the Heavenly Father, Peace, Mercy and Truth be multiplied among you all for ever, *Amen*.

Pray

"Pray for us that we may have boldneſs over our Enemies, to ſu'fil the righteous Will of our Heavenly Father, and be kept faithful in his Will, for ever, *Amen.* Streams of Love and Life floweth from a living Fountain, to you all my dear Friends; Our love remaineth ever with you all, *Amen.*

Preſent this to the hand of L. C.

L. C. *Thou Nurſing-Mother in* Iſrael, *peace be to thee for ever,* A. men. *Thy dear Brother* Daniel Baker, *in the Covenant of Life, in obedience to the* Lord, *hath viſited us, to the amazement of our Enemies,* Glory be to the Lord for ever, Amen; *He hath been a faithful Steward indeed, worthy to be had in remembrance in the Book of* Iſrael, *for ever,* Amen. *Whatſoever for the Truth we ſuffer, our reward is with us, and our innocent life will clear us,* Amen.

Written by me Sarah Cheven, a Priſoner in the Inquiſition, for the clear Teſtimony of the Lord Jeſus: This 11th. Month of the year 1681-

---

NOw after I had received theſe Papers, though not through a little ſtreights and difficulty, with jeopardy of my precious Life, which my God ſweetly through all preſerved, Glory to his Name; my heart was (as it were) overcome with the loving-kindneſs and ſalvation of the living Lord, and in his ſavory Life my mouth was filled with thanſgiving and praiſes to my God; and I ſaid in my heart on this wiſe, Who am I, oh Lord! or what was my Father's Houſe, or what is the Land of my Nativity, that I (a poor afflicted and deſpiſed Worm!) ſhould be raiſed up to ſee and perceive what mine eye, mine eye in thy Eternal Power and pure Life behold! Oh my God! thou haſt known the innocent travel of my ſoul, which I right well know the ſame is not hid from thee, even from the day of my birth, unto this moment, through no ſmall trials and tribulations, and through the exerciſe

cife of manifold temptations; yet behold, my Life is preserved a
at this time: And oh! my heart, my mind, my foul, my spirit, in
thy pure, undefiled Life and Virtue, blesseth thy Name, thy pure
Name, which thy Virgins love and live in, and in the same they
glorifie thy beloved, and the Wings of thy Majesty overshadow-
eth them, and their delight is under the secret shadow of thy
Almightiness, blessed be thy Glory, blessed be thy undefiled Power, blessed and magnified be thy pure Wisdom, and let the same be
so even in the Tabernacles of the just for ever, Thou Lamb of
Immortality, the Thrones, the Kingdoms, and Eternal Dominions are thine, and over all thy Throne is, and shall be exalted,
and thy Lambs behold thy glory and thy Majesty, in this the day
of thy terrible and glorious appearance; Wisdom, Riches, Glory, Power, Might and Dominion everlasting (with Eternal Salvation) over all, to thy Name, *Amen,* saith my Spirit, in
the Life which is, was, and for ever shall be, the same which liveth
and abideth for ever, and fadeth not away: In the same I commend thy dear, tender Lambs, to be preserved according to thy
unsearchable Wisdom, and counsel of thine own heart, to thy
everlasting Renown and Glory, and their Eternal comfort and
joy, and felicity with thy Saints and Angels in the Light of thy
countenance, and in everlasting remembrance in the powerful
and Eternal Kingdom of Immortality, if I be no more in this
World, when this body is gone to its place, according to thy E-
ternal Purpose and Decree, in thy Eternal Counsel; so be it, saith
my spirit, yea and *Amen* saith my foul, which blesseth and magnifieth thy Eternal Name, inasmuch as thou hast so far fulfilled thy
(living) Word of Prophesie, and not onely so, but much more also in the defire of my heart, in the behalf of thy dear, tender,
suffering, and long-suffering Seed of thine own bowels, for which
be innumerable Praises, Wisdom, Salvation, Glory and Dominion, to thy holy Name, *Amen, Amen.*

My

MY right dearly and well-beloved Friends of Eternal Life, of the Church of the first-born of the living God, which is the Pillar and ground of Truth, of which Christ Jesus our Lord is the alone and onely Head: Peace be unto you in him, who is arisen in his pure immortal life, and hath brought Life and Immortality to light, through the Word of his Power, and his Eternal Gospel of Peace, which is not hid from us, but it's clearly manifest in us by his coming, who ariseth with healing in his wings: Glory, Dominion, living, endless praises Immortal to his Name, now and for evermore; and let all the upright in heart, with my precious life say, Even so Amen.

Dear suffering, and long-suffering Lambs, ye know, that as I came in the Eternal Love and Peace of Immanuel, God's Lamb, to visit and serve you, and minister to your necessities, the which in the same Life and Peace, and in the integrity and uprightness of heart, and in its pure innocency, my God knoweth; and behold I call your Life that's manifest in you, (in which is our perfect unity as Members of one Body, to bear me record, That I have endeavoured in the good will of my God, to perform the same; and verily, the hand and blessing of Almighty God is with me, and hath blessed me, and so my reward is with me, and my work hath been manifest before me, even in the Light of his Countenance that liveth for ever; and this Scripture is fulfilled in me also, The Father worketh hitherto, and I work. So my dear Friends, I have honestly and nakedly before the Lord cleared my Conscience so far concerning you, and on your behalf, which is my reasonable service; and so I leave the same to the living Testimony of the Lord Jesus which you hold, and for which I am satisfied, (and in the behalf of the whole body of God's Elect you have so long suffered) So the Eternal God of Power, Dominion and Glory, of Heaven and Earth, consolate, support and strengthen you, (to the end) that your Testimony may be finished with joy, to his ever lasting praise to whom onely it belongs; and so my Spirit in the Light and Life Immortal, saith, Even so Amen. Farewel dear Lambs, I am your true Brother,   D. B.

Joseph was not made known to his Brethren the first time, though his Bowels earned towards and over them, till at last he could no longer forbear

bear crying out with tears, saying, I am Joseph your Brother; and lit-tle Benjamin *the youngest, he dearly loved you know.*

.This 5*th.* day of the Week, and the
30*th.* of the 11*th.*Mo.1661.

> *When my face you do not see ,*
> *Wait in the Eternal Life, and then remember me.*
>
> *So farewell, and feel the Well-spring of Life.*

This and many other Papers was communicated to each others hands, (which are seen meet not to be added hereunto) with the jeopardy of my life, and what else did attend us ; but magnified and for ever blessed be the living Lord and his Goodness, Wisdom and Salvation, who prospered his Work and Workers in his own Life of lasting Righteousness, through and over self, over all that which must dye and go to its place, *Amen*.

DANIEL.

Here followeth somewhat relating to the Travel and Service of D. B. which he hath freedom to give forth for the Truth's sake, and Friends satisfaction.

THe intent of the Spirit of the Lord within my heart and mind, stirring me up to write somewhat concerning my travel from my Native Countrey, Kindred and Father's House, being freely given up to serve the Lord, his Truth and People, in the Power and Gospel of God ; I having no imposition or necessity at all laid upon my Conscience, as from any mortal man, but

cer-

certainly it was a pure neceſſity from the living God of Heaven &
Earth, many of his faithful ſervants, Meſſengers, ſons & daughters
that were, & are as dear & precious to me as my own life, may bear
me record on the Lords behalf unto the truth of what I write on
this wiſe; & ſurely in the counſel everlaſting, the thing was hid from
me then whether ever I ſhould return to my Native Countrey or
not. However in the love and favour of God, and in his fear ſet up
within my heart, was I given up, with my body alſo offered as a
living Sacrifice, which was but my reaſonable ſacrifice, to give a
ſound to the Nations afar off, of the mighty day of our God,
and his bleſſed Truth, the Light of Jeſu manifeſt in every Conſcience, in which Light we have moſt aſſuredly believed unto ſalvation: And verily the Power and pure Preſence of his Eternal
Strength was with me, through many hardſhips, trials and tribulations; the right hand of the hiding of his Power did ſweetly
guide, ſtrengthen & ſupport me, even as it did, and doth his Lambs
whom he ſo ſend forth as among Wolves, in his Dovelike innocency, harmleſneſs & wiſdom, which is as wiſe, or rather wiſer than the
Serpents. And this Scripture have I well witneſſed fulfilled whilſt
travelling from one Nation to another people, as my Father did in
the ancient days. And on this wiſe, with three more Brethren, ſo
freely given up with one conſent in the behalf of the Goſpel everlaſting, that is now preaching again to the Nations, Tongues and
Kindreds.

We ſet forward the 16th. of the third Month, and we ſweetly
parted with our right dearly beloved Friends, Brethren, Fathers
and near Relations, that were fleſh of our fleſh and bone of our
bone, and from all our outward acquaintance, and Native Countrey, in the Will, Love and Spirit of our God, in the ſame day
from *Graveſend* we ſet forth; and at the end of 44. days, we arrived at *Legorn* in *Italy*, where we gave a certain ſound of our innocent ſervice and Meſſage of Salvation; and of its life and bleſ-
ſedneſs, coming upon the Nations as a weight either to condemnation or juſtification, as the ſame is received or rejected among
them.

And thus as we had opportunity, among the men of our own
Nation, the *Jews* and others, we gave a ſound and the bleſſing of
the God of Heaven, and his Preſence was with us, whether the
Nation

Nations of men did hear or forbear, but the Witness of God in sundry was reached, and the same answered in us. And herein we are so far well satisfied, whilst others were hardened, who defied us and our Testimony, as their uncircumcised Fathers always did resist and gain-say the truth that saves from sin, and so finally from its condemnation.

And it came to pass after that we had waited upon the Lord to understand his good will and pleasure, he answered us in the joy of our hearts, and we received his counsel, and communicated of the same to each other's satisfaction in the love of God, in which we were wel confirmed to obey the same until the death, as the Lord our God might have permitted for his Name's sake, who then further ordained us to be separated, *viz.* *John Stubs* and *Henry Fell* to pass on towards *Alexandria*, and my dear brother and companion, *Richard Scosstrop*, with me, to pass *Eastward*, to *Smyrna* and *Constantinople*, in *Asia*; and after a little season we parted in the goodness of God. And when 24. dayes were finished, having (in the mean time) touched a little season at the Island *Zant*, we arrived at *Smyrna*. But behold it came to pass, immediately at our coming there was not a little stir, together with the evil surmizings, and what else arising up as a flood, with threatnings breathed forth from the Apostate Christians, especially men of no small degree (of our own Nation) against us, when *Turks*, *Jew*, *Greeks*, *Heathens*, and others, were not altogether so evil affected as to let us from the exercise of our Conscience void of offence towards God and man, and so to hold forth the example of the harmless Life, and unblameable Conversation, in all equitableness in Doctrine, Life and Practice, of what we professed in the midst of them. But oh! how the Christians (by Name) in *Asia* (who should first have received the Word of saving-health) how did they defie and reproach not onely us, but our living Testimony and Message of Blessedness, which day by day was sounded in their ears notwithstanding; the Lord God lay not what they did against us, to their charge, when they have most need of Mercy and Peace with God, if happily repentance unto life be witnessed by them, who know not what they did; yea and my spirit is ready to say *Amen*, for their sakes that hated us without a cause, as the same unbelieving nature did our Lord and Master, whom

whom we love, ferve and honor in the fame, and therefore keep
his fayings, which are not grievous to us in that one and the felf-
fame Spirit which reproves the World for fin, in which we worfhip him as the Father, the which guideth into all truth, from all
evil, concerning which we well admonifhed their minds to fubjectto
the one, and to avoid and turn from the other, each having their
proper effects attending them; as anguifh, woes, judgements
and difquietments upon the foul and confcience that doth evil;
and contrariwife, bleffings, peace, glory, honor, and the goodnefs of God attending the foul of man which worketh good, in
the Light of the fame excellent Spirit of God which exercifeth
the Confcience in temperance and fobriety, meeknefs, and gentle-
nefs of Chrift.

And on this wife we befought the men of our own Nation, together with many more in them parts, that they may become a
fweet favour of the pure life of Chrift and Chriftianity, indeed
and in truth, which tends to anfwer the Witnefs of the Eternal
God manifeft in *Turks, Greeks, Jews, Heathens,* and Apoftate Chri-
ftians among the dark Nations, where they have their converfation: Yet I am conftrained to exprefs fomewhat of their manner of dealing with us to our good; Wherefore men of reafonable
and honorable underftanding, may bear with me, to the end that
the honeft-hearted may be informed to beware of a perfecuting
Spirit, which is not of God, neither ever was it born of him.

Their threatnings encreafed daily, and they burthened themfelves exceedingly with us, whofe deportment and behaviour they
were made to confefs to, as did the Conful and divers others,
which in truth they could not fay otherwife, but that it was tem-
perate, innocent, harmlefs and unblaméable in our converfation;
Magnified be the Lord, and bleffed be his Grace of Life, by which
we in fubmiffion to the fame were guided herein: But becaufe our
Teftimony was not for, but againft whatfoever might be faid in
truth to be evil, unjuft, or unequitable, (*which is difhonorable* therefore were we hated of the high and lofty ✱ to the difquieting of
their own reft day and night, becaufe they burthened themfelves
fo with the truth and innocency of the Lord's Teftimony, which
our Life held forth among them who received not the fame in his
love that they might be faved not onely from fin, but alfo from
the

the wrath to come. So they forthwith sent a Message from *Smyr-*
na, to the great City *Constantinople*, to the King's Embassador of
England, and besought him to expel us out from among them of
Asia, that we might not have a being in the extent of their Authority, in visiting them on this wise, as by the annexed Warrant
thou that reads the same, may understand.

A Copy of the Warrant which they produc't and prosecuted.

WHereas we are informed, that there is lately arrived with the
Zant Frigot, one Daniel Baker, *with his Companion,common-*
ly called Quakers, *with intention to come up to this Port ; and because*
we sufficiently have had experience, that the carriage of that sort of
people is ridiculous, and is capable to bring dishonor to our Nation, be-
sides other ill-conveniences that may redound to them in particular, and
to the English *in general :*

We therefore will and require you to give a stop to the said Quakers,
from proceeding any further in their journey either to Constantinople;
or the present Court of the Grand Signior, (viz. *the Great Emperor of*
the Turks) *or to any other place where our Authority extends, shipping*
them away either directly for England, *or any other part which they*
shall chuse to imbarque.

And we do hereby require all Officers and Members of the Factory,
and Masters and Officers of Ships, to be aiding and assisting to you
herein : And for so doing, this shall be your Warrant.

For our loving Friend, 'Antho-ny Isaacson, *Esquire,Consul for the* English *Nation at* Smyrna ; *By his Excellency's command,* Paul Ricoat, *Se-cretary.*	*Given under our Hand and Seal, at our Court at* Pare *of* Constan-tinople, *the* 19th. day of July, (*it should be* August, *for we were not in* Asia *in the Month called* July) 1661.Winchelf.4.

And forthwith this Warrant was dispatcht with a Messenger from the Embassador's Court at *Constantinople*, to *Smyrna*; and behold, the Merchants of the Earth, and others that could not endure to hear of the found of Truth, received the same not with little gladness,(poor me! wo and alas for them!) the end of which will not be peace, but contrariwise, wo and misery; and they put the same Warrant in execution, and fent a *Turkish* Janifary, and a *Drugerman*, that were Officers under the Conful of the *English* Nation; and they came with *Harmols*, (*viz.* called *Porters*) with *Cain's* Weapons, and fetcht us from our Lodging before the Conful; and the man was courteous and moderate, and had his ear open then to what we in the reverence and fear of the Lord then faid unto him, which was his honor, who then faw over and beyond that foolish Ceremony of the Hat, neither did he burthen himfelf with the fame, as many unwifely do, to the clouding or veiling of the nobility of a good underftanding, which hath a more noble refpect to Equity, Juftice and Judgement, without refpect of perfons in them, where it is fet up in its proper and peculiar Authority, than to fuch foolifh ceremonies which are below men of Wifdom; yet he defired that we might not take it ill as from him (in his place of Authority) in doing as he was obliged in the profecution of the Warrant, which fummoned all Officers and Members of the Factory, with Mafters and Officers of Ships, to be aiding and affifting to furprize and banifh two innocent, naked, harmlefs men, that had neither Bow nor Sword, nor any fuch like material, or vifible Weapon of War to refift evil, as *Paul* and *Barnabas* had not, againft whom the hard-hearted *Jews* cryed out with the fame voice, *Help men of Ifrael, &c.* and fuch like ftir there was; and we let the Conful firft know at our firft coming, that we owned his place of Authority, and were ready to fubmit to any thing that was juft or equitable; and at laft in this thing we could not fubmit without fuffering, forafmuch as in the uprightnefs of our heart, and in the innocency of the fame were we come fo far to do the Will of God, and to fuffer for it, as his hand permitted.

So with many other expreffions I cleared my Confcience, as alfo by Words, fufferings and Writings, to the whole Nation there; and the Conful feemed to be unwilling to ufe violence against us

that

that at our departure prayd for them that hated us without a caus, knowing not what they did; we seeing it could not at that season be otherwise, but what the Lord had permitted them to bring to pass, not to their justification, but as a Judgement among them from the living God, who did not onely dispence the visitation of his Love and Salvation day by day among them; but he visited them also with the strokes of his displeasure, even unto death and destruction: And surely he smote and took away of the chiefest, and others of them daily. And verily my heart often cryed, and besought the Lord for them (in secret more especially; though I was constrained not to cease uttering my voice openly among them, and for them) while they sought my hurt; as many of them (I know) by the Witness of God in them may remember. And so we were sent away as Prisoners, or rather as Lambs driven from the Dens of Lyons, or from the barren Caves of ravening Wolves, whose Nature wooried them.

Now we had spoken for a passage by a *Dutch* ship, to have gone from thence to *Constantinople*; but before the ship departed *Smyrna*, the Warrant came to the Consul's hands, which thou mayest see came not from either them called *Turks, Jews, Heathen, Greeks* or *Barbarians*, but even from the men of our own Nation. Alas! alas! yea wo and alas for them.

So the Reader may see what a stir there hath been in the Region of *Asia* against the appearance of Truth, and its innocency, in plainness, to expel and banish it, together with its Message and Messengers, out of their coasts or borders; and not to have any entertainment, or at least to come within the extent of their Authority, whatever becomes of them; let them go where they will, &c. So as in effect they say, We will not have this man, the Light, Truth, Temperance Innocency, its Life and Wisdom from above, to rule, or have its preheminence over us in our Consciences; We will rather chuse to live in the practice of our own evil hearts and ways; and therefore thus to their own hurt they say unto God, *Depart from us, for we desire not the*   Job. 21. *knowledge of thy ways, and as for the Word of the Lord, we have no delight in it.* Lo they have rejected the Word of the Lord, and what Wisdom is in them? And such the holy, perfect and upright man saw rebel against the   Job 24. 13

O   Light,

Light, and said, They are of those that rebel against the Light, they know not the wayes thereof, neither abide in the paths thereof.

And so with consent they joined together to banish Truth, its Message, and Messengers of Peace, which provoked them to jealousie that believe not, who scorned us as fools, and what else, not honestly considering, how that God is provoking the Nations to jealousie and wrath with a foolish people, as in the ancient days, *Deut. 22.* was prophesied. And such besought our Lord and Master, even Jesus, to depart out of their Coasts or Borders, who loved and fed their Swine upon the Mountains, even the *Gadarenes* besought him to depart, who saith, *He that loveth Father or Mother, or what else, more than me, is not worthy of me*; and Father and Mother, and such Relations, are of more honourable esteem than many Swine. And to his Disciples he also saith (that was dead, and is alive, and liveth for ever) *As they have done unto me, so will they do unto you; if they have persecuted me, they will also persecute you.* These are his faithful and true sayings; *He that receiveth you, receiveth me; and he that receiveth me,*

John 13.20 *receiveth him that sent me;* [mark that:] *Verily, verily I say unto you, Whomsoever receiveth whom I shall send, receiveth me; and him that receiveth me, receiveth him that sent me,* &c. *He that despiseth you, despiseth me; and he that despiseth me, despiseth him that sent me.* And it's to be understood, that such like dealing *J.S.* and *H.F.* our Brethren, found at *Alexandria*, from whom they also were banished.

And on this wise being rejected, despised, banished out of *Asia*, from *Smyrna*, in about eight dayes we arrived at the Island *Zant*, where my dear Brother and Companion, in sufferings, and not onely so, but in the Kingdom and patience of Christ, he was visited with sickness nigh unto death; but the Word and Commandment of the Lord ordered me to pass through part of *Italy*, and my face was set towards *Venice*; and we weighed the thing in the fear and counsel of the Lord, and were both given up in one to travel; yet it was so that the poor Lamb was not capable in body to travel with me, by reason of weakness; and he being fully perswaded and satisfied in his own mind, that I was to pass onward, in the tender Love of our God he did the more constrain

me;

me, I finding some unwillingnels to leave him in that condition, which was not a little crofs unto me. But in the Heavenly Will and Peace of our God, and joy of the Lord, out of all vifibly we parted afunder, and it came to pafs, that he laid down his body there in about two days after.

There being a Ship of *Venite* ready, I embarqued on the fame, and had a good paffage through the Gulf of *Venice*. After three Weeks were finifhed, was I admitted (together with the Ships company) to receive Product or Admiffion to come into the City as their manner is; and there I continued about eight days as a fign and wonder among many, and gave fomewhat of a found of the Lord's Day (in truth) among them; and from thence I travelled to *Legorn*, and my face was as if it were fet towards *England*, I being alone, as a Mourning-Dove in a defolate Wildernefs: Yet it came fo to pafs, when I arrived at the fame Port or City, that the everlafting Love of my God did fill and overcome my heart, and mine eye right dearly affected the fame, and verily the living Word and Commandment of my God founded in mine ear, and mine underftanding was quickened in the Spirit of Life from God, fo that I was made willing, and not to rebel againft the Heavenly Voice, [And what if I teftifie, that mine eye faw the Angel of his prefence?] which was exprefly for me to give up, and pafs away from thence, to vifit his long fuffering Seed of Innocency, fhut up in the Inquifition, in the Ifle of *Malta*, under the Pope's Authority, and to communicate to their neceffities; and verily the fweet promife of the Lord entered and poffeffed my heart, and my God made my way profperous; for in the Light of his countenance he had often fet thefe poor, afflicted, longfuffering innocents before my face: Wherefore my body and mind was freely offered up as my reafonable fervice, to ferve his Truth, and the leaft Member of it; and fo to the death of the Crofs, whereto I became obedient in uprightnefs of heart, as if I fhould never fee Kindred or Native Countrey more.

A Veffel of *France* being ready to depart from thence Eaftward, I embarqued thereon for the Ifle of *Cicilia* to *Mufena*, and from thence to the Ifle of *Malta* in a Veffel of the faid Ifland; and in my paffage the Veffel did bear in to *Syracufe*, where *Paul* abode three days in his paffage to *Rome*, (after he had fuffered

O 2

 fhip-

abode three days in his passage to *Rome* (after he had suffered a shipwrack on *Malta*;) and at *Syracuse* I abode five days, where I gave a sound of the Lord's Truth and Life: And so we immediately sailed from thence, and within 24. hours we arrived at the Island of *Malta*; and within some hours after I came upon the said Island, I had admittance to the Pope's Lord Inquisitor, to whom I delivered my Message in the *Italian* Tongue, on this wise, *I am come to demand the just Liberty of my innocent Friends; the two English women in prison in the Inquisition:* And he asked, if I were related to them as a Husband or Kinsman, and whether I came out of *England* on purpose with that Message. And I answered, I came from *Legorn* for that same end; and he replied at last, They should abide in Prison till they dye, except some *English* Merchants or others that were able, would engage or give obligation for the value of three or four thousand dollers, conditionally, that they should never return again into those parts.

On this wise was his reply divers times, with the Consul and many others; together and asunder, but in the Name and fear of the Lord God I withstood the same unchristian-like demand and cruelty, in the Word, Power and Travel of the Lord in his innocent, suffering Lambs behalf, albeit they daily threatned me with their cruelty and Inquisition of darkness, and followed me to and fro with their Officer and Black-Rod, and the Popes Deputy would have bound me that I should neither speak good nor evil to any one while I was on the Island, as the Consul said, save to him; neither to come to the Prison alone, except the Consul came also with me, or some of his Family at least: But their snares, Bonds and Covenants, in the Name of my God I defied, because the Spirit of Life from the Lord gave me Dominion through sufferings in Spirit, First, over their unjust, dark Impositions; yea, and in the same good authority, in the innocency and uprightness of my heart, I travelled through, and over the darkness, over its works, and ceased not to publish the end of my coming; which they would not have known abroad, & the sound of Truth, and its dread and same struck terror in their hearts, that both high, and wise great men together with the Popish Priests and Jesuits, knights them called of the Nobility, of the Pope's Dominion of *Spain* and *France*, and of many Nations; they did not but then themselves a little with my bodily presence, my clear te-
stimony

timony, and Friends in general, all which they defied and withstood; as it doth appear by the words of Truth in this Treatise.

And thus it comes to pass among the Nations, because we are not of this world, as our Life and Testimony also is not for, but against the same; therefore we marvel not if the world hate us, knowing its birth which is from beneath, earthly and sensual, persecuteth that which is from above, heavenly and spiritual, and so the Lord hath made me as a burthensome stone among them. My heart blesseth his Name that wonderfully preserved me. Yet some of them came to see somewhat of my innocency.

About 24. dayes I abode upon the said Island, they daily continuing their threatnings against me as aforesaid, and many times attempted me to take my passage to Cicilis, or to some parts of Italy, to produce the unreasonable and unchristian-like Obligation demanded by them; but in the fear of God I, with my dear friends, withstood them, and they were freely given up, rather to suffer, then to hurt God's truth and people thus to gratifie them, who (as it doth appear) the Spirit of the Lord God of truth rules neither in Pope, nor in any of his Lords, Priest or Jesuits, that exerciseth such Lordship over the innocent, long-suffering Heritage of the everlasting God. The time hasteneth, and behold it cometh to pass, that the weight of eternal Vengeance is coming over them, which the man of sin; and his sons of perdition will not be able to bear: For the doleful cry of the Innocent, it sighs and groans with tears, hath long uttered its voice, which hath ascended into the ears of the most high, who is higher hen the highest, yet hath he respect unto the needy, to uphold them, yea and to such as are of an upright, contrite, lowly, and trembling heart; What if I should say, the God of love and long-suffering dwels in such? and verily their sacrifice is acceptable in his bosome that liveth for ever; and I am a living witness, that the sweet testimony and innocent sufferings of these his long-suffering Lambs, is right dear and precious in his eye, which is the light of his countenance; and so is it not otherwise, but the same in oneness with his people concerning them.

And so in the endless Mercy, Blessing and Peace of our God we parted, and I came away with the love and peace of my God within my heart, having the answer and living testimony of a good Conscience; and in the wisdom of God brought away these their words and writings, which testifieth somewhat of their sufferings and faithfulness unto the Lord, his truth and people, which I right well know, cannot be shut out of the Record of life Eternal, unto which I bear record again, that they have been, and are a sweet savour unto the Lord God of faithfulness, and so their reward, which attends the same, is not onely with them, but with all the sons and daughters of truth and innocency, that are so travelling in their long-sufferings, which are but light and momentary in competition to the Eternal weight of glory which afterwards is to be revealed in the same that suffered in all generations, even from righteous Abel, unto this day of our God, to whom be wisdom, glory, salvation, and everlasting thanksgivings and dominion, for ever, Amen, saith my soul and spirit, even so Amen.

And it came to pass in the the third month of the year 1662. also after my God had well preserved me in my passage, and in his work and service from Malta to diverse places in Italy, till I came to the Straights Mouth (of the

Mediter-

Mediterranean Sea)at the place called *Gibralter*, it was the pleasure of the Lord God to suffer the wind and weather to continue contrary well nigh about 30 daies, in which season I suffered many trials and tribulations in spirit, having little or no rest in the same, because of the Vision and words of the Everlasting which soundest often up to my understanding, even as the roaring of a Lyon, which mine eye saw, and mine ear heard also [in the year --61. when I was a Prisoner for the pure Word and testimony of God and his Truth, in *Worcester* City [ayl, before I departed *England*] and the place was the high Mountain of *Gibralter* that stands within the King of *Spains* Dominion, which was the subject of the Vision; and ofen as I cast mine eye upon the scituation of the place, the pure life and power of God's Eternal presence did arise up in me, in the Word of Life, so that I saw clearly that some great exceeding weighty service for his Name and eternal Truths sake was to be done by me, which was so terrible and dreadful to me, when as I entred into reasoning, so that I was brought down even to the jaws of death in dust and ashes; and as Jonah turned his back upon *Niniveh*, the same temptation attended me also, to my wounding, before I could give up; for I fled often from the place to escape with my life from among such an unreasonable and bloody generation, and the Lord would not be intreated to let such a bitter Cup pass unfulfilled, but behold with the sound and stroak of his eternal Word, his Spirit of Life became awakened, quickned and mightily revived in me, in his Wisdom, over all fear of the Nations of men, and the same brake through the snares and bonds of death, and over destruction and the true seed that mourned, cried, *Not my will, but thy will be done, on earth as it is in heaven*; and so it was a hard thing to part with little *Isaac* which is received again in the Covenant of promise of Life, and that was offered up which fled so often (but at last was caught in a thicket). When the ships of diverse Nations attempted to pass through; but the God of heaven, whom the wind and sea obeieth, suffered them not, but they knew not what the matter was which was revealed within my heart, as the displeasure of God was against them, to humble them also, as I told them often by words and writings to clear my conscience; albeit they strove, being perplexed in their minds, and attempted often, to wit 7 or 8 times in about 21 daies, and could not pass but about 2 or 3 leagues, and on this wise it happened, it would ether prove calm, and then the current would drive them back into the Streights again sometimes, and otherwhile storms and tempests would scatter them, as a figure of *Pharaoh* and his Host of Egyptian darkness, so that the Charet-wheels mine eye saw struck off, so that they drove but heavily, within, and without; and at last I gave out among them, that God had service for me to do at that place, and my life was given up to do his will, if I never saw my Native Country, Kindred, or Fathers house at all any more; and therefore the pleasure of the Lord in his mighty power had made me willing, and also gave me dominion through and over the bonds and snares of death and destruction, as it were to lay down my precious life, that I may take it again, together with the body, which through his righteous judgments he had prepared to perform the good pleasure of his Almightiness, for his Truth and Names sake. Now the heavenly voice was often sounded within my heart en this wise, saying; O *Jerusalem, cut off thine hair*, and furthermore to gird sackcloth on my loins,

As to the Prophet
Jeremy, Chap.7.

and so I became obedient in the singleness and innocency of my heart, unto the God of Heaven, of my life, as a dreadful sign against the Whorish Church of Rome, and against all her Heads and Horns throughout the world: And I then signified to the Master of the ship in which I was a passenger, how that I did believe that God would soon give opportunity for the Fleet of ships to pass away after this service of God was performed & after I had used many perswasions, to the end that he might suffer my body on that wise to be cast among the wicked idolaters, lyars and murtherers, which are like the troubled sea. So the ship-Master let my body *Isaiah 57.20.* be on this wise cast over board from the ship, [God having provided a great Whale to swallow up that which fled from his presence so often] and so it happened, that it was upon one of their called, Holy-dayes, or Saints days, namely, the day called *Holy-Thursday.*

So I being cast on dry land, passed through their streets directly, until I came into the Mass-House or Idolater temple, among the Idolaters, where I found the Fryer, or Priest, at the high *Altar*, down upon his knees, in his white Surplice, adoring of the Host, (which is a *Chalice*, or a piece of bread, which they call the real substance of the body of Christ, after their unclean spirit of darkness hath muttered some words over it, which they call *Consecration*:) and after I had stood a season viewing this Idolatry with the indignation of the Eternal God set up within my heart against the same, I turned my back-part upon the Priest, and his dead God, and dumb Idols, at the high *Altar*; and in the holy Commandment of life eternal, my face was set towards the people, and I beheld them a certain season in the power of God in which I stood; I saw the multitude of ignorant people upon their knees also, worshipping the dark inventions and imaginations of their sottish leaders, and blind guides, and they know not what; and in the Lord's time (which mine eye had a circumspect heed unto) I then spread forth my arms, and stript off my Vesture, and rent the same from top to bottom, in divers pieces, and cast them from me with indignation. And then I took my Hat off my head, (which was the uppermost covering of the outside of a man) and cast the same under my feet, and stamped upon these things; and the nakedness appeared with the sack-cloath covering, to their astonishment; and then with a clear voice I sounded Repentance three times, and gave testimony as the sound of a trumpet among them, that the life of Christ and his Saints was arisen from the dead; and so passed away, sounding the same words of the Lord's Message, with Repentance, through the streets, as it were, flying from the Idols temple, and from Idolatry, and Idolaters, until I came to the sea-side, and there was I moved to kneel down and pray, and give thanks to the living Lord, who had so wonderfully preserved me in doing his pleasure and good will on earth; and he suffered no man to touch or do me harm,

And the next day following the Lord God gave opportunity accordingly as I had let the Ship-master know I believed would come to pass, and it was so, and all the Fleet did partake of the blessing: But how many of them rewarded me (men of my own Nation, to whom I also continued a sign, which they spake bitter things against) the Lord my God saw the same, and smote them with rebuke and astonishment in his displeasure, who in his wise determinate Counsel, ordained me for many dayes and nights to be tryed on this wise, and to fall among divers temptation: afterwards, the which as a mighty

Host

e f surrounded and beset me on every hand, immediately after I had done the good will in his all-sufficient power and strength; thus the Enemy with his subtilty in a mysterie was suffered to compass me about, to steale away my peace and reward with my God, in whom the same is hid; and then I was in a blessed condition, though sometime veiled for a little season, and then the Fathers countenance was hid from mine eye, and therefore was I troubled; Yet blessed are ye when you fall among divers temptations, saith one, and verily they were even as thorns in my flesh, yea as Messengers of Satan suffered to buffet me for a season, even as the servant of God witnessed, who was wrapt up into the third Heaven: What if I should somewhat testifie, so was it with me, lest I should be exalted above measure, so that I was made to bow and fall upon my face, and cry day and night to the Lord of Eternal life, that had respect to the tears of the innocent, and bowed the strength of his arm to support the lowly: And so his Almightiness gave ear to the sighs and groans of my distressed state, and had respect unto the voice of my mourning, as a Dove or Pelican in the Wilderness; and verily his Grace I found sufficient to save and preserve my innocency, in its sweet life of holiness to the Lord, through all this, and that which letted, salvation to his Name, Amen. So his strength is made perfect in weakness, even so it is in truth, in which I set to my seal of my right hand, that God is true, in which life I give thanks to his Name of Power and Defence, the which over all Nations is to be exalted in the hearts of his Saints, as in the ancient dayes, yea and much more abundantly in the Light of his bright-shining countenance, in which his Eternal and excellent glory, and pure dreadful Majesty, for ever hath his holy habitation; to whom be endless Dominion, with praises living and everlasting, over all, Amen.

Written in Newgate this 5th. Month, the 18th. day, 1662.. where he suffereth Bonds, together with many Brethren of Truth, for one and the same Testimony of the Lord Iesus, not for evil doing or speaking, but against the same: For we suffer because we cannot otherwise but meet together in the Name and Fear of God; neither swear at all, neither by Heaven, nor by Earth, nor by any other Oath, Matth.5. James 5.12.   D. B.

A Copy of a Paper which was written in the Spanish Tongue, and delivered the same day that I was upon the service, directed as followeth, Viz.

For the Governor and Inhabitants of Gibletore, in the Kingdom of Spain

BEhold, behold, the great day of God is come, and of his wrath, and of the wrath of his Lamb is come, and the hour of his Judgments is come, Wherefore Oh Inhabitants of the earth, Repent, Repent, Repent, and fear God, and give glory & honor to him that made Heaven and Earth, and the Fountains of Waters: Wo, wo, wo to the Inhabitants of the earth: And I heard another voice from Heaven, saying, Come out of her my people; that ye partake not of her sins, & that ye receive not of her plagues. These are the words of the power of Christ that is contrary to the false Church.

Behold, behold, Plagues, Plagues, Plagues are coming upon the Church of Rome, and upon her Heads in England, & in all parts of the world. And the Woman which thou sawest is that great City which reigneth over the Kings of the earth; and he saith unto me, the waters which thou sawest where the Whore sitteth, are Peoples, Nations, Multitudes and Tongues; &c

These words, with a Paper in Latine, with honest words of truth, was delivered with many more Scriptures in their own Language, that they may read, understand, repent, & cease from idolatry, & from all ungodliness, that the blessings of Eternal life might arise through Judgments, & have room among the Nations, to the eternal glory & renown of the Lord God over all who is blessed for ever. Amen.

A
CHRISTIAN
WOMANS
Experiences of the glo-
rious working of Gods free grace.

Published for the Edification of others, by
KATHERINE SUTTON.

Luk. 24: 24. *And they found it even so, as the VVomen had said.*

AT ROTTERDAM,
Printed by HENRY GODDÆUS, Printer in the Newſtreet,
Anno 1663.

COURTEOUS READER.

WHEN our Lord and Saviour JESUS CHRIST had fed many with a few *Loves*, he commanded his Disciples to gather up the *Fragments*, that nothing he lost, *Iohn.* 6. 12. And when God was pleased to poure out of his Spirit upon some of his faithful *Servants* in our Generation, he had also some of his *Handmaides*, who gathered up the *Crumes* of that spiritual Bread, which the Lord blessed and distributed among his Disciples: Of which Number this holy *Matron* was one. Now there are three Arguments whereby it may appear, that God would not have these *Fragments* (which she hath gathered into her Basket) to be lost, viz. *First*, Because, God made them (by his Blessing) food to her soul in the gathering, and receiving them into her own heart, and also to the soules of several young *Virgins* in her family, unto whom the Lord made some of these *Crumes* the bead of eternal Life. *Secondly*, Because when she had lost the manuscript (where in these and many other of her Experiences were written) in a sea storme wherein she suffered Shipwrack, yet God, who preserved her life, did also preserve these Experiences in her heart, where it seemeth they were written, not with ink but by his holy Spirit. *Thirdly*, Because she being pressed in Spirit to Communicate them more publikely, the Spirit of the Lord did bring them again to her remembrance, and she hath been made willing to publish them as her *Testimony* and witness of the free grace, and fresh *Anoyntings* of the Lords Spirit, whom he hath promised to poure forth upon his servants, and Handmaides in the last dayes, *Ioel* 2: 28, 29, 31, 32. Now for as much as this little Book is presented to thee, CHRISTIAN READER, as a Basket full of *Fragments*, be not offended with the broakenness of any matter, which thou mayest meet within the *Reading* thereof: considering, that God, who hath made them a blessing to others, may bless them unto thee. Thou mayest take notice of *three Things* in this little Book, which I judge worthy of every Christians observation, to wit, *first*, Her *extraordinary* Teachings of God by his holy Spirit and Word, when she could not enjoy the *ordinary* means of his own appointments. This godly Woman (after God hath begun the good work of grace in her soul) would not loose any opportunity she could get either in publicke or private for her precious soul, but would often break thorrow some difficulties and, endure some hardships to enjoy such opportunities; and this she did at that time, when many professors sleighted and neglected (O grievous Sin! yea contemned the Ministry of the word. Now observe, That as she followed the Lord, and waited upon him in the use of the means of Grace, when she could enjoy it, so the Lord was pleased (of the exceeding Richts of his free Grace) not onely to do her soul good by his presence and power therein: But also (when she could not enjoy the *Outward* meanes of grace) the Lord waited to be gracious unto her soul, and followed her with the *inward* teachings of his holy Spirit, and word, as she hath witnessed in many particulars in this her Book. And if thy experience, COURTEOUS READER, cannot seal unto the Testimony, that she gives of those Spiritual Teachings: Yet do not stumble at them, do not judge her, for she hath received an Unction from the

holy

holy One, and is taught of God. In the Reading of her Book, thou wilt meet with some suddain and unexpected Transition from one thing to another, (and thou mayest think it to be somewhat abruptly) yet Censure not too rashly, but rather consider, that even this also may, yea doth hold some proportion unto the course of Heaven and Heavenly communications. The Husbandman will not wonder to see showers and shinings, bright and dark Clouds succeed each other, knowing that the Rain which comes from Heaven hath its seasons and its measure too. Will the Marriner marvel to see the seas swell and rage in a great storme, or admire the stilness and smoothness of the deep watters in a great calme. Or will any who liv s upon the sea coast think the frequent Ebbing & flowing of the tyde a strange thing. Neither will any experienced Christian marvel at the suddain Ebbing and flowing of joyes, and sorrowes in the hearts of Saints. The operations and Administrations of the Spirit are various, 1. Cor. 12: 4, 5, 6, 7. Some times the Spirit is poured out upon the soules of Believers (*as floods upon the dry ground*) And those spiritual showers and shinings do make a spring of Grace in the wilderness of their hearts. Where of the Lord hath spoaken by his Prophets. *Isa.* 51:3. and 44: 3, 4. and 32: 15, 16, 17. *Ier.* 31: v. 12. But at other times the glory of the Saints comforts, joyes, and light is so clouded, and eclipsed, that they are under great desertions, *Isa.* 54: vers. 7, 8, 11. Yea and may for some time walk in dakness and have no light, *Isa.* 50: 10. *Secondly,* Another thing I judge worthy the Readers observation in this Book, is this Christian womans Experience of the presence and power of God, accompanying her consciencious endeavours to do good unto the souls of others both in her own family especially, and also in some other families, where she sojourned some time. I mention not this for her praise, who desires that God alone may have all the Glory of whatsoever he hath done for her or by her; (*she needs no Epistles of Commendation from men*) But seeing her Experiences are made so publicke, my hearts desire is, that Parents and Governours of families would follow her Example therein: Endeavouring (as she did) the Conversion and sanctification of them, whom God had committed to their charge, by Instructions, councel, and reproofe, which she administred, with so much love, wisdome, zeal, and tenter heartedness, that they proved by Gods blessing an effectual means of the conversion of many, some of whom are yet living witnesses of the truth hereof, and also of many other her Experiences related in this her Book. She was not onely a Governesse, but (as it were) a Prophetess in her family, for she prayed constantly with her children and Maidens, she also read the holy Scriptures daily unto them, and so spake from them, that many of them, who heard her (*in her family duties*) believed and turned to the Lord. She opened her mouth with wisdome, and in her tongue was the Law of kindness, as Solomon spake of the virtuous woman, *Pro.* 31: 26, 27, 28, 29. She did so Chatechise the young children, and instruct the elder maidens, tha t they all learned to know, and many of them to do their duty to God and man. *Thirdly,* there is yet one thing more, which I would have thee, *Courteous Reader*, to ponder in thy heart, *to wit*, the gift of singing spiritual Songs and Hymnes, whih she presents thee with some instances of in her Book, here and there occasionally touching, which Administration I am willing for thy edification to say; 1. That singing of Psalmes, Hymnes, and Spiritual Songs (*being an Ordinance of Gods worship*) ought to be performed by a gift, and the assistance of the Spirit, as well as prayer. 1. *Cor.* 14: 12, 15. What is it then? *I will pray with the Spirit*, &c. *I will sing with the Spirit*, &c. Now as to take a book and read a prayer out of it, or to say a prayer without the Book, is not to pray in the Spirit, so to read a Psalme in a Book, and sing it, or to sing the same Psalme without the Book is

not

not to sing in the Spirit: If the singing of Psalmes be a part of Gods worship (as doubtless it is) then it ought to be performed by assistance of the spirit, for the true worshippers ought to worship God in spirit and truth, John. 4: 23, 24. 2. That Christians ought to sing Spiritual Songs and Hymnes, *as well as Psalmes*; unto the Lord; And that with grace in their hearts, *Col.* 3: 16. for the melody (*which the Lord loveth*) is in the heart, rather then in the voyce, *Eph.* 5: 19. 3. They who performe this part of Gods worship, whether they speak unto themselves in private, or unto others more publickly, ought to have the word of Christ, to dwell richly in them, yea and to be filled with the Spirit, as the Apostle testifieth, *Ephes.* 5: *vers* 17, 18, 19, 20. and *Coloss.* 3: *vers* 16. I have known some other Godly and gracious Christians (*besides this grave and holy Matron*) who have this gift of Singing: and I my self have some experience of this kinde of Anoynting of the Spirit of praise, which will (*I hope*) ere long be powred forth upon the sons and daughters of Zion. And then they will praise Jehovah, singing to the Lord a new Song, and his praise in the Congregation of Saints, as is prophesied, *Psal.* 149: 1, 2, 5. and *Isai.* 51: 11. and 52: 1, 8. &c. The holy Spirit can dictate the Matter, yea and words of praise and singing, as well as the matter and words of prayer: And why may not the Lord assist a poor gracious humble soul to sing in the Spirit, as well as to pray in the Spirit: seeing there nothing too hard for God, to do? It was by many (and is still by some) denyed, that there is any such thing as a Spiritual gift of prayer, *save onely that which is acquired.* And yet the gracious experience of many Godly persons doth testify that there is such a gift of the Spirit, called a spirit of supplication, which is powred forth upon the Lords people. And although many nay most Godly Christians do not believe there is any such Spiritual gift of singing as I have here intimated, yet some few poor gracious humble soules have good Experience, that there is sometimes a measure of the holy Spirit powred upon them, whereby they are so filled with the Spirit, that they break forth into singing: Pray therefore that thou mayest sing, and praise the Lord, when the Redeemed of the Lord shall return and come with singing to Zion, *Isa.* 51: 11. And the Children of Zion be joyful in their King. *Psal.* 149: 1. Unto whom be glory and dominion for ever, AMEN. So prayeth he, who waiteth for his Kingdome and Coming.

HANSERD KNOLLYS.

ERRATA.

PAg. 1. Line 8, 9. *read* forbearance; *line* 16. *r.* sinned; *l.* 19. *r.* petty. *Pag.* 3. *line*. 1. *r.* I was stirred; *line*. 3. 4. *r.* to me towards Heaven. *Pag.* 4. *l.* 7. *r.* stumblest; *Pag.* 6. *l.* 1. *r.* heed; *Pag.* 7. *l.* 6. *r.* Christening; *Pag.* 8. *l.* 25. 26. *r.* unbelief: *Pag.* 9. *l.* 12. *read* renewings.

These and some other litteral mistakes the Reader is desired to mend in the perusal of this Book.

A

Christian Womans experiences of the glorious working of Gods free Grace.

 Had once hard thoughts of the people of God, yet being on a time perſwaded to go to hear them, I went though not out of love to them, but to vvatch vvhat I could obſerve; and being then over perſwaded againſt them, and the Miniſters Text (that then preacht) was Rom. 2: 4, 5, 6. or *Diſpiſeſt thou the riches of his goodneß, and forbeacance, and long ſuffering, not knowing that the goodneß of God leadeth thee uuto repentance; but after thy hardneß and impenitent heart treaſureſt up to thy ſelf wrath againſt the day of wrath, and revelation of the righteous Judgment of God, who will render to every man according to his deeds.*

Verily at this opportunity the dread of God did much ſmite upon my heart, that I had ſo long ſinnend againſt his patience and goodneſz. He had this paſſage, that the ſword of the Lord hung as in a twine threed, to cut of all pitty ſwearers; and I having been one that durſt not ſwear great oathes, (but ſmall ones I was addicted to) I thought it met with my particular condition : Then had I little acquaintance with any that feared the Lord; unleſs it were one family, and they were much afraid of me for a ſeaſon, becauſe I had been ſo vain.

Then was I caſt upon the Lord alone, who did much ſupport mee by his grace, bleſſed be his name; yet the very firſt night after he began to work upon my heart, I fell under this temptation, that I should not eat any more, but rather die, and then I should ceaſe from ſinning againſt the Lords goodneſs; I then caſt away my prayer-book, for it did not

reach

reach my neceſſities, and I cried unto the Lord alone to teach mee to pray; Then did I endeavour to keep cloſe to the beſt teaching miniſtery I could find; I was very ignorant, yet did ſearch the Scriptures diligently: but found them very dark to mee, I dayly ſaw a more clear diſcovery of my ſinful nature, and then began to be ſorely perplexed with fears thad I could not be a child of God, becauſe I knew not how to get victory over my ſin, and though I uſed all meanes I could, yet my corruptions would ſometimes break forth, which made mee often times ready to diſpare, and to caſt of all.

But one day amongſt the reſt the Lord made mee reſolve, though he kild mee, yet I would truſt in him; he made mee alſo deſire of him that if he would not ſave mee, yet that he would not let mee go back again into ſin (for the ſence of Gods goodneſs was much upon my heart.)

Then in ſeveral Sermons God was pleaſed to ſpeak peace to my poor ſoul, yet after through the violence of temptations, I often queſtioned my condition; ſometimes I was tempted to murder my ſelf, ſometimes to ſtarve my ſelf; yet the Lord upheld mee, for I could not make my caſe known to any but God for the ſpace of two years, all which ſeaſon I was wonderfully kept by the power of God alone. In this time was I called by my friends into a darck corner of the land full of ignorance, yet I was ſorely troubled, eſpecially when I was overtaken with any ſin, ſtill I fell down before the Lord bewailing my ſins; then did the Lord give mee much comfort from this place of Scripture. Jer. 31: 20. *Is Ephraim my dear ſon is he a pleaſant child, for ſince I ſpake againſt him, I do earneſtly remember him ſtill: therefore my bowels are troubled for him; I will ſurely have mercy upon him.* ſaith the Lord.

Now in the place where I was were many Papiſts, and they much endeavoured to have mee of their judgment: But God kept mee in a thirſting frame of ſpirit after the preaching of the word, and often caſt in my mind, that I ſhould, Matt. 6: 33. *Firſt ſeek the Kingdom of God, and the righteouſneſs thereof, and all other things ſhould be added.*

Wee had in that place a bad Miniſter, but to God I made my ſupplication, and uſed what means I could to obtain a better, and God was pleaſed to anſwer my deſires, and ſent a better to that very place, who remained there the time that I ſtayed, under whoſe honneſt teachings I often met with ſweet refreshing.

Then

Then was ſtirred up by my friends to change my condition, to be married to an husband; upon which I did earneſtly begg of God that I might have one that did fear the Lord, that he might be a furtherance to heaven, and indeed ſo hee was. For I married with a man that was much in practical diuties, yet ſome difference there was in our judgments, which often cauſed no ſmall trouble in my ſpirit: but it had this effect, it cauſed mee to cry to God, and to ſearch the Scriptures, ſo much the more, uſing all means for a right underſtanding in the things and wayes of God, and it became helpful to mee. And in this time of my earneſt ſeeking of God alone, he was pleaſed to diſcover to mee by dreames and viſions of the night, the ugglineſs of ſin in a far greater manner then ever I ſaw it before: and in dreams brought many Scriptures to mind that did anſwer ſome queſtions, and ſatisfy ſome doubts, that were in my heart: and ſo did cauſe darkneſs to become light before mee at that time: and this did the Lord do in the abſence of other meanes, ſoon after I gained information where the word was powerfully preached: but it being ſomething far from mee, I had ſome difficulty to get to it; yet it being (through grace) more to mee then my ordinary food: I keept cloſe to opportunities of the word there preached; which in an eſpecial manner God was pleaſed to make very uſeful unto mee. And I injoying often many ſweet taſts of the preſence of God in his ordinances, was carried out through all weathers to wait upon him; and this I can truely ſay from real experience that the worſt wheather I went through the more of God, I met within his ordinances, I remember one very wet day, I had much comfort from theſe words; (let this incourage others,) Joh. 1: 2, 3. *Now are wee the ſons of God, and it doth not yet appear what we ſhall bee:* And afterwards while my meditations were ſomething upon Hebrews 6: 5, 6. *I was much ſtirred up to mind, how far an Hypocrite might go in Religion:* And I began to conſider, whether or no I had gone any further then ſuch a one might go, for I ſaw plainly that a perſon might go very far, and yet be in a ſad ſtate, though they may be en'ightened and taſt of the heavenly gift, and be partakers of the holy Spirit, yea and taſt of the good word, and alſo hear the beſt Preachers gladly, as *Herod* did *Iohn* the *Baptiſt,* and as *Agrippa* did *Paul,* and yet be but almoſt a Chriſtian.

Then I being at a Sermon, the words of the Text were: Marc. 6: vers 20. *And he did many things:* That Miniſter then ſhewed, that an Hypocrite or a reprobate might do many things: but yet a true child of God can do more; he named two things in which a child of God goeth beyond an Hypocrite.

First, that he doth as much desire to be holy as happy.

2. That he doth as earneftly fet himfelf againft all fin as fome.

Then was I exceedingly taken up in my thoughts about this thing; but being carried out to feek the Lord earneftly, he was pleafed to give in this anfwer; Thou tumbleft fo much at the ftone of affurance that thou forgeteft to build, then did God let me fee that the foundation and top-ftone is Jefus Chrift, and that I muft ceafe from my own workes, and take Chrift upon his own termes, and then entred I into fome reft.

Oh, what a knotty piece was I to work upon! for until he put forth his mighty power I could not believe; and I found nothing ftronger then free grace to ftricke at the root of my fin.

Alfo on another fnowy day I going many miles to hear, I was re-freshed much from thefe words, 2 Cor. 12: 9. *My grace is fufficient for thee* .

And on another day from thefe words: Luke 10: 20. *But rather rejoyce, becaufe your names are written in heaven.* And another time aboundance of comfort from that Scripture: 1 Cor. 2: 9. *Eye hath not feen, nor ear heard nei-ther, hath it entred into the heart of man, to conceive the things which God hath pre-pared for them that love him* . It was a very fore day when I went to this op-portunity and a very bitter Journey I had, but God made it exceeding fweet unto mee.

Alfo I had a very great fit of a feaver, by reafon of the trouble of con-fcience I was under; and in the time of that great feaver, the Lord was pleafed to fet that Scripture upon my heart: Rev. 22: 17. *The Spirit and the bride faid comm, and let him that heareth fay, come; and let him that is a thirft come; and whofoever will, let him come, and take of the watters of Life freely:* Which did minifter fo much comfort & refreshing to mee from a fence of the freenefs of Gods grace, being fet upon my heart, with fo much power of the Spirit that I was (contrary to the Judgement of Phyficians) foon raifed to my health again. For indeed I had at that time been ex-ceedingly troubled in my fpirit about my fins, which I had been looking back upon; for I had made a Catalogue of them, and fpread them before the Lord for pardon: But thinking them to be fo many, that God would not pardon them; I did much defire I might die, and go out of the bo-dy, and not live any Longer in it, to encreafe mine iniquities. And although

although at this time a good Minifter did endeavour to comfort mee, yet I put comfort from mee, and faid, it did not belong to mee till the God of all grace was pleafed to give it in by the power of his Spirit, as before mentioned, and then after our good God had given mee a taft of the riches of his pardonning love and grace in Chrift Jefus: I was alfo carried out to pitty others, and begge that God would let them alfo taft of the fame; and a particular perfon was fet upon my heart to begge of God for, and in a short time the Lord was pleafed to anfwer my defire in working a work of grace in that foul.

Then I was called by providence to remove into a dark family, where I had lived fome time beofore; and I then finding much oppofition againft mee, was not willing to go thither again, but fet my felf to pray, not that I might be willing to fubmit to the will of God, but that I might not remove into that family, though had I then underftood it, my call was clear enough, being earneftly defired there unto by my husband, and invited by the family, who now profeffed they could not be without mee, though (when I was there before) they did not affect mee well, being lofty, and could not bear fuch admonitions that fometime letting fall among them, but upon the importunity of my husband and this family; I then at length fet my felf to feek the Lord, that my heart might be made to fubmit to his will, what ever it were; and that if I did go, I might fome way or other be ufeful to him in that place. Now that which made mee fo unwilling to go unto that family, was becaufe of the oppofition, that I had met with before in the wayes of God, and then a want of the means, both of preaching the word and fellowship with the Saints.

But upon my earneft feeking, to know the mind of God, and to be brought to fubmit unto it, my heart was foon made willing to go, which accordingly I did; and I had not been long there before, it pleafed the Lord to worke upon one of the family (to my great comfort and refreshing) who was one that I looked upon as unlike as any in the family.

Alfo the Lord was pleafed by death to take away a child from mee, which was to my cafting down, and for fome time I was under a cloud, and queftioned whither I were a child of God? and whither my child were faved? In that time a good man laboured to comfort mee, telling mee before, the Lord gave mee a fon, he gave mee his own fon; Oh, faid I, that I could fee that! A 3 Why

why said hee, if you will see that, take head of a cursting law, a slandring devil, and an accusing conscience; all which the Lord hath delivered you from, and therefore now wait upon the Lord I am confident the Lord will appear in this thing.

And the Lord was pleased after seeking of him, to set it upon my heart, that that child was well with him, and that he had such another mercy for mee on earth, which he gave mee faith in, notwithstanding great oppositions against at that present: yet after some half a years waiting upon the Lord I was assured of it.

A fit of desertion.

After this the God of comfort was pleased to withdraw and leave mee in a deserted condition, which I found to be very sad, and I was very much perplexed in my spirit, but could not speak of it unto any: But going to hear a Sermon, the Minister was upon that Text: *Lord forsake mee not utterly* (that is to say) *not overlong least the spirit should fail before thee*: hee then shewed what desertion was; and why God doth sometime seem to leave his own people.

Because (said he) throug some pride, they thougt they could walk alone, and so neglected their watch, then God hide his face, that they might see their own insufficiency: and know that all their peace, strength and comfort is in and from him: And this (through mercy) was a great help unto mee at that time.

Further, while I was under that ministry, God was pleased to convince mee of the falsness of their Worship, which in that place then was used, and having an opportunity to go with others to the communion (as they call it) I could not kneell as the rest did, but sat down as if I had kneeled; and as I there sat, it came upon my heart to think thus (as if it had been spoken to mee) why dissemblest thou a worship before the Lord, hee that commands thee to kneel there, may as well command thee to kneel at an Altar, (although at that time there was nothing known of setting up of Altars) which thing I made known to that Minister, and did warn him that if Altars should be set up, that he would not (for filthy lucre sake kneell at them himself, nor compel others so to do: But he told mee he could not believe any such thing should be: but if it should bee so he promised me

mee he would not conform to them.　But in a short time after he found
il too true, for Altarts were reared up, and he poor man (contrary to
his promife) did comform himfelf in that thing, and compelled others
fo to do: but the firft time he did fo, it pleafed the Lord to fmite him
with a fore languishing difeafe, that he went out no more.

Soon after I was at the Chriftenig of a child (as they call it) at which.
time God was pleafed to convince mee of the evil and falfenefs of
that piece of Worfhip alfo.

Then was there in the nation a publique faft proclamed, and by mans
invention there was a form of prayer made and appointed to bo read in e-
very affembly that faft-day, & this was a third conviction that I had about
their formal outfide way of worfhip; I had then an opportunity to come
into one of thofe affemblies that faft-day while that prayer was reading,
at which prefent this thought came ftrongly upon mee: Is this a worfhip in fpirit and truth which thy foul (when it is upon the wing with
God) cannot joyn with all ; for I could not joyn with the words
then read in that formoft prayer.

Upon which I even melted in my fpirit, and fell into shedding of tears,
refolving to feperate from, and come no more to joyn in fuch a way of
worfhip until I had very diligently fearched into the true way of Gods
worfhip, as it is written in his bleffed word; and in order there unto I made
ufe of all the beft books I could get, that were then published to that
purpofe, and alfo called in the help of many Godly Minifters of feveral
judgment: but when all this was done I was ftill unfatisfied in that behalf:
And then did I cry unto the Lord to teach mee, and it was by the Lord
fet upon my heart, that I muft not do any thing in the way of his worfhip
but what I had ground for in his holy word;& that Gods Servants were alwayes to obferve his pattern in all that they do to him, and that Scripture
was much fet upon my heart.　Rev. 22. vers 18, 19.　For I teftify unto
every man that heareth the words of the prophefy of this book, if any man
shall adde unto thefe things , God shall adde unto him the plagues that
are written in this book ; and if any man shall take away from the words
of the Book of this Prophefy, God shall take away his part out of the Book
of life, and out of the holy Citty, and from the things which are written in this book: well ftill I was put upon it to continue feeking the Kingdom of God and the righteoufnefs thereof, and the promife that all other
things should be added unto mee.

Then

Then did I with ſome others ſeek the Lord by faſting and prayer, for councel what we ſhould do, and wheter we ſhould go to injoy communion with the Lord, in the way of his pure worſhip, and the Lord was pleaſed in love to anſwer my deſirs in a wonderful manner, for being then intangled with a houſe of which my Husband had a leaſe for ſome years; and upon that account was unwilling to remove, not knowing how to diſpoſe of that houſe: But yet the Lord was pleaſed in a ſhort time to make him willing that I ſhould remove if I could get of that leaſe, and ſome goods I had; which the Lord ſoon holp mee in, by ſending one unexpectedly the very next day, after my Husband declared his willigneſs for my removal upon thoſe conditions, who took of the leaſe of the houſe of our hands with thoſe goods, and ſo I was made free; So forth with I removed to a place where I did injoy the hearing of a good man preach, and had the ſweet benefit of ſome private meetings, which was much refreshing unto mee: but yet two things I was very earneſt with God for.

1. One that I might be filled with the clear witneſs, and full aſſurance of the eternal Spirit.

2. And the other, that I might injoy more full and cloſe communion vvith God in all his bleſſed ordinances in both, vvhich God vvas pleaſed to anſvver mee in ſome meaſure; as to the firſt he did let mee ſee that I had ſinned againſt him, in that I again queſtioned that aſſurance vvhich before he had given mee in; and then he brought (vvith moſt vvonderful renevving povver) thoſe Scripturs, vvhich many years before at ſeveral times under ſeveral ordinances vvere ſet vvith much povver and evidence upon my heart: But firſt God vvas pleaſed to ſhevv mee that it vvas onely unbeïef that had cauſed mee (at the appearance of temptation and corruption) to queſtion his love and doubt about his kindneſs, and ſo to conclude againſt my ſelf: But the Lord did ſhevv me that all this doubting vvas from my evil heart of unbelief, the ſence of vvhich one morning eſpecially God did ſet upon my ſpirit to the breaking of my heart; ſo that for three dayes together I vvas greatly afflicted in my ſpirit: and continued crying unto God, as one that could not be anij longer contented vvithout the Light of his countenance vvith a renevving ſeal of his Love, long ſought vvith ſighes, prayers and tears, and in the third day morning he did ſend the comforther the Spirit, vvhich vvith invvard light, life, and povver ſet upon my heart theſe follovving Scriptures: 1 John. 3: 2. *Now are wee the ſons of God, and it doth not yet appear what wee ſhall be.*

But

But rather rejoyce, becaufe your names are written in heaven. Luke 10: vers 20.

And who foever will, let him come and take of the watters of life freely. Revel. 22. 17.

And my grace is fufficient for thee. 2 Cor. 12: 9.

Oh! I cannot utter the joy that then was in my heart by the mighty operation of the fpirit: And then after that, this word came upon my fpirit, and grieve not the holy Spirit, whereby thou art fealed unto the day of redemption; and then God did anfwer mee, that there was fufficiency in his grace in Chrift, to pardon all my fins paft, prefent, and to come.

Then as to my other defire which was after more communion with God in his ordinances. After waiting, the Lord was pleafed to fet it upon my heart, to believe that my habitation fhould be removed, and that I fhould injoy my defire by (the time called) Eafter, and fo it was accordingly; and I through mercy, after I had gotten the renewigs of the feal and clear witnefs of the Spirit, lived for about a quarter of a year as it were in Heaven upon earth, but then began a cloud again to araife, and I was under the buffetings of fome fore temptations, God withdrawing in a great meafure (though not the witnefs of the Spirit yet the com forts of his Spirit which before I did injoy; and I conceive this might be the caufe of it (which I wish all others may take heed of, for it coft mee deare) under that fweet foul refreshing communion I had with our heavenly Father, I gave way to fome doubtings and queftionnings, whither there was not a delufion in the thing I then injoyed.

This temptation lafted fome fix dayes, and I had no peace, day nor night when I was awake, to think that I should grieve fo good a God, and caufe him to depart from mee.

And Satan not changing his weapons, made mee think, that there was fomething in mee that I did not fo fully refift him, for when our dear Lord Jefus was tempted, he by his powerful refiftance made him to change them.

So I lay mourning before the Lord, but could not fet to praying for the violence of this temptation. Then my fleep departed, and I grew fick, & then God gave mee to mind that Abrahams wers lay before mee, when he

B   went

went to offer facrifice he was to drive away the fowles, Gen. 15. this work the Lord directed mee to do by laying hold upon Jesus Christ, who had prayed for mee, though I could not now pray for my self. Jo. 15: v. 17, 19. And so soon as my heart was brought to believe this, I was presently delivered, and in all this temptation the Lord hid not his face from mee, blessed be his name.

And then as the Lord carried mee over the Sea, where I did injoy further and fuller communion with himself in his ordinances, he gave mee another occasion for the exercise of faith and Patience.

For whilst I was upon that voyage, the vessel that I was in was pursued with enemies, and troubled with contrary winds, so that we were in great straits.

But God gave me to believe that he that delivered *Paul* out of his straits, would also deliver us out of ours, and so it was, blessed be his name; and so very safely was I carried unto that place that the Lord called mee unto.

But presently after I was there arrived the Lord was pleased to exercise mee with several afflictions.

First by taking away a child by death, and then by laying upon my self such a distemper that my joynts and sinnews were by fits bound up, that I could not stirre them, nor take any rest while it lasted, my pain was so great, no Doctor could do mee any good (though several physitians consulted what to do for mee) But concluded, there was no help but I must dye.

But when I heard that, I said, there is yet help in God, and it was set upon me to believe, that if I could but touch the hemm of the garment of Jesus Christ, that is believingly go to him, I should be healed, being also put in minde of that promise, that whosoever forsake any thing for his sake and the Gospels, Mat. 19: 29. should receive an hundredfold; then I cryed, Lord give me to be healed of this distemper by thee seing thou art pleased to deny help by man.

And one day our Pastor called in to visit me, as he was going to the meeting, whom I did desire to pray for me, and to stirre up the bretheren to joyn with him, and I much incouraged him that they should pray in faith, believing for what they asked, telling him that by faith and prayer he would assuredly heal me, and verily according unto my faith it was done unto me, for ever blessed be God for J. Christ, for as they were praying in his name the distemper departed.   Next

Next the Lord was pleafed to lay his afflicting hand upon another of my children, then did I much defire that all afflictions might be fanctified rather then removed, and that by all I might be made more conformable unto Jefus Chrift was I helped then to read and mind thad place in Job, Job 34: 32. *That which I fee not teach thou mee; if I have done iniquity, I will do no more.*

Then our Paftor coming again to vifit me, I asked him how we fhould know the mind of God in thefe many afflictions, he anfwered mee, that a man having an orchard or vineyard walkes therein, and among all the trees he makes choyce it may be of fome one tree, whofe ftanding is more pleafant and convenient then others; and that tree he chops, & hacks and makes an Arbour to fit in for his delight, and faid hee, if God wil do fo by you, will you not there with be content? Oh! yes faid I: if that be the good will of my heavenly father; and bleffed be God I did find it fo; for though I have fowed in tears, I have reaped in joy, and have found the times of greateft outward trouble, and affliction have been the onely times of greateft inward and fpiritual joy and foul confolation, verily I cannot exprefs with tongue nor pen the large experience I have had upon this account.

And this I have found, that when a poor foul is faithful and fingle hearted for God walking up to the light id hath received, this is the very way to injoy the prefence of God and his bleffing upon him, in what ftate and condition fo ever he is in; for this I can declare from mine own experience that lofe is the way to gain, trouble is the way to peace, forrow is the way to joy, and death is the way to life; he that loofeth his life for my fake, faith Jefus Chrift, the fame fhall find it, through the valey of tears lieth the way to the mountain of joy; for whilft I fet my felf in good earneft to feek the Lord for inftruction into the truth as it is in Jefus, I met with many difficulties; but yet our prayer hearing God was pleafed to come in by degrees; having through his grace given me faith in his fon (who was exalted as a Prince and a Saviour to give me repentance) made mee alfo willing to be baptifed for the remiffion of fins.

Now that which made me willing to obey the Lord, in this Ordinance was the Command of Jefus Chrift in Mat. 28: 19. and Act. 10: 48. and the example of Chrift and the practife of the Apoftles, and primitive Saints, together with the promife of the gift of the Holy Ghoft anexed thereunto. *Acts 2: 38.* And indeed this truth at laft was fo fet upon my

B 2   heart

heart by the Lord, that though many difficulties lay in the way, yet the Lord carried me through them all: and after I had obeyed the Lord therein (in very faithfulness I must declare that I did injoy the incomes of God in a more plentiful manner then before: But Satan for some time laboured to hinder mee in obeying the Lord in this piece of service, with this temptation, that by this meanes a death (in all likelyhood and in an eye of reason) would fall upon my livelyhood, but God made it a furtherance to mee and to others also, so that many of us were at that time (after waiting on God by fasting and prayer) baptized together.

And after that the Lord was pleased to bless mee in my imployment that following year, with more then ordinary success, by which the Devil was proved a lyar.

But afterward I had some fears, that my imployment might be a suare unto mee (as the world is to many) and that I should bee too earthly in it, for this Scripture did follow mee very much, (which I desire to give good heed unto) *Oh! Earth, Earth, hear the word of the Lord.* And often in prayer I did cry unto God, saying, speak Lord, for thy servant desires to hear; and was very desirous to know, what the Lord would have me to understand by this word; and when I had considered I found some thing in my imployment sinful, and a hinderance unto my spiritual injoyments, to convince mee of which, the Lord was pleased to with hold his blessing upon that imployment, which before I had found therein; to the convincing and converting of some to himself, so finding something in it contrary to his will, I was constreined to leave it of, and after much seeking of the Lord for councel, these Scriptures were much with mee, Math. 7: 7. *Ask, and it shall be given you: seek, and ye shall find: knocke, and it shall be opened unto you.*

If ye then being evil know how to give good guifts unto your children, how much more shall your father, which is in heaven, give good things to them that ask him. Math. 7: 11.

And on my servants, and on my hand maidens will I pour out of my spirit, and they shall prophesy. Acts 2: 18.

These promises did dwell with mee for a long season, so that I was much stirred up to pray to the Lord, that he would please to accomplish them upon mee, and pour out of his blessed Spirit upon mee. And after long seeking (especially one day) being very earnest and importunate with the Lord, after which I went out to walk, and on a sudden I

was

was indued with the gift of finging, in fuch a way and manner as I had not been acquainted with before; and immediately this following fong came in (as faft as I could fing) as followeth: it was in the year 1655. in the Moneth of February.

Come home, come home, thy work is done,
My glory thou shalt see;
Let all the meek ones of the earth
Come home along with thee.

Caft of the world, it is too bafe
And low for thee to dwell;
I have redeem'd thee from the pit,
And lowest place of Hell.

Admire, admire my love to thee,
VVhich took thee from so low,
And set thee in high places free,
VVhere thou my love might'st know

VVing thou aloft, and caft thy felf
Into mine Arms of love;
Look up, look up, and thou shalt see
My glory is above.

Let not the wicked know thy joy:
But let my servants hear
VVhat I have done for thee my love,
Since thou to mee drew'ft near.

My servants walk in clouds and bogg's,
They do not see my light:
The day draws near, and will appear,
That I will shine moft bright.

I will appear in my glory, and bea perfect light.
Admire, admire, the thing that I will do,
All nations shall it hear, and know
VVhat I am doing now.

I will a habitation be
To them that fear my name;
They shall lie down in safty, and
Give glory to the same.

All they that in high places sit,
And takes their honours low,
Shall be made tremble, quake, and pine,
VVhen they my Iustice know.

　　Come hide, come hide, come hide with me,
Come hide thee in the Rock;
Come draw thy Comforts high from mee,
I my treasures unlock.

Also it was agreed upon by some of the Lords people, with whom I was then present, that we should appoint and keep a day of solemn seeking the Lord by fasting and prayer; that wee might know what was the duty Gods poor Children ought to be found in at that time: but after this was agreed upon, and the day appointed: I was before the time came removed about 30 miles from them, and so that thing went out of my minde: but God by his Spirit set me upon the same work, by five in the morning the same day, and about the middle of the day God brought to my remembrance that agreement, so we were at the same work at the same time, though far distant one from another; and indeed the Lord was graciously present, pouring out much of the spirit of prayer and supplication; after which earnest seeking of God, was this following prophesye given in unto mee:

Shall light appear, and darkneß done away:
Shall Sommers green be cloathed all in gray:
Shall a bright morning set in shadowes dark,
Oh! England, Englands, take heed thou dost not smart.

And after this prophesy was set upon my heart that notable promise: 2 Chro.7: 14. *If my people, which are called by my name, turn from their wicked wayes; then will I hear from heaven, and forgive their sin and will heal their Land.*

Next morning, about four of the clock, being in my bed, I had this laid before mee, that God would afflict that nation with great afflictions: but I (not knowing what God would try the Nation with) did desire this of the Lord, that I might chuse with *David*, rather to fall into the hands of God, then into the hands of merciless men: it was much upon my heart at that time; that the Lord would turn a fruitful land into barreness, for the wickedness of them that dwell therein.

Then the Lord was pleased to lay upon mee a sore affliction, which I finding my self very unable to bear, did as it were repent mee that I in any
　　　　　　　　　　　　　　　　　　　　　　　　　　measur e

measure had chosen my condition, and did not rather wholy submit to the will of God; but the Lord did mee good by it, and his strength was made perfect in my weaknes.

Then was it much set upon my heart to consider what then were the sins of the nation, for which there was cause of great humiliation; and indeed the consideration of these following evils was much set upon my heart.

1. That great sloathfulnes, deadnes, and unfruitfulnes under the means of grace which we injoyed, for which the Lord threatened of old, Isa. 5: vers 5, 6. *To lay his vineyard wast, to plucke up the hedge and breake downe the wall there of.*

2. That great abounding sin of unbelief (notwithstanding the large experiences we had of Gods power for us, and love to us.) And this I saw did cause persons to seek themselves and the world. Unbelief cut them and us short of that rest that many (yea the most of us) promised to our selves, *As this unbelief of old cut Israel short of rest*, Heb. 3: 10, 11.

3. That Idolatry which mee thought I saw abounding in the nation in a threefold sence.

1. First in respect of false wayes of worship, contrary to the rule of the Gospel and primitive exemple.

2. Secondly in respect also of resting upon duty, and so not resting upon Iesus Christ that Rock of ages; this also was one of poor Israels evils, crying out the Temple of Lord, &c. Ier. 7:4.

3. In respect of coveteousnes, this in Scripture is called Idolatry also; Oh! that too too earnest desire! that was in some after the Foolish vanities of this present evil world, and in others after the vain profits of the world, and in others also after the vain glory and preferment thereof: these things were much upon my heart, and this was that for which God was angry of old with his people, and smote them; and hid his face from them. Isa. 57: 17.

4. Fourthly, That pride that I saw abounding in the lives of many, & I fear was in the hearts of others. Which appeared in their slighting the Councel of Gods Spirit: and their persisting to go on in seeking and setting up self, nothwithstanding the hand of God against them.

These sins being very much set upon my heart, with a deep consideration of many Scriptures: some of them was very great and sore threatnings: and other some were most sweet and precious promises to such as repent and departe from all iniquity; one of which I remember was that very remarkeable place, 2 Chron. 7: 14.

Then

Then I looked upon it as my duty to make this known, that people might be warned to depart from ſin, that ſo they might not partake of the great wrath and ſore diſpleaſure of God, which I much feared, was coming.

Then ſoon after I had an oppertunity to declare this to ſome that then were in high places, and in the very entring I had this added, which I alſo declared.

Didſt thou not hear a voyce from on high,
Deny your ſelves (take up the croſſe) or verily you ſhall die?

And this was approved on by ſome, and received as a very ſuitable and ſeaſonable word; but pour ſoules, for not hearkening unto councel in departing from ſin they were ſoon brought down, and laid low, yet there is mercy with the Lord that he may be feared, and he will manifeſt his love to all them that truely repent, and we may all make a good uſe of this experience; therefore let others harms become our warnings. Alſo about the year 1658. to the beſt of my remembrance [*for having loſt my book, in which I had ſet them down in order, I now wait onely upon the Lord, and as he by his Spirit helps mee, ſo I give an account of theſe things*) It was given in with aboundance of power upon my ſpirit, theſe few words following.

Awake therefore to righteouſneſs,
The Lord is near at hand: This was again brought to
And will afflict now very ſore   mind in January 1662.
By ſea and like by land.

And this ſeemes to agree with, and is a further addition to what was given mee in before in the Year 1657. which is as followeth.

There is a time approaching near at hand,
That men ſhall be in fear by ſea and land:
There is a time, there will be alteration;
And this ſame time doth haſten to this nation;
Let now my children hearken to my will,
And they ſhall ſee I will be with them ſtill.

Theſe with many more ſuch things came upon my ſpitit, and then after ſeeking the Lord he was pleaſed to ſhew mee by degrees what was the work of the day (for I am a ſtranger and a Pilgrim, therefore I ſeek for a
Kingdom

Kingdom whole Buylder and Maker is God. I defire not to fet up the Idol of coveteoufnefs, but to have it to be my meat and drink, to do the will of my Father, which is in heaven; and 'tis my onely defire to deny my felf, and to honor him) feeking to know the prefent work of the day: fome Scriptures with many waity confiderations were fet upon my heart, *Hezekiahs* prayers and tears, which were accepted of God, when his heart was broaken; *A broaken and a contrite heart is acceptable in the fight of God, and he will dwell with fuch.* Ifa. 57: 15. *rend your hearts and not your garments, and turn to the Lord; indeed when much of the form of Godlineß appears, but the power is wanting, then it is a time to mourn, and in fome it hath been fo in all ages, therefore Gods Prophet was bid cry aloud, and fpare not,* Ifa. 58: 1. *VVhen finlies hiden in the heart, nothing is accepted,* Ifai. 58: 2. *Yet you feek mee early and defire to know my wayes as a nation that did righteoufneß;* read and mind the whole Chap. Ifa. 15: 16. *Ceafe to do evil,* faith the Lord, *and learn to doe well, &c.*

But unto the wicked, God faith, what haft thou to do to declare my ftatutes, or that thou shouldeft take my covenant in thy mouth, feenig, thou hateft to be reformed? then it came upon my heart that the duty of the prefent time was for the people of God to be very much in thefe following things.

The work of the day.

1. Firft, to be watchful that the cares of this world, and the deceitfulnefs of riches make us not to forget the coming of Chrift, and the glory that shall then be revealed.

2. Secondly, be moderate in all things, the Lord is at hand; be patient, and act much faith; be much in prayer, do good, lay up treafures in heaven; thefe be all very weighty things.

3. Be much in humiliation, feek not great things for your felves, in a day when God is pulling down.

God pronounceth a woe to them that are at eafe in Sion, that put far away the evil day, and caufe the feat of violence to come near; Amos 6. vers. 3, 4, 5, 6. that lie upon beds of Ivory, and ftretch themfelves upon their couches, and eat the lambs out of the flock, and the calves out of the midft of the ftall, and fo fill themfelves in feafting, delighting in Mufick, and drinking wine in bowles, but are not grieved for the afflictions of *Jofeph*.

And the fame evil the Prophet *Ifaiah* complaines of alfo in the 22 of Ifa. vers. 5, 9, 12, 13, 14. *In that day the Lord God of Hofts called to weeping and mourning.*

C

mourning, and to baldness, and girding with sackcloath, and behold joy and gladness, slaying oxen, and killing of sheep, &c. In what day was this, you may see in the 5, and 9 verses; it was a day of trouble, and treading down and perplexity: But see how the Lord takes notice of this their contrary carriage in the 14 verse: he chargeth it upon them, as such an iniquity, as he tells them, shall not be purged from them till they dye verse the 14.

It is said, when the Judgments of God are abroad in the earth, the inhabitants thereof shall learn righteousness.

But it is threatened, they shall have no peace who go on in the wayes of sin and wickedness, but all that would have peace, must come from sin unto Jesus Christ, and walk in the way of peace, by this way we hide in the rock, and enter into the secret chambers, where God had promised to keep us till his indignation be over past.

Then, benig troubled in my spirit, the Lord was pleased to give in these following promises as special comforts against those great and publique calamities, which were coming.

I even, I am he that blotteth out thy transgressions for mine own sake, and will not remember thy sins. Isai. 34, 25.

I also will leave in the midst of thee an afflicted and poor people, and they shall trust in the name of the Lord. Zeph. 3: 12.

And they shall be mine, saith the Lord, in the day that I make up my Iewels, and I will spare them as a man spareth his own son that serveth him. Malachy 3: 17.

And the Lord shall guide thee continually, and satisfy thy soul in drought, and make fat they bones, and thou shall be like a wattered garden, and like springs of watter whose watters faile not. Isa. 58: 11.

And Moses said unto the people, Fear ye not, stand still, and see the salvation of the Lord, which he will shew to you to day; for the Egyptians, whom you have seen to day, you shall see them again no more for ever. Exod. 14: 13.

The name of the Lord is a strong Tower, the Righteous run into it, and is safe. Prov. 18: 10.

They, that wait upon the Lord, shall renew their strentgh, they shall mount up with wings as Eagles, they shall run and not be weary, and they shall walke and not faint. Isa. 40: 31.

Also the Lord set it upon my heart, how the people of God ought to carry it in such a day of calamity; namely, that they ought to have upon their hearts a deep sence of sin, which is the cause of sorrow, as Lots righteous soul was grieved with the unclean conversation of the wicked;
therefore

therefore God took care of him, and he was preserved when others were destroyed with the firy storme of Gods ~~displeasure~~ *Displeasure*

Also God is pleased to set a mark upon the fore-heads of them that mourn for the abomination of the times.

Also it was given me in to believe, that God would be a wall of fire about his people; with this promise : *That all things shall work together for good, to them that love God, who are the called, according to his purpose.* Rom. 8: 28.

And the Lord said, All things were made for himself, and nothing shall be destroyed without mee.

And God appeared unto Abraham, saying, I am God alsufficient, &c. Gen. 17: 1.

Let my word be a light to thy feet, and a Lanthorn to thy pathes, for I will keep them in perfect peace, whose mindes are stayed on mee, because they trust in mee.

And the Lord is the portion of his people.

And they are to him as the apple of his eye. Zech. 8: 2,8. And as a signe upon *signe* his right-hand : And he to them is a strong tower, a buckler, and shield, a Captain, and leader of his people, and it is written; *when ye see these things begin to come to passe, then look up, and lift up your heads, for your redemption draweth nigh.* Luke 21: 28.

If you had but so much faith as a grain of musterd-seed, you should say unto this mountain, be removed, into the Sea; Christ reprove Peter, for the smalness of his faith; All things are possible to them that believe.

Fear not them that can kill the body: but fear him that can destroy both body and soull in hell. Math. 10: 28.

Fear not little flock, it is your Fathers good pleasure to give you the Kingdom. Luke 12: 32.

See that you be not troubled, for these things must be; but the end is not yet, nation shall rise against nation, and Kingdom against Kingdom; and ye shall hear of warres and rumors of warres: but he that watcheth over Israel neither slumbereth nor sleepeth.

He that believeth on mee, as the Scriptures hath said, out of his bely shall flow rivers of living warter; but this spake he of the spirit, that they, that believe on him, should receive: and is promised to be poured out in the latter dayes.

After these promises and instructions followed this song, in the year 1658.

Oh, now my soull! give glory to the Lord.
  For this rich mercy he doth thee afoard;
    He made the heavens, and ordered every light;
    He takes the hearts up of his people quite.

And as I was on a Journey, this also was given in:
    VVhen that this green shall blosome bear,
   And birds shall pleasant sing;
   Then shall there be a knell most sad,
   In every place, beard ring:

Then did the Lord poure out upon me much of the spirit of prayer, and praising, with the knowledg of other things, which he is bringing to pass: In so much that I was much broaken before him, to see my own unworthyness, and his goodness, a sence of which I lay under for some season, not long after I had a great fit of sickness; and I was inquiring of God, what his mind should be in that affliction: he shewed mee, it was because I did not declare to the Church with whom I walked; those things he had made known unto mee.

But benig troubled at my own insufficiency; and they benig unacquainted with such things; and indeed my self did question at the first, whether it were the guift of God or no? (the guift of singing.) Then the Lord was pleased to set it upon my heart, that as those prophesyes were true, and should come to pass, so should I know that this was the true guift of God, given in unto mee.

And it was so when the spring came on, then began that sickness of agues and feavours, that have continued ever since, little or much; and there followed two dry summers one after another, and also we had many light appearances; but they set in dark shadows, till Christ our light shall appear, and in great mercy take away and remove our dark and sad afflictions, and sorrows; well now, I was at last so moved in my spirit, that I could not tell how to keep in these things any longer, and therefore went to the Church to that end, but I then could not find him that I would have spoken of it unto, for him to declare unto the rest, so I returned, and did it not.

Then the Lord afflicted mee again, and then I besought him again, and he gave mee to mind that I was justly afflicted for neglecting, to make it known, then being raised up again, I did declare something, but not so fully as I should; and indeed would have done fearing, it would not
be

be born, for which I was mourning before the Lord: and as I was mourning, I was put upon finging, as followeth:

Ceafe thou thy mourning, and fee thou doft praife,
For thou fhalt do my will in all my wayes:
Thy work fhall be praifes now for to fing,
Becaufe thou haft chofen Chrift to be thy King.

  Lift up your heads redemption draweth near,
Do not at all poffefs thy heart with fear:
Lift up your heads, and look to heaven high;
For God will make his people glorify.

  Draw water from the wells that are fo deep:
You fhall drink flaggons of my love, when others are afleep.

Then ftill fought I God what I might do to honnor God in my generation; and about three dayes after it was fet upon my heart in the night,
that I muft writte my experiences; but then I thought, oh, how should
I remember thirty years experiences! but then prefently came in thefe
promifes.

Fear thou not, for I am with thee; be not difmayed; for I am thy God, I will
ftrengthen thee; yea, I will help thee; yea, I will up hold thee with the right-hand
of my righteoufnefs. Ifaiah 41:10.

Fear not, thou worm Iacob, I will help thee, faith the Lord, *and thy Redeem-*
er the holy one of Ifrael. vers. 14. *Commit thy way unto the Lord, truft alfo in*
him, and he fhall bring it to pafs. Pfalm 37: 5.

Great things have I laid up for them that fear mee among the fons
of men.

The next day I fet my houfe in order, that I might go about this work
that the Lord had called mee unto, and until I went about it, this word
followed mee; *be inftructed leaft my Spirit depart from thee*; and as foon as
I fet upon my work, it left mee, and I found the Lord (according to his
promife) mightyly affifting mee, in bringing things to my remembrance
and I wrig them down, and had fome thoughts to put them in print; but
yet through the corruptions of my heart, and the advice of a friend, I was
not willing they should be published whilft I am living: my reafon was,
becaufe I am a poor weak worthlefs worm, and have not the parts and
gifts that fome others have.

And becaufe I am an old fruitlefs branch, my memory failes, and my
underftanding is fo dull, that I am (and was at the beft) a poor empty one,
which I cannot but acknowledg with tears and brokennefs of heart.

     Oh

Oh, that the Lord should be so good to mee! and I can bring no more glory and honnour to him; but yet notwithstanding I must give glory to God, for that he hath been pleased to poure out of his Spirit upon mee, and since that, to fill my soul with very sweet choyce, and heavenly injoyments from himself.

The most large measure of the spirit of prophesy was upon mee at two particular times, the one in the year one thousand six hundred and fifty five.

And the other in the year 1658. but at many times God was pleased to give me much of the spirit of prayer and praise.

Then by his hand of providence I was removed again out of *England* into *Holland*, and I brought the papers of my experiences with mee: which (the Ship being cast away) were lost, with the trunck in which they were: Then was it much set upon my heart, that God was displeased with mee, for not putting them in print, and then the guift of singing and praising was much ceased, and I was troubled; for the which I sought the Lord, and did begg', that if he were offended at mee, for not printing, and leaving them behind mee, that he would pardon it unto mee; and that, if it were his good pleasure, I should write them again. I did pray, that he would let his Spirit come to inable mee again in singing and prayer, as it was wont to do, and be my remembrancer to write again: and indeed it did so, not long after, in the night; both in song, and in prayer.

But then I having not time, was much hindered? yet notwithstanding (according to the time I had) I set my self to do it; and the Lord was pleased to assist mee, in bringing again to my remembrance things of long standing.

Now before I departed from *England*, I was satisfied in my spirit, that I had a clear call from thee Lord so to do; for indeed more then a year I had such a motion in my spirit, backed with many Scriptures for its furtherance.

Yet nothwithstanding in this Voyage we met wich some difficiulty, for the Ship I came over in was cast away; but in the time of the greatest trouble the Lord gave mee in these promises; that he would be with mee in six troubles, and in the seventh he would not forsake mee.

Call upon mee in the day of trouble, I will hear thee, and deliver thee, and thou shalt glorify mee.

With this sweet word also, thou shalt not die, but live, to see the mercy I will shew unto thee.

It was

It was in the night, and after some time (the Ship being a ground, and in great danger, and so were all the persons in it) one asked mee, if I were not afraid? I answered, the God of heaven my Father hath brought mee hither, and if he may have more honour in drowning of mee, then by preserving mee, his will be done.

Then, when the mast was cut down, and the Master with some others said, we are dead persons, and like to loose our lives, yet I had much hope in the Lord, because of his promise, and after that I (and some others in the Ship with mee) had committed our selves unto God by prayer, I being in the Cabbon, laid me down to sleep: but I had not (it seems) lien half an hour, but they called us, and said, there was Land not far of, if wee would seek for help? vvhich accordingly vve did.

But it being but about the break of the day, vve did vvander over the sands, but could find no vvay out of the sea, as it vvere, compassing us about round; then vve all returned to the Ship again, and some concluded vve must go in an perish there; so they vvent in again.

But vve said, if vve must perish, vve vvould be still seeking to save our lives.

And as our God (to whom we had committed ourselves) guided us, we went another way on the sands, and as I was going (looking to God to be my Pilot) not knowing whether vve vvent, for the sea vvas one both sides of us, and vvee had but a small vvay on the sands to vvalk in; and as I vvas begging of the Lord, to keep in the sea still vve found out a place, not onely for our ovvn escape, but that vve might see deliverance for our friends in the Ship also, the Lord vvas pleased to set this upon my heart.

As thy deliverance is, so shall Englands be, vvhen they are brought to greatest streights, then vvill deliverance be from God.

A hint of some night meditations and effects of prayer.

I being avvake one night, and very full of trouble in my mind, because I vvas no more spiritual, for I had found my self very dead-hearted in prayer over night; for the vvhich I vvas very sadly afflicted in spirit; and indeed then vvanting place of retirement (to send up strong cries unto the Lord) did much deaden my spirit, for I found it vvas the practice of Jesus Christ, sometime to be in the vvildernes, sometime in the mountain all night in prayer alone, and sometimes alone in the gardin; and I find prayer in fecret much accepted vvith God , according to that vvord, *Pray to thy Father in fecret , and he will reward thee openly* : Math. 6: 6. indeed fo full of forrovv vvas I that I uttered no vvords, but fighed and groaned to the Lord.

Then this came in..
Vpon the fountain thou shalt live ,
Fresh ſtreames of love I will the give :
Thou ſhalt be made all times to ſee ,
There is a ſountain ſlowes in mee.

Then did I groane before the Lord , that he vvould give in fome pro-mife : the Lord caſt in this that the grace of prayer vvas before the guiſt of prayer , and that this vvas the grace of prayer to give up our felves in faith to the guidance of the ſpirit, and fo by faith to have communion vvith the Father and the Son, in the Spirit, for Chriſt told the Woman. John. 4: v. 21,22,23. *Neither in this mountain, nor in Ieruſalem shall men worship the Father but the hour is coming, a now is, when the true worshippers shall worship the Father in Spirit and in truth, for the Father ſecketh ſuch to worship him ; God is a Spirit, and they that worship him muſt worship him in Spirit and in truth:* This Woman then could fay, that Chriſt vvould teach all things; vvhy should not vve look for the teachings of the Spirit novv, feeing Chriſt hath not onely been vvith us in the flesh, God and man, but had alfo promiſed us the pourings out of the Spirit, to teach us all things: and to bring all things to our remembrance.

Then further I vvas mourning that I could not injoy the ordinances of God in their purity ; and the Lord shevved mee that I muſt offer up my Iſaac : And vvhen *Abraham* vvent to do that, he left his fervants belovv the hill ; and confulted not vvith flesh and blood.

Alfo aftervvard I had fuch vvonderful experience of communion vvith God, through the Spirit, as I am not able to utter it.

I avvaking another night, vvas greatly complaining , that the flesh did fo puddel in the Spirits vvork, that vvhen I vvould do good , evil is pre-fent. Then did the ſpirit put me upon uttering many heavenly complaints in a vvay of finging, and after that, vvith the help of the Spirit, to pray vvith much enlarged nefs.

And after that there vvas by the fame ſpirit, vvith very much povver this vvord : *Be ſilent before mee all flesh.*

Oh ! and then follovved the vvonderful ſpeakings of God by his bleſſed Spirit to my poor foul, vvhich I cannot utter as to the manner of them , but the nature of them vvas exceeding comforting to my felf; and alfo fil-led mee vvith great hopes to all the people of God.   And

And now hereby do I know, that it was the Spirit of God and of truth that did work at this time, becaufe it did lay mee low, and flat before him, that is holy, and made me fee my own infufficiency, and his great al fufficiency, which did much humble mee, and broak, and melted mee exceedingly, then was this promife given in; *That they that waiton the Lord shall renew their strength, they shall mount up with wings as Eagles, they shall run and not be weary, and they shall walk and not faint.*

And my heart was very much drawn out to wait upon God, in a way of believing, both for my felf and people of God, having that word as it were whifpered in my ear: *If thou canst believe, all things are possible.*

Another time I was confidering, that though I had been a Profeffor many years, yet I though! indeed I was but a babe in Chrift, then that word came upon mee: *Out of the mouthes of babes and fucklings thou haft ordained praife.*

And indeed I can incourage the moft fimple and weak, to wait on the Lord, for his grace is fufficient.

At this time I was taught by the fpirit, that prayer was another thing then fome take it to be; it is of a divine nature, and they onely, whom God helpeth, can pray, for it is not words that is alwayes needfull, for a foul may pray and utter no words, and have fweet communion with God by faith; yet words fometimes affe&t the heart, and I have fometimes found the voyce cannot be kept in, the heart may be fo filled. Therefore I blame none, but defire to be tender of all, for God accepts what himfelf gives, outward performances is as the shell without the kernel; if the fpirit a&t not, but what of his own fpirit is in any duty that God doth accept. And we read of the poor woman in the Gofpel, who met with fome difcouragements, yet by the power of faith being inabled to hold on; oh! how greatly he commended her faith, and anfwered her defire, though her words were but few, onely, *Lord help mee, &c.*

And *Hannahs* prayer was heard, who did but move her lips: And although she was a woman of a forrowful fpirit before, yet she wentaway believing, and alfo rejoycing that God had heard her prayer.

So the defires of them that fear him shall be anfwered, and he will hear their cry.

Daniel, before he made his fupplication, was anfwered, the groaning of the fpirit before the Lord is a loud cry, the prayer of faith doth fave the fick.

The Lord is a very prefent help in the time of need.

They

They that truft in him, fhall not be difappointed.

Nay he takes pleafure in them that fear him, and that hopes in his mercy.

Therefore let them that call on the name of the Lord depart from iniquity.

Further, my heart being carried out long to wait for, and expect ther teachings of the fpirit more fully to be given mee : and therefore, if any thing comes in further, it is not of nor from my felf, but the Spirit of Gods working in and upon a poor weak creature, who though I be very unfit to publifh any thing of this nature to the world, yet according to my meafure I would with that poor woman do what I can with willingnefs and cheer-fulnefs, for God loves a cheerful heart in his work, and the Apoftle faith, if there be firft a willing mind, it is accepted, according to that a man hath, and not according to that he hath not.

Yet I am much incouraged to believe that this work is of the Lord, for I have found the flefh exceeding oppofet thereunto, and when I have ne-glected it, God hath withdrawn himfelf from mee, and when I fet to it in good earneft, then God returns and let mee injoy fweet communion with himfelf: And the more, the Lord appeared at the firft comings in of thefe things upon my foul, the more his love broake my heart, that I was wonderfully affected to behold the freenefs of his grace to fuch a one.

And verily the more watchful I was againft fin and unto duty, the more of his divine prefence was affoarded, which is fo glorioufly fweet to injoy, that the more I had, the more ftill I would have, and ftill longed for, not onely in the day, but in the night alfo, hearkening what God fpake, and in the night his vvay to my foul hath been to come in vvith many fvveet feafonable and povverful inftructions, ftirring me up to pray, teaching me hovv to pray, and vvhat to pray for, encreafing my faith and confidence, to believe for that I have praied for, both for my felf and others (and alfo ftirring mee up to prayfing him) and I find that giving my felf vvholy to the difpofing of God in prayer, is a very good thing: alfo this fear hath been upon mee fometimes, that I fhould offer unto God that vvhich coft mee nothing, that is, to lay ont the choifeft, and moft of the day about the vvorld, and then bring the fleepy head to God for a facrifice: I minding the fpirituallity of true prayer, and my unfitnefs for it, I have found the councel of our Lord Jefus Chrift very ufeful, vvhere he faith, *VVatch and pray.* Math. 26: 41.

And the Apoftle faith, *VVatch unto prayer.* Pet. 1: 4,7. yet I have found
often

often, when I have been to pray unto God, my heart have been very dead, and I could not get it into so spiritual a forme as I would, yet durst not neglect the dayly waiting upon God in that duty: but even then made it my work to petition the Lord, to compose my spirit and quicken me by his grace and holy Spirit, that I might not offer the blind the halt, and lame in sacrifice unto God: And indeed then God hath so, come in upon my spirit, that I have had more communion with him self yea more then at some other time, when I have been apt to think my self more fit.

At other times when I have not found God coming in to help mee, I have gone a way and waited his time, for unless God enlarge our hearts, it is not good for us to en large in words, for God is in heaven and thou on the earth, therefore *let thy words befew* (thy words mark that) *and bodily exercise profiteth nothing, my son give mee thy heart*, saith God. Ecclef. 5: 2.

The poor man that said, God be merciful unto mee a Sinner, went a way more accepted or rather Justified then the Pharise, in the time before the coming of Christ in the flesh, if Gods people could not bring a lamb so ra sacriffice, if they brought but two pigeons, or, a little flower, if it were brought to the Priest, it was accepted, so if we come to him that Justifies the ungodly, and hath promised to do all our works in us, and for us beholding his alsufficiency, and submit to him, and be content with that he will give us, as well in spirit uals as in temperals, the Lord will accept of us, onely believing we must flee unto the hornes of the Althar.

And I have found, when I have neglected prayer, my heart hath been very dead and full of unbelief: And again, I have found it no comfort to rest upon duties, for that is a dangerous evil to set up such an Idol in the heart; but here in lay my comfort, when I by faith could have communion with God, and coming near to him, could cast my burthen upon him, and go avvay quiet in my mind, that Christ vvould do all for mee; and vvhen I vvas vvilling, God shtould do vvhat he pleafed vvith mee, and my vvill vvas brought to his vvill; then have I had the mercy I have asked, and more also many times.

I have found retired places and vvatchings, the best opportunities and greatest advantages unto prayer.

Also I have had many temptations againft prayer, but the best vvay to overcome them, is to mind the command of Jefus Christ, vvhich is that vve should vvatch unto prayer, and pray alvvayes, keep clofe to the duty in the ftrength of Christ, and loofe not the motions of the Spirit neither grieve the Spirit by fin, but vvatch againft all appearances of evil, for I ha-

D 2   negle

have found that the neglect of vvatchfulneſs againſt ſin : and being over-come by it, doth greatly deaden the heart to duty; keep your eyes upon the promiſes by faith, look up unto Chriſt in prayer, and let all take heed of ſetting up prayer, or any other duty, above, or in the roome of Jeſus Chriſt.

If God aſſiſt you to pray for a mercy, though he give it not in preſently, yet hold on if your asking be according to his will, and your end the glo-ry of God, and ye find enlargment from the Spirit of life, you may be ſure he will be anſwer you in that thing or elſe in ſome thing better for you in his ovvn ſeaſon.

My ſelf ſought the Lord 20 years, for one thing, before I had an anſvver, but at laſt being at prayer, after I had done, God gave mee in a moſt gra-cious anſvver, and ſet dovvn the very time of deliverance, and did accor-dingly accompliſh it at the very time; to him be the praiſe.

And many other things I have ſought the Lord for, and he hath been pleaſed to grant my deſire, eſpecially vvhen he hath made me earneſt and importunate, and have aſſiſted me to hold on, and given me a ſpirit of faith, to believe for the thing prayed for.

Another time I ſought the Lord for a relation of mine, who was thought to be near unto death, and this vvas given in, call upon mee in the day of trouble, I vvil hear and deliver, and thou ſhalt glorify mee, and from that time that perſon amended, and life vvas continued.

Alſo I knew another young perſon that was, by the word preached, con-vinced of her ſinful ſtate, and ſet upon the performance of ſome duties: but not being acquainted with the wiles and temptations of Satan, afterward ſome deadneſs ceaſing upon her ſpirit, began to neglect her duty; but one in the family perceiving of it, adviſed her to preſent her ſelf before the Lord, and although ſhe found her ſelf dead, yet to pray that ſhe might pray, whoſe councel ſhee took, and ſhee continuing diligent, the Lord came in by the mighty witneſs of his ſpirit, fully ſatiſfying her ſoul in a very ſhort time.

Further: oh! let all that fear God be encouraged to continue in, and not neglect family duties, for I have found by good experience many wrought upon by inſtructions and prayer, when their lot have been caſt in-to thoſe families, where reading, praying, and Catechiſing, and ſuch duties have been faithfully performed; ô, many young ones have been brought home to God, by his bleſſing upon this meanes!

And amongſt many more I remember one who was very ſtrongly aſſalt-ed with many temptariones to keep her from coming to, and cloſſing with

Jeſus

Jesus Christ, and this temptation was most upon her, that she was too young, and it would be time enough afterward, why should she expose her self to scorne and reproach by being called a Puritan, and so become a luaghing stock to others: but the Lord was pleased to overcome her, and bring her to himself.

X Another also who set her self against them in the family, that wished her soules good, and used all meanes to get out of that family, to which end also she raised some lyes, which very evil the Lord set upon her heart, and then she came to be convinced of her sad sinful state, and was also brought home to God through his rich grace in Jesus Christ.

And another who by this meanes was wrought upon that, was a young maid, a Ministers Daughter, and had been well instructed and educated from a child, whereby she was informed of the evils of scandalous sins and avoided them, and was also very constant in the performance of duties; and indeed so walked as none could see ought a mise in her conversation, yet notwithstanding the poor heart was ignorant of her self, and of Jesus Christ; but she being under a family Catechising, and instruction was (by the mighty povver of the eternal Spirits vvorking) convinced of original sin, and then she savv that (for all her formality) she vvas a sinner, and had need of a Saviour, and so vvas brought home to close vvith Jesus Christ,

This also I have found, that a constant close seeking of God hath been crowned with his presence, for I my self was with some others desired to pray to the Lord for councel, and direction for them; but they would not tell mee in what it was that they sought direction, yet notwithstanding I did not know the thing, I set my self to seek God for them, and he was pleased to shew me what it was, (this was *Anno* 1657.) and I did pray God to let mee know his mind in that particular, and the Lord put it upon my heart to go and read, and the place of Scripture handed to mee, was quite against their work (at that time) which they had upon their heart to do, then I sought the Lord again, and the second answer was; go in and read; then I looked up to the Lord as I did before, and said, Lord, shew me where I shall read, and that Scripture also was flat against their work; and just so I had a third answer also: And the next day as I was at my work my heart and meditations were above, and my secret desire still to God for the further teachings of his good Spirit, and these following lines (with much more) came in as a further answer from the Lord:

As for

> As for the work of Babylon,
> It is a mighty work, and strong:
> But yet my power shall it compleat,
> For my wisdom is mighty great:
> They must sit still, behold my power,
> VVhich worketh for them hour by hour.

And novv my dear Chriftian friends, into vvhofe hands this my poor mite, shall come I defire you take notice of that great love and vvonderful grace of God, vvhich he hath been pleafed to manifeft in giving in fuch fweet returus of prayer, let him alone have the praife, and be ye all incouraged and ftirred up to pray continually, and be very watchful, that if at any time God do move you to do any thing, do it with all your might, according to the affiftance the Lord gives you; for I have found it a great grieving of the fpirit to put it of with delayes, through carnal reafonings of the flesh, which indeed vvould have hindreed mee in offering of thefe few experiences to the view of the vvorld: but vvhen God vvas pleafed to give me a heart to it, and I fet upon it vvith a refolution in his ftrength to go through it, not with ftanding all oppofition : Oh! then, was the Lord pleafed to come in again, and fill my foul with peace and joy unfpeakable, and full of glory; which was to my great refreshment I being then in a ftrange Land (Holand) feperated from Country, kindred, and fathers houfe; yea there, and then did our good God (according to what I had wont to have) give into my fpirit heavenly *Allelujas*, both night and day, with many fweet Inftruct̃ions from him felf (when it was with us as it were a time of famine of the word) our Teathers being removed into corners, and thrown into prifons (in the Year 1662.) O! how was I then ftirred up by the teachings of that good Spirit, often to praifing, and often to very earneft prayer (as for my felf, fo for his poor afflict̃ed perfecuted people) and then alfo I found my heart much enlarged to love, and to do good, and lay out my felf for fa ints of all perfwafions, yea and all others alfo as I had opportunity. And upon this ground becaufe my dear Redeemer, the Lord Jefus, hath fet mee a pattern to do good to all, and what talent foever we do recieve, we muft lay it out to his praife (if it be but one) and it shall be increafed: this I have had experience of, be not backward to improve thy talent, becaufe another may have more then thou, that fprings from a root of pride, and negligence is the way to loofe what thou haft, but look up to God for a bleffing upon the right ufe of what thou haft received, and if he feeth it good that thou mayeft better honnor him with more he will give in thee in his own way and

time,

time, for then shall ye know if ye follow on to know the Lord. Hofe. 6. 3.

It is alfo promifed, that they who be planted in the houfe of the Lord like a watered Gardin shall they grow and florish, and bring forth fruit in their old age: Pfa. 92: 12, 13. Further, o! let all the beloved of the Lord take a fpecial care of every Gofpel ordinance and commandment of our Lord, to hold forth what light you have received, for there is non of the ordinances of the Gofpel to be flighted, for they hold out unto us thofe choyce priviledges that vvere purchafed for us vvith the precious blood of Jefus Chrift, I have found great peace, and injoyed much of Gods prefence in vvaiting upon him in the vvay of his appointments, and I have found the Lord (not leaving but) teaching of mee, vvhen I out of confcience have forborn vvhere they vvere not tobe injoyed, according to the rule of the Gofpel, and expofe my felf to any fuffring to injoy them in the purity of them, and indeed God doth take fpecial notice of them vvho they be, and vvhere they dvvell, Revel. 2: 13. that in fore perfecuting and fuffering times hold faft his truths, and do not deny his name, Mal. 3: 16, and hath promifed that they vvho keep the vvord of his patience fhall be keept in the hour of temptation.

And vvhen he hath humbled us, he vvill shevv us the pattern of his houfe, the goings out, and the comings in thereof, and the fashions, Lawes, and ordinances thereof, that we may do them. Ezek. 43: 11.

And the time doth haften that God will turn to the people a pure Language.

And all shall know the Lord from the leaft to the greateft.

And he will lead the blinde in a way that they know not, he will make darknefs become light, and crooked things ftreight, and bitter things fweet, and hard things eafy; and this he will do, and not forfake us.

Further let none be difcouraged to do their duty, though never fo weak, yet if thou beeft acted by the Spirit of God, weak meanes oftentimes becomes effectual to accomplish great things, for by experience alfo I know when fome perfons have been praying together, that one being fenceable of the ftate of the other, and mourning over their fin before the Lord, God have made ufe of thofe very mournings and breathings, to convince the other of their finful ftate, with the danger of it, and thereby have been caufed to turn from fin unto the Lord, whofe eyes were never opened before.

One Maid who by this meanes was convinced, and faid nothing at prefent, but after prayer retiring herfelf to her Bible, with a purpofe to fee

what

what word of comfort she could find there, and it pleased God to hand to her that place, Rom. 8: 13. *For if ye live after the flesh ye shall die: but if ye through the Spirit do mortify the deeds of the body, ye shall live:* which word God did make very powerful and effectual to help forward his work upon her soul.

All these speak forth the freeness of Gods rich grace, therefore who ever readeth and understandeth what is in this free workings of Gods good Spirit, let him alone have all the praise and glory; and the Lord inclined my heart every day more and more to praise him: for his unchangeable love in Jesus Christ, therefore let them that read this give God praise for this undeserved mercy; and let me have a share in your prayers, that I may be filled with a spirit of praise; for none have more cause then I to speak well of his great and holy name, and that I may honour God that little time that I have to live upon the earth, and that in all changes.

For if God sees affliction to be good for mee, I desire not to dispise his chastizements; for I have found more strength in a great affliction then in a little one, and my soul hath been filled with joy out of measure.

Therefore if we be brought to this, take joyfully the spoiling of our goods, knowing we have a better inheritance, and the giving up all to the will of God, who gave all to us, we shall have all given to us with advantage, oh! the fulness of him that filleth all in all, but I am nothing, and can do nothing, no longer then he doth assist, therefore praise him for ever more.

And since I was taken of from my incumbrances in the world, and had more time to spend in the wayes and work of God: waiting on him for more of himself, the Lord (according to his promise) hath revealed himself more abundantly, and I have found that a chearfull watchful diligent spirit in ones general and particular calling is a great help to prevent mispending time, for of idleness comes no good, therefore it hath been my practice, that if I can do no good, nor receive good, not to stay in that place long.

Oh! let us be wary how we spend our precious time, for it hat a lock before, but none behind: I am of a fearful timerous spirit naturally, but I find it a great help to dash Babilons brats in the first rice.

I was about 14 years in the pangs of the new birth before I received the witness of the spirit, in which time I was exceeding troubled with my unbelieving heart through entertaining false fears: and indeed some thing of Jesus Christ was in mee all that while: Althoug sometimes I could not

with

with comfort behold him throughthat thick cloud of my many Iniquities and I never found Satan more foyled, and my own corruptions more fubdued, then when I by faith could look up unto Gods unchangeable love in Jefus Chrift, though I be a poor changeable creature, and verily I have found great gain in true Godlinefs.

And now friends, give me leave to tell you thefe are mine experiences, and I fear it would be burthen fome to you, if I should be larger, which I could be: but give me leave to tell you the conclufion of all what I endeavour after, which is to prefs after the mark of the high calling, to deny my felf, and look up to him that is perfect, and who prefents all his perfect without fpot or wrinkle.

Not to him that worketh onely, but to him that believeth, for he is holy, I defire to obferve all the Commands of Chrift as my rule of life, but I am not here by juftified, but alone by a righteoufnefs out of my felf, therefore I fay none but Chrift, not by workes of righteoufnefs that we do, but by faith are we faved, & that not of our felves it is the guift of God, for he that kindleth a fire and compofeth himfelf about with the fparks thereof, he shall lie down in forrow, Ifa. 50: 11. for a man may do much in outward performances, and yet not have a heart right with God: the foolish virgins had lamps of profeffion as well as the wife, but they had not oyle; fo the young man in the Gofpel faid to Chrift, he had obferved all the Commandments from his youth, what lacked he yet, but to deny himfelf, and to part with what he had for Chrift, to take up the crofs and to follow him, which he could not do, except Chrift had given him a righteous heart for all his outward feeming righteoufnefs?

So the Scribes and Pharifees blamed Chrift for all his righteous actions, but could not fee the Idol in thir own hearts, for all their righteoufnefs fprung not from a right root, nor was done by a right rule, nor to a right end.

1. Firft, they had not grace in their hearts.

2. Secondly, neither did they do what they did by the rule of the word of God, bnt by their own rule.

3. What they did was for their own glory to get them praife from men, and not to the glory of God, Amos 4: 4, 5, 6. the which is an abomination to the Lord; this facrifice God is weary of, it is as the offering of Swines blood, and the cutting of a Dogs neck before the Lord, this made Cains facrifice to be unacceptable in the fight of God; mans righteoufnefs is as monftruous cloathes, and filthy raggs, that comes ot

E from

not from a heart fanctified where Christ dwels; alt'though it be garnished with never so much parts and guists, the Lord looks upon the inward righteousnefs of the heart.

Parts and guifts may ceafe, but the least meafure of true grace shall hold out to the end.

And what foever is parts and not grace, bear not these following Characters upon them, such have not the fpirit, now the fpirit is Truth, light, and love.

1. Firft, the fpirit of truth joynes with the vvord of truth; if an Angel from heaven should bring any other doctrine, we are not to receive it, and them that believe and truft in the promife it leads into all truth, wait for the accomplishment of the promife of the fpirit, to teach you all things, and bring all things to your remembrance, which he hath promifed shall remaine with us alwayes, John 14: 16.

This is a good antidote against error, this teaching for the moft part, abides and formes the foul into it felf.

The more of this truth and light comes in, the more a foul abhorres it felf, fees it 's own emptinefs, and Chrifts fulnefs.

The more of this light comes into the foul, the more it thirfteth after light.

The more knowledg it hath of God, the more it loves God, which conformes it into his image, and the more it delights in God, and loves them moft that have moft of God in them, Pf. 16. all my delight is in the Saints, and them that are excellent in the earth.

The true fpirit delights in all the commands of God, which shews true love to God, if you love me keep my Commandments; Jo. 14: 15, 16. and I will pray the Father and he shall give you another Comforter, that he may abide with you for ever.

It is a meek and a quiet fpirit, it hates pride and lifting up; it fees enough in it felf dayly to humble it; Its full of love to all that God loves, though differing from them; by this shall all men knovv that you are my Difciples, if you have love one to another. Joh. 13: 35

We know that vve are paffed from death to life; becaufe we love the brethren. 1. Joh. 3: 14.

Now the reafon why we should cherish this grace of love to God, his people, and all men are these.

Firft, becaufe without love, which is charity, we are but as founding brafs or tinckeling Cymbals, all we do without this is nothing. 2 Cor. 13.

Second-

Secondly, becaufe Chrift hath faid, becaufe Iniquity fhall abound, the love of many fhall wax cold in the laft dayes. Mat. 24. 12.

Thirdly, becaufe it is one of Chrifts laft and great Commandments. John. 13: 34. 1. of Joh. 2. 7. 8.

Fourthly, it renders us much like unto our Mafter Chrift Jefus, Acts. 10: 38. who went about doing good to all; let us labour to follow his example, fhevv pitty to them, that God hath not yet fhewed fo much pitty to, as he hath done unto us; do good to them that hate you, and pray for them that difpitefully ufe you. Mat. 5. 44: 45.

Thefe were Gods teachings to mee in the abfence of faithful Teachers, when they were removed into corners; Which was a fore afflicion to mee, but I look at what mercy God afoards mee in all afflictions, feing I am un-vvorthy of the leaft mercy, for it vvere a righteous thing vvith God to cut us of, and I marvailed at his patience and long fuffering vvith mee, and all others.

I find by experience that reading theScripture before prayer many times quickeneth the heart to Chrift.

And to meditate on Gods mercies to our foules and bodyes; and what great things Chrift hath fuffered to purchafe thefe mercies for us : is a great help to ftir up to that heavenly duty of praifing and thankfulnefs : which is a maine duty I would ftir up my felf and others unto, becaufe our hearts are apt to be very backward unto it; and fecondly, becaufe it is a duty to be done at all times. In all things give thankes, yea in afflictions: For God hath promifed, all fhall worke together for good to them that love God. Thirdly, to be filled with the Spirit of praifes, makes the foul to live in heaven while it is on earth : verily, we had need be ftirred up to this duty; for he that offers praife glorifies God. *Pfal.* 50. *laft verfe.*

And Iefus Chrift complaines againft the neglect of it, in that place where the ten Leppers were clenfed, and but one did returne thankes : faith Chrift, was there not ten cleufed, but where are the nine? O! athank-ful frame doth compofe the heart to great contentednefs in every condi-tion : it is of a divine nature : it ftirres up the graces of God in the foul, as love and faith with hope in God and charity to others.

Therefore pray for the Spirit of God, to put the heart into a praifing frame for there's need of the exercife of much heavenly wifdome in the performance of this duty : for 't is a fpiritual work.

Another experience I have had that it is our duty, and very pro-fitable to watch againft all evil thoughs : thefe ften grieve the holy Spi-

　　rit of

rit of God; as of old he complained, how long shall vain thoughts lodg
within you, and God looking upon man, beholding what was in his heart,
and seeing his thoughts to be evil onely, and continually, and it repent
ed the Lord that he had made man on the earth, and it grieved him at
the heart; and God said, I will distroy man whom I have created from the
facre of the earth, *Gen.* 5: 6. And then down comes the flood of Gods
displeasure upon the old world, not for sinful actions only, but thoughts
also: Therefore keep your hearts with all diligence, *Prov.* 4: 23. For
out of the abundance of the heart the mouth speaketh: And in the multitude of words is fin.

I would desire all to take heed of idle words: and mind well what ye
speak, when and how; avoid all needless speeches: and put far away all
vain foolish jesting; an evil, which my self was some times very prone too,
and as too many do harm by, I endeavored to make my self and others
merry: but alas, 't is sinful mirth, and it will bring sadness here, or els
which is worse, end in sorrow hereafter: thus was I convinced of this evil
being upon a joyrney, meeting one that was a stranger to mee, thinking
to make him and my self laugh: spoake jestingly to him; but he presently
fella swearing and cursing, and railing; which when I heard, wounded me
to the heart, that I by my folly should provoke the poor man so to sin a-
gainst God, my mirth soon turned into mourning. And while I mourned
before the Lord over this my great evil, which had produced such a sad effect, God was pleased to set this upon my heart. Cannot I make thee
more merry with heavenly and spiritual joy, then thou canst make thy self
with such foolish vain and sinful mirth. And the Lord hath since filled
mee with that sweet refreshing joy: that is a thousand times better to mee
then all sinful mirth.

Further, in reference to words, I would commend unto yow some
Scripture rules: *Iam.* 1: 26. compared with *Math.* 12: 27. from whence
we may observe, that when any person doth utter words that be vain,
earthly, or froward, it doth plainly manifest that there is an earthly, vain,
and froward heart; whish is an abomination to the Lord, *Prov.* 11: 20.
and in *Iam.* 1: 19. The Apostle doth perswade Christians to be swift to
hear, but slow to speak, and slow to wrath. And Jesus doth exhort his
followers that their yea should be yea, and their nay nay; saying, that what
foever is more is evil: And *Iams* 1: 21. bids us lay apart all filthiness and
superfluity of naughtiness: that is to say, what ever is more then needful in words, apparel, and diet; yea, and in all things, and what ever
                                                                          pro-

profeffion any perfon may make, if they bridle not their tonge, they deceive themfelves and their Religion is vain; hath God through his free grace, paffed his diftinguishing love upon a little Remnant: doubtlefs 'tis their duty then to diftinguish themfelves from others, in their words habit, and in their whole converfatiou fo to walke as becometh the Gofpel: *Phil,* 1:27. Surely if perfons were awakened by the voice of God, that fpeaks lowd in the prefent afflictions, they would fo doe; 't now is not a time for any of Gods Children to continue their fuperfluities, when many do want neceffaries: Let me intreat fuch to read, and mind what is written in *Rom.* 12: 1, 2. And 1 *Pet.*2: 11. If we could but be moderate in the ufe of all things: what good Stewards fhould we be of the manifold bleffings of God; which he hath betrufted us with, and we muft give an account of in the day of the Lord.

Profperity hath made many to glory in the flesh; and exalt themfelves, in, which vain glory fome ftill do continue: although the great Eternal God hath and doth teftify from heaven againft it, but if it be not repented of, and departed from, God wil turn it into shame, *Hofea* 4: 7. As they were increafed, fo they finned againft me, therefore will I change their glory into shame: its now a trying time, and all perfons by their converfations will difcover what they are, and were ever the deeds and workes of the flesh appear, and are alowed, 'tis evident there is not the Spirit of God in them: And they who have not the Spirit of Chrift are none of his: And 'tis not a talking of, but walking in the Spirit, will help againft the fulfilling the lufts of the flesh, and manifeft who are the true Children of God. Oh! that perfons were wife, to confider their latter end, then furely they would not neglect the knowledg of thofe things that belong to their peace: but chufe that better part, that shall never be taken from them. Which would make them happy for ever.

Oh! that all would be perfuaded to commune with their own hearts, and confider their own wayes: And to mind the dreadful Judgments of God, and his vials of wrath that shall be powred out againft fin and finners, furely they would fee it is high time to departe from pride, vain glory, coveteoufnefs, oppreffion, hypocrify, mallice, and all fin: For verily, God is vifiting for thefe things, and for perfons ftill to continue therein, may it not be feared and juftly exfpected, that God should increafe his Judgments, and punish feaven times more: *Leit.*26: 21, 24. *They who departe not from fin God will departe from them:* and hovv fad that is let foules confider: read *Hofea* 9: 11, 12, 14.

E 3   The

Therefore who ever vvould not be eternally feperated from God, let them in time feperate from all fin : And let poor foules take fpeciall heed they live not in any knovvn evil, nor neglect any knovvn duty, but put on the Lord Jefus Chrift , and make no provifion for the flesh to fulfil the lufts thereof; for if ye live after the flesh ye fhall dye : But if ye through the Spirit do mortify the deeds of the body, ye fhall live, *Rom.* 8: 13. let me propound but this on queftion, and I vvifh all young and old, Rich and poor to mind it, vvhether or no it is not better to feparate from fin, then that fin fhould feperate thee from God for ever.

Oh! vvhat need is there, that all vvho love God and their ovvn foules, fhould hate, abhorre, and depart from all fin, becaufe 't is that vvhich God doth fo hate, as he vvill punifh it vvhere ever he finds it. Yea, if a *David*, a Man after Gods ovvn heart do commit any fin, he muft be reproved for it ; and God vvill fo frovvne as it may coft many figths, prayers, and tears, before God reftore unto him the joy of his falvation, and though fecretly committed, yet God vvill punifh openly that others may hear and fear. 2 *Sam.* 12: 12.

Oh! hovv have I found by fad experience, that pride is a breeding fin, and fpiritual pride is indeed the very vvorft; vvhen perfons come to have a little knovvledg of the things of God, and have fet a fevv fteeps in his vvayes : Many be too prone, then to be puffed up vvith felf conceite, and to judg all others to be in errors, vvho are not juft of their perfwafion; and fo to judge cenfure, and condemne them for Heretikes : and to perfecute them at leaft vvith the tonge, but though fometimes Paul did thus ; he acknovvledgeth it vvas from a Pharifaical fpirit, vvhich vve had all need to take heed of : and judg not ; and ye fhall not be judged. Alas ! our heavenly Father have many children, but there be babes and fome ftronge men : they are not all of an age, nor cannot all fee alike, nor acte alike ; let all the beloved of God (ceafe fmiting and) manifeft true love one another. And vvhat ever their perfwafion be all vvho are humble and holy, and do faithfully vvalke up to the light they have received, let them be beloved for the Fathers fake. Oh! that vve may be filled vvith that grace of true Charity ; for that is a fpecial antidote againft all pride, malice and any evil thoughts, and evil fpeakings, and prejudice, and offences one againft another. 1 *Cor.* 13: 1, 4. &c. There vve may read at large of the excellency of true charity. Oh! the more any one is filled vvith the good Spirit of God, the more fhall they be enabled againft all the vvorks and fruits of the flesh ; therefore I vvould counfel perfons vvhen they avvake

avvake, vvait for the teachings of the Spirit , and for the accomplishment of that promife made to the laft dayes. And vvhat the Spirit teacheth do ye commit to the Spirits keeping : and they, vvhith vvhom it is the day of Gods povver are made vvilling both to hear the Spirits voyce, and obey it.

And I vvould have all to endeavor diligently for the injoyment of the Spirit, and hearken every one that hath an ear : vvhat it fpeaks , for the teachings thereof are very glorious ; it makes a foul live as it vvere in heaven vvhile on earth. Surely vvhen *Daniels* faith vvas made ftrong by the injoyment of this bleffed Spirit of God , fo as nothing could hinder him from the vvorſhip of God. Oh! vvhat fvveet communion did he injoy vvith God , and although throvvn into the lions den , yet there vvonderfully and comfortably preferved, I have found this, that vve are too ready to difpife or flight the Spirit of God , vvhen it appears in fomething beyond us, or out of our reach, but let us take heed of this evil alfo.

This good Spirit of God is that vvhich vvill enable us to chufe to fuffer rather then to fin , and in all our fuffering it vvill vvonderfully affift and uphold us, and carry through the foreft firy tryals, and if vve be throvvn into fufferings for Chrift fake , be fure he vvil make one vvith us to uphold us in the furnis ; and vve need not ftudy hovv vve ſhall be delivered from our ennemies, for God vvill deal vvith them as he did vvith *Daniel*, and the three Children; for he will recompence the wickednefs of the wicked upon their ovvn heads; therefore fear not , but ftand ftill and vvait, and yovv ſhall fee the falvation of God. And I do not think that thefe things be given in to me from the Lord for my ovvne fake only, but for your benefit, to vvhom it may come; and I hope I am fo far from having high thoughts of my felf, that the more I fee of God, and injoy from God, fo much the more caufe I have to be humble ; and if others find theirhearts as bad as I have found mine , they vvill fee caufe enough to ufe all means vvith them ; and vvhen all is done; it muft be faith in Jefus Chrift muft remove this mountain; faith vvill carry us out of ourfelves unto Chrift, and caufe us to reft on him to do all our vvorkes for us , and in us, do ye cherish a holy fear againft fin, and an holy bouldnefs to come to God , and a holy confidence in him for vvhat we come for, and let not the fear of man hinder from any duty God calls thee unto ; to conclude , I only commend unto you that vvord in *Micha* 6: 8. So ſhal I leave this to the bleffing of the Lord, and the confideration of the vvife.

COUR-

COURTEOUS READER,

IF these my Experiences sute not with thy condition, yet let it have a patient view of thee, and pass by what is of the flesh, Own what is of the spirit, and Iudg not, what thou shalt meet with of the truth : because thou art not yet acquainted in that way, for the secrets of God are sometime with pore weak ones that fears him, and what is come to pass I hope you will believe; If it was not out of obedience to God, it should not have com'd to your vew, neither would I have put my name to it, if I could have avoided it, for fear of the rash Iudgment of some, Least it should be thought, I did it out of pride, or to own a propheticall spirit, which I know not, But I own a Propheticall voice of Christ, which if he pleases to speak, he can make mee to hear, yea to believe, this I have Experience of : And if these Crumes which I have gathered from my bountifull Lords table, you cann't find it savory to you, leave it to the hungry broaken hearted Christians, to whom ever crumbe of mercy is sweet, when it comes out of love from our blessed Saviour. And let not this be dispised, because it is the Spirits working in the weakest vessel; for Christ did not reject the woman though weak, ignorant, and sinful; and where he hath forgiven much, he maketh them love much, and follow him to the last, especially if they keep the word of his patience, holding fast to every truth of God, though it be in an evil time when truth is dispised.

Mary followed Christ to the last, and the Lord did so assist her with his Spirit, who shewed her strong affections to him, gonig early in the mornnig to the sepulchre, and Christ put this honour upon her, that she must bring the first glad tidings of the Gospel of the resurrection unto the Disciples.

And his appearance to her in that season, when she knew not where to seek him.

Christ herein shewed his great Love to sinners; for she being a poor ignorant woman, though full of affection, did as many of us do now a dayes, seek the living among the dead: but where Christ keeps up the affections of a soul to himself, he manifests more of the knowledg of himself; and Christ doth testify in Iohn. 4. That it was his meat and drink to do his fathers will, and that was to teach the poor the knowledg of his will. And when he made known himself to that poor woman, her affections where so enlarged that she goes and calls others ver. 34. thus Christ finished the work of his father, to take care of the weakest of his flock, that as the woman was first in the transgression, she might have first knowledg of the resurrection, the guift of the well of watter, which springs up unto everlasting life : and this guift God is pleased to give it unto women as well as unto men.

And he doth require that they should honour him as well as men, for the free grace
of

of God in Christ as well to the one as the other, and't is his free grace that I am what I am; and if this small mite be not accepted (by all,) I shall take it as an high honor to suffer for well-doing; for though in my self I am low, and find the flesh would hinder, and my memory bad, yet I can through grace say, the spirit hath been my remembrance, and in the simplicity of my heart I have done this, and out of obedience to my good God, which makes the Son of righteousness to shine on the weak and on the strong. And truely I have nothing to glory in, for I never did see my self so weak as now, and since I had communion night and day with God, I never was so much in self-loathing and abhorring as now; therefore praise the Lord with mee, for I am a poor sinful creature, and I desire that all that fear the Lord, to whom this shall come, would pray earnestly to God for me, that I may stand fast in this evil day, and may walk humbly, blamelesly, and very harmlesly towards all: so that I may honour him which hath honoured me, with his Son, to whom be glory and praise for ever.

Now, to testify to all that I have received (from the Lord) that gift of singing as well as the gift of prayer, and any other, therefore I shall present to your view some of those Hymnes and spiritual Songs : with an account how and when they were given in; and so shall leave it to the spiritual to Iudge.

As I was waiting on the Lord, in that Ordinance of the Lords Supper, this following short Hymne was immediately given in.

O Now my soul go forth with praise,
For God excepteth thee alwayes;
Thy life is bound up now in mee,
My precious death hath set thee free,
　2. This Testimony I thee give,
As this bread was broaken, so was I,
That thou in mee mightest never dye :
My blood doth justify the same,

That thou mayest praise my holy Name.
　3. My Covenant I have made with thee,
So that thou art now whole set free :
Sin nor Satan cannot thee charge,
Because my love hath thee inlarg'd,
So sure as I am plas't above,
So sure art thou now of my love.

Your waiting shall be upon me, till I your souls hath filled; and
in the way of righteousnes you shall be made to yeeld.

F

And

Another time I having been waiting on the Lord in breaking bread: And soon after was given in this following.

THE Spring is come the dead is gone,
Sweet streams of love doth flow:
There is a Rock, that you must knock,
From whence these stream do go.

2. The Banquets set, the King is come,
To entertain his Guest:
All that are weary of their sins,
He waites to give them rest.

3. Then come, and take your fill of love,
Here's joy enough for all,

To see our King so richly clad,
And give so loud a call.

4. Here's Wine without money or price:
Here's milk to nurish babes:
You may come to this banquet now,
And feede of it most large.

5. Then comfort you your selves in him;
Tis sweet to see his love,
That they, that are redeemed by him,
May live so free above.

And while the afflicting hand of God was upon mee in some measure, this following was given in one evening, as a song of instruction.

AFflictions are not from the dust,
Nor are they in vain sent:
But they shall work the work of him,
That is most nobly Bent.

2. Then let thine eyes look upon him,
Which worketh in the dark;
And let thine heart imbrace his love,
Least thou from him should'st start.

3. Although thou canst not see his work,
Yet waite on him with joy;
For none shall hinder now his work,
Nor none shall him Anoy.

4. Thou must be willing to take up
The cross, to follow him,
And waite till he will make his cup,
To flow up to the brim.

5. Seeing thou art now called unto
The purpose of his will,
Let not afflictions trouble thee,
Believe, and stand thou still.

6. If that the Lord did not thee love,
He would not this pains take,

To let thee see his grace in thee,
And also thee awake.

7. It scowers away the drosse from thee,
And takes away thy tinne:
It makes thy soul fit for to hear
The voice of thy sweet King.

8. It makes the soul further to know
The Sonship of his grace;
And weanes the soul from things below,
That it may seek his face.

9. It puts the wise to see his work,
And puts him in the way,
That he may forthwith seek the Lord,
Without further delay.

10. It makes him now resolve upon
Obedience to his grace;
And watchful in the way he goes,
That he may seek his face.

11. It makes him look for strengh from God,
To heale his sliding back:
It makes him look up to the Rock,
For that which he dos lack.

This

This was November the 20. in the Year 1656.

ZION *is God's precious plant*,
The Lord *vvill vvatter it every day:*
O ! *Zion is God's holy one*,
It shall not vvhet her nor decay.

2. *Zion is that fenced vvell*,
A Tovver that none shall throvv dov n :
O ! *Zion is that glorious hold*,
That God vvill keep both safe and sovvnd.

3. *Zion is that pleasant Plant*,
That God vvill hedg about each hour ;
O ! *Zion is Gods heritage*,
And he vvill keep it by his povver.

4. *Therefore let not thy heart novv faint*,
For Zions sake hold not thy peace ;
For our God vvill hear Zions Plaint ;
Therefore give thy God novv no rest ,
Till thou vvith Zion he hath blest.

5. *Let* Zion *knovv her time dravves near*,
She may look up novv vvithout fear :
Let Zion *knovv her God doth live* ,
That hath her portion for to give.

6. *Let* Zions *Children novv rejoyce*,
And lett hem praises sing:

O ! *let them lift up pleasant voyce*,
In honnor to their King.

7. *Let* Zion *knovv her God is true* ,
That vvill her mercies novv renevv ,
She shall receive great things from him ,
Who is her glory , *and her King.*

8. *Althoug afflictions should hold on* ,
And troubles should arise ;
Yet God vvill ovvn his precious one,
Their prayers hee'll not despise.

9. *Our King shall reigne in righteousness*,
His glory shall shine forth ;
He vvill come forth in Iudgment then, †
For his poor saints comfort.

10. *Our King shall reigne in glory then* ,
He shall himself come up ,
His ennemies then shall fall vvith speed
And be made but a puf.

11. *Then let my people quiet sit* ,
And vvait on him vvith joy ;
There is a time dravves near at hand ,
Nothing shall them Anoy.

† For the confirmation hereof do ye mind these two Scriptures
Esai. 45: 13. and *Psalm* 89: 19.

THE *poor then of the flock shall find a rest* ;
And I their God, and portion, will them bless :
And they shall to me for a refuge fly ,
And I will be their helpe continually.

2. *Then shall their souls alone in mee rejoyce* ,
That I have made of them my onely choyce ;
I vvill fill them in that day vvith my povver ,
So they shall vvait on me then every hour.

3. *Their soul shall be as vvattered plants vvith devv* ,
And I my mercy vvill to them renevv ;
Their beats shall be ingaged vvith my love ,
For I vvill move in them from povver above.

4. *This is the portion that I novv vvill give* ,
Vnto all those that strifes humbly to live ;
Therefore rejoyce in God your onely guide
VVhich in this day of trouble vvill you hide.

E N D.

Awake, awake, put on my strength,
  And mine owne comelyneß,
Look upon mee for I have
Wrought thy deliverance.
2. Thou art black, but comely in
  Mine eyes, that doth behold
Thee swearing mine owne righteousneß,
  Which glory cannot becould.
3. I waited long on thee, to see,
  When thou wouldst mee imbrace,
And when thou would'st look up to mee,
  To see my glorious face.
4. And now, what say'st thou unto mee?
  Have I not done thee good?
And have not spar'd to set thee free,
  Mine own Sons pretious blood.
5. Therefore let all thy life be now
  A sacrifice of praise,
And to my holyneß give up
  Thy self in all my wayes.

6. Let not the World so sad thy heart,
  Nor cast thee down so low,
For if thou wait upon my grace,
  My secrets thou shalt know.
7. Be watchful, and keep close to mee
  Thy Garments: do not staine;
And that will be to thy poor soul,
  A certain heavenly gain.
8. Take heed of glorying in my love
  But walk humbly and low,
For it is onely my fulneß,
  That makes thee thus to flow.
9. There is by pathes to wander in,
  That Sathan would advance,
But I will keep thee by my power,
  And be thy deliverance.
10. Be watchful and keep close to mee,
  My Garments do not soyl,
For they are thine to cover thee;
  Be watchful then a while.

OH! where shall I find now
  A people quicken'd still,
That seek all times to live on God,
  And eck to do his will.
2. A people that deny themselves,
  And eck the cross up take,
That doth delight in God alone,
  And eck the World forsake.
3. A people that abhor themselves,
  And over their sins weep,
A people mourning o'r the Land,
  And doth him dayly seek.
4. A people that believes in God,
  By faith drawes vertue still;
Lay hold on promise which is true
  Contented with his will.

5. A people that the word esteem,
  Keeping close there dayly,
And for a rule the same doth take,
  When others from it fly.
6. Their hearts are fastened on the Lord,
  They for a refuge fly,
That God would now help by his power,
  In their extremity.
7. Their cries are now unto the Lord,
  They seek in him to hide,
To take of now his heavy hand,
  And not let wrath abide.
8. With such a people would I spend,
  My life and dayes now here:
Oh! think upon thy servant Lord,
  And to me now draw near.

I assure you COURTEOUS READER these are not studed
things, but are given in immediately.

FIN.

Watts Bibliotheca Britannica
calls the "Claustrum Regale
Reseratum" a scarce and high-
priced curiosity"
of. Hughes "Boscobel Tracts"
Introduction, 27-28.

Mr Allan Fea (the authority on the
subject) says: —
"It is usually stated that this
Tract first appeared in 1680-1. The
only copy I know of the first edition
is in the Salt Library at Stafford".
"After Worcester Fight"
Introduction XIII.

CLAVSTRVM REGALE
RESERATVM

or.

The Kings Concealment
at Trent, published
by A.W.

In vmbrâ alarum tuarum sperabo
donec transeat iniquitas

LONDON, Printed for Will Nott at the
Queens Arms in the Pell Mell. 1667.

LATIBVLVM

Trent

Worcester

P. Williamson fecit

TO THE
QUEEN'S
Moſt Excellent
MAJESTY.

THis little Book having obtained liberty, after a long Impriſonment, to walk abroad, proſtrates it ſelf at Your Majeſties feet for patronage and protection. In it Your Majeſty may behold GOD's wonderful Mercy and Providence, in keeping and preſerving our Gracious Soveraign from the hands of His Enemies, when they ſo pleaſed

them-

To the Queen's Majesty.

themselves with the hopes of seising His Sacred Person after the Battel of Worcester, As they had invented and prepared new ways to afflict His Majesty , such as till then never entred into the hearts of the worst of Tyrants before them. But it pleased God to frustrate the hopes and designs of the Kings Adversaries, and to restore His Majesty to His Fathers Throne : Which that He may long enjoy with Your Majesty, in Health, Peace and Happiness, Is, and shall be the prayers of

Your MAJESTIE's

Most obedient, and most

Faithful Servant,

ANNE WYNDHAM.

Clauſtrum Regale Reſeratum :

OR,

The K I N G'S

Concealment

AT

TRENT.

Ow that after the Battel of *Worceſter,* His Sacred Majeſty moſt wonderfully eſcaped the hands of his blood-thirſty Enemies, and (under a Diſguiſe, in the company of Mrs *Jane Lane*) ſafely arrived at *Abbots-Leigh* in *Somerſetſhire,* (the ſeat of Sir *George Norton,* lying near to the City of *Briſtol*) hath been fully publiſhed unto the World. His Majeſtie's Journey from thence to the houſe of Colonel *Francis Wyndham* at *Trent* in the ſame County, his Stay there, his Endeavour

deavour (though fruftrate) to get over into
France, his Return to *Trent*, his final Departure thence in order to his happy Tranf-
portation, are the fubject of this prefent
Relation. A Story, in which the Conftel-
lations of Providence are fo refulgent, that
their light is fufficient to confute all the
Atheifts of the world, and to enforce all
perfons (whofe faculties are not pertina-
cioufly depraved) to acknowledge a watchful Eye of G O D from above, looking
upon all Actions of Men here below,
making even the moft wicked fubfervient
to his juft and glorious defigns. And indeed, whatfoever the Antients fabled of
Gyges's Ring, by which he could render
himfelf Invifible, or the Poets fancied of
their Gods, who ufually carried their chief
Favourites in the Clouds, and by drawing
thofe aerial Curtains, did fo conceal them,
that they were heard and feen of none,
whilft they both heard and faw others, is
here moft certainly verified. For, the Almighty fo clofely covered the King with
the wing of his Protection, and fo clouded
the Underftanding of his cruel Enemies,

that

that the moſt piercing Eye of Malice could not ſee, nor the moſt Barbarouſly-bloody Hand offer Violence to his Sacred Perſon: God ſmiting his purſuers (as once he did the *Sodomites*) with blindneſs, who with as much eagerneſs ſought to ſacrifice the Lords Anointed to their fury, as the other did to proſtitute the Angels to their luſt.

But before the ſeveral Particulars of this Story are laid open, two Queſtions (eaſily foreſeen) which will be readily asked by every Reader, call for an Anſwer. The one is, Why this Relation ſo much expect-ed, ſo much longed for, has been kept up all this while from publick view? And the other, How it comes to paſs, that now it takes the liberty to walk abroad? Con-cerning the firſt, it muſt be known, that a Narrative of theſe Paſſages was (by eſpe-cial command from his Majeſty) written by the Colonels own hand, immediately after the Kings return into *England*; which (being preſented to his Majeſty) was laid up in his Royal Cabinet, there to reſt for ſome time, it being the Kings pleaſure (for
reaſons

reasons best known to his Sacred self) that it should not then be published.

And as his Majesties command to keep it private, is a satisfactory answer to the first; so, his licence now obtained that it might travel abroad, may sufficiently resolve the second question. But besides this, many prevalent reasons there are, which plead for a publication; the chief of which are briefly these. That the implacable Enemies of this Crown may be for ever silenced and ashamed; who having neither Law, nor Religion to patronize their unjust undertakings, construed a bare Permission, to be a Divine Approbation of their Actions; and (taking the Almighty to be such a one as themselves) blasphemously entitled God to be the Author of all their wickedness. But the arm of God stretched out from heaven to the rescue of the King, cutting off the clue of their Success, even then when they thought they had spun up their thred, hath not left them so much as an apron of fig-leaves to cover the nakedness of their most shameful proceedings.

The next is, That the Truth of his Majestie.

jesties Escape (being minced by some, mistaken by others, and not fully set forth by any) might appear in its native beauty and splendor : That as every dust of gold is gold, and every ray of light is light ; so every jot and title of Truth being Truth, not one grain of the treasure, nor one beam of the lustre of this Story might be lost or clouded ; it being so rare, so excellent, that aged Time out of all the Archives of Antiquity can hardly produce a Parallel. Singularly admirable indeed it is, if we consider the Circumstances and Actors. The Colonel (who chiefly designed, and moved in this great Affair) could not have had the freedom to have served his Majesty, had he not been a Prisoner ; his very Confinement giving him both a liberty, and protection to act. For, coming home from *Weymouth* upon his Parole, he had the opportunity to travel freely and safely, without fear of being stopped, and taken up : And being newly removed from *Sherborne* to *Trent*, the jealous eye of *Somersetshire* Potentates had scarce then found him out, whose malevolent Aspect afterwards seldom suffered

B   him

him to live at home, and too too often furnished his house with very unwelcom guests.
Others, who contributed their assistance,
were persons of both sexes, and of very different conditions and qualities : And although their endeavours often proved suc-
cessless, though they received discourage-
ments on one hand, were terrified with
threats on the other ; That a seal of silence
should be imprinted upon the lips of Women, who are become proverbial for their
garrulity ; That faithfulness and constancie
should guard the hearts of Servants, who
are usually corrupted with rewards, or af-
frighted with punishments; That neither
Hope nor Fear (most powerful passions,
heightned by Capital animadversions proclaimed against All that should conceal, and
large Remunerations promised to such as
should discover the King) could work nothing upon any single person, so as to remove
him or her from their respective duty, but
that all should so harmoniously concenter,
both in the Design, and also afterward keep
themselves so long close shut up under the
lock of secrecy, that nothing could be discovered

vered by the moſt exquiſite art and cunning, till the bleſſed Reſtauration of his Majeſty to his glorious Throne, ſo filled their hearts with joy, that it broke open the door of their lips, and let their tongue looſe to tell this Miracle to the amazed World, would (were not the Perſons yet alive, and the Story freſh in memory) rariſie it into a Romance.

The reproaches and ſcandals, by which ſome envious perſons have ſought to dimi-niſh and viliſie the faithful ſervices, which the Colonel out of the integrity of his ſoul performed unto his Majeſty, ſhall not here be mentioned : Becauſe by taking up dirt to beſpatter him, they deſile their own hands, and the gun they level at his Repu-tation, recoils to the wounding of their own.

Theſe things thus premiſed, by way of Introduction, open the Gate, through which you may enter, and in the enſuing Pages (as in ſeveral Tables) take a full view of the Particulars.

The Diſguiſe his Majeſty put on, ſecured him from the Cruelty of his Enemies; but

could

could not altogether hide him from the pry-
ing eyes of his dutiful Subjects. For in the
time of his ſtay at *Leigh*, one *John Pope*
(then Butler to Sir *George Norton*, but formerly a Soldier for the King in the Weſt)
through all thoſe clouds eſpied the moſt
Illuſtrious Perſon of the King. With him
his Majeſty(after he ſaw himſelf diſcovered)
was pleaſed familiarly to diſcourſe; And
ſpeaking of the great Sufferings of very
many of his Friends in the Weſtern parts,
(moſt whereof were well known to *Pope*)
his Majeſty enquired if he knew Colonel
Francis Wyndham, who (in the time of
the late Wars) was Governor of *Dunſter-
Caſtle ?* Very well, Sir, anſwered *Pope*.
The King then demanding what was become of him ? *Pope* replies, That the Colonel had married Mrs *Anne Gerard*, one of
the daughters and heireſſes of *Thomas Gerard*
Eſq; late of *Trent* in *Somerſetſhire*, and that
he had newly brought thither his Mother
(the Lady *Wyndham*) his Wife and family,
and that he believed the Colonel intended
there to reſide and live. His Majeſty having
received this intelligence concerning the
                                    Colonel,

Colonel, together with an exact information of the scituation of *Trent*, sought an opportunity to speak with Mrs *Lane*, (from whom, the better to conceal himself, he then kept at a distance) and by means of Mr *Lassels* (who accompanied the King in this journey) obteining his desire, his Majesty with much contentment imparted to Mrs *Lane* what *Pope* had informed him concerning Colonel *Wyndham*, and his habitation ; telling her withall, That if she could bring him thither,he should not much doubt of his safety.

In this very point of time comes the Lord *Henry Wilmot* (since Earl of *Rochester*) from *Dirham* in *Gloucestershire* (the seat of *John Winter* Esq; a person of known loyalty and integrity) to *Leigh*. My Lord had attended his Majesty in his passage Westward, and on Friday morning (*September* the 13.) met accidentally Captain *Thomas Abington* of *Dowdswell* in the County of *Gloucester*, at *Pinbury* Park; and being known by the Captain, (who had served under his Lordship in the Wars) was that night by him conducted to Mr *Winter's*, from whom his
Lordship

Lordfhip (as he hath often fince acknowledged) received great Civilities. Mrs Lane
prefently reveals to the Lord Wilmot the
Kings refolution to remove to Trent : whereupon my Lord demanded of Henry Rogers
(Mr Winter's fervant, and his Lordfhips
guide from Dirham to Leigh) whether he
knew Trent ? He anfwered, That Colonel
Wyndham and his Mafter had married two
Sifters, and that he had often waited on his
Mafter thither. Thefe things fo happily
concurring, his Majefty commanded the
Lord Wilmot to hafte to Trent, and to
afcertain the Colonel of his fpeedy Approach.

His Lordfhip took leave, and continuing
Rogers for his guide, with one Robert Swan,
arrived at Trent the fixteenth of September.
Rogers was fent in forthwith to the Colonel
to acquaint him, that a Gentleman a friend
of his, defired the favour of him, that he
would pleafe to ftep forth and fpeak with
him. The Colonel enquiring of Rogers,
whether he knew the Gentleman or his
bufinefs ? anfwered, No, he underftood
nothing at all, but only that he was called
by

by the name of *Mr. Morton*. Then without further difcourfe the Colonel came forth, and found the Gentleman walking near the Stable; whom as foon as he approached, (although it was fomewhat dark) he faluted by the Title of *My Lord Wilmot*. His Lordfhip feemed to wonder that he fhould be known, but it was nothing ftrange, confidering the Colonels former acquaintance with him, being one of the firft that engaged under his Command, in his late Majefties fervice : Befides, his Lordfhip was not in the leaft altered, except a Hawk on his fift, and a Lure by his fide might pafs for a Difguife. This Confidence of his Lordfhip really begat admiration in the Colonel, calling to mind the great danger he was in, and whofe Harbinger he was ; For he advertifed the Colonel, that the King himfelf was on his way to *Trent*, intending that very night to lodge at *Caftle-Cary* (a Town fix miles thence) hoping by Gods affiftance, to be with him about ten of the clock next morning.

At this joyful news the Colonel was tranfported, (there having run a report, that his

Majefty

Majesty was slain in the Fight at *Worcester*)
and giving God thanks for his wonderful
mercy, he assured his Lordship, *That for his*
Majesties preservation he would value neither
his life, family nor fortune, and would never
injure his Majesties confidence of him; Not
doubting, but that God who had led his Ma-
jesty through the midst of such inexpressible
dangers, would deliver him from all those
barbarous threats, and bloody intentions of
his Enemies. With these and such like expressions, the Colonel brought the Lord
Wilmot into his parlour, where he received
an exact account of his Majesties condition,
and present affairs.

Next morning, the Colonel found it
necessary to acquaint the Lady *Wyndham*
his mother, and also his own Lady, with
the particulars the Lord *Wilmot* had overnight imparted to him, concerning the King.
The relation he gave them, did not (through
the weakness of their sex) bring upon them
any womanish passion, but surprized with
joy, they most cheerfully resolve (without
the least shew of fear) to hazard all, for the
safety of the King. And so (begging Gods
blessing

bleffing upon their future endeavours) they
contrive how his Majefty might be brought
into the houfe, without any fufpition to
their family, confifting of above twenty
perfons. Among them therefore, M*rs* *Julian
Coningsby* (the Lady *Wyndham's* Neece)
Elianor Withers, *Joan Halfenoth*, and *Henry
Peters* (whofe loyalty to the King, and
fidelity to themfelves, they had fufficiently
experienced) are made privy to their defign. Next they confider what Chambers
are fitteft for his Majefties reception. Four
are made choice of; amongft which, the
Lady *Wyndham's* was counted moft convenient for the day-time, where the fervants
might wait with moft freedom upon his
Majefty. Then a fafe place is provided to
retreat unto, in cafe of fearch, or imminent
danger : And laftly, Employments are de-
figned to remove all others out of the way
at the inftant of his Majefties arrival. All
which after a while, anfwered their defires,
even beyond their expectation.

Between nine and ten the next morning,
the Colonel and his Lady walking towards
the fields adjoining to the houfe, efpied the

King

King riding before *Mʳˢ Lane*, and *Mʳ Laſſels*
in their company. Aſſoon as his Majeſty
came near the Colonel, He called to him,
Frank, Frank ! how doſt thou do ? By
which gracious pleaſance the Colonel perceived, that though his Majeſties habit and
countenance were much changed, yet his
Heroick ſpirit was the ſame, and his mind
immutable. The Colonel (to avoid the
jealous eyes of ſome neighbours) inſtantly
conveyed the King and *Mʳˢ Lane* into the
Lady *Wyndham's* Chamber, where the paſ-
ſions of Joy and Sorrow did a while combat
in them, who beheld his Sacred Perſon :
For what loyal Eye could look upon ſo
Glorious a Prince thus eclypſed, and not
pay unto him the homage of tears? But
the conſideration of his Majeſties ſafety,
the gracious words of his own mouth con-
futing the ſad reports of his untimely death,
together with the hope of his future preſervation, ſoon dried them up. In a ſhort
time the Colonel brought the Lord *Wilmot*
to the King, and then the Ladies withdrew
into the Parlour, having firſt agreed to call
Mʳˢ Lane Couſin, and to entertain her with
the

the same familiarity as if she had been their near Relation. That day she stayed at *Trent*, and the next morning early Mr *Lassels* and she departed.

. His Majesty, after he had refreshed himself, commanded the Colonel in the presence of the Lord *Wilmot*, to propose, What way he thought most probable for his Escape into *France*; for thither he desired with all speed to be transported. The Colonel (the King giving him this opportunity) entertained and encouraged his Majesty with this remarkable passage of Sir *Thomas Wyndham* (his Father) *Who, not long before his death [in the Year 1636] called unto him his five Sons, (having not seen them together in some years before) and discoursed unto us [said he] of the long Peace and Prosperity this Kingdom had enjoyed under its Three last Glorious Monarchs : Of the the many Miseries and Calamities which lay sore upon our Ancestors, by the several Invasions and Conquests of Forein Nations, and likewise by Intestine Insurrections and Rebellions. And notwithstanding the strange mutations and Changes in* England, *He shewed,*

C 2   how

how it pleased God in love to our Nation to preserve an undoubted Succession of Kings, to sit in the Regal Throne. He mentioned the healing Conjunction of the two Houses of York and Lancaster, and the blessed Union of the two Crowns of England and Scotland, stopping up those fountains of Blood, which by National feuds and quarrels kept open, had like to have drowned the whole Island. He said, he feared the beautiful garment of Peace would shortly be torn in pieces through the Neglect of Magistrates, the general Corruption of manners, and the prevalence of a Puritanical faction, which (if not prevented) would undermine the very pillars of Government. My sons! We have hitherto seen serene and quiet Times: but now prepare your selves for cloudy and troublesom. I command you to honour and obey our Gracious Soveraign, and in all times to adhere to the Crown; and though the Crown should hang upon a Bush, I charge you forsake it not. These words being spoken with much earnestness, both in gesture and manner extraordinary, he arose from his chair, and left us in a deep consultation what the meaning should be of ---The
Crown

Crown hanging upon a Bush. *These words,
Sir,* (said the Colonel) *made so firm an im-
pression in all our breasts, that the many afflictions of these sad Times cannot raze out
their undelible characters. Certainly these
are the days which my Father pointed out in
that Expression: And I doubt not, God hath
brought me through so many dangers, that I
might shew my self both a dutiful Son, and a
loyal Subject, in faithfully endeavouring to
serve your Sacred Majesty, in this your greatest
Distress.*

After this Rehearsal, the Colonel (in
obedience to his Majesties command) told
the King, That Sir *John Strangways* (who
had given many testimonies of his loyalty,
having two Sons, both of them Colonels
for his Royal Father) lived but four miles
from *Trent*; That he was a person of great
fortune and interest in *Dorsetshire*, and therefore he supposed that either Sir *John*, or his
Sons, might be serviceable to his Majesties
occasions. The King, in prosecution of this
proposal, commanded the Colonel to wait
on them; and accordingly the next morning he went over to *Melbury*; the place
where

where Sir *John* dwelt. No sooner was he come thither, but he met with Colonel *Giles Strangways*, and after usual salutations, they walked into the Park adjoyning to the house, where Colonel *Wyndham* imparted the reason and end of his present Visit. Colonel *Strangways* his answer was, That he was infinitely grieved, because he was not able to serve his Majesty in procuring a Vessel according to expectation ; That he knew not any one Master of a Ship, or so much as one Mariner that he could trust : All that were formerly of his acquaintance in *Weymouth*, being for their loyalty banished, and gone beyond the sea ; and in *Pool* and *Lime* he was a meer stranger, having not one Confident in either. A hundred pounds in Gold he delivered to Colonel *Wyndham*, to present to the King ; which at his return, by command was deposited in the hands of the Lord *Wilmot*, for his Majesties use.

About this time the Forces under *Cromwell* were retreated from *Worcester* into the several Quarters of the Country ; some of which coming to *Trent*, proclaimed the

Over-

Overthrow of the Kings Army, and the
Death of the King, giving out that he was
certainly killed ; And one of them affirmed
that he saw him dead, and that he was buried
among the rest of the slain, no injury being
offered to his body, because he was a Valiant Soldier, and a Gallant man. This welcome News so tickled the Sectaries,
that they could not hold from expressing
their joy by making Bonfires, firing of Guns,
Drinking, and other jollities : And for a
close of all, to the Church they must, and
there ring the Kings knell. These rude Ex-
travagancies moved not his Majesty at all,
but onely (as if he were more troubled for
their madness, than his own misfortune) to
this most Christian and compassionate Expression, *Alas poor people!*

Now though the King valued not the
menaces of his proud Enemies, being confident they could do him no hurt ; yet he
neglected not to try the faithfulness of his
Friends to convey him out of their reach.
Thus the former design proving unsuccess-
ful, and all hope of Transfretation that way
being laid aside, the Colonel acquainted

his

his Majesty, that one Captain *William El-lesden* of *Lime* (formerly well known unto him) with his Brother *John Ellesden*, (by means of Colonel *Bullen Reymes* of *Wadden* in *Dorsetshire*) had conveyed over into *France*, Sir *John Berkley* (now Lord *Berkley*) in a time of danger. To this Captain therefore his Majesty sends the Colonel, who lodging at his house in *Lime*, took an opportunity to tell him, That the Lord *Wilmot* had made his escape from *Worcester*; that he lay privately near to him ; and that his Lordship had earnestly solicited him to use his utmost endeavours to secure him from the hands of the pursuers. To this purpose he was come to town, and assured the Captain, if he would joyn in this affair, his courtesie should never be forgotten. The Captain very cordially embraced the motion, and went with the Colonel to *Charmouth* (a little place near *Lime*) where at an Inne, he brought to him a Tenant of his, one *Stephen Limbry*, assuring the Colonel that he was a right honest man, and a perfect Royalist. With this *Limbry* Colonel *Wyndham* treated under the name of Captain

tain *Norris*, and agreed with him to tranf-
port himfelf and three or four friends into
France. The conditions of their Agreement
were ; That before the two and twentieth
day of that inftant *September*, *Limbry* fhould
bring his Veffel into *Charmouth*-Road, and
on the faid two and twentieth, in the night
fhould receive the Colonel and his company
into his Long-boat from the Beach near
Charmouth, from thence carry them to his
Ship, and fo land them fafe in *France*. This
the Colonel conjured *Limbry* to perform
with all fecrefie, becaufe all the Paffengers
were of the Royal party, and intended to
be fhipped without leave, to avoid fuch
Oaths and Engagements, which otherwife
would be forced upon them : And therefore Privacie in this tranfaction would free
him from Danger, and themfelves from
Trouble, the true caufe why they fo
earneftly thirfted (for fome time) to leave
their native Country. *Limbry's* Salary was
Sixty pounds, which the Captain engaged
to pay at his return from *France*, upon fight
of a Certificate under the Paffengers hands
of their landing there. To the performance
D of

of thefe Covenants, *Limbry* with many vows and proteftations obliging himfelf, the Colonel with much fatisfaction, and fpeed came back to his Majefty and the Lord *Wilmot* to *Trent,* who at the narration of thefe paffages expreffed no fmall contentment.

The bufinefs being thus far fuccefsfully laid, the King confults how it might be prudentially managed, that fo there might be no mifcarriage in the profecution. Neceffary it was that his Majefty and all his Attendants (contrary to the ufe of Travellers) fhould fit up all the night in the Inne at *Charmouth*; that they ought to have the command of the houfe, to go in and out at pleafure, the Tide not ferving till twelve at night. To remove therefore all fufpicion and Inconveniencies, this Expedient was found out.

Henry Peters (Colonel *Wyndham's* fervant) was fent to *Charmouth* Inne, who inviting the Hoftefs to drink a glafs of wine, told her, That he ferved a very gallant Mafter, who had long moft affectionately loved a Lady in *Devon,* and had the happinefs

nefs to be well beloved by her ; and though
her Equal in birth and fortune, yet fo unequal was his fate, that by no means could
he obtain her Friends confent : And therefore it was agreed between them, that he
fhould carry her thence , and marry her
among his own Allies. And for this purpofe
his Mafter had fent him to defire her to
keep the beft Chambers for him, intending
to be at her houfe upon the two and twentieth day of that moneth in the evening ;
where he refolved not to lodge, but only
to refrefh himfelf and friends, and fo travel
on either that night, or very early next
morning. With this Love-ftory (thus con-
trived and acted) together with a Prefent
delivered by *Peters* from his Mafter, the
Hoftefs was fo well pleafed, that fhe promifed him, her houfe and fervants fhould
be at his Mafters command. All which fhe
very juftly performed.

When the day appointed for his Majefties journey to *Charmouth* was come, he
was pleafed to ride before Mrs *Julian Coningsby* (the Lady *Wyndham's* Neece) as
formerly before Mrs *Lane :* The Colonel

was

was his Majesties Guide, whilst the Lord *Wilmot* with *Peters* kept at a convenient distance, that they might not seem to be all of one company.

In this manner travelling, they were timely met by Captain *Elesden*, and by him conducted to a private house of his Brothers among the hills near *Charmouth*. There his Majesty was pleased to discover himself to the Captain, and to give him a piece of forein Gold, in which in his solitary hours he made a hole to put a ribbin in. Many like pieces his Majesty vouchsafed the Colonel and his Lady, to be kept as Records of his Majesties favour, and of their own fidelity to his most Sacred Person in the day of his greatest Trial. All which they have most thankfully treasured up as the chiefest Jewels of their Family.

This Royal Company from thence came to the Inne at *Charmouth*, a little after night; where Captain *Elesden* solemnly engaging to see the Master of the ship ready, (the wind blowing then fair for *France*) took leave of his Majesty. About an hour after came *Limbry* to the Inne, and assured the

(:   Colonel

Colonel all things were prepared, and that about midnight his Long-boat should wait at the place appointed. The set hour drawing nigh, the Colonel with *Peters* went to the Sea-side (leaving his Majesty and the Lord *Wilmot* in a posture to come away upon call) where they remained all night expecting; but seeing no Long-boat, neither hearing any message from the master of the ship, at the break of day the Colonel returns to the Inne, and beseeches the King and the Lord *Wilmot* to haste from thence. His Majesty was intreated; but the Lord *Wilmot* was desirous to stay behind a little, promising to follow the King to *Bridport*, where his Majesty intended to make a halt for him.

When the King was gone, the Lord *Wilmot* sent *Peters* into *Lime*, to demand of Captain *Elesden* the reason why *Limbry* broke his promise, and forfeited his word? He seemed much surprised with this message, and said, He knew no reason, except it being Fair-day, the Seamen were drunk in taking their Farewell; and withall advised his Lordship to be gone, because his

ftay

ſtay there could not be ſafe. But ſince that,
Limbry himſelf hath given this account under his own hand : ——

That according to an Agreement made
at *Charmouth, September* the 19. 1651. betwixt himſelf and one Captain *Norris,* (ſince
known to be Colonel *Francis Wyndham*)
he put forth his Ship beyond the *Cobs-mouth*
into *Charmouth-rode,* where his ſervants on
the 22. of the ſame moneth were all ready
in her, waiting his coming ; That he going
to his houſe about ten that night, for linen
to carry with him, was unexpectedly locked
into a chamber by his Wife, to whom he
had a little before revealed his intended
Voyage with ſome Paſſengers into *France,*
for whoſe Tranſportation, at his return, he
was to receive a conſiderable ſum of money
from Captain *Eleſden.*

This woman (it ſeems) was frighted into
a panick fear by that dreadful Proclamation
(of the tenth of *September*) ſet out by the
Men of *Weſtminſter,* and publiſhed that day
at *Lime.* In this, a heavy Penalty was thun-
dred out againſt all that ſhould conceal the
King, or any of his party who were at *Wor-*
ceſter

cester Fight ; and a Reward of a Thousand pounds promised to any that should betray him. She, apprehending the Persons her husband engaged to carry over to be Royalists, resolved to secure him from danger, by making him a Prisoner in his own chamber. All the perswasions he used for his liberty, were in vain : For the more he intreated , the more her violent passion increased, breaking forth into such clamors and lamentations, that he feared if he should any longer contend, both himself and the Gentlemen he promised to transport, would be cast away in this storm, without ever going to Sea.

Thus a Design in a business of the highest nature, carried on with industry and prudence, even to the very last, still promising full hope of a happy production, by one mans single whisper (the bane of Action) proved abortive. For no doubt, had *Limbry* kept his counsel, he had gained the honour of Conveying over his Majesty ; of whose Noble Courage and Vertue , God was pleased to make yet farther trial, as the sequel will inform.

The

The King paſſing on upon *London* Road from *Charmouth*, met many travellers, among whom was one of his Fathers ſervants, well known both to his Majeſty and the Colonel; who were very well pleaſed that he was not guilty of ſo much Civility, as to give either of them the complement of a Salutation. As they drew near to *Bridport*, the Colonel riding a little before, and entring the town, perceived it full of Soldiers : whereupon ſtopping his horſe till the King came up, he inreated his Majeſty to keep on, and by no means to put himſelf into the mouth of them, who gaped greedily after his deſtruction. Neverthelefs, the King having engaged to the Lord *Wilmot* to expect him there, (without the leaſt apprehenſion of danger) rode into the *George*, and alighting in the Court, was forced to ſtay there, and in the Stable, near half an hour, before the Colonel could procure a Chamber. All this while his bloody Enemies were his onely Companions, with whom he diſcourſed freely without fear, and learned from them their intended Voyage for *Jerſey* and *Guernſey*, and their

Deſign

Defign upon thofe Iflands. Here may you fee the Purfuers overtaken, and the bitterest of Enemies friendly difcourfing with Him, whofe utter Ruine they accounted would compleat their Happinefs. He that fate in Heaven certainly laughed them to fcorn, and by the interpofition of his mighty Arm eclypfed their glory, and by his admirable Wifdom reproved and confuted their malice againft the King, and their blafphemies againft Heaven.

No fooner had the King withdrawn himfelf from this dangerous Company into a Chamber (with much difficulty obtained) but Mrs Coningsby efpied Peters riding into the Inne. He (being beckned up) acquainted his Majefty, that the Lord *Wilmot* humbly petitioned him to make hafte out of that place, and to overtake him flowly paffing on the road, and waiting his Majefties coming. Prefently upon the difmiffion of *Peters*, the King having taken fome fmall repaft, not far from the Town joyned in company again with the Lord *Wilmot*, and difcourfing of the feveral Adventures of that hopeful, and (as it fell out) moft

E   perilous

perilous Journey, concluded that *London-Road* was very unfafe, and therefore refolved to follow the next Turning which might probably lead towards *Teavill* or *Sherborn*, neither of which is computed to be above two miles diftant from *Trent*. Providence (the beft of Guides) directed thefe Strangers (for fo they were all to thofe parts) to a way, which after many hours travel brought them into a Village, in which was a fmall Inne for entertainment. This entred thefe mafqued Travellers, to enquire where they were. And to this purpofe calling for fome Beer, the Hoft of the houfe (one *Rice Jones*) came forth, and informed them that the place was called *Broadwinfor*. The Colonel knew the Innkeeper and his wife to be very honeft, loyal perfons, and that for their fidelity to the King and his party, they had (according to their condition) undergone their fhare of troubles. The King underftanding the affection of the people, refolves to lodge in the houfe that night, it being already fomwhat dark, and his Majefty and Company fufficiently wearied with their former nights watching,

and

and that days travel. The Colonel (while
the horſes were put up)deſired Mr. *Jones* to
ſhew him the moſt private rooms;the reaſon
he gave was, Becauſe his Brother-in-law
Colonel *Reymes* (whom the Lord *Wilmot*
perſonated) had been a long time impriſon-
ed, as well as himſelf; That they had lately obtained their Paroles, and to be ſeen
together ſo far from their homes, might
create new jealouſies, and ſo conſequently
cruſh them with new troubles. The good
Hoſt upon this brought them up into the
higheſt chambers, where Privateneſs recom-
penſed the meanneſs of the Accommoda-
tion, and the pleaſantneſs of the Hoſt (a
merry fellow) allayed and mitigated the
wearineſs of the Gueſts. Now the face of
things began to ſmile, which all the day
and night preceding looked ſo louring and
ill-favoured. But this ſhort Calm was on a
ſudden interrupted by a violent Storm. For
in comes the Conſtable with almoſt Forty
Soldiers to be billeted that very night in
the Inne : All the lower Receptacles were
thronged up with this unexpected Company; ſo that the King was in a manner

be-

besieged, there being no passage from a-
bove, but through those suspected Guards.
Thus every place brought forth its troubles,
and every period of time disclosed fresh
dangers ! Shortly after the Soldiers had
taken up their Quarters, a Woman in their
company fell in labour in the Kitchin. The
pangs she endured, made the Inhabitants
of that place very ill at ease, fearing left the
whole Parish should become the reputed
Father, and be enforced to keep the Child.
To avoid this charge, the chiefest of the
Parish post to the Inne, between whom and
the Soldiers arose a very hot conflict concerning provision to be made for the mother and the infant. This dispute continued
till such time as (according to orders) they
were to march to the Sea-side. This quar-
relsom Gossipping was a most seasonable
diversion, exercising the minds of those
troublesom Fellows, who otherwise were
likely to have proved too too inquisitive
after the Guests in the house ; the sad con-
sequences of which , every loyal heart
trembles to think on.

Surely we cannot, except we wilfully
shut

shut our own eyes) but clearly fee, and with all reverence and thankfulnefs adore the Divine Goodnefs for his Majefties fignal Deliverances in this Voyage. Efpecially if looking back upon *Charmouth*, we confider the dangers that threatned him, occafioned by the Lord *Wilmot's* fhort ftay there, after the Kings departure. For one *Hamnet* a Smith, being called to fhoe his Lordfhips horfe, faid, He well knew by the fafhion of the fhoes, that they were never fet in the Weft, but in the North. The Hoftler (a bird of the fame feather) hearing this, began to tell what Company had been there, how they fate up, and kept their horfes fadled all the night; and from hence they conclude, That either the King, or fome Great Perfons had certainly been at the Inne. The Hoftler (whofe heart was foured againft the King) runs prefently to one *Weftley* (of the fame leaven) then Minifter of *Charmouth*, to inform him of thefe Paffages, and to ask counfel what was to be done. This *Weftley* was at his Morning Exercife, and being fomthing long-winded, [*And by the way it may be obferved, that long*

*long Prayers proceeding from a Traiterous
heart, once did good, but by accident onely]*
the Hoftler, unwilling to lofe his reward at
the Gentlemans taking horfe, returns without doing his errand. As foon as my Lord
was mounted and gone, *Hamnet* tells *Weftley*
of the difcourfe between himfelf and the
Hoftler. Away comes *Weftley* upon full
fpeed to the Inne, and (almoft out of breath)
asks the woman of the houfe, what Guefts
fhe had entertained that night? She faid,
They were all ftrangers to her, fhe knew
them not. I tell you then (faid he) one of
them was the King. Then haftily turning
away from her, he and *Hamnet* ran to Mr.
Butler of *Commer* (then Juftice of Peace)
to have him difpatch abroad his Warrants
to raife the Country for the apprehending
of the King, and thofe perfons the laft night
with him at *Charmouth*. But he fpends his
mouth in vain, a deaf ear is turned upon
him, no Warrant would be iffued forth.
This check given to his zeal fo vexed him,
that it had like to have caufed a fuffocation,
had not Captain *Maffey* (as errant a Hotfpur
as himfelf) given it vent, by raifing a Party
and

and purfuing the King upon *London*-Road. But God preferved his Majefty by diverting him to *Broadwindfor*, whilft *Maffey* and his hot-mettled company outran their Prey as far as *Dorchefter*. And indeed, the report of the Kings being at *Charmouth*, was grown fo common, that the Soldiers (lying in thofe parts) fearch'd the houfes of feveral Gentlemen, who were accounted Royalifts, thinking to furprize him. Amongft which, *Pilefdon* (the houfe of Sir *Hugh Wyndham* Uncle to Colonel *Francis Wyndham*) was twice rifled. They took the old Baronet, his Lady, Daughters, and whole Family, and fet a Guard upon them in the Hall, whilft they examine every corner, not fparing either Trunk or Box. Then taking a particular view of their Prifoners, they feize a lovely young Lady, faying, fhe was the King difguifed in womens apparel. At length being convinced of their grofs and rude miftake, they defifted from offering any farther violence to that Family. And here it is much to be obferved, that the fame day the King went from *Charmouth*, Captain *Elefden* came to *Pilefdon*, and enquired of

Sir

Sir *Hugh* and his Lady for the King and Colonel, confidently affirming that they must
needs be there.

His Majesty having with an evenness of
spirit gotten through this rough passage,
safely anchored at *Broadwindsor :* Where
at length enjoying some rest, he commands
the Colonel to give his opinion what course
was to be taken, as the face of affairs then
looked. The Colonel (seeing Forces drawn
every where upon that shore) thought it
very hazardous to attempt any thing more
in *Dorsetshire* ; and therefore humbly besought his Majesty, that he would be pleased
to retreat to *Trent :* He hoped his Majesty
was already satisfied in the fidelity of his
servants ; and that he doubted not, his Majesty might lie securely in that Creek, till it
was fair weather, and a good season to put
forth to Sea. He humbly advised, that *Peters*
might conduct the Lord *Wilmot* to Mr *Huit's*
house at the *Kings-Arms* in *Sarum*, where he
and many of his friends had been sheltered
in the time of troubles. That *Peters* (being
at *Sarum*) should by a private token bring
his Lordship to Mr *John Coventry* (his Kinsman)

man) a Person Noble, Wise, and Loyal, with whom he had kept Intelligence in order to the Kings service, ever since his Majesty had set foot in *Scotland*; That he was assured Mr *Coventry* would think himself highly honoured to correspond in this matchless employment, *The King's Preservation*. He desired the Lord *Wilmot* to be confident of lying concealed; And likewise to treat with Mr *Coventry*, and by *Peters* to return his Majesty an account how he found that Gentleman affected towards this service.

This counsel being well relished and approved, 'twas resolved, That between *Sarum* and *Trent* (lying 30 miles distant and better) an Intercourse should be kept by trusty messengers, and a secret way of writing, to avoid danger in case of interception. All things being thus concluded, the King left his jovial Host at *Broadwindsor*, and returned with the Colonel and Mrs *Coningsby* to *Trent*. The Lord *Wilmot* with *Peters* went that night to *Sherborn*, and the next morning was waited on by *Swan* (who attended his Lordship to the Colonels) and that day got into *Sarum*; where he soon saluted Mr *Coventry*, in all

F   things

things fully anfwering his Lordfhips expectation: And (the 25.of *September*) *Peters* was
fent back with this joyful meffage from the
Lord *Wilmot* to his Majefty, That he doubted
not (by Mr *Coventry's* affiftance, and thofe
recommended by him) to be able in fome
fhort time to effect his defires.

Whilft his Sacred Majefty enjoys his peace
at *Trent*, and the Lord *Wilmot* (with thofe
other Worthies) is bufied at *Sarum* to procure its continuation, It cannot be imperti-
nent to mention a Circumftance or two,
which inferted in the midft of the web and
texture of this Story would have looked un-
handfom, but added, as a fringe may prove
ornamental.

Upon the Sunday morning after the King
came to *Trent*, a Tailor of the Parifh informed the Colonel, That the Zealots [which
fwarmed in that place] difcourfed overnight,
that Perfons of Quality were hid in his houfe,
and that they intended to fearch and feife
them ; and therefore he defired the Colonel
(if any fuch there were) to convey them
thence, to avoid furprifal. The Colonel (re-
warding the good man for his care and kindnefs

nefs towards himfelf and family) told him,
That his Kinfman (meaning the L. *Wilmot*)
was not private, but publick in his houfe,
(for fo his Lordfhip pleafed to be) and that
he believed he would fhew himfelf in the
Church at the time of Prayers. When the
honeft fellow was gone, the Colonel ac-
quaints the King what had paffed between
himfelf and the Tailor, and withall befought
his Majefty to perfwade the Lord *Wilmot* to
accompany him to Church, thinking by this
means not only to leffen the jealoufie, but alfo
to gain the good opinion of fome of the Fa-
naticks, who would be apt to believe, that
the Colonel was rather brought to Church
by my Lord, then his Lordfhip by the Colonel, who feldom came to that Place, fince
Faction and Rebellion had juftled out, and
kept poffeffion againft Peace and Religion.
He alledged moreover, that he fate in an Ile
diftinct from the body of the Congregation,
fo that the Parifhioners could not take a full
view of any of his company. Thefe reafons,
joined with his Majefties command, prevailed
with his Lordfhip; and (though he thought it
a bold adventure, yet) it not only allayed the

fury,

fury, but also took out the very sting of those wasps; insomuch that they who the last night talked of nothing but searching, began now to say, that *Cromwell's* late success against the King, had made the Colonel a Convert.

All being now quiet about home, the Colonels Lady (under a pretence of a Visit) goes over to *Sherborn* to hear what news there was abroad of the King. And towards evening, at her return, a Troop of horse clapt privately into the town. This silent way of entring their Quarters, in so triumphant a time, gave a strong alarm to this careful Lady, whose thoughts were much troubled concerning her Royal Guest. A stop she made to hearken out what brought them thither, and whither they were bound: But not one grain of Intelligence could be procured by the most industrious enquiry. When she came home, she gave his Majesty an account of many stories, which like flying clouds were blown about by the breath of the people, striving to cover her trouble with the vail of cheerfulness. But this the King perceiving to be rather forced then free, as at other times, was earnest to know the cause of her discomposure. And

to

to satisfie his Majesties importunity, she gave him a full relation of the Troop at *Sherborn*: At which his Majesty laughed most heartily, as if he had not been in the least concerned. Yet upon a serious debate of the matter, the Colonel and his Lady supplicated the King to take a view of his Privy chamber, into which he was perswaded to enter, but came presently forth again, much pleased, that upon the least approach of danger, he could thither retreat with an assurance of security. All that night the Colonel kept strict watch in his house, and was the more vigilant, because he understood from *Sherborn*, that the Troop intended not to quarter there, but only to refresh themselves and march. And accordingly (not so much as looking towards *Trent*) about two of the clock next morning, they removed towards the Sea-coast. This fear being over, the King rested all the time of his stay at *Trent*, without so much as the apprehension of a disturbance.

The strangeness of which will be much increased by the addition of what a Captain who served under *Cromwell* at *Worcester*, reported to two Divines of undoubted veracity, long before the King's blessed Restauration : That he was followed and troubled with Dreams for three
                                                                nights

nights together, That the King was hid at *Trent* near *Sherborn*, in a houſe nigh to which ſtood a Grove or patch of trees, and that thither he ſhould go and find him. This ſuggeſtion thus reiterated, was a powerful ſpur to prick him forwards : But the hand which held the reins and kept him back, was irreſiſtible.

Now the hands of his Majeſties enemies were not only reſtrained from doing him evil, but the hands of his friends were ſtrengthened to do him good. In order to which, Colonel *Eward Phelips* of *Montacute* in the County of *Somerſet*, came from *Sarum* to his Majeſty (*Septemb.*28.) with this intelligence, That his brother Colonel *Robert Phelips* was employed to *Southampton* to procure a Veſſel, of whoſe tranſaction his Majeſty ſhould receive a ſpeedy account.

In the mean time, Captain *Thomas Littleton* (a Neighbour of Colonel *Wyndham*) was diſpatch'd up into *Hampſhire*, where by the aid of *Mr. Standiſh* he dealt with the Maſter of a Ship, who undertook to carry off the Lord *Wilmot* and his company, upon the condition his Lordſhip would follow his direction. But the hope of Colonel *Phelips* his good ſucceſs at *Hampton* daſh'd this enterpriſe, and the Captain was remanded to *Trent*, and to make no progreſs till farther order.   Upon

Upon the first of *October*, Mr. *John Sellick* (Chaplain to Mr. *Coventry*) brought a Letter to his Majesty. In answer to which the King wrote back, That he desired all diligence might be used in providing a Vessel; and if it should prove difficult at *Hampton*, trial should be made farther: That they should be ascertained of a Ship before they sent to remove him, that so he might run no more hazards then what of necessity he must meet with in his passage from *Trent* to the place of his Transportation.

October the fifth, Colonel *Phelips* came from the Lord *Wilmot* and Mr. *Coventry* to his Majesty with this assurance, That all things were ready; And that he had informed himself with the most private ways, that so he might with greater probability of safety guide his Majesty to the Sea-side. Assoon as the King heard this message, He resolved upon his Journey. Colonel *Wyndham* earnestly petitions his Majesty, that he might wait on him to the shore: But his Majesty gave no grant, saying, It was no way necessary, and might prove very inconvenient. Upon the renewing his request, the King commanded the contrary, but sweetned his denial with this promise, That if he were put to any distress, he would again retreat to *Trent*.

About

. About ten next morning (*October* the sixth) his Majesty took leave of the old Lady *Wyndham*, the Colonels Lady and Family, not omitting the meanest of them that served him. But to the good old *Lady* he vouchsafed more then an ordinary respect, who accounted it her highest honour, that she had three Sons and one Grandchild slain in the defence of the Father, and that she her self in her old age had been instrumental in the protection of the Son, Both Kings of *England.*

Thus his Sacred Majesty, taking Mrs *Juliana Coningsby* behind him, attended by Colonel *Robert Phelips*, and *Peters*, bade Farewel to *Trent*, the Ark in which God shut him up, when the Floods of Rebellion had covered the face of his Dominions. Here he rested Nineteen days, to give his faithful Servants time to work his deliverance : And the Almighty crowned their endeavours with success, that his Majesty might live to appear as Glorious in his Actions, as Couragious in his Sufferings.

13

FINIS.

HEAVEN REALIZ'D

OR

The Holy Pleasure of daily
intimate Communion with

GOD,

Exemplified
In a blessed Soul (now in Heaven)
(Mrs. Sarah Davy.)

Dying about the 32 Year of her Age.

Being a part of the pretious Reliques,
written with her own hand.

(Stiled by her)

The Record of my Confolations, and the Meditations of my heart.

Published by *A. P.*

---

*Come and hear all you that fear God, and I
will tell you what he hath done for my foul,
66 Pfalm 16.*

Printed in the Year, 1670.

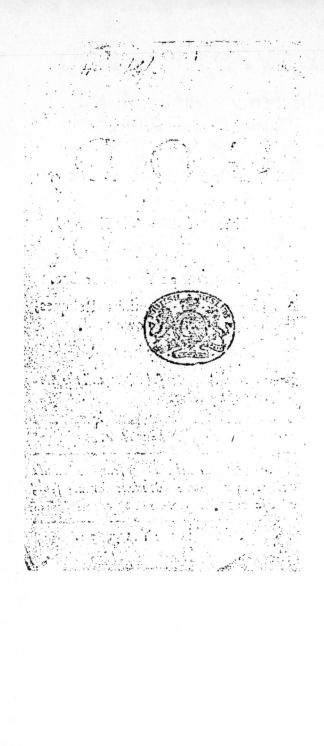

To all sort of Readers.

Whosoever thou art into whose hand providence may cast this small peice I have to beg o thee that thou wouldst no despise it before perused; it pleaseth th wisdom of God, thus to *chuse the fooli* *things of the world to confound the wise, an* *weak things to confound the things that a* *mighty, things that are not to bring to nough* *thing that are, that no flesh can glory in h* presence, especially when the wisdom t the flesh exalts it self against the *Wisde* *of God,* in the simplicity of the Gospe and the lusts of men against the *Holi* of it, when the mistery of God in Ch

A 2   ther

the dwelling of the Spirit, in *sanctified*
believers is denyed and called a delusion
I say, in such an hour of blasphemy, the
appearance of the *Spirit* in its clear enlightning, and *excellent workings*, in a weak
instrument is a blessed testimony against
the Atheism, Prophanity, Blasphemy, and
high derision of Godliness, that every
where abounds; If thou art one of those
who hast only a Form of godliness and
Worship, satisfying thy self with some
used of outward Worship, and so ma-
kest a sorry shift to still thy conscience
whilst in thy sins, and walking after thy
lusts, a Lover of pleasure, more then of
God, as the Character of the Apostle, of
uch is.

And hast thence a low and slight esteem
f serious Godliness, and deemest the
partings with the World, and pleasures
f sin and vanity like death it self, and
hat living with God in *self-denyal, mor-
tification of sin*, *holyness*, and Com-
union with God is a dark melancholly
and uncomfortable walk (as the Devil
and

and a carnal heart suggests) here thou hast a full confutation thereof; as also the experience of all the holy people of God in the world) in this pretious soul who realized that rich consolation and holy pleasure in serving God, and walking with him and choosing (very early) the dispised ways of God, rather then the pleasures of sin for a season, in a holy disdain and dayly trampling under her Foot the vanitie which the foolish hearts of most go after in a dayly solacing her soul, in *drinkin of the Rivers of the pleasures of God*, bein sick of Love to blessed Jesus Christ, whom she had chosen her *Saviour*, *Bridegroom Lord*, and *King*; whose *love*, *beauty*, an *glory* ravished her heart, who held him the gallery's, in his banquetting house whose banner over her was love, and i his blessed Ordinances came as to th *gate of Heaven*, there giving him h Loves.

Thou poor sinful soul, yet in darkne to these things, which are but as a soun of words to thee, In reading hereof (

A 3   th

he grace and power of the Lord may accompany it) caſt of thoſe mean and baſe
houghts of the deſpiſed ways of Chriſt
ind holineſs and believe theſe things to
 e *real*, and *ſatiſfyingly* injoyed by
his bleſſed Soul, and thereby break off
rom thy courſe of Vanity, and of this
World, *and fall in Love with* Heavens
rays; and *ſet thy ſelf* (the Lord helping
hee) to *ſeek* and *know* this *beloved Jeſus,*
tho was this Souls delight, and fall in
ve with him, and attend at Wiſdoms
ates (though blacked and ſcorned by
 e World.)

And thy own ſoul may come to expe-
ence the ſame things; to find out a *plea-*
nt life of ſweeteſt contentation in the Fa-
 ur of God, and injoyment of his good-
ſs and Love in his dear Son Jeſus
hriſt, the true wiſdom (as this Soul
th bleſſedly cleared) *that makes wiſe un-*
Salvation; with Jeſus Chriſt thou ſhalt
d the *Righteouſneſs* that can juſtifie thee,
 pretious blood that can cleanſe thee,
 Light that ſhall ſhine into thee, the

Love

Love that shall for ever endear thee, the *Life* that shall quicken thee, the *power and spirit* that shall *convert* and *change* thee, the *fulness* that shall satisfie thee; the *peace* and *joy* in believing that shall quiet and comfort thee in every condition here on earth, and assure thee of Eternal blessedness and glory hereafter ; If this be not to be chosen before making provision for thy deceitful lusts, that intice thee, flatter thee, in walking after them will certainly damn thee, to Everlasting terrours , and horrors, wailings, howlings, that will never have an end among the impenitent the careless, unconverted, the unholy in the lake provided for them, I say, if glorious delightful certain salvation from the *wrath to come*, be not to be chosen, imbraced, pursued, laid hold of in the first place let thy soul seriously weigh and consider take time apart every day to muse on it *pray and betake* thy self to the Scriptures and hearing Godly Ministers that give out the experience hereof, then let the word and conscience judge, &c.

A 4   Pa

Particularly; let *younger persons* (especially *young Gentlewomen*) be greatly *affected* with this precious example and be perswaded of the joy and sweetness this blessed Soul did find *in seeking the Lord in the days of her youth*, who received instructions betimes, *about the eleventh year* of her Age; began to know God as a holy God, to *fear* sin, to *pray in secret*, to delight in *dayly reading* the Scriptures, to fall in love with the beloved Jesus Christ, to choose him her Lord and Bridegroom, and to wait in the Ministry of his despised servants, to know him, and hear his voice, & became a Disciple and Follower of him; ravisht with his love, admiring his grace, and glory, diligently inquiring after his *feedings*, and betaking her to the following of his people, in a *congregation of believers*, where her soul delighted it self (and as she speaks in her Meditations here) *solaced* her self in Communion with her Lord, sitting at his Feet to hear his pretious words, going home with her heart filled from God, and in her retire-

ments

ments, praying meditating feeding on the word, making the day of the Lord a holy delight, go, tender soul, and through grace, be found in all these blessed practices, and thou maist live delightfully here, and be saved eternally.

When *thou art come to years,* to be capable to understand any thing, as 'tis said of *Moses, Heb. 11. 24. 25. Refuse the pleasures of sin,* which are but for a season, and choose the true wisdom, and to be found *in her paths, for her Merchandize is better then the Merchandize of silver, and the gains thereof then fine gold,* which this *Heavenly* Soul really experienc'd, and one part of her choice Meditations is of this *Wisdom,* as in the perusal of it; you will find ? Oh what is the pleasures of sin, and that but for a little, very little season, vanity, emptyness, a bubble, a pleasant dream, to such a *rich, solid, satisfying, durable, glorious enjoyment* of Jesus Christ, while here as but a taste of the glory shall be revealed ? Those vain pleasures of Youth must issue in sorrow, and deep repentance

pentance, and bitterneſs of Soul if ever
pardoned, and ſaved; but the pleaſure of
knowing, having, being in Chriſt Jeſus, and
the *delightful fellowſhip of* the Saints have
with him, iſſues a bleſſed, chearfulneſs,
and joy in God, without fear of Repentance, unleſs it be that we have no more
of Chriſt in us; and that we ſin againſt ſuch
Love and Grace ſo freely revealed to
us ?

Oh how happy are *younger Men and
Maidens* as the *Pſalmiſt* ſpeaks 148 *Pſal.*
that *begin* to fear the Lord from *their youth*
to ſeek early after Jeſus Chriſt ; for the
Lord to ſee their Faces, before the throne
and to hear their ſighs and cryes after
him, for Chriſt, the Spirit, ſaving grace,
power againſt all ſin, to take up a Croſs,
and chooſe ye affliction and reproach of
the Lords people, before the vanity's,
Pride of Life, and Fading Glory of this
world, this, oh this, is happineſs, ſoul-
happineſs, everlaſting happineſs, riches,
honour, peace, bleſſing, which none can
take away.

Eſpecially

Especially in an Age of the *great cor-*
ruption of youth, when Religion is made a
by-word and a scorn, when many hardned
and blaspheme, when so Few of the *youth*
of noble and generous familyes, Fall in with
serious Godliness, sobriety, but serving
divers lusts and pleasures, to all excess of
Riot, to the debasing of their Spirits, in a
degenerateness from true Nobility and
generousness of Spirit, which is in knowledge, good learning true wisdom and pi-
ety, as fitting them to serve God and their
Generation.

Oh in the midst of such impiety's, how
beautiful, how *honourable*, how *pleasing to*
the Holy God, for any younger persons,
especiall such as pretend to a *generous*
mind and education, such as are in Family's, where excess prophaneness abounds
or the Sons and Daughters of Godly Parents, to betake your selves to seek and
know and fear, & serve the great & blessed God betimes, to be an example and a
blessing to secure Christ and holiness, and
heaven, to walk in the truly noble, de-

light-

lightful, pretious ways, which this peice and *she that lived it* holds forth unto thee.

In order hereunto how should the Soul of Parents (unless they will be Soul Murtherers to their Children) be in travail for grace and Conversion for their Children, and not think it enough, to get them Estates, honours, and great things in this Life, and leave them and it under a curse, that all sorts of *Parents* not only give them liberty, but incourage them to Godliness, to pray and read the Scriptures, and attend upon powerful means of grace to tremble at sin, to dispose of them in the world in order hereunto, as this blessed Soul acknowledgeth the good use of Parents reproof and instructions unto her.

1. In this peice, you have first an account of her Conversion and calling, how the Lord gradually carried on her first convictions, her daily diligence in prayer and the word when a child, the discoveryes she had of the Free grace of the Gospel of the Mistery of Christ, of Righteous.

ousness by Faith, of being in Christ, of
the love of God, and Fellowship with
him, of which she gives an exact and di-
stinct account, discovering the choice and
spiritual understanding she had in the Mistery of the Gospel, not taking up only
from sin to duty, when Christ and grace
little understood, as it may be feared many do; nor yet turning grace into wanton-
ness, but under the constraints of the
choice discoveryes of Free and glorious
Grace, and the loves of God (in the *ad-
mirement* and *adoration* of which she lived)
to attend to most intimate Communion
with him, the breathings and partings of
her Soul, as you will see still running out
after more injoyment of and *likeness* to
her dear Lord Jesus, and exactest *holiness*,
bemoaning her self wherein she fell
short.

2. Next you will meet with her longing after the *real Communion of Saints,*
(which all profess to believe in the Creed
but will not bear the practice of) in the
pure ordinances of the Gospel) in a *con-
gre:*

Congregational Church, (so called) which when she enjoyed she expressed those blessed delights she had in Fellowship with the Lord Jesus, the *kisses of his Lips* she there met with his blessed Ordinances, and establishment of soul, in peace and joy in believing;

3. You have a choice discourse of *wisdom*, the true Heavenly Wisdom, which her Soul diligently sought after, and found, *which was more precious to her then Rubies*, and all the things *that are not to be compared to it*; the rich *experience* whereof she commends to the World in the debasement of all *fleshly Wisdom* in comparison of it!

Especially to her *dear Relations* in the flesh, which is the next *particular* in this discourse, to whose *acceptance* she commends it, with such bowels and gratious affection, and sweetness of Spirit, such powerful convincing motives, and from what of Heaven her own Soul hath tasted, as might become one very *skilful in the word* of Righteousness; to whose serious

perusal

perusal with the blessing of God, I would commend it as that which may lead you into the *path of Life*, helpt on by the singular *example of her Life*, in her *Holy*, sweet, acceptable, conversation towards you, which I hope you are convinced did arise *from a divine principle of Grace*, so to fill up every Relation to you, longing after all your Eternal Salvation in Christ Jesus, oh may all of you be ingaged not only to read but to beg of God; *the same Spirit of Wisdom and grace*, that was found in her, to walk in the *same steps* and *wayes* Heaven ward, that this be not a *witness* against any of you at the great day of Jesus Christ.

4. The next part is (as she stiles it) *the mistery of Godliness*, namely *of the mistery of God in Christ* , the *grace and love of* the Father revealed by him, in which I may take liberty to say, is as much of the Mistery of the Gospel, discovered as usualy I have met with in so little a Room, especially as to living in a delightful *fellowship* therewith which was

her

her great bufineſs, till taken up unto
him.

5. The reſt conſiſts of *occaſional Meditations*, *choice experiences*, *raviſhments* of
Divine Love, *admirations of grace*, *holy
praiſes*, *ſweet ſupports* under tryals, with
the *account* ſhe uſed to take of her ſelf
of hearing the word, and the *preparation*
of her ſoul thereto, in thoſe pretious
longings of her Soul, to meet with her
dear Lord in Ordinances and the high value ſhe put upon *Communion of Saints*,
in a *Church of Chriſt*, of which there is but
Room for the giving out of ſome taſtes,
in this little Treatiſe.

Laſtly, her *Meditations of death*, which
the ſpirit of Chriſt was preparing her for
in her time of health, whereby death was
made familiar to her, that ſhe *fell aſleep
in Jeſus*, even before we were aware of it
and indeed ſhe could hardly bear the
abſence from her dear Lord any longer; as in her laſt Poem you will perceive.

Surely

Of Readers.

Surely by such a despised Testimony, the *sleepy World is condemned*, and every Soul that peruseth it, should be provoked to take the *Kingdom of Heaven* by the *same violence*; And *Professors of Godliness* may hereby be convinced of *slightness of Spirit*, *sinful neglects*, *formality in duty*; *and ordinances Love of the World*, *decays in Grace*, *taking up with priviledges of Saints*, when *intimate Communion with the Lord, and growth of grace* is not so seriously attended to by them, against which this Treatise is also a living Testimony, and may be blessed of God to the quickning of them.

Let all such specially but remark that vein and Spirit runs through their short discourses, which was to prepare and keep her Soul *to God*, to be duly *calling in her own heart*, much in deepest humbling and self reflexion, Praying, Reading, Meditation, being her Morning and Evening exercise, highly esteeming every opportunity of enjoying the Lord, accounting *the feet of those beautifull* that

B   brought

brought the good tidings, having a high reverence and affection for the servants of Christ in that work, and an intire love to all Saints; as Saints, though of different persuasions at this day, in the weakness, Tenderness, Patience, Love of the Spirit; especially let me bespeak the *Congregation of Christ* whereof she was a *Member* in this City, as also all the Churches of Saints, to be following this Holy and pretious example and practice, which seemeth to be ordered by a hand of providence and grace, to awaken professors from the *evils mentioned*, which I fear have overtaken many, instead of their soul being *kept in life, and warmth*, and attending to *spirituallity*; and *growth in grace*, and being full of love and good works, under the loud calls they have thereunto by the word and providences of God they are under, that they may *witness a good profession*, as they are called thereunto, in the midst of a gainsaying generation.

Reader in a word thou maist here learn what

what it is to *live* and *dye,* comfortably, which is the great concernment before thee, which the Lord in his rich grace give unto thee, and bless the reading hereof for the ends for which it is published; as *prayeth,*

In the Year 1670. Thy Servant for
      Jesus sake.

       A. P.

     B 2 The

The Account of

her early conversation.

O my Soul, consider the wonderful goodness of God, revealing his free Grace and unbounded Love towards thee a poor Worm; oh how wonderful is this condescention, of his that thou shouldst be made an object of mercy? my soul forget not his unspeakable love, let it be recorded, keep in remembrance these choice blessings of a loving Father, bestowed so freely on me in the Lord Jesus Christ the dear Son of his Love, who hath born with thee in many weaknesses, infirmities, and ever seem'd to overlook all corruptions and set thee under his eye of pitty, and compassion; O let this be a means more to incite to a near closer walking with God, that thou maist be born up against the wiles of Satan, thy subtle enemy, whose aim is to destroy thee for ever.

IN the 11 Year of my Age the Lord was pleased to take away my dear Mother, my Parents were very dear and tender of

me and did not leave me without instructions of the things of God; At that time
the Lord was pleased to carry out my heart
to things I then knew not. For as soon as
my Parents had taught me *there was a God*, I
had an awe upon my heart concerning him, I
could then reason with my heart and said, *the
Lord made me, and he made me to serve him,*
and I must do it; so being young, the Lord
was pleased in the freeness of his Grace, to
kindle in my heart some *small sparks* of affections to himself; I remember on a time a little
Brother of mine was sick and my Mother being very tender of her Child, one Lords day
would not go to Church, which caused me
also to stay at home, but wanting employment, out of my Mothers sight went to work
about my babies, at night the Lord was pleased to take away the Child I standing by the
Cradle, which brought a fear upon me presently that I had been the cause, by my
working that day, of the Lords anger in taking away my brother.

I also remember that I went out and *wept
bitterly*, in the consideration of my days work,
but never let my friends know it, I was much
troubled at it, but hoped such was the ignorance of my heart that all would be well
again by my praying and going to Church,
which

which I was careful to do and fearful to omit one duty which might hinder the means of my salvation, and cause the Lord to be displeased with me.

The Ten Commandments was much *upon my heart* making that my only rule to walk by, and was earnest with the Lord that he would help me to the daily observing and fulfilling of them for I then knew there must be a greater power then my own to inable me to the performance of it, also my Parents taught me *in my Catechism* what was my duty towards God and towards my Neighbour, & by my continual saying of them the Lord was pleased to work them upon my spirit, and into my affections and then in mercy to take notice of me in the freeness of his Grace, and tender mercy to own me in the Lord Jesus Christ, whom I was ignorant of as to what he had done and undergone for my soul, but now I can't but admire to behold the infinite goodness and tender love of God, who was then pleased *to chose me from amongst my Brethren,* and his own self took care of me, *leading me by* many paths of providence, passing over all my Corruptions, my weaknesses and my failings caused me to find a tender hearted Father of a great and Holy God, oh how sweetly hath the Lord been

plea-

pleafed to carry on the work of Grace in my
poor unworthy Soul! How exceedingly doth
his Glory fhine and his goodnefs appear in
that he who i the high and mighty One, the
Great God of Heaven and Earth, the King
of Kings, and the Lord of Lords fhould con-
defcend fo far as to caft his eye upon a
Worm, much more *His love* upon a diftreffed
creature, About the fame year of my Age,
the Lord was p'eafed to take away my dear
Mother by which I had a great lofs, yet knowing it was my duty to truft God at all times
I laboured therefore to be content and the
Lord was pleafed to bear me up by confiderations of his *love*, I was in the time of my
Mothers life fickly and weak, fubject to divers bodily infirmities, which made my Mother the more tender of me, hence I was
more fenfible of my great lofs, but fuch was
the goodnefs of God that he was pleafed then
wholy to take away my diftemper and fo
heal me that I have through his mercy never
fince been troubled with it; I fell under fome
other tryal but the Lord was pleafed to in-
large my heart to lay open my cafe before
him and in mercy caufed me to fee that he
did not difpife my poor furplications, but
wa sgracioufly pleafed to fweeten my troubles, and by this to comfort me in that they
carried

carried me nearer to the Lord, sometimes he was pleased to mittigate them, but mostly gave me strength to go through them and patiently to bear them, thus was the Lord pleased to exercise his loving kindness, and tender compassions to my poor soul carrying of it as a Lamb in his Arms; But oh why was my heart so dead that I was so long contented in a state of Ignorance, and not more desirous to come to the knowledge of his ways? but thou O Lord art good and thy ways past finding out, thy tender compassions never fails those whose hearts are upright before thee; O blessed is the Soul to whom *thou imputest no sin* for certainly O Lord shouldst thou have been so just as to mark what was done amiss, O Lord my sins, my corruptions, my daily actings, besides that guilt of original sin brought into the world with me was enough to have sunk me into the bottomless pit for ever.

I *could not see the need* I had of my troubles, nor the *end* for which they were sent, but blessed be thy Name O Lord, who in thy righteousness and goodness, and tender mercy didst afflict me, thou mightest have spared thy pains and have bestowed those sweet discoveries of thy *love* on such who would have better improved it, and have let

me

me perish to all Eternity.

Oh how is my soul bound for ever to extol the *riches of thy grace*, now I have seen his glory, I *abhor* my self in dust and ashes, oh how *unworthy* am I to appear before thee? but blessed be thy name who have not left me in despair, but in the sight of my unworthiness and the wretchednes of my condition, caused me to see that there was hope concerning this matter, that thou hadst *laid help upon one who was mighty to save.*

About a years time I lived very contentedly and in much ease, in my outward conditions, but I began to be unmindful of the Lord who had done so much for me; O how apt was I to forget the rock of my salvation, I began to find these things indifferent to me, which before I had prosecuted with much zeal, the dishonoring of Gods name by others being so common where I was, I did not find my self so affected as before, nor so much troubled at it, till the Lord was pleased by new allarums *to awaken my drowsie soul*, which was so willing to be lulled asleep by *Satan* in a sinful security, and by afflictions some outward trouble, brought me truly to consider my wayes, and to lie low again before the Lord, often spreading my condition before him in private, who was gratiously pleased

one

once more to look upon me and caused me
to see the tenderness of his love towards me.

Then did I begin to grieve at their disho-
nouring God by their profane walkings,
and the Lord was pleased to cause an aw upon
my spirit concerning him and his ways I was
mighty desirous to receive the Lords Supper,
but I dared not, I wondred at some that made
so light a thing of it; when I found
it to be of much weight upon my spirit, I
found them in their ways very prophane and
cold to any good duty, I then began to apply
my heart unto the Scriptures, desiring the
Lord to give me an understanding therein, it
was much upon my spirit to desire that the
Lord would be pleased to open my heart as
he did *Lydia's* that so I might attend unto the
things that were of God.

It pleased the Lord, my time being expired at School, to return me home to my Fathers house Mr *Pierce* being then *Minister*, the
first Sermon I heard from him did much take
upon my affections and raise up my desires
unto the ways of God, preaching from the 4.
Cant. 7. 8. *thou art all fair my love, there is no
spot in thee*, wherein he opened the beauty of
a Soul in Christ, and the love, the Lord was
pleased to honour such a Soul withall, this
filled me with desires and longings to be such:

a

a one, but how to attain unto it I did not
know, then was I full of fears and doubtings,
and Satan brought into my mind my evil and
unworthy walkings, under so much of the
love of God as I had been partaker of this
made my Soul walk heavily under much
dispute a long time and when the Lord was
pleased to come into my heart by a word at
any time which did refresh me, it lasted but
a little time.

The Devill would be ready to tell me, that
was not my part, I was too apt to catch at
Childrens bread and think that my own which
did not belong to me, thus did he follow me
a long time, robbing me of the comfort of
many a sweet Sermon, making me walk in
such sadness which was taken notice of by
my friends, I would fain have related my
condition, and declared my doubts but could
not do it, yet in these doubts found some
comfort, I found my Soul much carried out
in love to Christ, I could delight to sit alone
and meditate on the love of Christ, held forth
in the Gospel to poor sinners, and in the former testimonies of his love wherewith he had
followed me in every outward providence
my soul would be many times carried out to
admire the freeness of his love, my soul
longed for such a heavenly communion which
                                        put

put me much at the throne of Grace to desire
one glimps of his Glory, one testimony of
his love in Christ, but Satans suggestion put
me to a loss in my comfort he would often
perswade me I was a *Hypocrite*, and that I was
fallen from Grace, this was a sad and great
burden upon my spirit, and I thought my
sins was so great I must cry out with *Cain, my
punishment should be greater then I can bear,* yet
was the Lord in his goodness pleased *not long
to leave me* in this condition, but to incline my
heart more, and with much affection to the
word, remembring the deadness of spirit I
had been under.

There was few I was acquainted with whom
I could in the least have any converse with in
the whole Town, thus did I labour to keep
my troub'es to my self, I remember a sentence which did something refresh me (which
was) *He will lead sinners in the right way,* and
the Lord was pleased to come into my heart
with this truth, *I never said unto the house of Jacob seek ye me in vain,* then did I go unto the
Lord and earnestly desire the assistance of his
spirit to seek counsel, in this matter I sought
over the book of God and begged of the
Lord with tears, that he would be pleased to
give me a *right understanding* in what I could
not well apprehend, so gratious was the Lord
                                                            at

at that time to give in answer to my poor request and caused me to find much sweetness and comfort in reading, which before I never had found, this raised up my heart to praise the Lord for his mercy towards me and gave me much comfort in that I hoped the Lord had not forgotten to be gratious but had in mercy owned himself to be my God hearing prayer, and that the poor weak prayer of a wretched miserable creature (who was looked upon with the eye of scorn and much dispised) this carried up my soul to joy in the Lord with praises to him, in which I found much comfort and incouragement, then did I in my heart resolve to wait upon the Lord with my poor petitions for strength till he should please to give me a clearer evidence of his love, and the true knowledge of his wayes, which I desired to know above all earthly things, thus was the Lord pleased to come in with a gratious influence of his holy spirit whereby I received comfort *from every Sermon* I heard, for about 2 Months space.

But then how was my sinful and deceitful heart *puffed up*, what thoughts did I begin to have of my self how had the Devil changed his note and told my proud heart, my state was now good and my graces were much increased, for which I ought to be much esteemed, how ready I was to do any thing which might

secretly

secretly make me bethought well of by such
as knew it, then did I walk as one that was
well principled in Religion and a great professor.   O wicked wretch that after so much
love should dare to be so careless as to let Satan steal away my heart, yet the goodness of
the Lord whose mercies indure for ever,
would not suffer me to rest in this condition,
but was pleased by a Sermon to make me behold my condition and search into with a
single eye, the subject he preached from
was the 25 of *Matthew*, the parable of the ten
virgins, whereby he shewed how far a carnal
outward professor might be like a *real*
Christian, and yet have never a dram of grace
which the Lord was pleased to fasten upon
my soul making me to weigh my actions and
the thoughts of my heart with the pure word
of God where I found much unsoundness and
rottenness, then was my heart cast into its
former sadness, then was the Lord pleased
to *humble* my soul under the sence of a *proud
disobedient heart* and made me to be more
watchfull to my ways and apply my heart to
reading and prayer which before it was much
streightned in.

Thus did I look into the waies of some o-
ther professors, where the Lord discovered
to

to me many weaknesses and failings by comparing of their wayes unto the pure word of
God, I saw a shortness of that Gospel spirit
the whole Gospel so sweetly treats of, this was
a stumbling block to my soul thus was my
trouble greatly increased wherein *Satan was
very busie to destroy the comforts I had formerly
had*, None could I find to declare my trouble
so malicious was the fire brand of hell to cause
several jealousies in the hearts of people what
might be the cause of my trouble, and as *David saies my humbling became a reproach unto
me*; I cared not for company but most to be alone;
in which I did contemplate the sweetness of
his Divine Mercy, yet desiring the Lord would
ease me of my burden, which I thought to be
very great often should I sit and bewail my
sad condition; and be ready with *Job* to curse
the day of my birth, yet in this my distress
the Lord was pleased to bring me to his feet,
then wou'd I come with tears and offer up
my poor supplications before the Lord, where
I found my heart much inlarged being affected with the love of God to sinners, and
carried out much upon those words, *call upon
the Lord and he will hear thee, he is nigh unto all
that call upon him, to deliver them out of trouble,*
and many more sweet and seasonable *Scriptures* was the Lord pleased graciously to bring
in·

into my remembrance, and powerfully to apply unto my heart, which made me go often
unto the Lord and spread my condition before the Throne of his Grace, having much
incouragement to hope in his mercy, thus
did I find much comfort and sweetness in
my secret communion with the Lord and
found much ease in my troubles, which I took
as gratious returns of my poor broken prayers, and was much carried out to trust in him
and to wait upon him, then could I sit and call
to remembrance the mercies of old as a tender and a loving father, who nourished up my
poor soul, which made me exceedingly admire the infinite riches of his Grace and the
freeness of his love in Christ Jesus to my poor
Souls, which made me often cry out, Lord
what am I that thou shouldst take such notice
of a poor creature, that thou shouldest cast
thine eye of love upon me; (though the Devil would yet be busie and often cast into my
thoughts doubtful fear;) what was there in
me should cause the Lord to pitty me, and
indeed I could do nothing in my self, which
began to increase my trouble, yet I remem-
bred it was the saying of *David* when *my father and my Mother forsook me, then the Lord
would look upon me*, this did at first revive me,
but then I considered *David* was a holy man

C   after

after Gods own heart, how dare I to lay claim
to any thing belonged to him.

Thus was my bafe diftruftful heart exerci-
fed with variety of tempta ions by the Devil,
as to diftruft the goodnefs of the Lord; and
to rob my foul of the comforts he was pleafed many times to come in withall, many
times has the Lord been pleafed to come in
by a Sermon to my foul, and as it were fpake
unto my prefent condition, but oh how dull
have I been to remember, and how did my
unworthy walking caufe thofe bleffed truths
to flip out of my mind, yet was the Lord in
mercy pleafed to keep my heart fincere before him, to plead for mercy for the Lords
fake, for whofe fake he was gracioufly pleafed to continue his tender and compaffionat:
love unto me,

The

The sweet experiences of the tender love of God to my Soul, at *Mrs. W.* at School.

THen was the Lord pleased in much bounty to appear very gracious to my poor Soul and drawed out my heart much to long after the knowledge of his waies, now being yet under the old way of Worship, I besought the Lord truly to convince my Judgement as well as my affections of the way which is of his own setting up, but for a small time the Lord was pleased yet to leave me to my self that I found my self at a loss being dead and dull yet performing outward duties but with little spiritual life, and my heart also was carried out after vanities, then I found that I had lost the former sweet incombs of the Lord, and the refreshings of his blessed spirit, and was as one lulled a sleep by the *deceitful inchantments of Satan,* and malitious devices.

C 2

O

O *wicked and deceitful heart*; how couldst thou so soon forget such *bondage* delivered from such *snares* as the Devil had so often got thee into, how soon hast thou forgot the God of all thy mercies how hast thou made the Lord to serve with thy sins.

Yet once more was the Lord pleased to call me out of my benumbed conditions and shewed how I was running my self into my own destruction.

Oh the *goodness of the Lord* who never did leave me! but to *see my own inability* to live without his help, then did the Lord in mercy convince me of the emptiness of all Earthly vanities and also of that way of formal worship that it was a dead carnal lifeless thing under which my soul could not prosper and so growing weary of it more and more at length besought the Lord to guide my poor ignorant Soul which was so easie to be led away with every wicked and subtile device of Satan, my heart desired much to *hear good men*, and when I could with convenience, which some took notice of and said I was one whom the Apostle speaks of, *having itching ears, ever learning, &c.*

This did much afflict me, about which the Lord was pleased to give me a heart to seek him and that earnestly for his assistance in the know-

knowledge of his truth;

One more experience of the providence of God appeared unto me, as an incouragement to trust in his mercy and to wait upon him by prayer for all things, I had at that time a distemper upon me of which I saw no hope of cure, yet one day particularly being in a serious meditation of the infinite goodness of the Lord, toward me, the Lord was pleased to direct my eye upon a place of Scripture where I found the woman coming to the Lord, confessing that she had spent all she had to be cured of her infirmity, and one touch of Christs garment had done it, from thence may not I come trembling that have received so many testimonies of his love & tryed so many medcines before I came unto the Lord, or looked up to him for help then did I, bewail my unprofitableness yet went unto the Lord in the language of the Lepper and said Lord if thou wilt thou canst make me clean, who was not deaf to my poor request but in some small time was graciously pleased as I may say without means wholy to clear me of it, this mercy carried up my heart more to praise the Lord then any yet I had received who notwithstanding all my weaknesses and sinfulnesses was graciously pleased to follow me with many mercys.

C 3   O

Of further discoveries of Christ.

Then was the Lord pleased in his gratious Providence to remove me to a place in H. Sh. where I had much more advantage of means and helps for my poor Soul.

WHere the Lord was pleased to give me through his grace, a little more insight into the *mind of Christ*, evidencing himself to be a God *gratious and mercyful, abundant in goodness, &c.* I was filled with admiration, to see the holy glorious God, abase himself to so poor a wretchless Creature as I then was, I cryed out with earnest desires and longings after more of the knowledge of this God, but here came I under strong temptations, Satan

was

was powerful in raising up of spiritual Pride,
but the Lord whose goodness never failled
me, did then take care for me; *thou O Lord
who broughtest me out of the Pit of despair, O suffer me not to climb up to the Mount of Presumption;* then was the Lord pleased in the tender-
nels of his love to convince me that the *poor
in Spirit,* were heirs of the Kingdom; that the
lowly Soul was his *habitation,* then I besought
God, begging at the Throne of Grace, for the
affistance of his gratious Spirit, without which
I could do nothing, and that he would *humble* me even to the dust, that so my Soul might
not loose the fight of that *Glory revealed in the
face of Jesus Christ.*

This the Lord was gratioufly pleased to
grant, and sweetly bring me to see a riches in
Chrift Jesus and that this was more to be defired then all the treasures upon Earth.

C 4   The

The longings of her Soul after Church Fellowſhip, and all the Ordinances of Chriſt.

THen did I long after God, and the injoyment of him in his own way, and ſaid Lord, thou haſt made me, O lead me in *that way* wherein I may bring moſt glory to thy ſelf, I durſt not truſt my own judgement but reſign'd my ſelf unto his will, and continued my petitions at the Throne of Grace, and at length he was pleaſed graciouſl to anſwer my poor prayer, *bleſſd be thy name O Lord, O let my Soul be inlarged in thy praſes.*

One day the Lord was pleaſed by a ſtrange providence to caſt me into the company of one that I never ſaw before, but of a ſweet and free diſpoſition, and whoſe diſcourſe ſavour'd

vour'd so much of the Gospel, that I could
not but at that instant bless God for his goodness in that providence, it pleased the Lord
to carry out our hearts much towards one a-
nother at that time, and a little while after,
the Lord was pleased to bring us together
again for the space of three dayes, in which
time it pleased God by our much converse
together, to establish and confirm me more
in the desires I had to jyn with the people of
God in society, and enjoy Communion with them
according to the order of the Gospel, she was
of a society of the Congregational way called
Independants, and gave me so clear a demon-
stration of their wayes, that upon considerations and searching of the Scripture for the
understanding of which I earnestly besought
the Lord) I was cleerly convinc't in my judgment, that this was the way which came
nearest to the rule of the Gospel, and the
commands of Christ, then were our hearts
firmly united, and I blessed the Lord from
my soul for so glorious and visible an appearance of his love, for I had many sweet refreshments given me at that time, when she
was gone, I was sensible of the great mercy
the Lord had been pleased to show me, but
in an instance snatcht it from me again, at
which I began to be troubled, but after a few

re-

reflections to this purpose, why do I not patiently submit to the will of my Father, who knows what is best for me, my soul was again filled with hungrings and thirstings after God for a more clear and full injoyment of *him*, and that in that blessed ordinance appointed for a seal to *confirm the Covenant* he hath gratiously made, through his dear Son with all believers, this was at a time, when the Lord was pleased as to outward appearance to frown upon his people, it seemed an hour of darkness to me, my heart was troubled, then was I earnest with the Lord further to direct me in the way that he should choose, and the Lord was pleased to shine in with some Gospel light, and cause me to see a vast disproportion between a superstitious way of worshipping of God and a spiritual sincere way, in which spiritual Christians serve him, then I said O that God would please to bring me into the fellowship and Communion of his own people, and if he hath appointed them to suffer. Oh that I might be one that he would count worthy to suffer for the name of Christ, Oh how doth my Soul desire to bear part in the affliction of *Sion*, much rather then to injoy the mirth and pleasure of an earthly Kingdom, then did I cast my self upon the Lord and offer up my

Soul

Soul to him who knows how to frame it according to his own blessed will, then I said Lord hast not thou the hearts of all creatures in thy hand, and hast power to turn them into what frame soever thou pleasest, bring mine into a conformity to thy blessed will, O do it Lord for thy mercies sake, then I made known my desires unto my friend by letter to joyn in society with that congregation whereof my friend was a member.

For about that time the Minister of the Parish intending to give the Sacrament preached a preparatory Sermon from 1 *Cor.* 11. 27, 28, 29, *&c.* Shewing the sweet nature of that blessed ordinance, the danger of unworthy receivers and how a Christian ought to be qualified before partaking thereof at the hearing of which I was awakened and the Lord was pleased to come in with sweet comfort and refreshments considering the blessed provision God had gratiously made for those that prepared to meet him therein; but I was troubled when I considered that very few or none of his Communicants were so quallified to appearance which was my great burden, for I longed much to partake of that ordinance but dared not to do it in that manner and with such persons

None

None could I use freedom with in this matter but those who I feared would make my trouble greater but thou O God who art ever ready to help in time of neeed thou the wise counsellor wilt not be far from the Soul that truly seeks thee, then I called upon the Lord who was gratiously pleased to grant an ear to my request, and through the help of my friend to bring to remembrance, 1 Cor. 10 16. 17. v. by which I was much establish d, but more when I saw the number of his Communicants whom he had examined and accepted such as was very blind , ignorant, formal creatures then I came to a resolution through the blessing of God to wait with patience till he should see good to open a way wherein I might injoy such ordinances in power and purity and so as I might expect Gods presence and blessing, which at last he was gratious'l p'eased to do making that my friend an instrument thereof.

Oh let my heart be more carried out to God with praises, and put a new Song into my mouth, make it my work to glory that thy great name, since thou art thus pleased to own me in thy dear Son.

Of Recording her Experiences.

O My Soul thou hast found by sweet experiences how good a thing it is to wait upon the Lord let not the gratious taft of his love flip out of thy remembrance but whilst he hath given thee life improve these mercies and the talent he hath lent thee, to his own glory, and let the gratious workings of the Lord as he is pleafed to honour thee with incomes of his love, and the sweet breathings of his holy spirit, recount them here in order as the Lord shall give thee leave that they may be *upon record against an evil day, a day of temptation*, for how many pretious evidences hast thou lost, for want of *remembring* them, but now O Lord help me to deal faithfully with my

soul

Soul in declaring thy power and the riches of thy Grace in the *daily remembring* of thy mercies, O cause me to see the *growth of my Soul*, in Grace and in the *knowledge* of my gratious God, that my Soul may only aim at the Glory of my redeemer.

The Lord was thus pleased to carry on his gratious work with much power in my poor Soul, notwithstanding the Devils suggestions, many fears, &c. As that my condition surely was not yet so good as I did hope it to be, and to doubt whether my joy was not meer presumption, but the Lord in his goodness was pleased in a little time to clear it more fully to me and cause me to see by the workings of his holy Spirit, sweet evidences of his tender love and brought into my meditation many blessed promises, which he was pleased to bless unto my *Soul, and confirm unto me with much establishment.*

The Lord being thus pleased by his wise Councel and his tender love thus *to guide my unworthy Soul*, at length by his gratious providence brought me to the place where the Church met though they were strangers to me yet was he pleased to cause me to find much love and tenderness, and there I had that blessed opportunity to receive that sweet refreshing Ordinance which my Soul had so

much

much longed after. Blessed be his Holy name:
O thou my Soul since thou hast seen the gracious dealings of the Lord towards thee be not
thou unmindful of his praise.

Improve thy talent to thy Masters use; lay
out thy strength for God, and let thy heart
be carried out for ever to remember the
tender and unspeakable love of thy dear Lord
unless thou put thy hand to help, my strength
is nothing, I am a poor weak nothing not
able to do any thing if thou shouldest once
leave me never so little.

The

The Choice Discoveries of Christ to her Soul, when joyned to a Church, in the Lords Supper.

OH how was the Lord in mercy pleased to manifest his Glory and goodness to thee O my Son in this Ordinance, in which he was gratiously pleased by faith to draw thee up to recive those outward elements the bread and wine as presenting the immediate *body and blood of the Lord Jesus broken and shed for thy sins,* O thou

un.

unworthy Soul how gratiously was the Lord
pleased to come with power, raising thee up
to praise and admire the exceeding riches of
his Grace in choosing thee to be partaker of
so great a blessing, how was he pleased to fill
thee with spiritual joy at thy returning home,
and give thee leave to come into his presence
to return him thanks with joy that he was
pleased so gratiously to manifest himself unto thee poor unworthy Soul, as a God hearing
prayer and answering thy poor request with
so much mercy, which the Lord inable thee
for ever to remember to his Glory thou
knowest I desired to do so even from my
Youth and if my deceitful heart deceive me
not I dare appeal unto thee for the sincerity
of it oh that thou wouldest make me *usefull*
to thee in that way or any way thou shalt be
pleased to choose that I might glorifie thy
great and holy Name.

D   Sweet

Sweet Discoveries of the Love of God in Jesus Christ.

Oh how good a God have I, who is pleased every day to bear up my Soul with the sweet influences of his gratious Spirit, and pretious incomes of his tender Love, O how could I sit and meditate of thy loving kindness all the day long, where can I find any comfort in this World but in thy presence, there have I Lord indeed through thy Grace found a fulness of Joy, a time of endless pleasures; O what am I or what is my Fathers House, that I should be the daughter to a King that I a worm a poor detestable creature made up with clay and dust nay worse then a worm they being creatures which shall prey upon me for that I am appointed for their food, yet that the Lord of Hosts the Holy One of Israel the High and Mighty God, the King of Glory, the King of Kings, who is a King over the whole Earth should

yet

yet be pleased thus to abase himself as to have
thoughts of love for such a poor unworthy wretched creature as I am, oh how unworthy am I of
thy favours, yet Lord because thou hast bid me
hope in thy mercy I dare do no otherwise, nay Lord
thou hast commanded me to believe, Lord I believe
pardon my unbelief, that should in any ways cause
me in the least to distrust the riches of thy Grace
or thy unspeakable goodness which is thy Glory,
since thou art pleased dear Lord to make a worm
the object of thy grace, Oh let my Soul enjoy these
sweet transcendant pleasures which lye discovered
to my soul in the rich treasury of thy unbounded
love whilst others take their fill of Worldly vanities.

When I considered the sinfulness of my nature, my weaknesses, my frailties, and my
many infirmities, oh what is there in me
should ever cause the Lord to pitty me or yet
to coutinue his favour to me, in so unspeakable a manner, N my Soul bless thou the Lord
for Jesus Christ in whom the Lord is pleased
richly to look upon thee? O happy is the soul
that is born up by such a support; how
wretched had my soul been, had not the Lord
laid help on one who is mighty, hadst not
thou had the Lord to be thy Saviour, Christ
the dear son of God to be thy Redeemer I. O

blessed

blessed be the Lord, and blessed be my Rock who hath thus looked upon sinful mankind, and thus loved the Sons of Men as to give his only dearly beloved Son to dye for such poor miserable wretches as I! *O the wonderful goodness of God the transcendant, and unspeakable riches of his grace in Jesus Christ!* O my Soul canst thou but be filled with holy admiration at the infiniteness of his Glory, the unspeakable and transcendant beauty of thy dear Redeemer, this indeed is rich mercy. That the Lord should come into the World and give his life a ransome for poor sinners, but that thou shouldest be one for whom the Lord was pleased to leave his glory to take upon him the habit of a servant, the nature of a sinful man, that thou shouldest be one for whom the Lord became himself, a curse to redeem thee from the curse, that was due to thee and from that which there was no Redemption but through the blood of that pure and spotless Lamb, that Christ the Son of God should give himself to dye a shameful death for thee that thou mightest live, that thou mightest be partaker of those glorious benefits and gracious priviledges which came by him? O my soul that thou shouldbe one to whom such exceeding love is shown! O my soul how doth the love of Christ constrain

blessed   thee

thee to love him, O my poor unworthy soul how
art thou bound for ever to admire, and only.
aim at and seek the glory of thy dear Redeemer! O my dear Redeemer how is my
poor unworthy heart carried out to admire
thy dear and tender love?

Lord if to injoy the Communion with thy
Saints, and people here on earth be such a
glorious priviledge which thou hast made my
soul to long after; O then what is it to injoy
Communion with thy Saints and Angels to all
Eternity in the presence of my Lord and Saviour ? What darkness can Eclipse that glory or rather will not that glory quite put out
that glory which the World but falsly yeilds;
what is all the glory of the World, or all the
Kingdoms of the Earth compared to the ap-
prehention of a Heavenly Kingdom in the
soul here, much less to the full injoyment of
it to all Eternity ? What is all the glory of.
the world, but poor empty husks, poor deceitful vanities; a very lie, which at the best
makes but ashamed, but Lord how glorious
art thou in the *beauties of holiness, my Soul* hath
found enough in thee to fill it with a holy admiration: O that I might forever be admiring
of thy glory: what are the treasures of the
earth poor low base things, that we should
have our hearts so much carried after them?

D 3   what

What is it the hearts of the World runs out so
much after, as if there was their greatest happiness? Is it not that they may gain abundance of riches? and what are they when they
are gotten but thorns to put out their own
eyes, they toyl and labour hard in the
world for that which is at best of no indu-
ring substance, and if they make a shift to
keep it whilst they continue here,
yet at the Grave this the great happiness
must leave them; O misserable are they whose
chiefest good consists in worldly vanities,
what is all the treasure upon Earth to that in
estcemable Riches, which are only to be
found in Jesus Christ, of how much greater
value is that *one pearl of great price*, then all
the Pearls and Diamonds and the richest treasure upon earth. *Lord fill thou my heart with
Heavenly Treasure and let my Soul be rich in
grace, oh that it might be such in which I
might bring glory to thy Name,*

Meditations upon my Saviours Love.

How excellent a thing is Love, how doth it adorn a Christian and comes most near the Image of a loving Saviour, never was any love like to his love, he loved us not because we first loved him, no we were enemies, yet even then he loved us and had compassion on us; O the riches of divine Love, see the sweet indearments of a loving Saviour, greater love can no man show then to lay down his life for his friends, yea but our dear Lord laid down his life for us when we were enemies, and from being enemies he is pleased to stile us friends, and not only so, but behold what manner of love the Father hath bestowed upon us that we should be called the sons of God and if sons, then Heirs of God, and Coheirs with Christ in Eternal Glory.

O blessed change from enemies to friends,

D 4   from

from *friends*, to *Sons*, and so *heirs* with the
Lord Jesus of an eternal inheritance ; O the
gratious effect of this tranfcendant love, Now
are we Sons of God, but yet it doth not appear what we fhall be, why can greater
teftimony of love be fhown then this, to be
taken into the number of Gods Children ?
to be counted Sons and Daughters of the
Great and Glorious God ? the Lord of
Hofts; the High and Mighty King of Kings,
Oh yes, it doth not yet appear what we fhall
be, now we fee but darkly as in a Glafs, but
here is mercy, this is tender love, that when
he fhall appear who hath fo loved us, even
our dear Redeemer in his Glory, we fhall be
like him for we fhall fee him as he is , our
dear Saviour who was content not only to
lay down his life for us that we might be
partakers with him of his Son-fhip and alfo
of the Glory.

*Oh the tranfcendant and unfpeakable love, of
God to poor Souls,* whom the Lord Jefus is
pleafed out of the rich treafury of his divine
Love to reconcile unto God by the blood of
the Crofs, and what hath the Lord required
again of us poor Worms for all his benefits,
but that we fhould return him love again, and
this is the love he requires that we fhould
keep his Commandements, oh bleffed Lord, and
thy

thy commandements are not grievous but delightful to the Soul that loves thee, and what is thy Commandement dear Lord *this is my Commandement* (and it is a *new Commandement*) that you should love one another my Commandements are not grievous it is only love that is required, and that you should manifest it in obedience to my commands; one of which is that you *love one another*, but how dear Lord shall we manifest our love to thee in loving one another, how hast thou required that we should love one another, have not I set you an example.

Did not I *first love you?* and therefore give you this new Commandement, that as I have loved you so you would love one another, with a sincere pure unbounded love, such a love as seeks not your own things, but the good of others, such a love as is inward and not in outward show only, but in *deed*, and in *truth*, in the sincerity of your hearts, such a love as seeks the good and spiritual advantage of one anothers Souls, to love one another as I have loved you, or to love thy friend, as thou lovest thy self, most willing to do that which may be for thy friends good, although it be to some prejudice to thy self; this is love and by this you shall know that you are my Disciples, if that you
love

love one another ; and by this men shall know that you are mine, such as I have loved from the beginning, *Oh dear Lord how art thou pleased thus to plead with poor clods of clay what sweet arguments of thine own matchless goodness.*

Art thou pleased to lay down thy life to *draw* poor sinful Souls to thy self, O Lord whom didst thou ever bless with a clear sight of the least glimps of thy most gratious goodness, that yet would not love the Lord, are not our hearts harder then stone, How many is there do profess to love thee but in works deny thee, even in this great matter of love even in loving one another,

Do we not rather back-bite, and discover one another; where is that *tender bearing* one anothers burthens? Where is that sweet convincing spirit to reprove as should be in Christians? how few are to be found but such as fear both to reprove and to be reproved, to exhort or to be exhorted in that sence; where is that love which hides a multitude of faults ? that *love* that *works* no *thinks no ill* to his neighbour, where is that spirit of mourning over one anothers infirmities, that spirit of supplication in one anothers behalf, Lord where is this Spirit to be found in the measure it ought.

sure

Sure but in few that do make profession of thy name Lord! is there not *secret pride* lies hidden through Hippocricy in our base deceitful hearts; whoever saw the Lord that could not love, who Lord hast thou ever brought under the power of thy *constraining love*, that are not willing there to rest, but Lord unless thou teachest by thy holy spirit, and give us daily supply from thine own self we can do nothing. *O Lord we are not able to do one good action without thy especial grace*, but here lies our fault still we have not power no strength, Lord *we have not because we ask not*, Our dear Lord hath said, *Ask and you shall receive*, O how largely is he pleased to make promise unto poor worms, *Whatsoever ye shall ask in my name I will do it*; and again repeats it, *And if ye shall ask any thing in my name I will do it*, is not there a gratious promise from the mouth of him in whose power it is to make it good; Is it not from the Lord himself who is the only giver of all good, whose word the least tittle of which shall not fall to the Ground, O then, why are we not more at the throne of Grace, since he is pleased in mercy to afford unto us so glorious a priviledge, O that my

soul

soul may abide seeking of thee; that my
heart may still more and more be carried out
with this *sincere love*, unto thee and thine; O
suffer me dear Lord once more to say with
boldness through thy Grace I will not let
thee go until thou herein wilt bless me,